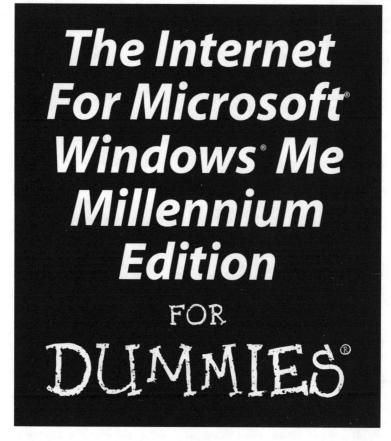

The Internet For Microsoft® Windows® Me Millennium Edition

FOR DUMMIES®

by John R. Levine, Margaret Levine Young, Jordan Young, Carol Baroudi

IDG BOOKS WORLDWIDE

IDG Books Worldwide, Inc.
An International Data Group Company

Foster City, CA ◆ Chicago, IL ◆ Indianapolis, IN ◆ New York, NY

The Internet For Microsoft® Windows® Me Millennium Edition For Dummies®

Published by
IDG Books Worldwide, Inc.
An International Data Group Company
919 E. Hillsdale Blvd.
Suite 400
Foster City, CA 94404
www.idgbooks.com (IDG Books Worldwide Web Site)
www.dummies.com (Dummies Press Web Site)

Library of Congress Control Number: 00-102527

ISBN: 0-7645-0739-7

Printed in the United States of America

10 9 8 7 6 5 4 3 2 1

1B/RV/QZ/QQ/IN

3 3113 01980 4261

Distributed in the United States by IDG Books Worldwide, Inc.

Distributed by CDG Books Canada Inc. for Canada; by Transworld Publishers Limited in the United Kingdom; by IDG Norge Books for Norway; by IDG Sweden Books for Sweden; by IDG Books Australia Publishing Corporation Pty. Ltd. for Australia and New Zealand; by TransQuest Publishers Pte Ltd. for Singapore, Malaysia, Thailand, Indonesia, and Hong Kong; by Gotop Information Inc. for Taiwan; by ICG Muse, Inc. for Japan; by Intersoft for South Africa; by Eyrolles for France; by International Thomson Publishing for Germany, Austria and Switzerland; by Distribuidora Cuspide for Argentina; by LR International for Brazil; by Galileo Libros for Chile; by Ediciones ZETA S.C.R. Ltda. for Peru; by WS Computer Publishing Corporation, Inc., for the Philippines; by Contemporanea de Ediciones for Venezuela; by Express Computer Distributors for the Caribbean and West Indies; by Micronesia Media Distributor, Inc. for Micronesia; by Chips Computadoras S.A. de C.V. for Mexico; by Editorial Norma de Panama S.A. for Panama; by American Bookshops for Finland.

For general information on IDG Books Worldwide's books in the U.S., please call our Consumer Customer Service department at 800-762-2974. For reseller information, including discounts and premium sales, please call our Reseller Customer Service department at 800-434-3422.

For information on where to purchase IDG Books Worldwide's books outside the U.S., please contact our International Sales department at 317-572-3993 or fax 317-572-4002.

For consumer information on foreign language translations, please contact our Customer Service department at 1-800-434-3422, fax 317-572-4002, or e-mail rights@idgbooks.com.

For information on licensing foreign or domestic rights, please phone +1-650-653-7098.

For sales inquiries and special prices for bulk quantities, please contact our Order Services department at 800-434-3422 or write to the address above.

For information on using IDG Books Worldwide's books in the classroom or for ordering examination copies, please contact our Educational Sales department at 800-434-2086 or fax 317-572-4005.

For press review copies, author interviews, or other publicity information, please contact our Public Relations department at 650-653-7000 or fax 650-653-7500.

For authorization to photocopy items for corporate, personal, or educational use, please contact Copyright Clearance Center, 222 Rosewood Drive, Danvers, MA 01923, or fax 978-750-4470.

Cartoons at a Glance

By Rich Tennant

"I did this report with the help of a satellite view atmospheric map from the National Weather Service, research text from the Jet Propulsion Laboratory, and a sound file from 'The Barking Longworms' new CD."

page 7

"I don't mean to hinder your quest for knowledge, however it's not generally a good idea to try to download the entire Internet."

page 105

IT'S FRICASSEE OF PYTHON WITH FRIED ANTS AND CRISPY GRASSHOPPERS.

YOU'RE GETTING RECIPES OFF THE INTERNET AGAIN, AREN'T YOU?

page 173

"It's a letter from the company that installed our in-ground sprinkler system. They're offering Internet access now."

page 255

"He found a dog site over an hour ago and has been in a staring contest ever since."

page 347

Fax: 978-546-7747
E-mail: richtennant@the5thwave.com
World Wide Web: www.the5thwave.com

Dedication

John dedicates his part of the book (the pages with the particularly dumb jokes) to Sarah Willow, and to several women named Margaret.

Margy and Jordan dedicate their part of this book to Professor Jordan Young and Dionir Sousa Gomes Young.

Carol dedicates her part of the book to Joshua, with all her love, and to her friends, who remind her that there's more to life than writing books.

Authors' Acknowledgments

As you can tell from the cover, writing this book was a collaborative process. Arnold Reinhold's was the principal hand behind several chapters, and he put four more into their current form. Kathy Werfel originated one chapter. By the time it's done, though, everybody's fingerprints are pretty much everywhere. Hy Bender was also involved in thinking about this book in its early stages. Rima Regas revised the entire book from cover to cover, and she'd gladly do it again.

All the authors particularly thank our editors at IDG Books Worldwide, Inc., especially Rebecca Whitney, Diane Steele, and Mary Bednarek. There's much lamenting nowadays for the lost art of editing, and we thank Rebecca for shoveling against the tide. You're about to read a much better book because of her efforts. It's a cliché to say that it takes a cast of thousands to make a big project like this one happen, but it's true. We've met only a few of the dedicated folks listed on the Publisher's Acknowledgments page, but we're very thankful that they and their coworkers are making this book happen.

The entire contents of this book were submitted by the authors to the publisher over the Internet. Edited chapters were returned for review the same way. We thank the Finger Lakes Technology Group (Trumansburg, New York), LightLink (Ithaca, New York), STCO.NET (Shoreham, Vermont), SoVerNet (Bellows Falls, Vermont), and FlashCom DSL (Washington, D.C.), our Internet providers.

Many thanks to the Internet community for its support.

Publisher's Acknowledgments

We're proud of this book; please register your comments through our IDG Books Worldwide Online Registration Form located at http://my2cents.dummies.com.

Some of the people who helped bring this book to market include the following:

Acquisitions, Editorial, and Media Development

Project Editor: Rebecca Whitney

Acquisitions Editor: Steve Hayes

Proof Editors: Teresa Artman, Dwight Ramsey

Technical Editor: Bill Karow

Editorial Manager: Mary C. Corder

Editorial Assistant: Sarah Shupert

Production

Project Coordinator: Regina Snyder

Layout and Graphics: Elizabeth Brooks, Jill Piscitelli, Heather Pope, Jacque Schneider, Julie Trippetti

Proofreaders: York Production Services, Inc.

Indexer: York Production Services, Inc.

Special Help
Constance Carlisle

General and Administrative

IDG Books Worldwide, Inc.: John Kilcullen, CEO

IDG Books Technology Publishing Group: Richard Swadley, Senior Vice President and Publisher; Walter R. Bruce III, Vice President and Publisher; Joseph Wikert, Vice President and Publisher; Mary Bednarek, Vice President and Director, Product Development; Andy Cummings, Publishing Director, General User Group; Mary C. Corder, Editorial Director; Barry Pruett, Publishing Director

IDG Books Consumer Publishing Group: Roland Elgey, Senior Vice President and Publisher; Kathleen A. Welton, Vice President and Publisher; Kevin Thornton, Acquisitions Manager; Kristin A. Cocks, Editorial Director

IDG Books Internet Publishing Group: Brenda McLaughlin, Senior Vice President and Publisher; Diane Graves Steele, Vice President and Publisher, Consumer Education and Reference Group

IDG Books Production for Branded Press: Debbie Stailey, Director of Production; Cindy L. Phipps, Manager of Project Coordination, Production Proofreading, and Indexing; Tony Augsburger, Manager of Prepress, Reprints, and Systems; Shelley Lea, Supervisor of Graphics and Design; Debbie J. Gates, Production Systems Specialist; Steve Arany, Associate Automation Supervisor; Robert Springer, Supervisor of Proofreading; Trudy Coler, Page Layout Manager; Kathie Schutte, Senior Page Layout Supervisor; Janet Seib, Associate Page Layout Supervisor; Michael Sullivan, Production Supervisor

Packaging and Book Design: Patty Page, Manager, Promotions Marketing

◆

The publisher would like to give special thanks to Patrick J. McGovern, without whom this book would not have been possible.

◆

ABOUT IDG BOOKS WORLDWIDE

Welcome to the world of IDG Books Worldwide.

IDG Books Worldwide, Inc., is a subsidiary of International Data Group, the world's largest publisher of computer-related information and the leading global provider of information services on information technology. IDG was founded more than 30 years ago by Patrick J. McGovern and now employs more than 9,000 people worldwide. IDG publishes more than 290 computer publications in over 75 countries. More than 90 million people read one or more IDG publications each month.

Launched in 1990, IDG Books Worldwide is today the #1 publisher of best-selling computer books in the United States. We are proud to have received eight awards from the Computer Press Association in recognition of editorial excellence and three from Computer Currents' First Annual Readers' Choice Awards. Our best-selling *...For Dummies®* series has more than 50 million copies in print with translations in 31 languages. IDG Books Worldwide, through a joint venture with IDG's Hi-Tech Beijing, became the first U.S. publisher to publish a computer book in the People's Republic of China. In record time, IDG Books Worldwide has become the first choice for millions of readers around the world who want to learn how to better manage their businesses.

Our mission is simple: Every one of our books is designed to bring extra value and skill-building instructions to the reader. Our books are written by experts who understand and care about our readers. The knowledge base of our editorial staff comes from years of experience in publishing, education, and journalism — experience we use to produce books to carry us into the new millennium. In short, we care about books, so we attract the best people. We devote special attention to details such as audience, interior design, use of icons, and illustrations. And because we use an efficient process of authoring, editing, and desktop publishing our books electronically, we can spend more time ensuring superior content and less time on the technicalities of making books.

You can count on our commitment to deliver high-quality books at competitive prices on topics you want to read about. At IDG Books Worldwide, we continue in the IDG tradition of delivering quality for more than 30 years. You'll find no better book on a subject than one from IDG Books Worldwide.

John J. Kilcullen

John Kilcullen
Chairman and CEO
IDG Books Worldwide, Inc.

Eighth Annual Computer Press Awards ≥ 1992

WINNER

Ninth Annual Computer Press Awards ≥ 1993

WINNER

Tenth Annual Computer Press Awards ≥ 1994

WINNER

Eleventh Annual Computer Press Awards ≥ 1995

IDG is the world's leading IT media, research and exposition company. Founded in 1964, IDG had 1997 revenues of $2.05 billion and has more than 9,000 employees worldwide. IDG offers the widest range of media options that reach IT buyers in 75 countries representing 95% of worldwide IT spending. IDG's diverse product and services portfolio spans six key areas including print publishing, online publishing, expositions and conferences, market research, education and training, and global marketing services. More than 90 million people read one or more of IDG's 290 magazines and newspapers, including IDG's leading global brands — Computerworld, PC World, Network World, Macworld and the Channel World family of publications. IDG Books Worldwide is one of the fastest-growing computer book publishers in the world, with more than 700 titles in 36 languages. The "...For Dummies®" series alone has more than 50 million copies in print. IDG offers online users the largest network of technology-specific Web sites around the world through IDG.net (http://www.idg.net), which comprises more than 225 targeted Web sites in 55 countries worldwide. International Data Corporation (IDC) is the world's largest provider of information technology data, analysis and consulting, with research centers in over 41 countries and more than 400 research analysts worldwide. IDG World Expo is a leading producer of more than 168 globally branded conferences and expositions in 35 countries including E3 (Electronic Entertainment Expo), Macworld Expo, ComNet, Windows World Expo, ICE (Internet Commerce Expo), Agenda, DEMO, and Spotlight. IDG's training subsidiary, ExecuTrain, is the world's largest computer training company, with more than 230 locations worldwide and 785 training courses. IDG Marketing Services helps industry-leading IT companies build international brand recognition by developing global integrated marketing programs via IDG's print, online and exposition products worldwide. Further information about the company can be found at www.idg.com.

1/26/00

Jordan Young has been knocking around the computer industry for about 25 years now. He learned to program by flipping the switches on the front panel of a PDP-8 one night, and since then it's been second nature. Early on, he realized that he enjoyed explaining computers more than using them, and he has been helping people use them effectively ever since. That included a stint in what he fondly calls IBM's State Department and a few years in International Marketing at Data General (it used to make minicomputers). Over the years, he's done everything from software product development to press conferences announcing new computers to operating systems training courses in English and Spanish to lectures on OLAP software in Portuguese. Most enjoyable has been watching two children grow, a long trip down the Amazon river, a weekend spent on Easter Island, and camping in the Andes. Now he spends his time helping Margy with the occasional *For Dummies* book, working on their Internet storefront at GreatTapes.com, and teaching computer classes. When he's not writing about or explaining computers to people, he likes to cook, tend to the chickens, and contemplate the nature of life, God, and the universe.

Carol Baroudi first began playing with computers in 1971 at Colgate University, where two things were new: the PDP-10 and women. She was lucky to have unlimited access to the state-of-the-art PDP-10, on which she learned to program, operate the machine, and talk to Eliza. She taught Algol and helped to design the curricula for computer science and women's studies. She majored in Spanish and studied French, which, thanks to the Internet, she can now use every day. In 1975, Carol took a job doing compiler support and development, a perfect use for her background in languages. For six years, she developed software and managed software development. For a while, she had a small business doing high-tech recruiting (she was a headhunter). Though she wrote her first software manuals in 1975, she has been writing for a living since 1984. Carol has described all kinds of software, from the memory-management system of the Wang VS operating system to e-mail products for the PC and Mac. For the past several years, she has been writing books, *E-mail For Dummies* (published by IDG Books Worldwide, Inc.), for ordinary people who want to use computers. She enjoys speaking to academic, business, and general audiences about the impact of technology on society and other related topics. (Check out her home page, at `http://iecc.com/carol`, to see what she's up to.) Carol believes that we are living in a very interesting time when technology is changing faster than people can imagine. She hopes that as we learn to use the new technologies, we don't lose sight of our humanity and feels that computers can be useful and fun but are no substitute for real life.

About the Authors

John R. Levine was a member of a computer club in high school — before high school students, or even high schools, had computers, where he met Theodor H. Nelson, the author of *Computer Lib/Dream Machines* and the inventor of hypertext, who reminded us that computers should not be taken seriously and that everyone can and should understand and use computers. John wrote his first program in 1967 on an IBM 1130 (a computer roughly as powerful as your typical modern digital wristwatch, only more difficult to use). He became an official system administrator of a networked computer at Yale in 1975. He began working part-time, for a computer company, of course, in 1977 and has been in and out of the computer and network biz ever since. He got his company on Usenet (the Net's worldwide bulletin-board system) early enough that it appears in a 1982 *Byte* magazine article on a map of Usenet, which then was so small that the map fit on half a page. Although John used to spend most of his time writing software, now he mostly writes books (including *UNIX For Dummies* and *Internet Secrets,* both published by IDG Books Worldwide, Inc.) because it's more fun and he can do so at home in the tiny village of Trumansburg, New York, where he is the sewer commissioner (Guided tours! Free samples!), and play with his baby daughter when he's supposed to be writing. John also does a fair amount of public speaking. (See his home page, at `http://iecc.com/john1`, to see where he'll be.) He holds a B.A. and a Ph.D. in computer science from Yale University, but please don't hold that against him.

Unlike her peers in that 40-something bracket, **Margaret Levine Young** was exposed to computers at an early age. In high school, she got into a computer club known as the R.E.S.I.S.T.O.R.S., a group of kids who spent Saturdays in a barn fooling around with three antiquated computers. She stayed in the field throughout college against her better judgment and despite her brother John's presence as a graduate student in the computer science department. Margy graduated from Yale and went on to become one of the first micro-computer managers in the early 1980s at Columbia Pictures, where she rode the elevator with big stars whose names she wouldn't dream of dropping here. Since then, Margy has co-authored more than 16 computer books about the topics of the Internet, UNIX, WordPerfect, Microsoft Access, and (stab from the past) PC-File and Javelin, including *Dummies 101: The Internet For Windows 98, Dummies 101: Netscape Communicator, Internet FAQs: Answers to Frequently Asked Questions, UNIX For Dummies,* and *WordPerfect 8 For Windows 95 For Dummies* (all published by IDG Books Worldwide, Inc.). She met her future husband, Jordan, in the R.E.S.I.S.T.O.R.S., and her other passion is her children, Meg and Zac. She loves gardening, chickens, reading, and anything to do with eating and lives near Middlebury, Vermont (see `http://www.gurus.com/margy` for some scenery).

Contents at a Glance

Introduction 1

Part I: Getting on the Net with Windows Me 7
Chapter 1: What Is the Net? What Is the Web? 9
Chapter 2: How May I Connect to Thee? Let Me Count the Ways 25
Chapter 3: Setting Up Your Internet Account 49
Chapter 4: Dialing In and Out 81

Part II: Mail and Gossip 105
Chapter 5: All about E-Mail 107
Chapter 6: Advanced E-Mail Stuff 133
Chapter 7: The World According to E-Mail: Electronic Mailing Lists 153

Part III: Windows Me Web-Whacking 173
Chapter 8: Windows Me Meets the World Wide Web 175
Chapter 9: Working Web Wonders 197
Chapter 10: Finding Stuff on the Net 213
Chapter 11: Unlikely Ways to Use and See the Web 235

Part IV: Other Stuff You Can Do on the Internet 255
Chapter 12: More Shopping, Less Dropping 257
Chapter 13: Downloading, Uploading, and Other File-Flinging Fun 275
Chapter 14: Online Chatting: How to Make Friends and Influence People 299
Chapter 15: Getting Together with NetMeeting 327

Part V: The Part of Tens 347
Chapter 16: Ten Problems and Solutions 349
Chapter 17: Ten Frequently Asked Questions 355
Chapter 18: Ten Cool Places on the Internet 365
Chapter 19: Ten Stupid Internet Moves to Avoid 369

Glossary 381

Index 393

Table of Contents

Introduction *1*

    About This Book 1
    How to Use This Book 2
    Who Are You? 3
    How This Book Is Organized 4
    Icons Used in This Book 5
    What Now? 5
    Feedback, Please 6

Part I: Getting on the Net with Windows Me *7*

Chapter 1: What Is the Net? What Is the Web? **9**

    So What's All the Hoopla? 11
    A Few Real-Life Stories 13
    Why Is This Medium Different from Any Other Medium? 15
        Anybody can access it 15
        It's politically, socially, and religiously correct 15
        The Net advantage 16
    Electronic Commerce 18
        Security in general 18
        Security in specific 19
    Banking 19
    Some Thoughts about Safety and Privacy 20
        Safety first 20
        Protect your privacy 21

Chapter 2: How May I Connect to Thee? Let Me Count the Ways ...**25**

    Ways to Connect to the Internet from Windows Me 26
        Prodigiously computing and serving America online 28
        The pros and cons of AOL and CompuServe
            as Internet Service Providers 29
        Serving up the Internet 31
        And then there's the cable guy 32
        Wait! There's more! Now there's the DSL guy 32
    Hacker Heaven or Surfer Salvation? 34
    What You Need to Connect Windows to the Internet 35
    Choosing a Modem 36
        When is a modem not a modem: Part 1 36
        Shapes, sizes, and speeds 37
        When is a modem not a modem: Part 2 39

Take the ISP Plunge (Ahhh!) 39
    Who's eligible to be your ISP? 40
    Hippie access 40
    Choosing from among the eligible 42
    Don't let the Windows Me Internet
        Connection Wizard push you around 44
    Signing up for your Internet account 45
All Dressed Up and No Place to Go, So Which Programs
    Talk Over the Internet? 46

Chapter 3: Setting Up Your Internet Account 49
Introducing the Connection Wizard 49
Care and Feeding of the Internet Connection Wizard 50
    The wizard wants to recommend an Internet Service Provider 51
    Signing up with an ISP using the wizard 53
    Telling the wizard that you're already signed up 54
How the Wizard Can Get Lost and Other Exciting Adventures 58
Making Sure That Windows Me Sees Your Modem 60
    Letting the Modem Wizard do the work 60
    I'll do it my way 61
Casting Internet Connection Spells Yourself 65
    Controlling modems from the Control Panel 66
    Network spell 1: The networking pieces of Windows Me 69
    Network spell 2: Setting up TCP/IP 71
    Information about your ISP 74
Getting to the Internet from an Online Service Like AOL
    or CompuServe 76
    America — and the rest of the Internet — Online 77
    AT&T WorldNet 77
    CompuServe 77
    Prodigy Internet 78
    The Microsoft Network (MSN) 78
    Moving on 78
Avoiding the Connection Wizard Altogether 79

Chapter 4: Dialing In and Out 81
Starting Up Your Dial-Up Networking Connection 82
Hanging Up in (Not on) Windows 85
Telling Windows to Connect to the Internet Whenever It Darn Well
    Pleases! 85
Telling Windows How Long to Stay Connected 89
Monitoring Your Dial-Up Networking Connection 89
Making Dial-Up Networking a Little More Convenient 90
    Putting your connection on your desktop 91
    Putting your connection on your Start menu 92
    Canceling your Internet account 93

Fine-Tuning Your Connection 93
    Making sure that the telephone number is local 94
    "Why doesn't Windows Me save my Dial-Up
        Networking password?" 94
Location, Location, Location 96
    Dialing from your desktop computer 96
    Dialing from your laptop computer 98
Whom to Call (and Whom Not to Call) for Support 101
    Call your Internet Service Provider 101
    Get Windows Me help 101
    Call Microsoft — maybe 102
    Call the folks who made your computer 102
    Call your friends 103

Part II: Mail and Gossip *105*

Chapter 5: All about E-Mail **107**
Addresses, Domains, and Mailboxes 107
    What's in a username? 108
    What's in a domain name? 109
    Address tips 110
Where Mail Lives 110
More E-Mail Programs Than You Can Shake a Stick At 111
    PPP, DSL, and cable Internet accounts 111
    America Online (AOL) and CompuServe 112
    Free e-mail accounts 112
    Web-based mail 113
    LAN and other mail 113
What Your E-Mail Program Needs to Know 113
Sending and Receiving Mail with Outlook Express 114
    Running Outlook Express the first time 114
    Sending mail with Outlook Express 119
    Reading mail with Outlook Express 120
Sending and Receiving Mail with Netscape Messenger 122
Sending and Receiving Mail with Netscape 6 123
Sending and Receiving Mail with Eudora 125
Getting Eudora 126
    Setting up Eudora 126
    Sending mail with Eudora 127
    Reading mail with Eudora 129
Where Are the Etiquette Ladies? 131
    Flame off! 131
    Laugh and the world laughs with you 132
What's Next? 132

Chapter 6: Advanced E-Mail Stuff **133**

Here's What We Think: Replying to Mail 134
Is this the party to whom I am replying? 134
Here's what you just said 135
Keeping Track of All Your New Friends 135
The Outlook Express address book 135
The Netscape address book 136
The Eudora address book 137
This One's for You: Forwarding Mail 138
For All You Pack Rats: Saving Mail 140
Filing with Outlook Express 141
Filing with Netscape Messenger/Mail 142
Filing with Eudora 142
Recycle Those Electrons: Deleting Mail 142
Fancy Mail and Getting Attached 143
Slinky links 143
Mail attachments 143
Outlook Express attachments 146
Netscape Messenger/Mail attachments 146
Eudora attachments 147
Robot Mail 147
Your Own Personal Mail Manager 148
Can the Spam 149
Why call it spam? 149
Is it so bad? 149
Can I do something? 150
"Is There a Trick to Using E-Mail Effectively?" 151

Chapter 7: The World According to E-Mail:
Electronic Mailing Lists **153**

You Say You Never Get Any Mail? 153
Signing On to and Getting Off Mailing Lists 154
The human touch 154
LISTSERV, the tyrannosaur of mail managers 156
Make LISTSERV do stuff 158
Majordomo at your service, madam 160
Majordomo does stuff too 161
ListProc — yet another list manager 162
Sending your first message 163
Reply Like a Pro 164
Some Lists to Whet Your Appetite 165
Running Your Own List (?!) 168

Part III: Windows Me Web-Whacking **173**

Chapter 8: Windows Me Meets the World Wide Web **175**

All Hyped Up and Someplace to Go 177
What's in a Name? 178

Browsing Around 179
Surfing the Web with Windows Me 179
    Anatomy of a browser window 181
    Click when ready 184
    Do you know where your browser has been? 184
    Picture this 185
    There's no place like home 186
    A few good links to start with 187
    If at first you don't succeed 187
    Time to quit 188
Getting and Installing Internet Explorer or Navigator
   or Communicator 188
    About downloading a browser: Who, what, where 189
    Downloading your browser 191
    Got it! Now what? (The installation) 194

Chapter 9: Working Web Wonders **197**
Where Did I See That? 197
    Playing Favorites in Internet Explorer 198
    Bookmarking Netscape 199
Making the Paint Dry Faster 201
    Pick a faster place to start 201
    Skip the pix 202
    Catch up with your cache 203
Clear the Deck 204
Forms, Forms, Forms 205
Save It for a Rainy Day 206
Touch Your Nose and Rub Your Belly 207
Making Treeware (Printing) 208
Keep Your Cookie Crumbs Off My Computer 208
Plug In to What's Happening 210
    Popular plug-ins 211
    Using plug-ins 211

Chapter 10: Finding Stuff on the Net **213**
The Five-Minute Guide to Searching 214
Searching in Depth 216
    Yahoo! 216
    More Yahoo 218
    It's also a cheese grater 219
    AltaVista 220
    AltaVista hints 223
    Yahoo and AltaVista — what a pair! 223
    AltaVista away 224
But Wait — There's More 225
    AskJeeves 225
    Google 225

WebCrawler 225
The GO Network 226
Excite 226
HotBot 226
Lycos 226
Northern Light 227
Other Web guides 227
Looking for Businesses 227
WHOIS is a wiz 228
Hoover is not a vacuum cleaner 229
Your tax dollars at work — EDGAR 229
A bounty of business directories 230
Person to Person 230
Call me 231
On the Net 231
Yahoo People Search 232
WhoWhere 232
Canada 411 232
Bigfoot 232
Mail, one more time 233
Where do I buy an aardvark? 233

Chapter 11: Unlikely Ways to Use and See the Web 235

Multimedia and Other Web(by) Gizmoids 236
RealPlayer 8 237
QuickTime 4 240
Flash and Shockwave 241
Windows Media Player 242
Watch Out for Flying Protocol Handlers! 243
The (Hyper-)Active Desktop 244
Putting a tiger in your tank and a Web page on your desktop 246
Care and feeding of your Active Desktop items 248
I want what I want the way I want it when I want it 249
Help on the Web 252
Updates on the Web 252

Part IV: Other Stuff You Can Do on the Internet *255*

Chapter 12: More Shopping, Less Dropping *257*

Shopping Online: Pros and Cons 257
The Credit Card Question 258
Let's Go to the Store 259
Simple shopping 260
Fancy shopping 262
Up, Up, and Away 263
The general theory of airline tickets 263
More about online airlines 265

Taking It to the Bank 265
Moving Money Around 266
Pure Money 266
    Mutual funds 267
    Stockbrokers 267
    Tracking your portfolio 268
Even More Places to Shop 268
    Books and such 268
    Clothes 269
    Computers 270
    Auctions and used stuff 270
    Food 272
    All-In-One 272
The Shopping Update 273

Chapter 13: Downloading, Uploading, and Other File-Flinging Fun . . .275

Why Download Files? 276
Why Upload Files? 276
Downloading Web Pages 276
    Downloading pictures 277
    Downloading programs 277
    Downloading other files 278
File Transfer in Theory and in Practice 279
    Anonymous downloads 279
    Text files versus everything else 280
    Choosing an FTP client program 280
Downloading Files By Using Your Web Browser 280
    The URL of FTP 281
    Giving your browser an FTP URL 281
Real FTP with WS_FTP 283
    Downloading WS_FTP 284
    The big WS_FTP picture 285
    Connecting to an FTP server 285
    "It won't speak to me!" 287
    Local and remote 287
    I am outta here! 289
    Connecting again 289
    FTP-ing wrong 289
Uploading Is Cool Too 290
    Uploading with Netscape 291
    Uploading with WS_FTP 291
After You Download a Program 292
    Getting WinZip for unzipping 292
    Running WinZip 293
    Unzipping files 294
    Zipping around 294
    Easy? Windows? Hurray for Aladdin Expander! 294
    Scanning for viruses 296

Installing the program you downloaded — finally! 297
Configuring the program 298
Finding the Good Stuff 298

Chapter 14: Online Chatting: How to Make Friends and Influence People 299

What's Chatting All About? 299
"Is there a room for me?" 300
"I didn't catch your name" 301
Getting Ready to Chat 301
Chat etiquette 302
A serious chat about safe chatting 303
Abbreviations, emoticons, and smileys 304
There is always some jerk 305
Ways to chat 306
Chatting on AOL 306
Walk on in 306
Rooms with a view 307
People power 308
"Who am I now?" 309
For members only 309
Meet me under the sign of the rose 310
The chat police at your service 311
Cruising IRC with Microsoft Chat 311
"Serve me some chat" 311
Roaming the channels 312
You too can be jolly Saint Nick 314
Installing Microsoft Chat 314
Connecting on chat 316
"What's on the channels tonight?" 317
"Join me" 318
Telling chat who you are 318
"Whisper in my ear" 319
Own your own channel 319
By invitation only 320
Command performance 320
You're not in Kansas anymore 322
Web-Based Chat 322
MSN Chat 323
Chatting in 3-D Worlds 325

Chapter 15: Getting Together with NetMeeting 327

Setting Up NetMeeting 328
Your ID, please 328
Getting connected 331
Anatomy of the NetMeeting window 332
Trying another server 333

Making a Call 334
    Talk to me 335
    Watch what you say 336
    I see you! 337
Answering a Call 338
Let's Chat 338
    Sending a file 340
    Talking privately 340
You Gotta Have Art 341
    Tempted to change the drawing? 342
    Edit my drawing? I don't think so 342
Sharing with Your Friends and Associates 343
Collaborating with Your Partners 343
Meeting Adjourned 345

Part V: The Part of Tens 347

Chapter 16: Ten Problems and Solutions 349

"Loading Web Pages Takes Forever on My Computer" 349
"My E-Mail Inbox Is Filled with Junk Mail" 350
"I Don't Want My Kids Exposed to Online Porn and Weirdos" 350
"I'm Afraid to Use My Credit Card Online" 351
"My Computer Crashes Frequently While I'm Online" 351
"I Can't Find a Friend's E-Mail Address" 351
"I Keep Getting '404 File Not Found' Messages" 352
"My Eyes Hurt, My Back Aches, and My Arm Is Sore" 353
"I Don't Have Enough Time to Try All Those Interesting Web Sites" ...354
"I Spend Too Much Time Online" 354

Chapter 17: Ten Frequently Asked Questions 355

"How Important Is This Internet Stuff?" 355
"Why Bother with the Internet, and What Can I Do with It, Anyway?" ...356
"Are the Internet and the World Wide Web the Same Thing?" 357
"How Much Does It Cost to Be on the Internet?" 358
"Who Should I Sign Up with to Be on the Internet?" 359
"What's an Internet Address?" 359
"Are There Any Good Places to Shop on the World Wide Web?" 360
"Is It Safe to Use My Credit Card on the Net?" 361
"How Can I Make Money on the Net?" 362
"Can People Steal Information from My Computer
    If I'm on the Internet?" 363

Chapter 18: Ten Cool Places on the Internet 365

A Fact-Filled Feature for Flick Fans 365
The Spook's Almanac 365
Getting There Needn't Be a Pain 366
Old-Fashioned Books 366

All the News That Links 366
Read the Future 366
Get a New Computer Custom-Built for You 367
Share That Ware 367
Lost Romance 367
Ring Around the Web 368
Immerse Yourself in Cyberspace 368
If You Liked This Book 368

Chapter 19 : Ten Stupid Internet Moves to Avoid **369**

Fitting In 369
Netiquette 101 370
    Speling counts 370
    STOP SHOUTING — I CAN HEAR YOU 371
    If you don't have anything to say, don't say it 371
    "Can someone tell me how to unsubscribe from this list?" 372
    The netiquette police: Police yourself 372
    Signing off 373
    Don't get attached 373
    Warning: Do not use e-mail in the presence of open flame 374
Junk Mail — Retail and Wholesale 375
    The chain gang 375
    Wholesale junk mail, also known as spam 376
Don't Cause a Run on the Bank 376
    Hang up, already! 377
    Audio and video pigs 378
Some Web Wisdom 378
    Small is beautiful, Part I 378
    Small is beautiful, Part II 379
    If we want the White House, we know where to find it 379
    Let a hundred viewers blossom 379
    Don't be dumb 379

Glossary *381*

Index *393*

Book Registration Information ....*Back of Book*

Introduction

● ●

*W*elcome to *The Internet For Microsoft Windows Me Millenium Edition For Dummies.* We think that it's vital for people to understand what the Internet is, especially if it turns out to be as important as we think it is (and we have a great deal of company in thinking that it will stay important). The Internet is about more than just computers. Sure, it started as a way to connect some computers, but what no one realized at the time is that when computers are hooked together, they provide people with a new way of communicating. That's why, sooner or later, almost every discussion about almost any subject seems to come around to the Internet and the World Wide Web: The Net and the Web are really about communication, and communication is relevant whenever two or more people try to do something, understand something, talk about something, buy or sell something, or do practically anything together.

Yes, this book is about the details of getting your computer hooked up to the Internet and learning how to surf the Web, but it's also about the ways that people communicate on the Internet and what kinds of information you can find out there.

About This Book

Microsoft would like to include with Windows Millenium Edition everything you need to use the Internet and the World Wide Web. As you may have heard, however, this development has created some controversy, everywhere from the U.S. Department of Justice to the Senate to the attorneys general of quite a few states. (In fact, Presiding Judge Jackson decided that Microsoft needed to be broken into two separate companies.) It may be bad for business to have all this software wrapped up in one package, but it certainly is convenient for us tyro computer users. We've been writing about the Internet for quite some time now, and for the first time we can give you step-by-step instructions for how to get your computer hooked up to the Net and how to get information from the Net because, for the first time, all the software you need is already on your computer.

We don't limit ourselves to Microsoft software, however. You may have some choices of what software to get when you buy a computer with Windows Millenium Edition on it. Even if the Netscape Navigator program and

Communicator suite of programs don't come as options on your new computer, though, they provide excellent alternatives for people looking to surf the Web. Also, Eudora, from Qualcomm, has set the standard for e-mail programs. We talk about all these software programs in the book.

Different people will want different things from this book, and you yourself will want different things from it at different times. Here's an overview of what you'll find:

- ✔ An explanation of what the Internet is
- ✔ Tips for figuring out which service to use to connect to the Internet
- ✔ Instructions for sending and receiving e-mail (electronic mail)
- ✔ The World Wide Web explained without (we hope) too much jargon
- ✔ Straight talk about subscriptions, cookies, and other World Wide Web hype
- ✔ The ins and outs of shopping on the Web

How to Use This Book

This book is designed so that you can read just the parts you're interested in. If you're just starting with Windows Millenium Edition and the Internet, however, you'll probably find that you want to read Part I first. (That's why we put it at the beginning.) It steps you through the process of selecting, signing up with, and setting up an Internet connection on your Windows Millenium Edition system. From there, you can hop around the book as you please. Sometimes a topic is too big to fit in one chapter and you find chapters with words like *More* or *Advanced* in their titles. You may want to read the chapter preceding these first, unless you already know what's going on.

Although we try hard not to introduce a technical term without defining it, sometimes we slip. Sometimes too, you may read a section out of order and find a term we defined a few chapters before that. To fill in the gaps, we include a glossary.

Because the Internet is ever-changing, we have expanded our book to include an online area to help keep it up-to-date. Whenever you see our special Whoosh icon, it means that we have more up-to-the-minute information available on our Web site, at

http://net.gurus.com

Whenever you have to type something, it appears in the book like this: **Hello, Internet!** Or else we put it on a line of its own, like this:

```
cryptic command to type
```

Type it just as it appears. Use the same capitalization we do — some systems care deeply about CAPITAL and small letters. Then press the Enter or Return key. The book tells you what should happen when you give each command and what your options are.

If you have to follow a complicated procedure, we spell it out step by step wherever possible, with the stuff you have to do also highlighted in **boldface.** We then tell you what happens in response and what your options are.

When you have to choose commands from menus, we write File⇨Exit when we want you to choose the File command from the menu bar and then choose the Exit command from the menu that appears.

Who Are You?

In writing this book, we assumed that

- ✔ You have a computer running Windows Millenium Edition.

- ✔ Your computer has a modem, and you've plugged your modem into the telephone line.

- ✔ You're pretty comfortable using Windows Millenium Edition. You don't have to be a whiz at Windows; you just have to be able to get around.

- ✔ You have or would like to have access to the Internet.

- ✔ You want to get some work done with it. (We consider the term "work" to include the concept "play.")

- ✔ You are not interested in becoming the world's next great Internet expert, at least not this week.

How This Book Is Organized

This book has five parts. The parts stand on their own — although you can begin reading wherever you like, you should at least skim Part I first to get acquainted with some unavoidable Internet jargon and find out how to get your computer on the Net.

Here are the parts of the book and what they contain:

In Part I, "Getting on the Net with Windows Me," you find out what the Internet is and why it's interesting (at least why we think it's interesting). Also, this part has stuff about vital Internet terminology and concepts that help you as you read through the later parts of the book. Part I discusses how you get on the Internet, gives some thoughts about children's use of the Net, and tells you everything (we think) you need to know to sign up with an Internet Service Provider. For most users, by far the most difficult part of using the Net is getting to that first connection, with software loaded, configuration configured, and modem modeming. After that, it's (relatively) smooth sailing.

The rest of this book deals with what you can do on the Internet. Part II, "Mail and Gossip," jumps right to the heart of what the Internet is about: people talking to people. We get you set up with an e-mail account, teach you some e-mail tricks, and tell you how to fill up your e-mail box with messages from all sorts of mailing lists.

Part III, "Windows Me Web-Whacking," dives into the World Wide Web, the part of the Internet that has powered the Net's leap from obscurity to fame. We discuss how to get around on the Web, including how to look at all sorts of things people never expected you to want, like radio broadcasts and movies. We also talk about finding stuff (which is not as easy as it should be).

Part IV, "Other Stuff You Can Do on the Internet," looks at the other important and useful Net services. Getting a file full of information from the Internet to your computer is something you have to (or want to) do at some point. Sitting down at the keyboard and typing messages while others do the same is a way many people have found to meet like-minded souls. From there, it's just a short hop to conducting a business meeting "live" on the Internet.

A compendium of ready references and useful facts is in Part V, "The Part of Tens" (which, we suppose, suggests that the rest of the book is full of useless facts).

Icons Used in This Book

Lets you know that some particularly nerdy, technoid information is coming up so that you can skip it if you want. (On the other hand, you may want to read it.)

Indicates that a nifty little shortcut or time-saver is explained.

Gaack! We found out about this information the hard way! Don't let it happen to you!

Points out a resource on the World Wide Web that you can use with Netscape, Internet Explorer, or other Web software.

Points you to more up-to-the-minute information on our very own Web site. Hey, this book is *alive.*

What Now?

That's all you need to know to get started. Whenever you hit a snag using the Internet, just look up the problem in the table of contents or index in this book. You'll either have the problem solved in a flash or know where you need to go to find some expert help.

Because the Internet has been evolving for almost 30 years, largely under the influence of some extremely nerdy people, it was not designed to be particularly easy for normal people to use. Don't feel bad if you have to look up a number of topics before you feel comfortable using the Internet.

Feedback, Please

We love to hear from our readers. If you want to contact us, please feel free to do so, in care of

IDG Books Worldwide, 10475 Crosspoint Boulevard, Indianapolis, IN 46256

Better yet, send us Internet e-mail at internetme@gurus.com (our friendly robot answers immediately; the human authors read all the mail and answer as much as we can), or visit this book's Web home page, at http://net.gurus.com. These electronic addresses put you in contact only with the authors of this book; to contact the publisher or authors of other ...For Dummies books, visit the publisher's Web site at http://www.dummies.com, send e-mail to info@idgbooks.com, or send paper mail to the address just listed.

Part I

Getting on the Net with Windows Me

"I did this report with the help of a satellite view atmospheric map from the National Weather Service, research text from the Jet Propulsion Laboratory, and a sound file from 'The Barfing Lungworms' new CD."

In this part . . .

Someday, you will get a computer, plug it in, and have access to the Internet. That day is not now. As a prelude to getting connected to the Net, we talk a little about what the Internet is, what you can do there, and how it got that way. Then we dive in to the nitty-gritty of getting your Windows Me system connected to the Internet: the choices you have to make and the magic spells you have to cast. After you're on the Net, we give you some tips on how to keep the Netty bits of Windows Me out of your hair.

Chapter 1

What Is the Net? What Is the Web?

●●●

In This Chapter

▶ What, really, is the Internet?

▶ For that matter, what is a network?

▶ What is the Internet good for?

▶ Banking, briefly

▶ Is the Internet a safe place?

▶ Where did the Internet come from?

●●●

*W*hat is the Internet? What is the Web? Are they the same thing? The answer (one you'll see more often in this book than you might expect) is, it depends. The Internet, the Web, and the technologies that make them work are changing faster than anyone can keep track of. This chapter begins with the basics and tells you what the Internet and the Web are and, just as important, what has changed during the past couple of years so that you can begin to have an understanding of what it's all about.

If you're new to the Internet, and especially if you don't have much computer experience, *be patient with yourself.* Many of the ideas here are completely new. Allow yourself some time to read and reread. It's a brand-new world with its own language, and it takes some getting used to. Many people find it helpful to read through the entire book quickly one time to get a broader perspective of what we're talking about. Others plow through a page at a time. Whatever your style, remember that it's *new* stuff — you're not *supposed* to understand it already.

Even if you're an experienced computer user, you may find the Internet unlike anything you've ever tackled. The Internet is not a software package and doesn't easily lend itself to the kind of step-by-step instruction we could provide for a single, fixed program. We are as step-by-step as we can be, but the Internet resembles a living organism that's mutating at an astonishing rate more than it resembles Microsoft Word or Excel, which sit quietly on your computer and mind their own business. After you get set up and get a little practice, using the Internet seems like second nature; in the beginning, however, it can be daunting.

The Internet — also known as the *Net* — is the world's largest computer network. "What is a network?" you may ask. Even if you already know, you may want to read the next couple of paragraphs to make sure that we're speaking the same language.

A computer *network* is basically a bunch of computers hooked together to communicate somehow. In concept, it's sort of like a radio or TV network that connects a bunch of radio or TV stations so that they can share the latest episode of *The X-Files*.

Don't take the analogy too far. TV networks send the same information to all the stations at the same time (it's called *broadcast* networking); in computer networks, each particular message is usually routed to a particular computer. Unlike TV networks, computer networks are invariably two-way: When computer A sends a message to computer B, B can send a reply back to A.

Some computer networks consist of a central computer and a bunch of remote stations that report to it (a central airline-reservation computer, for example, with thousands of screens and keyboards in airports and travel agencies). Others, including the Internet, are more egalitarian and permit any computer on the network to communicate with any other.

The Internet isn't really one network — it's a network of networks, all freely exchanging information. The networks range from the big and formal (such as the corporate networks at AT&T, General Electric, and Hewlett-Packard) to the small and informal (such as the one in John's back bedroom, with a couple of old PCs bought through the *Want Advertiser*) and everything in between. College and university networks have long been part of the Internet, and now high schools and elementary schools are joining up. In the past few years, Internet usage has been increasing at a pace equivalent to that of television in the early 1950s; the Net now has an estimated 100 million computers and something like 380 million users, growing at 40 to 50 percent per year. It's estimated that by 2002, nearly *one-half-billion* users will be online.

Of course, it's important to keep in mind that more than 6 *billion* people are living on our planet, and half of them haven't ever used a telephone. This concept is humbling when you consider that we are among the privileged few who can claim access on a global scale. We can only hope that everyone will soon get the chance to be online.

So What's All the Hoopla?

Everywhere you turn, you hear people talking about the Net and the Web — as though they're on a first-name basis. Radio shows give you their e-mail addresses, businesses give you their Web site (starting with "www" and ending with the ubiquitous "dot com"), and strangers ask whether you have a home page. People are "going online and getting connected." Are they really talking about this same "network of networks?" Yes, *and* there's more.

With networks, size counts for a great deal because the larger a network is, the more stuff it has to offer. Because the Internet is the world's largest interconnected group of computer networks, it has an amazing array of information to offer.

The Internet is a new communications technology that is affecting our lives on a scale as significant as the telephone and television. Some people believe that when it comes to disseminating information, the Internet is the most significant invention since the printing press. If you use a telephone, write letters, read a newspaper or magazine, or do business or any kind of research, the Internet can radically alter your entire worldview.

When people talk about the Internet today, they're usually talking about what they can do, what they have found, and whom they have met. The Internet's capabilities are so expansive that we don't have room to give a complete list in this chapter (indeed, it would fill several books larger than this one), but here's a quick summary:

- ✔ **Electronic mail (e-mail):** This service is certainly the most widely used — you can exchange e-mail with millions of people all over the world. People use e-mail for anything for which they might use paper mail, faxes, special delivery of documents, or the telephone: gossip, recipes, rumors, love letters — you name it. (We hear that some people even use it for stuff related to work.) Electronic *mailing lists* enable you to join in group discussions with people who have similar interests and meet people over the Net. *Mail servers* or *mailbots* (programs that respond to e-mail messages automatically) let you retrieve all sorts of information. Chapters 5, 6, and 7 have all the details.

- ✔ **The World Wide Web:** When people talk these days about surfing the Net, they often mean checking out sites on this (buzzword alert) multimedia hyperlinked database that spans the globe. In fact, people are talking more about the Web and less about the Net. Are they the same thing? Technically, no. Practically speaking, for many people, yes. We tell you the truth, the whole truth, and nothing but the truth (this year), in Chapter 9.

The Web, unlike earlier Net services, combines text, pictures, sound, and even animation and lets you move around with a click of your computer mouse. New Web *sites* (sets of Web pages) are growing faster than you can say "Big Mac with cheese," with new sites appearing every minute. In 1993, when we wrote the first edition of this book, the Internet had 130 Web sites. Today, it has many millions, and statistics indicate that the number is doubling every few months.

The software used to navigate the Web is known as a *browser.* The most popular browsers now are Netscape Navigator and Microsoft Internet Explorer. You may have also heard of Opera and of some hoopla over something called Netscape 6. We tell you all about them both in Chapters 9 and 10, along with some other less popular but worthy competitors.

✔ **Chatting:** People are talking to people all over the globe about everything under the sun. They enter *chat rooms* with several other people or one special someone. They're using the America Online chat facility, the CompuServe version of the same thing, or *Internet Relay Chat (IRC),* a chat facility available to almost anyone on the Internet. We tell you how in Chapter 14 and discuss *paging* programs like ICQ and AOL Instant Messenger, which let you send messages that "pop up" on the recipient's screen.

✔ **Information retrieval:** Many computers have files of information that are free for the taking. The files range from U.S. Supreme Court decisions and library card catalogs to the text of old books, digitized pictures (nearly all of them suitable for family audiences), and an enormous variety of software, from games to operating systems.

Special tools known as *search engines, directories,* and *indices* help you find information on the Net. Lots of people are trying to create the fastest, smartest search engine and the most complete Net index. We tell you about two of the most useful, AltaVista and Yahoo!, so that you get the picture. As mentioned in the Introduction to this book, you see a Web icon here and there; it points to resources you can retrieve from the Net, as described in Chapter 10.

✔ **Electronic commerce:** This term is just a fancy word for buying and selling stuff over the Net. It seems that everybody's doing it, and now the software is available to make the process of sending your credit card number over the Net safe and secure. You can buy anything from books to stock in microbreweries. We talk about the relevant issues later in this chapter and in Chapter 12.

✔ **Games and gossip:** An older but still quite popular type of multiuser game called a *MUD (Multi-User Dimension* or *Multi-User Dungeon)* can easily absorb all your waking hours and an alarming number of what otherwise would be your sleeping hours. In a MUD, you can challenge

Where did the Internet come from?

The ancestor of the Internet was the *ARPANET,* a project funded by the Department of Defense (DOD) in 1969, both as an experiment in reliable networking and to link DOD and military research contractors, including the large number of universities doing military-funded research. (*ARPA* stands for Advanced Research Projects Administration, the branch of the DOD in charge of handing out grant money. For enhanced confusion, the agency is now known as *DARPA* — the added *D* is for Defense, in case anyone had doubts about where the money was coming from.) Although the ARPANET started small, connecting three computers in California with one in Utah, it quickly grew to span the continent.

In the early 1980s, the ARPANET grew into the early Internet, a group of interlinked networks connecting many educational and research sites funded by the National Science Foundation, along with the original military ones. By 1990 it was clear that the Internet was here to stay, and DARPA and the NSF bowed out in favor of the commercially run networks that comprise today's Internet. Some of the networks are run by familiar companies like AT&T, Worldcom/MCI, IBM, GTE, and Britain's Cable and Wireless; others belong to specialist companies like PSI and Exodus networks. No matter which one you're attached to, they all interconnect, so it's all one giant Internet.

For yet more Internet history and gossip, visit our Web site at net.gurus.com/history.

other players who can be anywhere in the world. Of course, this is the technology of ten years ago, when text was King (Queen?). Today, gamers revel in the 3D action of Quake III: Arena and Unreal Tournament, where you shoot or die, pilot starships from *Star Trek* in battle with Klingons and other alien hostiles, and blast other "Mech jockies" out of their pods with a few well-placed LRM hits in Mechwarrior 3. Then again, you may appreciate the simple strategy of Backgammon or even Checkers while engaging a faceless opponent who can be anywhere.

A Few Real-Life Stories

Seventh-grade students in San Diego use the Internet to exchange letters and stories with kids in Israel. Although it's partly just for fun and to make friends in a foreign country, a sober academic study reported that when kids have a real audience for their stuff, they write better. (Big surprise.)

For many purposes, the Internet is the fastest and most reliable way to move information. In September 1998, when special prosecutor Kenneth Starr suddenly delivered his report to the U.S. House of Representatives, the House quickly put the report online, allowing millions of people to read it the day it came out. (We can still debate whether it was a good idea to do that, but the Internet is what made it possible.) And Matt Drudge's *Drudge Report* online gossip sheet broke much of the scandal first.

During the 1991 Soviet coup, members of a tiny Internet provider named RELCOM sent out stories that would have been in newspapers, statements from Boris Yeltsin (hand-delivered by friends), and their personal observations from downtown Moscow.

Medical researchers around the world use the Internet to maintain databases of rapidly changing data. People with medical conditions use the Internet to communicate with each other in support groups and to compare experiences.

The Internet has more prosaic uses, too. Here are some from our personal experience:

When we began writing our megabook, *Internet Secrets* (published by IDG Books Worldwide, Inc.), we posted notices on the Net asking for contributions. We got responses from all over the world. Many of these contributors became our friends. Now we have people to visit all over the world. It could happen to *you.*

We get mail every day from all over the world from readers of our ...*For Dummies* books and are often the happy recipients of readers' first-ever e-mail messages.

The Internet is its own best source of software. Whenever we hear about a new service, it usually takes only a few minutes to find software for our computers (various computers running various versions of Windows and a Power Macintosh), download it, and start it up. Most software available on the Internet is free or inexpensive shareware.

The Internet has local and regional parts too. When John wanted to sell a trusty but tired minivan, a note on the Internet in a local for-sale area found a buyer within two days. Margy's husband sold his used computer within a half-hour of posting a message in the relevant Usenet newsgroup.

Lastly, and you've likely heard this and thought that it was a rumor, but we are friends with a couple who met in an Internet discussion group and soon got married. As of this writing, that was four years and one child ago. The Internet can be many things to many people.

Why Is This Medium Different from Any Other Medium?

The Internet is unlike all the other communications media we've ever encountered. People of all ages, colors, creeds, and countries freely share ideas, stories, data, opinions, and products.

Anybody can access it

One great thing about the Internet is that it's probably the most open network in the world. Thousands of computers provide facilities that are available to anyone who has Net access. This situation is unusual — most networks are extremely restrictive in what they allow users to do and require specific arrangements and passwords for each service. Although pay services exist (and more are added every day), most Internet services are free for the taking. If you don't already have access to the Internet through your company, your school, your library, or a friend's attic, you probably have to pay for access by using one of the Internet access providers. We talk about them in Chapter 2.

It's politically, socially, and religiously correct

Another great thing about the Internet is that it is what one may call "socially unstratified." That is, one computer is no better than any other, and no person is any better than any other. Who you are on the Internet depends solely on how you present yourself through your keyboard. If what you say makes you sound like an intelligent, interesting person, that's who you are. It doesn't matter how old you are or what you look like or whether you're a student, a business executive, or a construction worker. Physical disabilities don't matter — we correspond with people who are blind or deaf. If they hadn't felt like telling us, we never would have known. People become famous in the Net community, some favorably and some unfavorably, but they get that way through their own efforts.

Every continent?

Some skeptical readers, after reading the claim that the Internet spans every continent, may point out that Antarctica is a continent, even though its population consists largely of penguins, who (as far as we know) are not interested in computer networks. Does the Internet go there? It does. A few machines at the Scott Base on McMurdo Sound in Antarctica are on the Net, connected by radio link to New Zealand. The base at the South Pole is supposed to have a link to the United States, but it doesn't publish its electronic address.

At the time this book was written, the largest Internet-free land mass in the world is probably Queen Elizabeth Island in the Canadian arctic. We used to say New Guinea, but we got e-mail from a reader there in 1997 telling us about his new Internet provider.

The Net advantage

Maybe it's obvious to you that Internet technology is changing so quickly that you have barely had time to crack the spine of *The Internet For Windows 98 For Dummies,* and here you are holding the Windows Me edition. (We said the same thing last time.) "Could it possibly be all that different?" you ask yourself. Trust us — we've asked ourselves the same thing. The answer, by the way, is a resounding "Yes." It's *that* different again this year. This year, we have to say that the Internet is totally mainstream, and you're falling further behind the curve faster if you haven't yet gotten started. Increasingly, news gets out on the Internet before it's available on other media, and the cyber-deprived are losing ground.

Here are some of the ways the Internet is being used:

- **Finding people:** If you've lost track of your childhood sweetheart, now's your chance to find him or her anywhere in the country. You can use one of the directory services to search the phone books of the entire United States. We tell you more about this subject in Chapter 10.

- **Finding businesses, products, and services:** New yellow page directory services enable you to search by the type of company you're looking for. You can indicate the area code or zip code to help specify the location. People are shopping for that hard-to-find, special gift item. A friend told us of her search for a bear pendant that led her to a company in Alaska that had just what she was looking for.

- **Research:** Law firms are realizing that a great deal of information they formerly paid $600 an hour to find from commercial services can be found for almost nothing when they go directly to the Net. Real estate appraisers use demographic data available on the Net, including unemployment statistics, to help assess property values. Genetics researchers and other scientists download up-to-date research results from around the world. Businesses and potential businesses research their competition over the Net.

✔ **Education:** Schoolteachers coordinate projects with classrooms all over the globe. College students and their families exchange e-mail to facilitate letter writing and keep down the cost of phone calls. Students do research from their home computers. The latest encyclopedias are online, including the entirety of the *Encyclopedia Britannica* (http://www.britannica.com).

✔ **Travel:** Cities, towns, states, and countries are using the Web to put up (post) tourist and event information. Travelers find weather information, maps, transportation schedules and tickets, and museum hours online.

✔ **Marketing and sales:** Software companies are selling software and providing updates via the Net. (The folks making money from the manufacture of floppy disks are looking for new products. Aside from the large pile of AOL disks we now use as coasters, most software distribution is migrating to the Net.) Companies are selling products over the Net. Online bookstores and music stores enable people to browse online, choose titles, and pay for stuff over the Net.

✔ **Love:** People are finding romance on the Net, as evidenced by our aforementioned friends. Singles ads and matchmaking sites vie for users. Contrary to Internet lore, the Net community is no longer just a bunch of socially challenged male nerds under 25.

✔ **Healing:** Patients and doctors keep up-to-date with the latest medical findings, share treatment experience, and give one another support around medical problems. We even know of some practitioners who exchange e-mail directly with their patients.

✔ **Investing:** People do financial research, buy stock, and invest money. Some companies are online and trade their own shares. Investors are finding new ventures, and new ventures are finding capital.

✔ **Organizing events:** Conference and trade-show organizers are finding that the best way to disseminate information, call for papers, and do registration is to do it on the Web. Information can be updated regularly, and paper and shipping costs are dramatically reduced. Registering online saves the cost of on-site registration staff and the hassle of on-site registration lines.

✔ **Nonprofits:** Churches, synagogues, and other community organizations put up pages telling about themselves and inviting new people. The online church newsletter *always* comes before Sunday.

Electronic Commerce

We hear many new buzzwords and phrases aimed at confounding the inno-cent and filling the pockets of would-be consultants. We hear about "digital commerce," "electronic commerce," "digicash," "virtual checks," and "smart cards." If you care, entire books are being written about these subjects. The one topic in this area that you need to know about is buying stuff over the Net. Chapter 12 tells you all about it. (If you plan to set up your own business and sell stuff over the Net, you need more info than we have pages in this book to cover it.)

The earth-shattering, startling new idea of how to buy things over the Net lies buried in the inner meaning of the following phrase: "Enter your credit card number." We're not saying that you shouldn't exercise caution, but our expe-rience of buying stuff over the Net in the past years tells us that you have no great cause for alarm. What have we bought? Books, CDs, clothing, software, videotapes, encyclopedia subscriptions, and matchmaking subscriptions. Here's what you need to know.

Security in general

Some folks seem particularly wary of sending their credit card number over the Net. On the other hand, these same people hand their actual physical cards with their handwritten signatures to gas station attendants wearing distinctive outfits in bright colors not typically found in nature, to servers at restaurants, and to clerks at all sorts of stores. Do you know what they do with the card before they give it back to you? Do you worry about it? We don't. We do know someone who used to run a restaurant and later ran an online store, who assures us that he had far more credit card trouble at the restaurant.

If you use a credit card, remember that the credit card companies are even more concerned than you are about the idea of any kind of credit card fraud, on or off the Net. All cards have a limit on the amount of fraudulent use for which you're liable; if you're a U.S. resident the limit is $50 or less. But remem-ber that a debit card is not the same as a credit card and we suggest that you stick with credit cards because debit cards are not protected in the same way.

The point is that if you're comfortable using a credit card for other uses, you don't have to get scared about using it over the Net just because it's new. We do recommend that you take sensible precautions, and we tell you all about them in Chapter 12, which talks about shopping on the Net, with or without a credit card. Meanwhile, look for the little padlock on a Web page that tells you you're running in secure mode.

If possible, use credit cards rather than checks when ordering over the Net. If you have a dispute with the vendor, you can ask your credit card company to reverse the charge or to refuse charges from that company.

Security in specific

To avoid the possibility of bad guys or gals electronically listening to the bits of your private information whirring across the Net, stripping them off, and redirecting them to purchase their dream vacations, schemes have been invented to encode info sent over the Net so that even if the villains intercept the info, it doesn't do them any good. The information gets all mixed up and hidden in such a way that only the legitimate recipient can decode it. The software that processes this information safely, hiding everything from possible perverse perusal, is known as *SSL* (Secure Sockets Layer) which lets you connect to a *secure server*. We just call it encryption. Most Web browsers (you can read more about them in Chapter 8) have SSL encryption built right in. If you're the least bit antsy about sending your card number over the Net, stick to secure servers.

Software that takes your credit card number (or any other information) over the Net without encoding it is known as *insecure*. Insecure services are perfectly adequate for many transactions. We use them all the time as long as we know that the business behind the server is reliable. If you don't know the business behind the server, the fundamental reliability of the business should be of more concern than what flavor of server they use.

Banking

Over the past year, more and more banks have made their online banking services prominent on the list of services they provide. The first bank to do this, in the mid- to late 1980s, was Citibank. You can obtain information about your checking and savings accounts, loans, and credit card and CD accounts. Even small banks now offer this kind of service. Most, but not all, offer their services under the most secure conditions available, and most offer their online banking services in three ways, via the Web or using Quicken or Microsoft Money. The key term you should look for in any of your bank's brochures or ads is *128-bit encryption*. If this term is used in your bank's promotional material about its online banking, it's likely to be kosher. The transmission of your banking information is made under the very secure technology that is in use today. Is it foolproof? No, but nothing is. You can read more about banking online in Chapter 12.

Some Thoughts about Safety and Privacy

The Internet is a funny place. Although it seems completely anonymous, it's not. People used to have Internet usernames that bore some resemblance to their true identity — their name or initials or some combination in conjunction with their university or corporation gave a fairly traceable route to an actual person. Now, with the phenomenon of screen names (courtesy of America Online) and multiple e-mail addresses (courtesy of many Internet providers and countless free e-mail service providers), revealing your identity is definitely optional.

Depending on who you are and what you want to do on the Net, you may, in fact, want different names and different accounts. Here are some legitimate reasons for wanting them:

- ✔ You're a professional — a physician, for example — and you want to participate in a mailing list or newsgroup without being asked for your professional opinion.

- ✔ You want help with an area of concern that you feel is private and would not want your problem known to people close to you who may find out if your name were associated with it.

- ✔ You do business on the Net, and you socialize on the Net. You may want to keep those activities separate.

A warning to those who would consider abusing the anonymous nature of the Net: Most Net activities can be traced, and a significant number of people have the skills to trace abusers. If you start to abuse the Net, you'll find that you're not so anonymous.

Safety first

The anonymous, faceless nature of the Internet has its downside too.

We advise that you do not use your full name or ever provide your name, address, and phone number to someone you don't know over the Net. Never believe anyone who says that he is from "AOL tech support" or some such authority and asks you for your password. No legitimate entity will ever ask you for your password. Be especially careful about disclosing information about kids. Don't fill out profiles in chat rooms that ask for a kid's name, hometown, school, age, address, or phone number because they are invariably used for "targeted marketing" (junk mail).

Though relatively rare, horrible things have happened to a few people who have taken their Internet encounters into real life. Many wonderful things have happened, too. We've met some our best friends over the Net, and, as mentioned, some people have met and gotten married — no kidding! The Net is a wonderful place, and meeting new people and making new friends is one of the big attractions. We just want to make sure that you're being careful. Just use common sense when you set up a meeting with a Net friend. Here are a few tips:

- ✔ Talk to the person on the phone before you agree to meet. If you don't like the sound of the person's voice or something makes you feel nervous, don't do it.

- ✔ Depending on the context, try to check the person out a little. If you've met in a newsgroup or chat room, ask someone else you know whether they know this person. (Women, ask another woman before meeting a man.)

- ✔ Meet in a well-lit public place. Take a friend or two with you.

- ✔ If you're a kid, take a parent with you. Never, ever meet someone from the Net without your parents' explicit consent.

Protect your privacy

Here in the United States, we've grown up with certain attitudes about freedom and privacy, many of which we take for granted. We tend to feel that who we are, where we go, and what we do is our own business as long as we don't bother anyone else. Well, it seems that a whole bunch of people are extremely interested in who we are, where we go (on the Net, at least), and, most especially, what we buy. Here are a few hints to control how much or how little info you give them.

Please pass the cookies

To enhance your online experience, the makers of Web browsers, such as Netscape and Internet Explorer, have invented a type of special message that lets a Web site recognize you when you revisit that site. They thoughtfully store this info, called a *cookie,* on your very own machine to make your next visit to the same site smoother.

This info can usually make your next transaction smoother, in fact. When you're using an airline-reservation site, for example, the site uses cookies to keep the flights you're reserving separate from the ones other users may be reserving at the same time. On the other hand, suppose that you use your credit card to purchase something on a Web site and the site uses a cookie to remember your credit card number. Suppose that you provide this information from a computer at work and the next person to visit that site uses the same computer. That person could, possibly, make purchases on your credit card. Oops.

It may be true that cookies can make your life more convenient. You have to be the judge. Every Web server can offer you cookies, and most do (you'd be surprised at the sites that deposit cookies on your computer). You need to know that this kind of software exists so that if you're concerned about your privacy, you can take steps to protect it.

Cookie files usually have the name *cookie* associated with them — cookies.txt on Windows and MagicCookie on a Mac, for example. You can delete your cookie files — your browser will create a new, empty one. Modern browsers can tell you about cookies and ask you whether to accept them as servers offer them to you. When Carol checked her Macintosh, she found two cookie files — one from Netscape and one from Internet Explorer. If she hadn't been looking for them, she never would have known that they were there.

Contrary to rumor, cookie files cannot get other information from your hard disk, give you a bad haircut, or otherwise mess up your life. They collect only information that the browser tells them about.

In addition to the cookie file, Internet Explorer keeps a history file of where you've been on the Web. (Look in your Windows folder for a subfolder named History.) If anyone other than you uses the computer you use, you may want to delete its contents after your use, unless you don't care who sees it. Courts have ruled, by the way, that companies own their computers and their contents. You have no "right to privacy" at work, even though most of us find the idea creepy. Companies can eavesdrop on phone calls, read your e-mail (going and coming), and read anything on your computer, including a history file detailing where you've searched. This situation can be problematic if you've done a little unofficial surfing at lunchtime.

Encryption and pretty good privacy

When you send information through the Internet, it gets relayed from machine to machine, and along the way, if someone really cares, she may be able to take a look at what comes across the wire. Whether you're sending your credit card number or sending e-mail love letters, you may feel more comfortable if the absolute secure nature of the transmission were guaranteed.

You can guarantee security by using *encryption,* which is high-tech-ese for encoding — just like with a secret decoder ring. You know — codes, spies, secret messages. Software exists that helps you package up your message and send it in a way that nobody except the intended recipient can read it.

Encryption is the virtual envelope that defies prying eyes. In practice, we rarely encrypt e-mail, though we're happy to know that the option exists. One reason we don't encrypt it is that, at this point, it's too darned cumbersome. Some e-mail software comes with encryption built-in — notably, Microsoft Outlook Express — so many more people will choose to use it. Also check out PGP, which stands for *pretty good privacy*, the most widely used encryption scheme on the Net. Because PGP is complicated enough to require pages of explanation, we don't have room in this book to go into the details; check out our *E-Mail For Dummies,* 2nd Edition, and *Internet Secrets,* 2nd Edition, where we give you blow-by-blow details. New, easier-to-use versions of PGP come out every month or two, so a PGP add-in is probably available for your favorite mail program.

Chapter 2

How May I Connect to Thee? Let Me Count the Ways

• •

In This Chapter

▶ Connecting from Windows Me

▶ Avoiding not-so-heavenly hackers

▶ Making phone, LAN, cable, and DSL connections

▶ Choosing an ISP

▶ Choosing a modem

▶ Choosing which programs to use

• •

*W*ith an ominous-sounding name like Windows Millenium Edition (Windows Me), you may think that your computer already knows and does everything you want it to. If you do, you'll be a bit disappointed. Although you won't be spending many hours tweaking and cajoling your computer to connect to the Internet, you will still have to make some choices and enter some information.

Your computer most likely came with Windows preinstalled. However, no Internet connection comes preloaded because you can connect your computer to the Internet in too many ways for one of them to be the "obvious" choice, even for Microsoft. The reason is, in part, that no single Internet Service Provider (ISP) is a local telephone call from everywhere in the United States and partly that an Internet connection is a service you pay for every month rather than software you buy once. The best deal for you depends on what you are going to do, how much support you want, where you live, and often what local or long-distance telephone plan you have.

In this chapter, we introduce you to the different ways you can connect to the Internet, and we tell you what tools normally found around the home you need in order to connect. *Hint:* A hacksaw is *not* one of them, and you don't have to raid the toolbox either. We're talking about software tools here. In Chapter 3, we give you step-by-step instructions for getting connected using these software tools.

If you already have an Internet account you're happy with, and for which you don't pay huge long-distance bills, we give you permission to skip this entire chapter and go directly to Chapter 3. On the other hand, you may want to read this chapter anyway, to find out what new alternatives may have become available. Besides, we think that this chapter is fascinating and just know that you'll enjoy it.

Ways to Connect to the Internet from Windows Me

To connect your computer to the Internet, you have anywhere from two to four major choices, if you're lucky:

✔ **Choice 1: Sign up with an online service, such as America Online.** Online services tend to be easier to use, and they provide information in a more organized way. They usually give you the full range of Internet services, which can make them quite attractive. They all also provide their services at a flat rate, albeit one that is a little higher than the average Internet-only Internet Service Provider's. Because demand is growing faster than some providers can support, access is sometimes slow, although this situation is changing. The players in this field are America Online (AOL), CompuServe, and, to some small degree still, Prodigy.

Although you pay $24.95 per month, services like CompuServe and Prodigy have archived many years of accumulated knowledge and know-how from their longtime users. The information, help, and tips you can find in the CompuServe user forums alone are well worth the extra $5 per month.

✔ **Choice 2: Sign up with an Internet Service Provider (ISP) for an Internet account.** These folks are the main on-ramp to the Internet nowadays. They are generally considered the access portals for people with technical "chops" and give you the basic account you need to put your computer on the Internet. If you decide that you want to deepen your Internet experience, most ISPs allow you to put up a Web page, though exactly how varies from provider to provider. What these folks give you is a PPP account (we promise to explain it in a few paragraphs), which is what you need to use a Web browser (Internet Explorer or Netscape Navigator), an Internet mail program (Outlook Express, Eudora, or Netscape Communicator), and all the other new things cropping up on the Internet, from telephones to whiteboards.

✔ **Choice 3 (if you're lucky): Sign up for cable TV access.** We say "if you're lucky" because cable access is not widely available yet. If it's available in your area, however, all you have to do is call your cable company and arrange for someone to come and install a network card in your computer and some cable in your home (if you don't already have cable TV.) If you choose this option, you can skip the rest of this chapter and just gloat. You don't need a phone, you don't need a modem, and you don't need a TV.

✔ **Choice 4 (if you've been smiled upon by angels): Get xDSL installed.** What's that you say? xDSL is a way to get ridiculous Internet access speeds from your old, groggy phone line. Don't worry about the technical details; just know that you can surf the Web more than 30 times faster than with an analog modem. Although xDSL is hooked up to an existing phone line, it doesn't use the line. We know — this really sounds weird. Suffice it to say that you can order pizza while you're watching a QuickTime movie trailer online at `www.trailers.com`. xDSL is fast, cheap, and always on. Depending on whom you ask, it may be faster or slower than cable access, but it's definitely much faster than any other alternative.

This section takes them one at a time.

Are you already on the Internet?

If you have access to a computer running Windows, it may already be on the Internet. If you're just upgrading to Windows Me from Windows 95 or Windows 98, you may also already be on the Internet. Here are some ways to check.

✔ If you have an account on an online service, such as CompuServe, America Online (AOL), Prodigy, Microsoft Network (MSN), or MCI Mail, you already have a connection to the Internet. At the least, you can send mail, and some online services provide relatively complete Internet connections.

✔ If you use a computer at your company or school, it may well have an internal e-mail system. If it does, it can probably send mail

to and from the Internet. Ask your friendly neighborhood nerd (don't worry — you can say "nerd" to them as often as possible. The term is now considered a badge of honor).

✔ If your company or school has a local computer network or Local Area Network (or LAN), it may be connected directly or indirectly to the Internet, for either just mail or a wider variety of services. Because networks of PCs (including all flavors of Macintosh, various examples of UNIX, and other tints of Windows) use the same type of networking as the Internet does, connection is technically easy. Some networks of PCs use different types of network setups (most commonly, Novell).

Prodigiously computing and serving America online

Back in the not-so-old days, the Internet was only for the government, college students and professors, and scientists. Although a few hardcore nerds were online, the Internet was mostly unknown. Everyone else who wanted to be online used The Source or, later, CompuServe or, even later, America Online and Prodigy. Those online services did a few important things to earn the two or three (or, early on, even ten) dollars an hour they charged their customers.

First, they provided local telephone numbers in most of the major regions where people live. That capability was often important. Even if your company or university had a computer you could dial in to from home, if you lived any distance away, the long-distance telephone charges could mount up fast (for more about long-distance charges, the sidebar "How important is my ISP's telephone number, really?" later in this chapter). Even if you were adventurous and signed up with a bulletin-board system, after you traveled away from home, it was long-distance time again.

Second, the online services provided easy-to-use software for electronic mail. For a long time, you could trade mail only with people on the same online service as you, although that capability could still be useful. Third, they provided chat facilities and the same online kind of CB-type chats we talk about in Chapter 14. Fourth, they created communities of people with similar interests, ranging from the technical to the social. Online services were a decent deal: you got to use many of the most popular Internet services with much less hassle.

With the growth in popularity of the Internet and new packages that make it easy to sign on, CompuServe, AOL, and Prodigy decided to make themselves "gateways" to the Internet, providing all the services they had traditionally provided and adding Internet access.

After many years of competition between AOL and CompuServe (some would even say that Prodigy was once a contender), AOL *bought* CompuServe. Since then, nothing at CompuServe has changed except the access software. All the original forums and other unique aspects of CSI, as it is still called by its long-time user community, are still intact.

The pros and cons of AOL and CompuServe as Internet Service Providers

Here are some reasons you may want to use AOL or CompuServe to access the Internet:

- ✔ **You already have an AOL or CompuServe account.** It's the best reason we can think of. If you've been using these services, you already have an e-mail address that people may know, and you probably have found stuff on these services you like (such as chat rooms or investment advice or movie reviews). Why bother learning that all over again? Continue to use what you know *and* use new things on the Internet: It's the best of both worlds.

- ✔ **AOL or CompuServe have local-access telephone numbers in your area, and no one else does.** This situation is very unlikely. Take Burlington, Vermont (population 35,000), for instance. It has three local numbers for AOL and only one for MindSpring. Then again, with an excellent local ISP like SoVerNet, you can safely and happily choose to support your local business community.

- ✔ **You travel frequently, particularly overseas.** CompuServe in particular has an excellent network of service points all over the world. Both AOL and CompuServe provide good national coverage in the United States. Using AOL or CompuServe enables you to get on the Net without having to rip out your Windows Me Internet setup every time you visit a new location. (On the other hand, if you travel frequently, the AT&T Business Internet service, formerly the IBM service, has even more international service points than CompuServe does.)

- ✔ **You want to post your own Web page without becoming an Internet whiz.** Although we take you through as much of the posting-your-own-Web-page procedure as we can, every Internet Service Provider (ISP) is a little different. AOL makes it pretty easy.

- ✔ **You want to keep access to some of the proprietary AOL content, particularly investments.** AOL does have a little-known $9.95-per-month rate for unlimited access called BYOA (Bring Your Own Access), if you access its services from your connection with an ISP. To be honest, it's a great way to go. It may be $30 as opposed to $25 with AOL alone or $20 for a regular ISP, but you get unfettered access to the Internet using any software you like *and* unlimited access to online AOL content and community. It's quite the deal.

Here are some reasons you may *not* want to use AOL or CompuServe to access the Internet:

- Some Internet services they provide are new to them, and our experience is that their technical support sometimes isn't up on the latest details.

- It takes a very long time to get through to technical support over the phone or online.

- Access to Internet features, from searching the World Wide Web to downloading files, can be slower because everything you're doing has to go from the computer you're looking at to their computers, out to the source on the Internet, back to their servers, and back again to your computer. It's similar to when you got mad at someone in high school and used someone else to talk to the target of your fury while that person was standing next to you. ("You tell *her* that I will *not* be held responsible for anything that may happen to *her* pom-poms. Humph!!"). Not exactly efficient.

- Your computer has an extra layer of software and although it's not *supposed* to get in the way, sometimes it does.

- Internet access isn't their main business, so if that's what you want to concentrate on, you may not have their full attention.

What about Prodigy and MSN?

You may have noted that we've allotted a great deal of space to AOL and CompuServe. We have a good reason. Because both are mainly *proprietary*, their services are incompatible with Internet standards across the board. Does this statement mean that you should not consider signing up with them? No! Both are quite good at what they do, and they offer Internet access. AOL is entirely outside the realm of the Internet, and CompuServe uses a number of Internet standards to integrate the CompuServe and Internet experience (to great effectiveness, we might add).

So where do Prodigy Internet and MSN (Microsoft Network) fall in regard to this situation? Easy — they're real Internet Service Providers that base their systems on real Internet standards. You can use any software you want in order to access your Prodigy Internet or MSN account. Of course, both offer enhanced services. Prodigy has a long history and a vast amount of accumulated data to offer its users through members-only Web pages. MSN has recently added a completely new interface to its service (and offers it freely to anyone, of course, members or not), hoping to make everything easier to use — and more dependent on Microsoft services. Shameful.

You've probably concluded that both Prodigy Internet and MSN are nothing more than ISPs that compete directly with the likes of MindSpring, AT&T WorldNet, and other national services and *not* with AOL or CompuServe. We cover traditional ISPs in depth in Chapter 3, so we save this discussion for that chapter.

As you can probably tell from this list, we think that using AOL or CompuServe as your ISP works, although we're not enthusiastic about it. Although we have accounts on both online services, we mainly use a *real* ISP (read on).

Serving up the Internet

Companies that sell Internet accounts and accounts that connect your computer to the Internet are called *Internet Service Providers* and are even more often abbreviated as *ISPs*. (We computer types just love TLAs, *three-letter acronyms*.) An ISP is similar to an online service, but with the important difference that its primary business is hooking people to the Internet. Because almost all ISPs buy their equipment and software from a handful of manufacturers, the features and services one ISP offers are much like those of another, with such important differences as price, service, and reliability. Think of it as the difference between a Ford and a Buick, with the differences between your local dealers being at least as important in the purchase decision as the differences between the cars.

What an ISP sells you is known as a *PPP account.* For all you TLA fans, PPP stands for Point-to-Point Protocol, if you must know. (An earlier scheme named SLIP worked in a similar fashion to PPP, although PPP is now universally offered and is more reliable. Not to mention that there's not much room in this world for FLAs (*four-letter acronyms*) — four-letter words don't go over well with parents). When you connect to your provider with PPP, your computer becomes part of the Internet. You type stuff directly to programs running on your computer, and those programs communicate over the Net to do whatever it is that they do for you.

The big advantage of PPP access is that you're not limited to running programs your ISP gives you. You can download a new Internet application from the Net and begin using it immediately and your provider acts only as a data conduit between your computer and the rest of the Net.

The disadvantage of PPP accounts used to be that they were difficult to set up. You had to know many arcane numbers and fiddle around in the guts of your computer's operating system. Windows Me makes this process much easier with its wizards, and we lead you through the process in Chapter 3.

If you're the type of person who likes to live on the edge, technologically speaking, you probably want the fastest Internet connection available so that you can play with all the fancy graphics and download sound and video. Graphics, video, and sound are all bits of information, and lots and lots of bits of information are too many for most dial-up connections to handle. High-speed connections can provide greater *bandwidth,* the amount of data transferred in a specific amount of time. The good news is that high-speed connections are becoming affordable and available to mere mortals. And, at least for the moment, they are available from ISPs, not from online services.

And then there's the cable guy

Cable television companies have been working to provide Internet access and in some areas are successfully providing service. If cable Internet access is available in your community, it's worth checking out.

Here's how it works in the Boston area. You call the cable company. The technician comes and installs a network connection thingy (very technical term) where your cable comes into your house, installs a standard network card in your computer if it doesn't already have one, brings a cable modem (Carol's looks like a laptop computer with a spike hairdo), and hooks them together. Magic.

If you have cable television, the cable is split, and one segment goes to your computer. If you don't have cable television, the cable company may have to install the actual cable too. When the technician goes away, however, you have a permanent, high-speed connection to the Internet (as long as you pay your bill, about $40 a month on top of your regular cable bill). In addition to the speed and constant access at a fixed price, you aren't tying up a phone line.

Essentially, the cable TV company serves as your Internet Service Provider. This setup is nice because it gets one company out of your Internet equation. With a PPP account from an ISP (that's what we describe in the preceding section), you use the phone company to get in touch with the Internet. With a cable modem, your computer talks directly to the cable company's box. Because they're the folks supplying the Internet data to you, one less company is involved (the telephone company gets left out of the play).

Wait! There's more! Now there's the DSL guy

As though the choices we present in this section aren't enough, here's one more for you to mull over. DSL service is a new kind of service that is now being deployed rather aggressively in most large metropolitan areas. The companies that offer it are either your local telephone company or a handful of national or regional companies like Flashcom, Covad, and Northpoint. If you're already connected to the Internet or know someone who is, go to http://www.dslreports.com to see a full listing of DSL providers nearest you and reviews from users.

DSL service is as fast or faster than cable, although the faster you get, the more you pay. The advantage of DSL over cable is that you don't have to try to recable your house with coaxial cable wire to get the connection where

Firewalls: Computing inside a box

Lots of PCs in big companies are loaded up with Internet software and have network connections with a hookup to the Internet, so, if you're so blessed, you can run programs on your computer and hook right up to the Net. Right? Not quite.

If you're in a large organization that has (not altogether unreasonable) concerns about confidential company secrets leaking out by way of the Internet, a *firewall* system placed between the company network and the outside world may control and limit outside access to the internal network.

Because the firewall is connected to both the internal network and the Internet, any traffic between the two must go through the firewall. Special programming on the firewall limits which type of connections can be made between the inside and outside and who can make them.

In practice, you can use any Internet service that is available within the company; for outside services, however, you're limited by what can pass through the firewall system. Most standard outside services — such as looking at Web pages, copying files from one computer to another, and sending and receiving electronic mail — should be available, although the procedures, involving something called a *proxy server,* may be somewhat more complicated than what's described in this book.

Often, you have to log in to the firewall system first and from there get to the outside. It's usually impossible for anyone outside the company to get access to systems or services on the inside network (that's what the firewall is for). Except for the most paranoid of organizations, electronic mail flows unimpeded in both directions.

Keep in mind that you probably have to get authorization to use the firewall system before you can use *any* outside service other than e-mail.

you computer already is. DSL is just as expensive as cable, though, and can cost considerably more if you opt for very high-speed service. DSL is usually added to your existing phone line and does not interrupt your voice service, even when you use it.

In our experience, the NetGear FA310TX 10/100 is *the* most reliable and compatible network interface card that can be had for $30. We would pay $50 for a card, but that's not what they charge. You can find them almost anywhere, although we know that you can get them at CompUSA.

Because it is so new and in such high demand, DSL service is typically installed within four to six weeks of the initial order. Unless you already have it (which is likely), you will have to get temporary Internet service for a month or two from a local or national provider before your DSL gets installed.

Full-service DSL

When you're shopping around for DSL service, you should look for a free DSL modem in exchange for signing a two-year commitment for the service. A DSL modem can cost $300. We expect that you will be able to find providers offering terms similar to these throughout 2001. Keep in mind that you will be signing a binding contract, so if you think that you may move out of the area within the two years, you will want to choose a national provider. You should also make sure that, if you move to a different area, the company will continue the contract without any penalties.

Most DSL accounts come with an e-mail account and access to Internet newsgroups, just like a dial-up ISP. At about $40 per month, the basic level of service should be sufficient for most home users. The basic plans have some limitations, however, and one of them is not being able to run your own Web and mail server. This would mean that you would have to house

any web page or domain (yourown.com) at a Web hosting service at additional costs which may run higher than simply buying the next level of service. The next level, at about $80 per month, typically allows you to serve Web pages or e-mail from your DSL connection location without restriction.

Make sure that your computer is equipped with a network interface card (NIC). If it isn't, you can purchase one for as little as $30 and have it installed at a local computer repair shop or a major computer retail store, such as CompUSA. Hooking up DSL is the provider's responsibility. Typically, the phone company comes in to check the line, and after the line has been deemed fit for DSL usage, the DSL installer comes in, installs your modem, fiddles with the phone wiring, and generally makes sure that everything is in working order. You may have to make a phone call to technical support to set up the connection in your Windows Me software.

Hacker Heaven or Surfer Salvation?

You may have heard of hackers and their illegal exploits into various computers around the world. They're actually *crackers,* but that's another story for another time. These things do happen, and people lose credibility, data, or both. You may think that you're nobody to a hacker. Why would anyone want anything from you? What could anyone possibly gain from crashing your home computer? Nothing, really. A hacker can, however, co-opt your computer for a denial-of-service (DoS) attack, where large numbers of computers make so many requests for information from one service as to bring it to a dead stop.

These types of attacks were made on several very large sites in early 2000. A site that was stopped dead in its tracks was Yahoo, one of the largest Web sites in the world that services millions of people every day. How did the hacker or hackers do this? Unfortunately, it was done very easily. Using readily available software, these malicious individuals were able to take over a large number of computers and instruct them all to direct a very large number of requests at Yahoo. It's like going to McDonald's and having a few hundred people all shouting their orders at one time. Lots of people want something all at the same time.

After the attacks were stopped and the ruckus was quelled, it was determined that almost every single computer in this attack was used unwittingly from remote locations. Here's where you come in. Cable modems and DSL service use a *static* IP address. Think of it as your home address on the Internet: Like your real home, that address almost never changes, and certainly not while you're still there. With a dial-up account, a new IP number is assigned to you every time dial up, and it's usually different.

If your address were to change all the time, it would be hard to keep track of you, right? When your address does *not* change, you can *always* be found, which is partly what hackers count on. A computer that sits still makes the best candidate for inspection, intrusion, or even destruction, if not all three. Cable and DSL no longer sound very appetizing? Don't worry because if your computer is the only one to have access to that connection and you have not activated any server software or shared your computer (trust us — you'd know if you had), a hacker has no way to get at your files.

If, on the other hand, you have more than one computer or are contemplating home networking, you could have a problem. We're not saying that anyone with cable or DSL *will* get hacked, although there's a greater chance of it happening. Fortunately, there are ways of preventing unwanted attacks and intrusions, and some of them are quite good. We mention unauthorized access later elsewhere in this book, but for now, suffice it to say that you can have your cake and eat it too.

So, when your nervous friend comes running to you, urging you not to destroy your life and your files by getting cable or DSL access, rest assured that the friend is wrong and that you can get what you want without having to give anything up. Meanwhile, get access to the Internet and check out Steve Gibson's Shield's Up! service, at `http://grc.com`, where he offers a veritable mountain of information on protecting yourself from hackers (who are really crackers, but again, that's another story entirely).

What You Need to Connect Windows to the Internet

Just about any computer that can run Windows Me can connect to the Internet. In addition to your Windows Me machine, however, you need three items to make this Internet trick work:

> ✔ A modem to hook your computer to the phone line
>
> ✔ An account with an online service or ISP, to give your modem somewhere to call
>
> ✔ Software to run on your computer

We look at each of these items in turn.

Choosing a Modem

If you went the cable TV or DSL routes we talk about in the preceding section, you don't need a modem, so skip this section.

No matter whether you sign up with AOL, CompuServe, or an Internet Service Provider (ISP), your computer calls that computer over the telephone. How fast information comes and goes to and from the Internet is determined by three things: how fast your computer can squirt the information into the telephone, how fast the telephone company can carry that information to the provider you signed up with, and how fast it can suck that information from the phone. The "thing" that connects your computer to the telephone (and, on the other end, the telephone to the service's computer) is a *modem*.

When is a modem not a modem: Part 1

You may have heard that you can connect your computer to the Internet in faster ways than using a modem. In theory, that's true, although reality is usually another story. Here's the scoop: The pair of phone wires that runs between your house and the phone company has remained unchanged in design since about 1900. They work just fine for voice applications, such as ordering pizza, but leave something to be desired for transmitting Internet data. In the early 1980s, AT&T developed what was supposed to be the next generation of telephones, called *ISDN,* alleged to be short for Improvements Subscribers Don't Need. (AT&T, if it still were, would swear up and down that the term stood for Integrated Services Digital Network). ISDN uses the same phone wires (which is important because phone companies have about 100 million of them installed) and puts boxes at each end that transmit *digital* data rather than the older, *analog* data. In this arrangement, an ISDN line can transmit 128K bits per second, a considerable improvement over the 33K or 56K a regular line permits.

Although the idea was good, phone companies, unfortunately, utterly botched the way they made ISDN available. For one thing, ISDN installation is fantastically complicated; we know full-time telecom managers who have been unable to find anyone at their local phone company who knows how to install it. For another, ISDN is overpriced in most places: in New York, for example, an ISDN line costs about twice as much as a regular line, and every call you make, even a local call, costs extra. For this reason, unless you have a local ISP that arranges the details of an ISDN connection for you and knows the incantations to mutter at the phone company to make the per-call charges go away (phrases such as "multilocation Centrex"), we don't think that ISDN is worth the bother.

Shapes, sizes, and speeds

Modems come in all sorts of shapes and sizes. Some are separate boxes, known as *external* modems, with cables that plug in to the computer and the phone line with power cords. *Internal* modems are inside the computer, with just a cable for the phone. The newest ones (*PC Card* modems) are tiny credit-card-size things you stuff into the side of your laptop. (They still have a cable for the phone — some things never change.)

Matching the variety of physical sizes is an equal variety of internal features. The speed at which a modem operates (or the rate at which it can stuff computer data into a phone line) ranges from a low of 2400 bits per second (bps, commonly but erroneously called baud) to 33,600 and even 56,000 bps. (These big numbers are usually abbreviated as 33.6K and 56K, and the bps part is dropped.) Notice that in all these cases, we're talking *bits* per second here; divide by eight to get bytes (or characters) per second. So your 56K modem transfers a maximum of 7,000 characters per second from the Internet (and that's if you're *very* lucky) and even less *to* the Internet, a process we call *sending* and the nerds call *uploading.* Some modems can act as fax machines, and some can't. Some have even more exotic features, such as built-in voice jail, er, mail.

Those 56K or V90 modems aren't really what they seem to be. The 56K (meaning 56 kilobytes per second) is actually limited to *53K* because of FCC (Federal Communications Commission) restrictions on how much juice can be crammed through a phone line. Sending is even worse because a so-called 56K modem can *upload* at only 33.6K!

Nearly any modem made in the past five years is adequate for an initial foray on the Net, and most computers sold in the past several years come with built-in modems. If you already have a modem, use it. If you have to buy a modem, get the best darned 56K modem you can afford. While you're shopping, be sure to get a cable to connect the modem to your computer if you're buying an external modem, and be sure that it has connectors that match the connectors on your computer. (You use either a parallel port or, on newer computers, a USB port.)

Note to laptop computer owners: If your computer has credit-card-size PC Card slots (called PCMCIA or CardBus) but no built-in modem, get a PC Card modem that fits in a slot so that you don't have to carry around a separate modem when you take your computer on the road. Although it costs more, it's worth it. Then again, most newer laptops already have them — the card kind, we mean.

Does your computer need its own telephone line

No. If you're planning on doing serious surfing, however, you may want to get it one. You don't *have* to, but let's clear up some common misconceptions. Then you can decide whether you *want* to.

When your computer is connected to the Internet, it is talking on the telephone. Even though nobody in the house has a handset glued to an ear, your telephone is in use. People calling you get a busy signal, just as though the cat had knocked the receiver off the cradle. If you pick up the telephone, you hear a great deal of static, which is what information actually sounds like as it streams down the telephone line. The computers (yours and the one you called) usually resent the intrusion and hang up on each other, each likely blaming the other. If you've been getting a large program from the Internet for later use on your computer (downloading, as explained in Chapter 13) and you're 45 minutes into a 50-minute download, you won't be very happy about the hangup.

Think about the following when you're deciding whether to get a second telephone line: If you live with other people, is it okay with them for the telephone to be tied up for hours at a time? Even if you live alone, is it okay with you not to be able to receive telephone calls for hours at a time? Finally, if you're new to computers and need some technical support about an Internet program, it can be convenient to talk to technical-support people *while* you're on the Internet and using their program. You can do that only if you have two telephone lines.

If you can afford it and if you think that you'll be online for any length of time, we strongly recommend a second telephone line. Check with your telephone company; most now have an affordable two-line pricing plan specifically for home Internet users. If you decide not to get one, however, you may want to get voice-mail service from the telephone company if it's available in your area. Although we normally like our trusty answering machine, if you're on the Internet, people calling you get a busy signal and the answering machine never gets the call. With voice mail, the telephone company takes the message while you or your computer are on the phone, without the caller's ever getting a busy signal. Then, when you're done surfing the Net, you can deal with the dozens of irate friends wondering who the heck you were talking to on the telephone for all those hours.

When is a modem not a modem: Part 2

Modem is short for *mo*dulation–*dem*odulation, which is exactly what modems do to communicate with one another. We hear it as horrible screechings and other beeps and whistles. Digital systems do *not* communicate in such out-moded fashions. Digital means 1s and 0s (ones and zeros), on or off — even ying and yang. Of course, we wouldn't be human if we didn't get stuck on call-ing a class of things by a single name. (Quick — show us a Q-Tip.) We still call all these nifty, new digital devices modems. Why? Because it's a familiar word and the "modem" still performs at least a similar function; transmitting and receiving data to and from the Internet. Because of all of this, you will always hear references to cable and DSL as "modems."

Take the ISP Plunge (Ahhh!)

Okay, you've decided not to go the cable-modem route, and you've decided not to go the AOL or CompuServe route. Your decision means that you have to pick an Internet Service Provider. This selection may seem as mystifying to you as picking a dentist from the telephone book seems to some of us. We can shed some light on the problem, however. This section tells you what to think about and what to keep an eye out for.

First, it would be nice to get your selection right the first time. Because your ISP's name is part of your e-mail address, you don't want to change too often, or else your friends will get tired of trying to follow you around. Still, if you find that you have to move, it's not too big of a problem if you do so before 600 people have your e-mail address in their address books.

If you have experience with bad luck, or if receiving poor customer service runs in the family, you can take advantage of a free mail.com service. It's one of the best-known e-mail *forwarding* services. Whenever mail arrives at your mail.com address, at `snazzy-dresser@mail.com`, for example, it can be automatically sent to your current address, at `snazzy@dresser.com`. Using a mail-forwarding service is helpful because after you feel "settled in" with an ISP, you can put out the word that you have a new e-mail address. Of course, you can keep your mail.com address as long as you want.

Second, it's almost impossible to substantively compare ISPs, although there is one place where you can find comprehensive information on locating one, as well as other services. A little mini-industry of programs and services claims to measure ISP performance, although they really rate only national or large regional ISPs, and the performance they measure may or may not have anything to do with the performance you experience. The one that shines in this group is, or was, InternetList.Com, which is now owned by C|Net (`http://www.cnet.com`), arguably *the* largest presence on the Web. Go to `http://www.internetlist.com`, click on Dial-up Access near the upper-left corner of the home page, and enter your zip code in the appropriate field. You're rewarded with a comprehensive list of national *and* local ISPs.

Third, the most important thing about an ISP is its telephone number. If an ISP isn't a local telephone call for you, don't consider it. In most places, that cuts the list to a handful of potential ISPs.

Who's eligible to be your ISP?

A bunch of national ISPs exist and companies have set out to provide Internet access over most (if not all) of the country. Their thinking is that, just as you want to use a long-distance calling card anywhere in the country, you will want to use your Internet account anywhere in the country. They also figure that if they own their own network, they can provide better-quality service than smaller companies. Not surprisingly, many of these national companies are in the communications business. Some of the more well-known are AT&T WorldNet, Concentric, MindSpring, and Earthlink.

Finding a local Internet Service Provider is much like finding any other small- or medium-size business serving your community. Try the following:

- ✔ Check the business pages of your local newspaper for advertisements from local-access providers.

- ✔ Ask your public library's research librarian or online services staff.

- ✔ Look in your local yellow pages under Internet Services.

- ✔ Use a friend's Internet account, an Internet computer at the local library, or a trial account from a commercial provider to access the World Wide Web. Search for "Internet Service Providers." You can find numerous lists of them that you can then search for something close to home. We've compiled our own list of lists for you. Check our Web page about ISPs (at `http://net.gurus.com/isp`) for Web sites that list ISPs by state, area code, or country.

- ✔ Ask anyone you know in your area who already has access what she's using and whether she likes it.

Hippie access

In the 1960s, rebellious youths, called hippies, advocated free love and called for an end to the Vietnam War. Although few people now display such passion for freedom and all it stands for, at least there's still free "love," in the form of

How important is my ISP's telephone number, really?

If you're not careful, you can end up paying more for the phone call than you do for your Internet service. One thing you do when you sign up for an online service is to determine the phone number to call. *If at all possible, use a provider whose number is a free or untimed local call. Some telephone companies (namely, Bell Atlantic in Vermont) offer only metered local service with a monthly cap on charges, so it may be called metered, although it can still act like free local calling.* If you use a local or regional Internet Service Provider, that provider has a short list of phone numbers you can use. Of the national providers, IBM, AT&T, and CompuServe have their own national networks of dial-in numbers; the rest piggyback on other networks, such as Sprintnet, from Sprint; Tymnet, from MCI; and Alternet, from WorldCom. If one national provider has a local number, therefore, they probably all do because it's a Sprintnet, Tymnet, Alternet, or CompuServe number that works for any of them.

If you cannot find a provider that's a local call for you, your options are limited. If you have a long-distance plan, such as Sprint Sense (Sprint) or Friends and Family (MCI), you can put your provider's phone number on your list of frequently called numbers and get a low rate that should be less than ten cents per minute for nights and weekends. (That's still more than $5 per hour.) Be sure to compare rates for in-state and out-of-state calls because an out-of-state call is cheaper in many cases, even though it's farther away.

Here's a real-life story that happened to one of our readers, who wrote to ask us to warn other people. She bought a new computer with Internet software already installed. When she started up the software, it said that it would find a local-access number for her. She entered her area code and the first three digits of her phone number to aid the search. The software found a number and configured her program to dial it automatically. She believed it, not unreasonably, when it said that it had found a local-access number. She found out differently, however, when her $500 phone bill arrived. To be sure that this situation doesn't happen to you, if you let your ISP's software find a local-access number for you, check that number before you let your computer dial it. Check for the availability of a truly local provider, as explained in the section "Who's eligible to be your ISP?" Call your long-distance carrier and find out, at minimum, your charge per minute.

local, free, unlimited Internet access. Many cities have what are called *freenets,* a type of local community computer system that usually has a link to the Internet. Most freenets are indeed free, though some charge startup fees or regular "dues" of a few dollars a month (although they don't turn down contributions if you want to support them).

Another option is to join one of the two national freenet operations. Although both FreeWWWeb and WebCOMBO offer unlimited free access in perpetuity, they differ in one significant manner: FreeWWWEeb is truly free. You can download its software and open an account for literally nothing, except for your time. WebCOMBO, on the other hand, charges what seems like a whopping $179.95 (U.S. dollars) for its software package (which contains mostly free software, one inexpensive commercial software package, and a commercial demo, all of which are certainly are not equal in value to $180). After paying this "fee," WebCOMBO members are guaranteed free access for the rest of their lives — with never any additional fees.

More importantly, both these services host a great number of very satisfied users. It seems that a service does not have to cost $20 per month in U.S. dollars to be reliable. It can also be free. Of course, you may be asking yourself "What's the catch, man?" Apparently, none. Lots of other "free" services — such as Netzero, Freei, and Juno — use special software displaying an ad banner box that floats above everything else, cannot be closed without stopping the service, and cannot even be moved off of the screen (they automatically pop back into view).

The best of two worlds? Sure. Get a free Internet access account, and then sign up for the AOL BYOA (Bring Your Own Access) offer and get it for only $9.95 per month. Otherwise, you pay $20 for the Internet access *and* $24.95 for AOL. That does *not* sound like a deal to us.

Choosing from among the eligible

After you've determined which companies are in your handful of ISPs, here are some things to think about as you try to select from among them. As usual, no hard-and-fast rule applies for choosing between a national ISP and a local one. National ISPs are convenient because they have lots of dial-in numbers across the country; this option can be handy if you travel much. AT&T, for one, has a handy 800 number you can call that automagically tells you what telephone number to dial for Internet access, and it even makes a stab at telling you whether it's a local call. National ISPs also usually (but, sadly, not always) have an extensive support staff to help you. On the other hand, because local ISPs tend to compete in pricing more than the national ones do, you may get a better deal. And, because they stick to one geographic area, many offer community-oriented online materials.

When you're doing your comparison shopping, consider the following factors.

Price

Pricing schemes have become standard over the past couple of years. Some providers offer services that charge you by the hour while most have a flat rate per month. Many have *blended* schemes: For a monthly charge, you get a set number of hours, and you pay by the hour if you use more than that. We recommend the providers that have a flat rate of $20 per month or less, even if they also have a lower blended rate. If you do pick one with limited free hours, studies have shown that the average Internet use is about 18 hours per month. A few providers charge more for daytime use than for nights and weekends, although that's much less common than it used to be.

If you or your kids become regular online users, you will find that time stands still while you're online and that you use much more online time than you think you do. Even if you think that you will be online for only a few minutes a day, if you don't have a flat-rate plan, you may be surprised when your bill arrives at the end of the month. Some ISPs charge $10 or less per month; they're probably depending on a temporary quirk of phone politics called "reciprocal compensation." When that quirk goes away in a few months or years, their price will also probably go up to $20.

Support

Call and talk to members of the support staff before you sign up. Good support means support 24 hours a day. That's a level of support you're probably not going to get from a local ISP, so you have to decide whether that single factor is enough to make you go with a national provider. Even if you do decide that it is, make sure that your national provider doesn't put you hold for a long time. Perhaps even more important than the number of hours of support available is the *kind* of support you get. Your ISP should provide support people who don't think that your questions are stupid and can actually answer them. You would be surprised at how often they don't. We don't say this to knock support people; it's a hard job, and the people who do it are usually at the bottom of the pecking order. (We know; we've done it.)

Load

Two things concern you here: Do you get busy signals when you call, and does the information you're receiving from the Internet get stuck behind other people's information somewhere inside your ISP's facilities? Busy signals, you can test yourself. Even before you have Windows Me all set up to call the Internet, you can call the ISP's access number (the number your computer calls) and see whether you get a busy signal. You shouldn't, even between 7 p.m. and 10 p.m., which is probably the Internet's busiest time. How fast information makes it through your ISP facility is hard to test, so this factor is just one to be aware of. If you're talking to someone who uses an ISP you're considering and they say that things seem slow for them, this could be the problem.

Modem speed

Modem speeds have pretty much stood still at 56K, that V90 thing we mention earlier in this chapter. We haven't heard of an ISP that hasn't upgraded to V90, although it's possible. One trick we do know of is allocating certain modem speeds to certain dial-up numbers. AOL does this, reserving certain access numbers for slower modems. (It wasn't long ago that AOL still supported 2400 bits per second access.) It's a good idea to check whether an access number has a limit to the speed it supports, even though this situation is increasingly uncommon.

800 numbers

A few providers (typically the national ones and some regional) have 800 numbers for use when you're on the road, but there are a handful of local ISPs that offer toll-free access as well. Their hourly rates have to be high enough to cover the cost of the 800 call, however, so it's almost always cheaper to dial direct back to your usual "local" number and pay for the call yourself. After all, someone has to pay for the 800 call, and that someone is you. Access to an 800 number can be attractive to people who travel frequently but who sign on to the Internet only occasionally while they're on the road.

In the end, whom you choose as an Internet Service Provider probably isn't that important. Within broad limits, they all work, although some more quickly than others. Just make sure that you have a pricing plan you can live with and that the Internet is just a local call away.

A point and a gold star are awarded to CompuServe for having dial-up access on a somewhat global scale. Another point and gold star go to the top-flight ISP MindSpring for its Global Roaming service, with more than 2,384 places where you can dial in (be careful — this service costs extra).

Payment plans

All ISPs (that we have ever heard of) take credit cards. For ISPs, and for most customers, that's the easiest way to pay. If you're on a fixed-rate plan, your card is charged once a month. Some smaller ISPs even wait and charge you for the *preceding* three months, so you can get ahead a little. Other, larger ISPs have quarterly or yearly plans where they give you a little price break for paying in *advance*.

For some people, however, credit cards are not a good option. You may use a bank-issued Visa check card rather than a credit card. Some ISPs, usually smaller local ones, can arrange for you to pay ahead with a check. It's not a particularly common arrangement (computer types hate dealing with pieces of paper), although if you call around, you can probably find an ISP that's willing to do it.

Don't let the Windows Me Internet Connection Wizard push you around

Windows Me comes with a nifty wizard that helps you get on the Internet. A *wizard* is the mechanism by which Windows Me asks you a bunch of questions and then sets up something based on your answers. Most hardware installation (and some software installation) in Windows Me is done through wizards. The process of getting connected to the Internet can have so many steps that the Internet Connection Wizard may actually call on the services of several other wizards along the way. It's all confusing, although if you just keep answering questions, you end up on the Internet.

We go through all the steps in the Internet Connection Wizard in Chapter 3, although you should know about one important aspect of the wizard. It's actually a nice feature: the Internet Connection Wizard asks for your area code and the first three digits of your telephone number and then tries to find a local ISP for you. It may or may not succeed; if it can't find a local ISP, it finds the closest one it can, which can result in hefty long-distance charges if you surf the Internet much.

More important, the list from which the wizard selects an ISP is far from complete. It includes many national ISPs and some regional ones, although none of our favorite local ISPs appears. If you select an ISP for yourself, you can still use the Internet Connection Wizard and its friends to set up Windows Me to connect to your account.

Signing up for your Internet account

If you have decided to use AOL, AT&T WorldNet, CompuServe, the Microsoft Network, or Prodigy Internet, wait: We take you through their automated sign-up procedures in painful (just kidding) detail in Chapter 3. If you decide to use a local Internet Service Provider, you have to call; it usually signs up people over the telephone or sometimes by mail using actual pieces of paper. A local ISP takes your credit card number (or check) and all the contact information it needs and then mails you a packet. The packet usually contains at least four items:

- ✔ The technical information you need in order to tell Windows Me how you're planning to connect to the Internet.

- ✔ A list of telephone numbers your computer can call to connect to the ISP.

- ✔ Some cryptic instructions for how to get all this stuff set up. (In fairness, some of the instructions are getting better.)

- ✔ A great deal of software, including a Web browser.

Your chosen ISP may also send you a ton of promotional material, special offers for other services, and the other typical stuff people try to get into your hands after they think that there's some chance you'll read it. This advice is important: *Unless the instructions they send you specifically discuss Windows Me and are crystal-clear to you, ignore the software and their installation instructions!* The software is usually old, and you probably have better

Winsock? Like at an airport?

No, Winsock is short for *Win*dows *sock*ets. It's like this: Back in the dark ages of PC networking, about 1990, several different software vendors wrote PC Internet packages. Each package provided functions so that other people could write Internet applications of their own that worked with the vendor's package.

Because each vendor's functions were, unfortunately, slightly different in the details, even though functionally they all did the same things, applications that worked with one didn't work with another. In 1991, a bunch of network vendors got together at a trade show and thrashed out a common, standard set of functions for Windows Internet applications. Every Internet software vendor, even Microsoft, quickly agreed to support this Windows sockets standard, or Winsock. (It's called *sockets* because its design is based on a well-established UNIX package by that name.)

In practice, therefore, any Windows Internet application you find that is *Winsock compatible* (whether it's commercial, shareware, or free) should work with Dial-Up Networking, the Winsock-compatible Internet connection program that comes with Windows. If you have a PPP or cable Internet account, you can use any of a huge variety of Winsock-compatible programs. All the famous programs you've heard of, like Netscape Navigator and Internet Explorer, are Winsock-compatible, as are the Internet programs that come with Windows Me. America Online and CompuServe work with Winsock-compatible programs too.

In the annals of software development, this degree of compatibility is virtually unprecedented, so let's hope that it's a sign of more good things to come.

software on your Windows Me system. The instructions range from the absurdly complicated to the pretty good. Even when they're good, however, they have to cover Windows 3.1, Windows 95, Windows 98, Windows Me (if you're lucky), and the Macintosh. Chapter 3 covers only Windows Me and does so in great detail. We think that you'll find it easier to follow.

You need much of the technical information the providers send you; a list at the beginning of Chapter 3 helps you figure out just what you need.

All Dressed Up and No Place to Go, So Which Programs Talk Over the Internet?

You have an account with an online service or an Internet Service Provider. You have a modem. You have a phone line. You're ready to roll. Wait — what about the software?

Internet software lets you do most of the important things that people like to do with the Internet, and those folks at Microsoft are no fools! They've worked hard to make sure that you have almost every category of Internet software to avoid the horrifying (to them) possibility that you may use or, even worse, buy software from someone else. Still, they represent only one entrant in each of those categories. Let's review those categories with some looks at the other entrants:

- ✔ **Connection software:** Dial-Up Networking, the Windows Internet connection program, works great. You have no reason we can think of to use any other connection program. We tell you how to set it up in Chapter 3.

- ✔ **Web browsers:** Although Netscape Navigator has lost its crown to Microsoft, it is still a popular Web browser that holds almost 40 percent of the market. To the casual (or even the not-so-casual) user, both browsers are equivalent. One or the other or perhaps even both almost certainly came with your Windows Me system. Netscape isn't down and out; it's just down — at least until recently. Enter Netscape 6. You may as well call this version "Navigator: The Next Generation" with lots of fanfare and fireworks booming in the sky. At the time this chapter was written, Netscape, which is owned by America Online, wowed the Internet world with a preview release of its next Netscape Web browser (and then some). Netscape used to rule the roost, but was sent to the showers by Microsoft because Microsoft gave away its Web browser, Internet Explorer, while Netscape had to sell its browser. Internet Explorer, which holds around 60 percent of the browser market, is now at version 5.5, and the last version of Netscape Communicator was 4.72.

  Interestingly enough, Netscape called its new Web browser Netscape 6. Confused yet? The generally accepted belief is that Netscape jumped a version number because it would leapfrog the next version of Internet Explorer. Microsoft hasn't even announced a version 6.0 of its Internet Explorer. That makes Netscape look pretty cool (and it is). We talk all about browsers in Chapters 8 and 9.

- ✔ **Helper applications and Web browser plug-ins:** Stand-alone applications — such as RealPlayer, Shockwave, and QuickTime — and their friends the plug-ins, also serve time as "helper" programs for your Web browser. These programs have miniprograms called plug-ins. *Plug-ins* are installed in and work inside Web browsers. You don't have to run Netscape Navigator or Internet Explorer to use the programs we just mentioned. However, their plug-ins work only with a browser. For the most part, they merely add to an already rich experience; some, however, like QuickTime and RealPlayer, can actually entertain (especially with a cable or DSL connection). Unless you care about the innards of the technology, you can just think of most of these programs as part of the World Wide Web. Still, because they require some care and feeding, and because so many other plug-ins are available, we talk about them in Chapter 9.

- **E-mail:** Outlook Express is the latest of several attempts Microsoft has made at conquering the e-mail market, and it is homing in on it. Does anyone remember Microsoft Mail? Eudora is still the queen of the hill, in our eyes, however. Netscape Messenger (part of Netscape Communicator) also holds its own in this category. Read more about them in Chapters 5 and 6.

- **Usenet, the Internet bulletin board:** Outlook Express does double duty for Microsoft, covering this category as well as e-mail. The other program to consider is Free Agent. Both these programs are great for reading Usenet newsgroups. You can also read your newsgroups over the World Wide Web, at Deja.com. Netscape Messenger weighs in here too. We talk all about Usenet on our Web site.

- **Chat:** We talk about the CB-radio-like features of the Net in Chapter 1. The Internet calls these online, real-time, flying-purple-conversations with lots of people at the same time *IRC,* or *Internet Relay Chat.* mIRC is the most widely used Windows program that lets you do it. Microsoft even has a product for Windows Me, named Chat, that lets you participate in IRC conversations *and* pretend that you're in a surreal comic strip at the same time. (We are not making this up!) Because Microsoft has recently migrated to the Web, however, MSN Chat has taken over and actually runs in your browser. Sadly, MSN Chat has no silly comics. You can, however, download Comic Chat from the Microsoft download center. If silly comics are your thing, look at Chapter 13.

- **Instant messaging:** Somewhat similar to chat, instant messaging has become quite popular. You simply join a service, download and install the software, and, if (and only if) your friends or family members come online, you know about it instantly. You can even send messages back and forth and engage in live chat. Popular entries in this field are ICQ (it's a play on words — just spell it out), AOL Instant Messenger, and even Microsoft's own MSN Messenger Service (of course), in addition to others. We describe them in Chapter 14.

- **Collaborative working:** This category is one of the more interesting Internet applications to come along recently. Windows Me comes with the Microsoft NetMeeting program, which rolls several Internet communications functions into one package: Internet phone, videoconferencing, IRC, whiteboarding, and application sharing (where one person in a meeting controls an application that appears on the screens of all participants in the meeting). This package is surprisingly cool, and we talk about it in Chapter 15.

Chapter 3

Setting Up Your Internet Account

● ●

In This Chapter

▶ Making simpler connections with the Internet Connection Wizard

▶ Stepping through the Internet Connection Wizard

▶ Telling Windows Me about your modem

▶ Signing up with an online service

▶ Telling Windows Me about an account you already have

▶ Knowing when you don't need the Connection Wizard

● ●

*F*or most people, the most difficult part of using the Internet is getting their Internet account set up. For approximately 10 percent of the U.S. population, a painfree alternative exists. If you're curious about whether you may be part of that lucky 10 percent, jump to the end of this chapter and read the section "Avoiding the Connection Wizard Altogether." If you know that you're part of the 90 percent who doesn't have the option of cable access or you naturally prefer doing things yourself, read on.

Introducing the Connection Wizard

To make the process of connecting to the Internet simpler, Microsoft created the Internet Connection Wizard. Its job is take you through all the steps in this chapter, from making sure that your modem is installed to signing you up on the Internet to getting you connected. Unfortunately, like all wizards, it's a little short on the explaining part of things and just takes things into its own proverbial hands. Also, you can cast many of the same spells the wizard uses, which can be handy when the wizardry flies by faster than you want.

In this chapter, you use the Internet Connection Wizard, which offers to take you down one of three separate paths: one to sign you up for a new account with an Internet Service Provider (ISP), one to use an existing account with an ISP, and one to use an Internet connection you may already have. We describe all three paths. We also show you how to cast all the same spells without using the Internet Connection Wizard.

The wizard does not think highly of online services such as CompuServe, Prodigy Internet, and AOL, although your choice of providers is your own. Later in this chapter, we guide you through the process of signing up for one of those services and preparing to use one as your Internet connection.

You probably don't have to read this entire chapter. If you're lucky, Windows Me correctly identifies your modem and loads its Internet dialing software so that you speed right through and quickly and easily sign up for an Internet account. In that case, you read about one-third of what's in this chapter. On the other hand, if things don't go so well, you may read the entire chapter, perhaps several times. When you think that you're done, however, you're done.

Care and Feeding of the Internet Connection Wizard

Running the Internet Connection Wizard is usually the easiest way to set up your Internet connection. As with all wizards, your first problem is to find it. If you're lucky, it's right on your Start menu, and you click the Start button and give the command Programs⇨Accessories⇨Communications⇨Internet Connection Wizard. In the unlikely event that the command isn't there, try wandering around your menus to see whether you find something that says Connection Wizard. You know that you've found the Internet Connection Wizard when you see a screen that looks like the one shown in Figure 3-1.

Figure 3-1:
How do you want the Internet Connection Wizard to serve you?

The wizard wants to recommend an Internet Service Provider

As you can tell from Figure 3-1, the Internet Connection Wizard does one of three things for you: It can set up an account for you with an ISP, set up a connection to an account you already have, or leave your accounts well enough alone. Click the appropriate option, conveniently explained in the following list, to indicate what you want the wizard to do for you:

✔ If you already have an account with an ISP and you (or someone else) have set up that account on your computer, choose the last option, I already have an Internet connection set up on this computer. Then click the Next button. In this case, the wizard disappears and you can skip to the beginning of Chapter 4.

✔ If you already have an account with an ISP but it's not set up on this computer, choose the second option, I want to set up a new connection to my existing Internet account. Then join us again later in this chapter, in the section "Telling the wizard that you're already signed up."

✔ If you need to choose an ISP, choose the first option, I want to choose an Internet Service Provider. Then click Next to go comparison shopping, by letting the wizard gather the information for you.

You have *plenty* of time to have second, third, and fourth thoughts before you spend any money. Windows Me may have to reassure itself that it has all its marbles. If so, you see a screen telling you that the wizard is beginning its automatic setup. Windows Me may tell you that it needs to install some additional components so that it can get the information it needs to set up your Internet connection. On the other hand, it may not. It all depends on what got installed when Windows Me was first put on your computer. If it has to install some additional components, it may also restart your computer, so make sure to close all other programs you may have been using.

You may, in fact, see various screens (or the same screen several times) if Windows has to make many behind-the-scenes changes. Among other things, Windows may want to know which modem it should use to connect to the referral service. Even if you have only one modem, make sure that the wizard selects the one you want to use to dial into the Internet, and click OK. It may also want to confirm your area code so that it can look for local ISPs. If you see other messages, just keep pressing the Next button. Sooner or later, you see a dialog box that says Location Information.

When the wizard is all done, the dialog box is replaced by a box similar to the one shown in Figure 3-2. On the left side of the window, you're looking at a list of providers the wizard thinks that you may be interested in; it may show you enough that you have to scroll up and down the list to see them all. The right pane shows you information about each Internet Service Provider. Click on the ISP's name on the left to see the information about it. You may need to scroll up and down to see all the information about a provider. Be prepared to spend some time with this list if you really want to comparison shop; a great deal of information lives here.

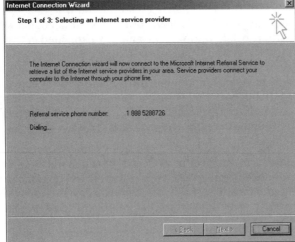

Figure 3-2:
The Internet Connection Wizard is fetching a list of Internet Service Providers for your consideration.

Rather than see a list of recommended ISPs, you may see one of two other screens. If you see a dialog box that looks like Figure 3-3 and says "Could not connect," check out the advice in the section "How the Wizard Can Get Lost and Other Exciting Adventures," later in this chapter. If you see a dialog box labeled Install new modem, skip over to the section "Making Sure That Windows Me Sees Your Modem," a couple of sections ahead.

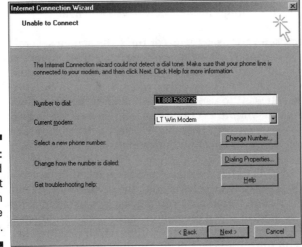

Figure 3-3:
The wizard couldn't get through on the telephone.

Signing up with an ISP using the wizard

When it comes to deciding which ISP to sign up with, the choice is always personal. We've heard of most of the companies that appear on the lists for our area codes, and all the ones we saw there are perfectly reputable. If you have friends who are already connected in your area, ask them which provider they use and whether they're happy with the service. Another thing you can do to boost your confidence (or confirm fears) is to call and talk to several providers on the phone and ask about the services they provide. If they're courteous and helpful before you buy, that's a good place to start. If they're not, forget about them and find somebody who is.

After you've chosen a service, highlight its name in the left pane of the Internet Connection Wizard's window, and click the Next button. Because the sign-up procedure is a little different for each provider, we can't give you step-by-step instructions after that. In general, you need to fill in some forms containing the information the ISP needs in order to set up your account, including a credit card number. If you have read Chapter 1, you know how we feel about entering credit card numbers over the Internet: _It's plenty safe._ If you're still not comfortable with it, some of the sign-up pages may have a telephone number you can call to talk to a live human being.

Before you decide to go forward, we remind you one last time that the telephone number the ISP picks for you may not necessarily be a local telephone call. This situation should be clear if the wizard lets you pick a telephone number from a list — you can check before you confirm that you want to use that telephone number. If the wizard just picks a telephone number for you, however, be sure to check that the connection phone number is a local call — look on the confirmation screen before you let it charge your card. If the ISP doesn't tell you the telephone number it's going to dial, you just have to trust it. After your account is set up, you can check the number and cancel if you need to. We show you in Chapter 4 how to cancel your Internet account.

The information you need for each ISP is slightly different, although not particularly exotic. Here's what we provided to the ones we tested:

- ✔ Name.
- ✔ Address.
- ✔ Telephone number.
- ✔ The telephone number the computer is connected to. This number helps the ISP figure out what number your computer should dial. Some ISPs let you pick from a list of numbers in your area.
- ✔ A credit card number with expiration date.
- ✔ Some ISPs let you pick your own username and password, and others assign a username and password to you. (We give you more info about this subject in a minute.)

✔ An e-mail mailbox name. Although you can read more about this subject in the e-mail chapters, briefly, your e-mail address is whatever you pick, with your provider's name at the end. For example, our e-mail address here for *The Internet For Windows Me For Dummies* is internetME@gurus.com; gurus.com is the "company," and internetME is the e-mail mailbox name.

Somewhere in the sign-up process (usually at the end), you see a summary screen with your login name, password, e-mail mailbox name, and perhaps some technical information. *It is very important that you keep all this information!* Unfortunately, Microsoft makes it very difficult to print this information. If you're feeling adventurous, you can press the Print Screen key on your keyboard to capture the information on your screen. Then click the Start button and choose Programs⇨Accessories⇨Paint to use the paint program that comes with Windows Me. Finally, use the Edit⇨Paste command in Paint to create a new Paint picture with your Internet account information. Finally, use the File⇨Print command in Paint to print the information on your printer. On the other hand, if you're not feeling adventurous, you can just copy this stuff down with pencil and paper.

This screen of information is the only place where this information appears. If you need to call your ISP, you need this information. If you need to change any of the settings in your Internet setup, you must have this information. Please don't lose it.

At the end of the sign-up process, your Internet Service Provider may offer to set up an Internet connection for you using your new account. By all means, allow it to. You should be all set to start sending and receiving e-mail (see Chapter 5) or surfing the World Wide Web (see Chapter 8), although you may want to take a look at Chapter 4 just to get the big picture of when your computer connects to the Internet and what you see when it does.

Things do not always go smoothly when you're sending information over the Internet, and you may as well learn that now as later. It's possible to get all the way through the sign-up process and, just before you think that you're done, have the whole process come to a grinding halt. (It has happened to us.) Make a note of the telephone number to call for customer assistance; it's on one of the sign-up screens.

Telling the wizard that you're already signed up

Whether you got help from the wizard in choosing an ISP or told it to skip that part, you should now see the an Internet Connection Wizard dialog box labeled Set Up Your Internet Connection. If you don't, take a quick look at the beginning of the section "Care and Feeding of the Internet Connection Wizard," earlier in this chapter. Choose one of three options depending on whether you're shopping for an account, have an account you need to set up, or already have your account set up. If you're shopping, go to the section "The wizard wants to recommend an Internet Service Provider," earlier in this chapter. If you already have an account with an Internet Service Provider *and* you (or someone else) have set up that account on your computer, skip to Chapter 4.

You may already have an account with an ISP, although it's not set up on this computer. The reason may be that you just signed up and have a welcome package from the ISP on your desk or that you were using the Internet from another computer and you're moving to a new computer. Or you may have an account set up on this computer but want to change some of the settings for it. In any case, you're in the right place. Follow along to see what the wizard does next:

1. **In the Internet Connection Wizard's Welcome dialog box, choose the second option, I want to set up a new connection — to my existing Internet account. Click the Next button.**

   The wizard asks whether you are using just any old Internet connection or an Internet connection through Microsoft Network (MSN) or America Online (AOL). Microsoft Network and AOL have their own configuration programs that have nothing to do with the wizard. To avoid confusion, the wizard gets out of your way right now if you're using one of those services. If you're using one to get to the Internet, click on the second option, and then click the Next button and then the Finish button to make the wizard disappear. The section "Getting to the Internet from an Online Service Like AOL or CompuServe," near the end of this chapter, has more information about these services.

2. **Select the first option in this dialog box or the one labeled Select this option if you are accessing the Internet using and Internet Service Provider or a local area network (LAN). Then click the Next button.**

   That's assuming that you're using a *real* Internet Service Provider and not Microsoft Network or AOL.

   You see the Set Up Your Internet Connection dialog box, in which you can tell the wizard whether you have a LAN connection or a telephone connection. You have a LAN connection if you're at the office (or school or the like) and your computer is connected via a high-speed network connection to other computers in the building, one of which is connected to the Internet, or if you have a cable or DSL modem installed. (We mention this subject briefly in Chapter 2 and later in this chapter, in the section "Network spell 2: Setting up TCP/IP.") We assume that you will connect over the telephone.

3. **Make sure that the Connect using my phone line option is selected and then click the Next button.**

   The Internet Connection Wizard asks you to choose a modem. In most cases, you have only one modem connected to your computer, and Windows Me is showing you the correct modem. If Windows Me did not detect a modem attached to your computer, you are taking a detour into the Install New Modem Wizard, so take a detour to the section "Making Sure That Windows Me Sees Your Modem," just ahead.

4. **Verify that Windows Me is showing you the correct modem, and press the Next button. (*Hint:* If you're not sure how many modems are installed, pull down the list. If you can choose from only one item, it's likely that there's only one modem and little chance that you'll make a wrong selection.)**

   If a Dial-Up Networking connection is already set up on this computer, the wizard displays a dialog box. You can change the characteristics of this connection by selecting it, or you can create an entirely new connection. If you don't have a Dial-Up Networking connection on this machine, the wizard skips directly to the Phone Number screen, where you tell it what number to dial; skip Step 6.

5. **If the wizard asks you what to do about an existing connection, decide whether you want to create a new one or modify the existing one. Select the appropriate option, and click Next.**

   If you select an existing connection, the wizard asks whether you want to change the setting for it. This question strikes us as kind of silly because you wouldn't have selected this connection unless you wanted to change it, but hey, perhaps things in Redmond, Washington, are different from the way they are in other places. It does rain a great deal up there. If you decide that the answer is No, make sure that that option is selected and click Next. Skip ahead to Step 13, where we tell you why you should ignore mail for now. If you decide that you do want to change the existing connection, select the Yes option and click Next.

   The wizard may have to pause here to mess with the guts of your Windows Me system. If it does, you see a message along the lines of "Installing files."

6. **Make sure that you have your Windows Me CD handy, and let the wizard do its thing.**

   When it's all done, you're looking at the Phone Number dialog box of the Internet Connection Wizard.

   The entries here are fairly straightforward, with the exception of the check box labeled Dial using area code and country code. This entry is the telephone number that you want to make sure is a local call from where you are. If you never move your computer, it doesn't matter whether you check the check box labeled Dial using area code. Most people leave it checked, and that's fine. (This check box tells Windows

Me whether to use the dialing rules, which we talk about a little in Chapter 4, in the section "Location, Location, Location.") Click the Next button when you've filled out everything; then you see the User Name and Password dialog box.

7. Fill in the username you got from your ISP, along with the password it gave you, and click Next.

ISPs usually let you select your own username (except that you can't have one that's already in use) and often let you select your own password. Click Next when you've filled in the information; then you see the Advanced Settings dialog box.

8. How brave are you? With most modern ISPs, you don't have to mess with this advanced stuff, so you should probably click No and then Next and move on to Step 13.

If your connection doesn't work, you can always get back here by starting the wizard again and telling it that you want to change the settings for your Internet account.

If you're still here, you're either curious or your setup didn't work on the first try. Click Yes in the Advanced Settings dialog box, and then click Next.

The following four screens require information from your ISP, so if you don't have that stuff, you're out of luck. First, Windows Me asks whether you have a SLIP or PPP account. As far as we can tell, no one should be using a SLIP account anymore; if you have one, your ISP can usually change it to a PPP account in one brief telephone call.

9. Click on the PPP option and click on Next.

You also have to know how to log on. Some providers require you to enter a collection of nearly incomprehensible text that is called a *script*. If your provider requires it, you have to get it there. Generally, you can type by hand what you need. Most services don't require anything.

10. Select the appropriate script option (if you're lucky, it's labeled I don't need to type anything when logging on) and click on Next.

You have to know whether you have a permanent IP address. Most people *don't* have one, and that's okay. (Most nerds call this type of address *static,* as in the opposite of dynamic — not the kind that sticks to your leg at exactly the wrong time.)

11. If you do have a permanent IP address, type it here. Otherwise, leave the My Internet Service Provider automatically assigns me one option selected. In either case, click on Next.

The same rules apply for the DNS server address. We give you more detail about these four options in the section "Deep spells within TCP/IP, or reading the entrails," later in this chapter, where we cast our own spells.

12. **Click on Always use the following and enter the DNS addresses you got from your ISP. Alternatively, leave the option labeled My Internet provider automatically sets this set. In either case, click on Next.**

13. **If you're creating a new Internet connection, you need to give it a name. Click Next when you've chosen something. You don't need to name anything if you're modifying an existing account.**

    We usually use the name of the ISP just so that we don't forget what's what, although you can get as cute as you want.

14. **Now come three questions, to which you should answer No: No, you don't want to set up your Internet mail account; No, you don't want to set your Internet news account; and No, you don't want to set up your Internet Directory service.**

    We talk about mail in Chapter 5 and finding people in Chapter 10. Meanwhile, hold your breath.

Congratulations! Your Dial-Up Networking connection is all set to call your ISP. In Chapter 4, we tell you how to make the connection, and we throw in a few tips to help you get connected more easily. The rest of this chapter gives you the ins and outs of the wizard, along with details to help you out if problems with your Internet connection crop up.

How the Wizard Can Get Lost and Other Exciting Adventures

The Internet Connection Wizard must be able to dial the telephone if it's going to connect to anything. Figure 3-3 shows the dialog box you see if the wizard can't get through on the telephone. If you don't see a dialog box that looks like that one, check to see whether Figure 3-4 looks more like it. If so, skip ahead to the next section; that's where we talk about setting your modem up in Windows Me.

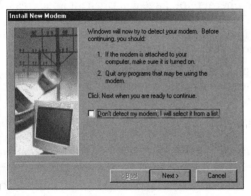

Figure 3-4:
The Modem
Connection
Wizard
magically
appears.

The wizard may not be able to get through to its list of ISPs, for any number of reasons. Here are the most common:

- ✔ The modem is turned off. Most external modems have an on–off switch somewhere on them. Some of the most popular have a little rocker switch right on top that's easy to reach. Check to see whether the modem has lights and, if it does, whether any of them is on. Also check the power cable to the modem and the power brick at the outlet.

- ✔ The cable from the computer to the modem is another place to check. Usually, it has little screw knobs that most people don't bother to screw in to the back of the computer or the back of the modem. Make sure that the screw knobs are tight.

- ✔ If the screws are loose or the cable just doesn't tighten nicely, pull the cable out and take a look at the pins. It's unlikely, but possible, that one or more of the pins is bent. It's better that you don't try to bend them back into position and simply replace the cable (at $9 to $15, they're not expensive); if you do, however, be prepared to break off a pin or two. Like we said. . . .

- ✔ The preceding are two reasons that internal modems are becoming more popular. It's still a good idea, however, to check both the connection from the telephone line to the modem and the telephone line at the wall jack.

- ✔ Does the telephone line have a dial tone? Plug in a telephone rather than the modem, just to check.

- ✔ Are you calling from inside an office? Do you have to dial 9 or something similar to get an outside line? You could press the Dialing Properties button in the Dial-Up Networking Connect dialog box and become an expert. If your computer is a laptop that travels from place to place, that's just what you may have to do. We help you at the end of Chapter 4, in the section about making Dial-Up Networking a little more convenient. To sign up for an Internet account, you have to get this stuff right just one time. Click in the Number to be dialed portion of the Could Not Connect dialog box (the one that was shown in Figure 3-3), and type the digits you have to dial to get through to the wizard's phone number.

- ✔ Do you have call-waiting? Did someone try to call while the wizard was on the telephone? The wizard doesn't take kindly to being interrupted. In the same Number to be dialed portion of the dialog box, enter the magic code you need that turns off call-waiting, usually *70. If you have to wait for a second or two afterward (most call-waiting systems pause the dial tone a few times to indicate that it's been turned off), follow the *70 with two commas — ***70,,** — each comma pauses the process for a couple of seconds. Sometimes, 1170 works too.

None of those things helps? You need your neighborhood telephone guru. After you can get through to the phone number the wizard is trying to call on a regular telephone and you hear the whistle and hiss of the modem on the other end, go back and try the wizard again.

Making Sure That Windows Me Sees Your Modem

When Windows is installed, it puts an immense number of drivers in your system and pits each one against the components inside your computer. If you received your computer with Windows Me already installed, the modem is already configured. Likewise, if you have upgraded from Windows 95, Windows 98, or Windows 98SE and your modem was working there, then Windows Me is already using that driver. Beyond this, it all gets a little sketchy. We explain.

Vast numbers of modems are available from a large number of manufacturers. Each one needs a translator (the driver) to tell Windows Me and the modem how to communicate with each other. If neither of the above scenarios applies to you, you either purchased a new modem to replace an older, slower model or got it as a gift. So now Windows Me will try to figure out what kind of modem it is and install the proper drivers for it. This is where another wizard comes in.

One other possibility is that a bug (a bug in Windows?) is causing a problem. If this is the case, we cannot help, no matter how much we want to. Your computer maker probably is aware of the problem and has issued a fix for it. Because you can't get online, it would be silly for us to suggest that you go to the company's Web site and download the fix, so we think that you should call them. Sometimes, it's possible to fix a problem *without* downloading something.

More wizards? Well, unbeknownst to you until now, Windows Me has not just one wizard inside it, but rather a whole coven of them. The Install Modem dialog box, as shown in Figure 3-4, is the face of yet another one of those wizards. If you reached this dialog box from the Internet Connection Wizard, your modem wasn't installed in the Windows Me software. No problem: The Modem Wizard is here to help. You can invoke it in a couple of other ways; we talk about them in the section "Casting Internet Connection Spells Yourself," a little later in this chapter.

Letting the Modem Wizard do the work

In most cases, the wizard can get your modem installed for you. If it can't, you can wade in to the details and do it yourself. Before you click Next and let the wizard look for your modem, follow its advice and make sure that it's turned on and plugged in, and in general look at the list of things that can go wrong, as described in the preceding section, "How the Wizard Can Get Lost and Other Exciting Adventures." If you prefer to wade in directly without even giving the wizard a chance, look at the following section, "I'll do it my way."

Letting the wizard search for a modem is the best thing to do, for several reasons. First, sometimes the wizard can identify your modem more specifically than you can. Are you *sure* that you know the difference between v32, v32bis, v42, v42bis, v90, and vEverything modems? And which exact one do you have? Who makes it? The wizard can figure these things out. Second, the wizard somehow occasionally identifies and installs a modem that doesn't appear on that list. Third, by letting Windows find the modem, you know that Windows can communicate with it, and that's a good thing.

Not much is involved in letting the wizard find the modem. It may ask you for a hint about whether it's looking for a PC Card modem (also known as a PCMCIA modem card), although that's about it. PC Card modems are popular on laptop computers, so if you have a desktop computer, the answer is probably no. (See Chapter 2 for the lowdown on modems.) Windows Me knows a great deal about PC Card devices, so as soon as you insert a PC Card modem, Windows Me tries to install the relevant software for you. That's all the wizard does for PC Card modems: tells you to stick them in and then waits for Windows Me to do all the work.

If you're not installing a PC Card modem, the wizard goes around to all your hardware's "doors" and eventually lets you know who has gone out and who stayed home to talk. If it picked the right one, click Next to see a final dialog box that tells you that you're all done. If you don't agree with its choice, you can click the Change button and follow along in the following section, "I'll do it my way."

After you click the Finish button in the last Modem Wizard dialog box, you go back to where you came from — either the Internet Connection Wizard or the Modems Properties dialog box from the Control Panel (if you're casting your own spells).

I'll do it my way

You're doing it your way by telling Windows Me exactly which modem you have if the wizard couldn't find your modem or if it chose the wrong modem or if Windows Me doesn't come with software to support your modem. No matter how you get here, you see a dialog box like the one shown in Figure 3-5.

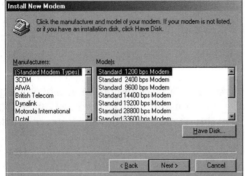

Figure 3-5:
Picking your
modem
yourself.

Having a modem that connects at only 28.8K speeds when it's a 56K modem is like someone's stealing $20 from you when you have only $40. We don't like it, you don't like it, and nobody should be forced to live with it. Of course, a few modems are not represented by Windows drivers. These are given the generic, or (in Windows terminology) Standard, modem drivers. They represent the lowest common denominator, a simple language that all modems are usually required to understand, although they are often inadequate for the job. Contact the company you purchased the computer from, and have it identify the modem maker and model and even provide a driver for it, if at all possible. All the biggies do so. If you call Hewlett-Packard, Dell, Compaq, Micron, Quantex, Gateway, or another large company, you usually can get some good assistance and a quick pointer to installing the problematic driver.

This dialog box has two columns. On the left, scroll down until you see the manufacturer of your modem. When you do, click its name. As soon as you click, you see in the list on the right a list of modems it makes (at least the ones that Windows knows about). Scroll through that list until you see your modem and then click it. If you see too many modems with similar names, you may have to guess. It generally shouldn't make much difference if the modems are very similar. If you're not sure, pick the one that sounds the simplest because it's the one most likely to work. Another trick is to check out the marketing material for your computer and whether it says anything about fax or voice-modem capabilities. You often find different drivers for the same modem *model* that has different features. *Fax* or *voice* or *fax/voice* is often appended to the model's name.

Your modem may not appear on the list. In fact, the list may not show any modem remotely like your modem. For that matter, the manufacturer of your modem may not even appear on the list. If that happens, don't despair. *If* your modem came with a floppy disk or CD-ROM containing the *driver files* (those translators we spoke of) that Windows Me needs in order to carry on a conversation with your modem, you're in luck. That's what the Have Disk button is for.

With a double-click here and a single-click there

With the Internet taking more and more of people's attention, Microsoft wanted to make the Windows Me desktop look as much like a part of the Internet as it could. One aspect of the Internet that it adopted was the *single-click action.* Although in earlier versions of Windows a single-click *selected* something and a double-click *activated* it, most of us found that distinction impossible to remember. Web pages on the Internet do away with that foolishness and just use single-clicks for everything: You point to something, you click it, it does its thing. (Of course, some silly people thought that it would be terribly clever if they made their Web sites work like Windows, so they don't count.)

People who have used computers for a while and who are familiar with double-clicking hate the change. People who are just learning about computers love being able to click just once. Not wanting to offend anyone, Microsoft lets you have it both ways, which means that your computer may be set up differently from your neighbor's. In this book, we use single-clicks because we assume that most of you are just learning.

Here's how to make sure that your Windows Me expects single-clicks:

1. **Click the Start button, choose the Settings⇨Control Panel command, and select Folder Options.**

   This step opens the Folder Option control panel, which offers a number of desktop-interaction-related options. The one we talk about is the last one, Click items as follows.

   Unlike in previous versions of Windows, you do *not* have to activate the Active Desktop to use single-clicking. If this issue was a problem for you (older computers don't work as quickly with all the extra work they're asked to do by Active Desktop), you can now turn it off. We like this idea. It never

occurred to us that cluttering the desktop was productive. It's like embedding a television into the top of your desk so that it gets covered in papers and the keyboard and stuff.

2. **Click on the button next to the top option, Single-click to open an item (point to select).**

   That round button is called a radio button because you can have only one option selected at a time, like being able to listen to only one radio station at a time.

3. **Make a choice from the options that are offered.**

   The first option is Underline icon titles consistent with my browser. Don't worry about the confusing language. It simply means that you want your desktop icons to look like your Web links. The real issue is whether you want them underlined all the time, which is the effect of the second option, Underline icon titles only when I point at them.

   If you click OK here, the option becomes active. Try it out a few times before moving on. The big hurdle you have to get used to is selecting. Just point at it and wait a second. When you move the cursor away, the option remains selected. You can still drag-select, although you have to practice with multiple selections in a list. We work on that later.

   With a little practice under your belt, you can now move on to the next task — making your computer look like the Web. First, open the Folder Options control panel. You'll see several sections where there are options:

   ✔ **Active Desktop:** This choice is up to you. We prefer browsing in a window.

   ✔ **Web View:** This view makes your folders look like a Web site. Web view displays a

(continued)

(continued)

bar along the left side of the window, inside of which information about the selected item appears. Pictures show up as little miniatures so that you can tell what they are before opening them. You can always go back later and change this or any other setting.

✔ **Browse Folders**

Are you getting the idea? All the options in this control panel are simply parts of the whole Web thing-a-ma-bob looking whose-a-whats-zis for your Windows desktop. This one in particular makes surfing your computer possible by causing each folder's contents to appear in a single window, like moving from Web page to Web page. With all the toolbars and other elements active, you would be hard-pressed to tell the difference between Windows Explorer and Internet Explorer.

Unfortunately, the Web page that can take up your entire desktop (okay, some icons can live on the far left side) isn't really a browser. It's more of a page holder for whatever page or location you specify. The default is your home page. Don't fall into the trap of believing that this is seriously cool. It's not, unfortunately. After you click on a link — *any* link — it opens a regular browser window. It's quite a disappointment.

Now you're really ready to single-click.

The Have Disk button tells Windows to look wherever you tell it for drivers for your modem. Usually, you tell it to look on a floppy disk (in drive A) or on a CD-ROM (usually in drive D). If the people who created the disk or CD have been cooperating, you can just type **A:** or **D:** in the box labeled Copy manufacturer's files from. If they've squirreled away the drivers somewhere on the disk or CD, you have to fill in that box *and* press the Browse button. You have to click different folders until you get to one that has files ending in .INF. Windows doesn't let you click OK until you find one. After you do find a folder with .INF files in it and you click OK, the manufacturer's list and the modem list are replaced with just the items that are on your floppy disk or CD-ROM.

Whether you're selecting from the list that Windows Me came up with or from the list for items on your floppy disk or CD-ROM, you're asked how this modem is connected to your PC. The wizard didn't have to ask because it found the modem and knows where it found it. Your choices are usually COM1, COM2, or LPT1, and the answer is almost always COM1 or COM2. How can you tell which? Fortunately for us, Bill Gates answered our cries of frustration and gave us System Information. Huh? Okay, it's not a magic wand, although it *is* helpful. Click the Start button and choose the Programs⇨Accessories⇨System Tools command. (Phew!) Then select System Information. Down the left side is a column of text items, one of which is named Components. You should see a small box with a + inside. Click it and another list of items rolls out. Click on the Modem item (of all things), let it grind away for a minute or so, and read the fifth item from the top. Voilà! Select that, and you're done (at least for that part).

After you click Next in this dialog box, your modem is installed, although you have to click the Finish button in the next box to get the Modem Wizard to go away. Just like when you let the wizard do all the work, you whisk back to wherever it was you called the wizard from.

Casting Internet Connection Spells Yourself

Wizards are wonderful things when they work. Unfortunately, much like wizards in the real world (you know what we mean), the Windows Me wizards can be a little temperamental. In this section, we lay out all the separate spells you have to cast to get your Windows Me PC on the Internet. Here are the things that must be installed and configured in Windows Me in order for you to get on the Internet:

- ✔ A modem
- ✔ The networking pieces of Windows Me
- ✔ TCP/IP, the "language" computers speak to one another over the Internet
- ✔ Information about your Internet Service Provider (ISP)

For each of these elements, you may also have to know how to find out whether it has been set up properly in Windows Me and, if not, how to fix it. At the end of this section, we tell you how to dial out to your ISP. The starting place for the first three items is the Windows Me Control Panel; information about your Internet Service Provider has its home in a thing called Dial-Up Networking. The Windows Me Control Panel is so important that it has its own place right on the Windows Me Start menu: You click the Start button and choose Settings⇨Control Panel. Figure 3-6 shows the Control Panel.

Figure 3-6: The Windows Me Control Panel.

The special Start menu blue-light special

Because nothing is ever perfect, of course, Microsoft was able to improve on the Control Panel. Here's how to get it. Click the Start button and choose Settings⇨Taskbar & Start Menu, which opens the Taskbar and Start Menu Properties dialog box. At the top are two tabs. Select the Advanced tab (don't worry, it's not *that* bad). In the lower section of the dialog box is a collection of check boxes with labels. Each one turns on or off a feature of the Start menu and the taskbar.

To have all the widgets on the Start menu turned on, make sure that all the options are checked. Most either show or hide a feature of the Start menu. The others activate cascading menus. It's easier for you to see than to explain, so turn on all the options you want; just make sure that you turn on the Expand Control Panel options, or else this won't work. Click OK, click the Start button, choose Settings⇨Control Panel, and then wait a second. (Note the new little black arrow to the right of the text.) When a list of control panels appears, move to another item with a black arrow (Printers, for example) and point at it (or click). The item you chose opens too, showing you its contents.

Each of these is a folder with stuff in it, so, as long as there are folders inside of folders, you can keep digging deeper and deeper. You'll find that, with a little practice, this method is much easier than opening window after window. After you reach the place you want to open, you can just open double-click the name or right-click it and choose Open.

Controlling modems from the Control Panel

The Control Panel contains Modem Central for your Windows Me system. Clicking the Modems icon shows you everything that Windows Me knows about modems on your computer. (This is the first time we've done any clicking where the new Windows Me *Web style* makes a difference. If you click Modems and nothing happens, look at the sidebar titled "With a double-click here and a single-click there," earlier in this chapter.) After you click Modems, if Windows Me doesn't know about *any* modems on your computer, it launches — as a bonus — the Modem Wizard we describe in the section "Making Sure That Windows Me Sees Your Modem," earlier in this chapter.

If Windows Me knows that you have a modem, you see the Modems Properties dialog box, from which you can add new modems, remove old ones, and find out about the ones you already have. Figure 3-7 shows both tabs in the Modem Properties dialog box.

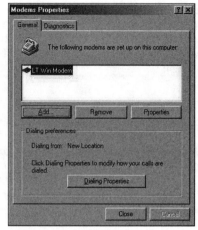 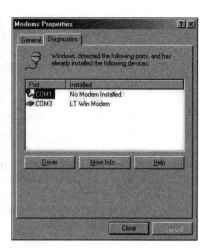

Figure 3-7:
Both tabs in
the Modems
Properties
dialog box.

This dialog box lists each modem installed on your system. If a modem is
plugged in to your computer and it's not listed here, Windows Me doesn't
know about it. Fortunately, that situation is easy to fix. Just click the Add
button, and the handy Modem Wizard appears. The section "Making Sure
That Windows Me Sees the Modem," earlier in this chapter, talks about that
process.

Testing your modems

In the section "Making Sure That Windows Me Sees Your Modem," earlier in
this chapter, we tell you that the only good way to tell where your modem is
connected is by looking in System Information. (Just a friendly reminder:
Click the Start button, choose the Programs➪Accessories➪System Tools
command, select System Information, open the Components item, and select
Modem.) The Diagnostics tab in the Modem Properties dialog box is the
place to view all connected devices. There, Windows Me lists all the ways
that it thinks a modem can be connected to your computer — it calls those
ways *ports* for getting data into and out of your computer. It also lists what it
thinks is currently connected to each port.

Click the port you want to test and click the More Info button. If you see a
dialog box full of information, your modem is working. (The exact information you get is arcane and not all that interesting to most of us.) Alternatively,
you may see a message saying that your modem is not responding. Windows
Me gives you two suggestions: one for internal modems and one for external
modems. For internal modems, Windows Me recommends that you check for
interrupt conflicts. Fixing interrupts gets you deep into the guts of Windows
Me — we strongly suggest calling whoever installed your internal modem in
your computer, your local computer whiz, the people who made your
modem, or the people who made your computer.

For external modems, check to ensure that the modem is turned on (although we figure that you already tried that suggestion). Our bet is that you've told Windows Me that your modem is connected to the wrong place. Check out the modem's properties to see whether it matches what System Information says and change it to match if it doesn't.

The properties of a modem

On the General tab in the Modems Properties dialog box is a Properties button. Highlight the modem you want to find out about and then click this button. You see a dialog box with several tabs full of information about this particular modem. Figure 3-8 shows the properties for a typical external modem. The dialog box you see may have more tabs because the properties depend on the modem and the software driver that was written for it. The General tab contains the only stuff you're interested in for purposes of this discussion.

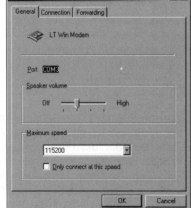

Figure 3-8:
The
properties
for a
particular
modem.

For an internal modem (including a PC Card modem), all you can usually do is turn the speaker on and off. For an external modem, however, you can click the Port setting and choose among the ports where Windows Me thinks that your modem can be (usually COM1 and COM2). If you get no response from the port you have picked, try picking another one. Then click OK to close the properties for this modem, and try the diagnostics again. (For the danger-ously curious, we talk about dialing properties in Chapter 4, in the section about making Dial-Up Networking a little more convenient.)

Network spell 1: The networking pieces of Windows Me

As you know, Windows Me comes with everything you need to get connected to the Internet. Unfortunately, some of that stuff may still be on your Windows Me CD, not loaded into your computer. You can find out by looking for Dial-Up Networking on your Window Me Start menu. Usually, you can find Dial-Up Networking by clicking the Start button and choosing Programs⟹ Accessories⟹Communications⟹Dial-Up Networking. If you don't find Dial-Up Networking there, click the Start button and look around on your Programs menu; it may be somewhere else. If you do find Dial-Up Networking, you're in luck: You can skip this whole spell and move on to the next, checking to determine whether TCP/IP has been set up on your computer.

If you're still here, you have to see whether Windows Me Dial-Up Networking was installed when Windows Me was installed on your computer. Just as with modems, the Control Panel is the place to check:

1. **If your Control Panel isn't already running, click the Start button and choose the Settings⟹Control Panel command to open it or simply choose Control Panel if you've set up the Start menu to open the Control Panel's menu. (This feature is very cool. We urge you not to pass it up. Look for instructions in the sidebar "The special Start menu blue-light special," earlier in this chapter).**

2. **Open the Add/Remove Programs icon.**

   You see the Add/Remove Programs Properties dialog box with three tabs; on the middle tab, labeled Windows Setup, you can investigate which parts of Windows Me got installed on your computer.

3. **Click the Windows Setup tab, and be prepared to wait a little while Windows wanders around your computer, looking for parts of itself.**

   When Windows Me is done, you see a list like the one shown in Figure 3-9. Each of the major topics with a check box beside it represents a part of Windows Me. Most of these parts are made up of subparts. A white, blank check box means that the entire part of Windows Me was *not* installed; a white, checked check box means that the entire part and all possible sub-parts of Windows Me *were* installed. A gray check box (with a check mark) means that only some subparts for that part of Windows Me were installed.

4. **Look for the Communications part of Windows Me; in most cases, its check box is gray with a check mark in it. Click the word *Communications.***

   Do *not* click the check box; that action prepares your computer to remove all the parts of Windows Me that have to do with communications. If you do clear the check box by mistake, click Cancel immediately, and then open the Add/Remove Programs icon again.

5. **After you click the word *Communications,* click the Details button.**

   You see a list of Windows Me subparts having to do with communications. One of the first is Dial-Up Networking.

6. **Make sure that this box has a check mark in it and click OK. The Add/Remove Programs dialog box returns, and you can click OK again.**

   If Dial-Up Networking was not installed on your computer, it is now. You may have to find your Windows Me CD, and Windows may decide to restart your computer.

Now you're ready to tell Windows Me how to talk over the telephone. You may be able to do it by using the Internet Connection Wizard. Try going to the section "Care and Feeding of the Internet Connection Wizard," earlier in this chapter, and telling the wizard that you already have an Internet account you want to set up. The wizard may do the plumbing and deep spells for you.

Network spell 2: Setting up TCP/IP

This procedure is, without a doubt, the most complicated piece of setting up an Internet connection, and one of the major benefits of using the Internet Connection Wizard is that it saves you the trouble of doing this part of the job. If you have to read this section, either the Internet Connection Wizard didn't do its job for you or for some reason your Internet connection doesn't work or you're just curious. No matter; we go through the procedure one step at a time, and you will, in all likelihood, get online eventually. Setting up TCP/IP has two parts. One is just getting TCP/IP on your computer and hooked up right. The other is making sure that Windows Me is, deep in its guts, looking in the right place for the right Internet stuff. We discuss each aspect in turn.

Getting TCP/IP hooked up to the plumbing

As with most of the other spells we cast here, the Windows Me Control Panel is the place to begin. (Here's a great place to use your new Start menu skills with the Control Panel.) Here are the tasks in front of you:

✔ Make sure that the Dial-Up Networking adapter is installed; if it isn't, install it.

✔ Make sure that TCP/IP is configured to talk to another computer using the dial-up adapter.

Here's how you do it:

1. **Open the Network icon in the Control Panel.**

   You see the Network dialog box, as shown in Figure 3-10. What you're looking at is a list of the ways in which Windows Me is prepared to talk to other computers. The list in this illustration is fairly extensive; your list may be much shorter or even blank. No matter: What you're looking for is an entry that says Dial-Up Adapter and another entry that says TCPIP -> Dial-Up Adapter.

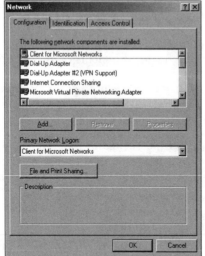

Figure 3-10:
The
Network
dialog box
and how to
add network
hardware.

Notice that the list shown in Figure 3-10 does contain a dial-up adapter and a TCP/IP entry, although both are for use with the Microsoft Virtual Private Network (VPN). If you don't see a line that says simply Dial-Up Adapter and another that says simply TCP/IP -> Dial-Up Adapter, you have to install them. On the other hand, if you *do* see those two lines, you're all set. Proceed to the section "Information about your ISP," later in this chapter.

2. If you don't have a dial-up adapter, click the Add button.

You see the Select Network Component Type dialog box.

3. Select Adapter and click the Add button.

You see the Select Network Adapters dialog box.

4. Scroll down the list of manufacturers until you see Microsoft and click it. In the box on the right, click Dial-Up Adapter.

(We know — Microsoft didn't make your modem, although it did write the software you're about to install.) Figure 3-10 illustrates this series of steps.

5. Click OK to finish.

6. If you don't have a TCP/IP -> Dial-Up Adapter, click the Add button.

You see the Select Network Components dialog box.

7. Select Protocol and click the Add button.

You see the Select Network Protocol dialog box.

8. **Click Microsoft in the list of manufacturers. In the box on the right, scroll down to Dial-Up Adapter and click it.**

9. **Click OK to finish.**

10. **Click OK to close the Network Properties dialog box.**

Windows Me may ask you to restart your computer, or it may ask for the Windows Me CD-ROM; when Windows Me is done whirring and clicking, you're almost ready to talk on the Internet.

This is also the last you see of the Control Panel (at least for setting up your Internet connection). Use the File⇨Close command (or the Close button, the X, in the upper-right corner of the window) to close the Control Panel. Note the added freedom of never again having to close the Control Panel if you have been using the special Start menu blue-light special mentioned earlier in this chapter. Isn't progress great?

Deep spells: The guts of TCP/IP, which you should ignore if at all possible

Whenever your computer calls your ISP, your computer connects to the Internet. Several million computers worldwide may have to be capable of finding your computer and talking to it more or less instantaneously. To enable the rest of the computers on the Internet to find your computer, you have to enter some additional information if it hasn't been set up automatically. You may have received one or more of the following pieces of information from your ISP:

✓ **A permanent IP address:** Your computer's address on the Internet — in the form 123.45.67.89 (computers love to think in numbers). If you didn't get one, every time your computer calls, your Internet Service Provider assigns it a temporary IP address.

✓ **One or more Domain Name Server (DNS) addresses:** The address (or addresses) of computers your computer can use to ask for the IP addresses of other computers — kinda like 411 directory assistance for the Internet, but fast and reliable.

✓ **A domain name:** The name of the family of computers your computer is a member of. It's usually a name related to your Internet Service Provider. Because one of our ISPs is TIAC, for example, one of our domain names is tiac.net.

✓ **A hostname:** The name by which your computer is known on the Net. You don't use the hostname unless you do some really geeky stuff.

All your Dial-Up Networking connections live together in your computer. You can peek at them by clicking the Start button and choosing the Programs⇨ Accessories⇨Dial-Up Networking command. You see the Dial-Up Networking window, as shown in Figure 3-11. You can tell Windows Me about this technical stuff from the Dial-Up Networking windows.

Figure 3-11:
The Dial-Up
Networking
window
and the
properties
for a Dial-Up
Networking
connection.

Figure 3-11:
The Dial-Up
Networking
window
and the
properties
for a Dial-Up
Networking
connection.

1. **From the Dial-Up Networking window (refer to Figure 3-11),** *right*-**click your connection name.**

   You see a pop-up menu that includes a Properties command.

2. **Choose Properties.**

   You see general information about this connection.

3. **Click the Server Type tab.**

4. **Click the TCP/IP Settings button.**

   This dialog box is the place to type your permanent IP address and your Domain Name Server IP addresses, if you know them. In many cases, neither Windows Me nor your Internet Service Provider cares if you don't bother.

5. **If your ISP gave you this information, type it in the box. If your ISP didn't tell you a permanent address, click Server Assigned IP address.**

6. **Click OK until you're back at the Dial-Up Networking window.**

When you're looking at the properties for a connection, you can click the Server Type button. Notice that the Server Types dialog box, as shown in Figure 3-11, has check boxes for NetBEUI and IPX/SPX Compatible. You can clear these check boxes and speed up your network communications a little. It's just more geeky stuff.

Information about your ISP

You may have wondered just what it was that the Internet Connection Wizard was offering to do for you at the end of the sign-up process, when it asked whether it should set up an Internet connection for you. You're about to find out. It's not all that grisly, and it's a good thing to know about so that your Internet connection isn't entirely magic.

Making a LAN connection to the Internet

Although this entire subject can be mind-numbingly complicated, all the pieces you need to connect a PC that's already on a LAN to the Internet are part of Windows Me, so you can probably get things working with the help of your local network manager.

Here's a one-sentence summary: You set it up the same way as Dial-Up Networking, except that rather than use a dial-up adapter, your network connection uses whatever networking card is installed in your computer. Connecting via a LAN is a little simpler than dial-up because you don't need phone numbers, logins, or passwords and all that mess. Whoops — that was more than one sentence; it really is kind of complicated.

Windows Me collects all the information it needs to dial an Internet Service Provider into a thing it calls a *Dial-Up Networking connection*. You're about to create one. To do it, you must be signed up with an ISP and know the telephone number to dial to connect to that ISP:

1. **Click the Start button and choose Programs⇨Accessories⇨ Communications⇨Dial-Up Networking from the taskbar.**

   If this is the first time you've run Dial-Up Networking, another wizard immediately appears to guide you through the process of creating a connection.

2. **If a wizard doesn't appear, invoke it by clicking the Make New Connection icon in the Dial-Up Networking window.**

   The wizard wants to know only three things about your Internet connection.

3. **Give your connection a name. Don't just say it out loud — type it in the box.**

   What's it called? Because our Internet Service Provider is named the Sovereign Vermont Network, we call ours *SoVerNet*— creative, eh? (The preceding "Eh" was courtesy of Canada and the province of Quebec. Bonjour!)

   You see the description of your modem on the list. If you have only one modem, skip Step 4.

4. **Choose the modem you want this connection to use.**

   Click on the modem name. If you see a list of modems installed on your computer, select the one you want to use.

5. **Click <u>N</u>ext to proceed to the next step in the wizard.**

6. **Type the telephone number your computer dials to connect to your ISP. Make sure that the Country code is right.**

   Notice the boxes for your area code and country. Windows wants to know where your ISP is so that it can figure out whether to dial the area code and things like that. That's all in Chapter 4, in the section about making Dial-Up Networking a little more convenient.

7. **Click Next to proceed to the next step in the wizard.**

8. **Click Finish.**

   The wizard adds your connection to the list of available connections, and you're done.

That was painless, right? In Chapter 4. we talk about *using* that Internet connection.

Getting to the Internet from an Online Service Like AOL or CompuServe

In Chapter 2, we go over a couple of reasons you may want to get your Internet access from an online service like AOL, CompuServe, Microsoft Network (MSN), or Prodigy Internet. Briefly, although they are just becoming *full* Internet Service Providers, if you plan to spend most of your time using their special services (like the AOL chat rooms) and want the flexibility to occasionally use any Internet programs you want, using your online service as an ISP may be a good solution for you. Online services have spent more time and effort in becoming easy to use and easy to sign up for than most ISPs, so we don't go step-by-step through each sign-up procedure. This section gives you the overview of what you have to do, along with some pitfalls.

You can click the Start button and choose Programs⇨Online Services to find all the online services that come with Windows Me. If you live outside the United States, you may see a different list from the ones we describe here.

Both CompuServe and Prodigy Internet used to be services like AOL that employed proprietary software rather than web browsers and e-mail clients. They were networks apart from the Internet and did not offer access to it either. Both CompuServe and Prodigy Internet are now (as the latter's name implies) Internet Service Providers in the true sense of the word, and they still offer content and services available only to their users.

America — and the rest of the Internet — Online

The AOL sign-up process is easy to use and thorough; by the end, you're signed on to America Online and can, through that service, access the Internet. (Chapter 2 has instructions for starting an Internet connection using AOL.) For ease of use, AOL is hard to beat. We still get more busy signals there than with most ISPs, though. Of course, that may have something to do with the estimated 17 *million* users that AOL supports. (That's a ton of users, but it's no excuse!) Also, because the AOL connection is not really an Internet connection, some software may not work seamlessly with it — we occasionally have to tell programs that we really are connected to the Internet. We also find that it's slow during peak hours (6 p.m. to 1 a.m.). A major disadvantage at the time we write this book is that you're stuck with the AOL mail program. On the other hand, AOL integrated the Microsoft Internet Explorer 5.0 software into its program, and it offers a far richer experience on the Internet than its previous measly offerings. (Although Version 4.0 was decent, the version before that was abysmal.)

AT&T WorldNet

Unlike America Online and CompuServe, AT&T WorldNet is a real, honest-to-goodness Internet Service Provider. We include it in this part of the chapter because it has a good sign-up package you can reach by clicking the Start button and choosing Programs⇨Online Services from the menu. Just like the Internet Connection Wizard, it creates a Dial-Up Networking connection for you. It also creates its own Dial-Up Networking connection if you click the Start button and choose Programs⇨AT&T WorldNet Software⇨Connect to AT&T WorldNet Service. Although some of its dialing screens therefore look a little different, deep down, they're doing the same thing as Dial-Up Networking.

CompuServe

CompuServe has taken a middle route between AOL and AT&T: With CompuServe, you get the value-added content from an online service along with a true Internet connection. The connection is reasonably fast, and all standard Internet programs — including e-mail programs — are perfectly happy to work with CompuServe. After AOL bought CompuServe awhile back, we had written that you could expect CompuServe to eventually become more AOL-ish. Nothing could be further from the truth. If anything, it has gotten more CompuServe-ish; its brand-new version 5.0 has loads of new features that highlight the primary strength of CompuServe; community. CompuServe has thousands of *forums,* which are groups of like-minded people who simply spend time communicating with each other.

Prodigy Internet

Prodigy started as an online service, later called Prodigy Classic, that was turned off in late 1999. Its ISP service is Prodigy Internet, which is the sign-up that comes with Windows Me. It's hard to distinguish between Prodigy Internet and other ISPs because it *is* an ISP. Like MSN and AT&T WorldNet, it's an Internet-based service, and like MSN and AT&T WorldNet, it creates a true Dial-Up Networking connection for you so that other Internet programs work well. The sign-up process is not flashy, although it works well.

The Microsoft Network (MSN)

The Microsoft service began as an online service competitor to AOL and CompuServe but quickly became Internet based. As with AT&T, you can sign up either from the Internet Connection Wizard or by clicking the Start button and choosing Programs⇨Online Services from the taskbar. As with CompuServe, you end up with a real Internet connection, so other programs work well. MSN is so Internet oriented, in fact, that you use it through the Microsoft Explorer web browser (described in Chapters 8 and 9). Using a browser is nice because it means that you don't have to learn how to use another program in order to use MSN. (Because both AOL and CompuServe came out before web browsers even *existed,* the program you use to communicate with them is their own — one more thing to learn.) MSN Internet mail is the most standard of the three online services, although not as standard as a regular ISP's.

Moving on

By hook or by crook, you have a connection to the Internet now. You're either going through an online service, in which case things were probably simple to set up, or you chose one of the Microsoft-recommended ISPs, or you're using an ISP you chose yourself. In any case, you have a Dial-Up Networking connection. In Chapter 4, you get online and learn some tips about making dial-up connections more convenient under Windows Me.

Avoiding the Connection Wizard Altogether

For some small but ever-growing percentage of the population, high-speed access to the Internet is available using cable and DSL connections, collectively called *broadband*. In many areas of the United States, cable television, local telephone providers, and other enterprising companies are providing broadband access to the Internet. Here's what's cool about that:

- ✔ Broadband is significantly faster than dial-up modems.
- ✔ The service provider comes to you and installs your cable modem and sets up your Internet connection. You could skip this whole chapter as well as the next.

The cost and availability of broadband access varies all over the country. For some, it costs as little as $25 a month; for others, it's close to $60. Before you plug your ears and run away, however, listen to why the cost may be worth it to you.

Cable access does not use a telephone line. (Some providers do. Ask your cable provider whether you need a modem to upload to the Internet. If the answer is yes, wait. Otherwise, you *get* the Internet at very high speeds, but you *send* at only the comparative pace of a snail and you're still out a phone line or the cost of an additional line). Cable access means that you can use your computer and talk on the phone at the same time. (Or someone else could use the phone, or someone could call you.) DSL does this too; rather than use cable TV "cable," however, it "piggy-backs" on your phone line. (Although it *uses* your phone line, you can still use it as a phone at any time with no interruptions to either voice or Internet.) People who use the Internet frequently install a second phone line. Broadband access may be cheaper than a second phone line. (To get an accurate comparison, add the monthly cost of the second phone line to the monthly cost of your Internet Service Provider.)

Broadband access is always there — you're always connected. You don't have to have your computer dial in every time you want to check your e-mail or look at a Web site. You click — it's there.

Unfortunately, we can't tell you whether cable is available in your area. You have to call your cable television company and ask. We do know that it's available in the greater Boston area and parts of upstate New York, and we like it.

DSL access is also becoming widespread. We've found that http://www.dslreports.com is a great Web site that reviews DSL providers and technology and provides pointers to said providers. Most DSL providers have an online form you fill out that tells you whether you're within spitting distance of what's called a Central Office. Others require you to call them. No matter what you do, though, haggle as much as possible.

Get the free modem, the unlimited access, and the free setup and installation, and shoot for one or two free months of access and additional months for referred friends. And don't pay anything more than $50 a month for anything called ADSL, XDSL, G.Lite, or SDSL, or anything with advertised speeds of "384 kilobits per second" or "1.5 megabits per second," for example.

One bit of warning, however, if you do go the cable route. Cable technology puts you on a Local Area Network connecting all cable-modem customers in your neighborhood. Make sure that your computer doesn't have file sharing or print sharing enabled, unless you really want all your neighbors to look at your disk or print on your printer.

Here's the fast bit on disabling file- and print-sharing on your computer. Click the Start button, choose Settings⇨Control Panel⇨Network, and click the File and Print Sharing button near the bottom of the Network dialog box. If either check box is checked, uncheck them. Click OK twice and be on your merry way.

Chapter 4

Dialing In and Out

● ●

In This Chapter

▶ Starting up, monitoring, and hanging up your Dial-Up Networking connection

▶ Letting Windows Me know when you want to dial and for how long

▶ Making Dial-Up Networking a little more convenient

▶ Knowing whether to bother with the Windows Me Location feature

▶ Figuring out whether Windows Me remembers your password

▶ Deciding whom to call (and not to call) for help

● ●

*G*etting ready to dial out to the Internet can be quite an adventure. You may have created a Dial-Up Networking connection, successfully confronted the Internet Connection Wizard, cast some Internet connection spells, and who-all knows what else. Now you're ready to see whether the whole thing works. In this chapter, we go through the basics of how to use your Dial-Up Networking connection. We also give you some tips on what can go wrong when you try to get connected. After you're connected, hanging up isn't hard to do, although you have to know where to click. We also talk about programs that are smart enough to hang up for you and ones you have to tell that you're through. Also, if you ask nicely, Windows Me can tell you how things are going with your Internet connection, and we tell you how to ask.

We hereby notify you that from now on we will be using the term Windows Me rather than the space-consuming Windows Millennium Edition. Plus, we think it's kind of cute.

You can make Dial-Up Networking more convenient in a number of ways, including making your connections easier to find and making Windows Me dial automatically without bothering you. We tell you how to do these things, and we talk more about local telephone numbers and dialing locations. In case you haven't noticed, new area codes are springing up like mushrooms after a spring rain, and now you may have to dial an area code just to make a local call about as often as you're not *allowed* to dial an area code to make a local call. The Windows Me dialing locations deal with all this stuff, but to do so, they have to be kind of complicated. Still, they're probably worth reading about, just so that you know what they're about when you need them.

Starting Up Your Dial-Up Networking Connection

Until you spruce up your desktop and menus (described later in this chapter, in the section "Making Dial-Up Networking a Little More Convenient"), the Windows Me Dial-Up Networking window is your key to getting on the Internet. Here's how to use it to get online:

1. **If the Dial-Up Networking window isn't open, open it by clicking the Start button and choosing Programs➪Accessories➪Comunications➪ Dial-Up Networking from the taskbar.**

   Figure 4-1 shows our Dial-Up Networking window after we've created dial-up networking connections for all the online services that came with our copy of Windows Me, plus our local ISP. Your Dial-Up Networking window probably has only two icons in it: Make a New Connection and the connection for the ISP or online service you signed up for. Note that we have no AOL icon even though we signed up for it. The reason is that, as we say in Chapter 3, AOL doesn't give you a true Internet connection.

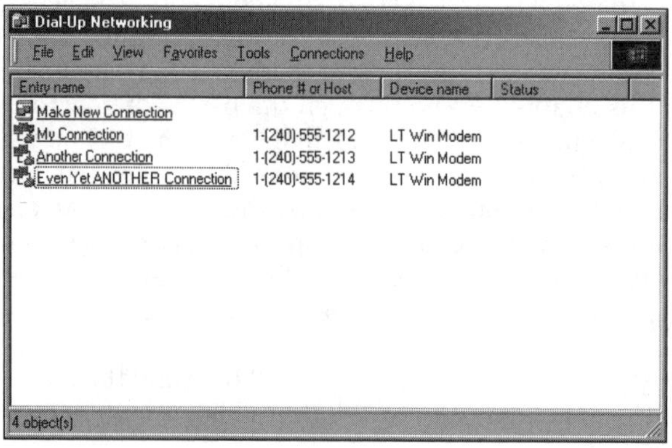

Figure 4-1:
The Dial-Up
Networking
window with
a number of
dial-up
networking
connections.

2. **Click the connection name.**

   Back when you created the connection, Windows Me suggested My Connection for the name, although we hope that you were more creative.

   You see a Connect To dialog box, as shown in Figure 4-2. Windows Me may or may not suggest a username, depending on whether you have other (non-dial-up) networking connections set up on your computer.

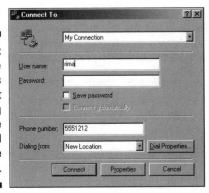

Figure 4-2:
The
Windows
Me Connect
To dialog
box dials the
phone and
makes the
connection.

3. **Make sure that the right username is in the box, and remember that cApiTaliZaTioN matters!**

   Keep in mind that this statement could also mean the opposite. Just for fun, suppose that your username is <pumpernickel> (the brackets are often used to show you where you put information, although you never type the brackets themselves) and you type Pumpernickel but are rejected. Why? Pumpernickel is a proper name, after all. Your ISP doesn't care about that fact — it just wants pumpernickel (in lowercase letters!).

4. **Enter your password in the Password box.**

   For security reasons (who's that looking over your shoulder?), the password appears as asterisks, one per character you type.

5. **Decide whether to check the Save password check box so that you don't have to enter your password again.**

   Advantage: You don't have to type your password every time you want to call the Internet. *Disadvantage:* Anyone can walk up to your PC and sign on to the Internet as you. If you're at home, don't laugh. Keeping your Internet access password-protected means that your children don't have unsupervised access. The Save password check box may be gray and may not allow you to check it. If that's the case, read the section "Why won't Windows Me save my dial-up networking password?" near the end of this chapter.

6. **Change the Phone number and Dialing from boxes, if you need to.**

   The phone number should be familiar from using the Make New Connection Wizard. You can type a new telephone number here, although you probably don't want to — you're better off modifying the telephone number permanently (see the section "Making Dial-Up Networking a Little More Convenient," later in this chapter) or creating a new connection.

The Dialing from box contains the name of the location where Windows Me thinks that you are right now. It's usually New Location, unless you have a portable computer and have already set up different dialing locations for it (see the section referred to in the preceding paragraph).

7. Click the Connect button.

You see a series of messages beginning with Initializing and ending with Connected. Finally, you see the Connection Established dialog box, as shown in Figure 4-3.

It's a perfectly nice dialog box, although it's just a reminder about what we tell you in the following section: how to disconnect from the Internet. If you don't mind seeing the dialog box, skip Step 8, which makes this dialog box go away forever. We prefer to click as few dialog boxes as possible when we want to get on the Internet. (Our thoughts turn to reading our e-mail or looking at whatever Web page it was that brought us to the Internet, not the care and feeding of Windows Me, although Microsoft may prefer, of course, that it were the other way around.)

Figure 4-3:
At last!
Connected
to the
Internet.

8. Click the Do not show this dialog box check box, if you want not to see this particular dialog box every time you connect.

9. Click the Close button to make this dialog box go away.

10. Celebrate — you're finally connected to the Internet!

What Microsoft is trying to tell you with the Connection Established dialog box, with its little icon of two computers, is that a new little icon appears on the system tray part of your Windows Me taskbar (way over to the right, next to the clock). We call it the *dial-up icon,* and whenever Dial-Up Networking is connected to the Internet, that icon appears on the taskbar.

Hanging Up in (Not on) Windows

It doesn't take much *effort* to hang up your Dial-Up Networking connection, though it can be kind of hard to figure out *how* unless you know where to look: *Right*-click the dial-up icon (the little picture of the two computers on your taskbar, as shown later in this chapter, in Figure 4-5) in the system tray part of the taskbar (way over to the right). You see a menu with two items on it: Status, which shows you the connection statistics we just talked about, and Disconnect. Clicking the word *Disconnect* does just that. The astute reader (that's you) also notices the Disconnect button in the Connection Statistics dialog box. Clicking it does the same thing.

Telling Windows to Connect to the Internet Whenever It Darn Well Pleases!

Whenever you connect to the Internet, you want *Internet* things, such as e-mail or the Web, not Windows Me dialog boxes. You can tell Windows Me to connect automagically to the Internet whenever you ask for Internet-based information. Windows Me remembers how you want to be connected to the Internet, and *most* (but not all) programs that access the Internet can induce

Are we done yet?

Some programs (most notably, Internet Explorer) offer to disconnect you from the Internet when you're done using them. A program generally does this only if it was the one that initiated the connection to the Internet in the first place. We generally find this to be a nice feature.

This feature can be a little confusing, however. For example, what happens if you start using Internet Explorer to browse the World Wide Web and then get involved in reading your e-mail? As soon as you decide to leave Internet Explorer, it offers to shut down your Web connection. If you're in the middle of downloading some mail, you probably don't want to disconnect just yet.

You don't have to *do* much about this situation — it just happens. What you do need to remember (if you told Internet Explorer *not* to disconnect from the Internet) is to disconnect yourself when you're done reading your mail (or whatever else it was that you were doing). Take a look at the section "Telling Windows How Long to Stay Connected," just ahead, to find out how to have Windows Me disconnect from the Internet after you've walked away from your computer for a while.

Windows Me to get connected all by itself. When you set up a dial-up Internet connection, the Dial-Up Networking Wizard automatically assumes that you want to use this connection for automatically dialing the Internet — or *autodialing.*

Even though we jump ahead a little here, you can start yourself down the autodialing path by asking Internet Explorer to show you a Web page. We talk all about Internet Explorer in gruesome detail in Part III of this book, but just getting it started can't hurt, right? Here's what to do:

1. **Make sure that you are not connected to the Internet (disconnect if you need to).**

2. **Click the Internet Explorer icon, which is usually on your desktop or right beside the Start button on the taskbar, or you can click the Start button and choose Programs⇨Internet Explorer from the taskbar.**

   The first time Windows Me decides that it has to dial out to the Internet, you probably see the Internet Autodial dialog box, as shown in Figure 4-4. If you see this dialog box, you see it only once. After you tell Windows Me that you want it to dial the Internet automatically, it is content to do so until you tell it to stop. (That's what the following sidebar, "Get your hands off my telephone — turning off Internet Autodial," is all about.) This is your chance to tell Windows Me if you *don't* want it to dial out by itself.

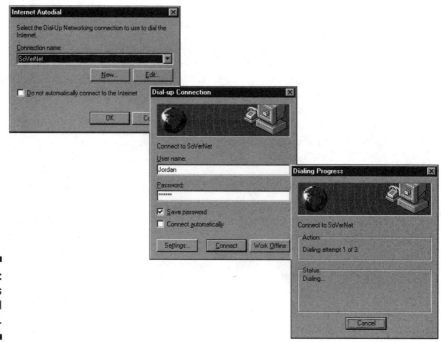

Figure 4-4:
Three steps
to autodial
the Internet.

3. **If you *don't* want Windows Me to connect to the Internet when it thinks that you may want to, click the Do not automatically connect to the Internet check box. If you *want* Autodial to work, leave this check box blank.**

   Our opinion is that you *shouldn't* click this check box. It's kind of nice to have Windows start up your connection whenever you ask to check your e-mail or see a Web page. When Windows Me wants to dial out, you have another chance to figure out whether your teenager is on the telephone.

   Whenever Windows Me tries to dial out to the Internet, you see the Dial-Up Connection dialog box, the middle dialog box shown in Figure 4-4. The username is the name you used to sign on to Windows Me.

4. **If the name you use with your Internet Service Provider doesn't appear in the User name box, type the username it gave you.**

   The first time you see this dialog box, the Password box is blank because you have never told Windows Me what your password is for this account.

5. **Type your password in the Password box (asterisks appear as you type).**

   After you enter a password, the Save password check box is available, so you have to decide whether to trust that password to Windows Me. The first time you see this dialog box, the Save password check box is *not* checked.

6. **Decide whether to click the Save password check box.**

   Convenience definitely dictates that you should click it. Your comfort level with the people who pass by your computer whenever you're not around determines whether you do.

   If you let Windows Me save your password, anyone who walks up to your computer can sign on to this ISP or online service as you. You get hasslefree connection to the Internet, however. Windows stores your password on your hard disk in an encrypted form, which means that casual passers-by can't read it, although it won't slow down the National Security Agency for long. Your computer is still protected by your Windows Me password, which you typed when you turned the computer on. We always let Windows store our password because we like uninterrupted access to the Net. We figure that the Windows password is good enough and that the number of malicious strangers who wander into our home office is usually low.

7. **Decide whether to click the Connect automatically check box.**

   Plusses and minuses abound. On the plus side is uninterrupted access to the Net. On the minus side is the fact that your computer may pick up the telephone at odd times, without knowing whether anyone else in the house is using it. If your computer is on its own telephone line, we definitely recommend automatic connection. If your computer shares a telephone line with human beings (you, for example), it depends on how upset people will get if the computer occasionally picks up the phone while they're talking. Although it doesn't do any harm, it can be annoying.

If you decide on automatic connection, you see the Dialing Progress screen from the right side of Figure 4-4 every time Windows Me decides to dial out to the Internet. If you change your mind and decide that you don't want to connect automatically at that time, you can click the Cancel button. Rather than go away entirely, the Dial-up Connection dialog box appears (the one in the middle of Figure 4-4). From there, you can uncheck the Connect automatically check box.

8. **After you've entered your identifying information and decided what Windows Me should do with your password and connection, you're ready to click the _C_onnect button.**

   You see the Dialing Progress dialog box, as shown on the right side of Figure 4-4. After you're connected to the Internet, the dialog boxes go away, and you're all set. Only the dial-up icon on the system tray part of the taskbar indicates that you're connected.

Get your hands off my telephone — turning off Internet Autodial

You can turn off Internet Autodial in a slightly roundabout way. The key is in the Windows Me Control Panel (click the Start button and choose Settings⇨Control Panel from the taskbar to open it). Click the Internet icon in the Control Panel to see the Windows Me Internet Properties dialog box, and then click the Connection tabs in the dialog box. If you told Windows Me to autodial the Internet, the button beside the Connect to the Internet using a modem option contains a check mark. You can disable autodialing by clicking the button beside the Connect to the Internet using a local area network option, _even if you don't have a Local Area Network!_ (Local Area Networks, unlike telephones, don't have dials.) Click OK to close the Internet Properties dialog box, and close the Control Panel, by either choosing the File⇨Close command or clicking the Close button (the X) in the upper-right corner of the Control Panel.

Programs that need to access the Internet behave in one of two ways: They either tell you that they can't get to the Internet (like Internet Explorer) or go ahead and dial whatever Dial-Up Networking connection they think they need (like Outlook Express). You always have the option of connecting manually, which is, after all, what you said you wanted to do.

Telling Windows How Long to Stay Connected

One way to disconnect from the Internet is not to send or receive any information for a while. How long "a while" is depends. The nearby sidebar, "Get your hands off my telephone — turning off Internet Autodial," contains the key: On the Connection tab in the Internet Properties dialog box in the Control Panel, click the Settings button. You see the Dial-Up Settings dialog box, where you can specify the name of the connection you want Windows Me to use when it connects automatically, a check box to enable automatic disconnection, and a number box that says how many minutes to wait to disconnect. Before you are disconnected, however, you always have a chance to say something about it. After the required period of Internet inactivity, Windows Me displays a dialog box telling you that it will disconnect in 30 seconds. You can either watch the time count down if you enjoy the suspense, disconnect immediately, or cancel the disconnect. If you cancel the disconnect, you remain online.

Monitoring Your Dial-Up Networking Connection

If the Internet were less congested and if modems were faster, you probably wouldn't care what goes on with your Dial-Up Networking connection. Instead, you would ask for information and it would appear instantly, and then you would send information out to the Internet, and it would transmit in a flash.

Alas, most of us don't live in that world; we live in a world in which access to Web pages has been called the World Wide Wait. You click a Web page or request some information from the Internet or check your mail, and your Internet connection seems to stop. Although the rest of your computer seems to be humming along fine, who knows what's happening between you and the Internet?

If your modem has lights, you can look and see whether any information is coming or going; external modems usually have SD (send data) and RD (receive data) lights that blink as data goes by. Most modems nowadays are internal, though, which means that they have no lights. (Who could find them in the dark inside a computer?) You may need some important information that you can't find out just from lights, anyway. Luckily, Dial-Up Networking can give you a little information about what's going on with your connection.

Remember the dial-up icon that appears near the right end of the taskbar when you are connected? The icon represents your computer and the computer you're dialed in to; when their screens flash, information is coming or going. (Are these guys cute or what?)

You can get some more specific information about your connection, too. If you pass your mouse pointer over the dial-up icon and pause for a second, a little message pops up telling you how many bytes your computer has sent and received. The message also tells you the speed at which your modem is communicating over the telephone, although we find the speeds it reports to be wildly optimistic. Figure 4-5 shows the taskbar with a dial-up icon on it, with the cursor on the icon and the pop-up information displayed.

Figure 4-5:
Connection
statistics
from the
dial-up icon
and the
Connected
to dialog
box.

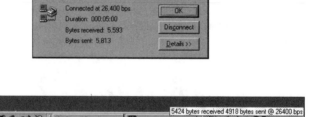

If you double-click the dial-up icon, you see the dialog box shown in Figure 4-5. Unlike the pop-up information, the information in the dialog box is "live." As information flows to and from your computer, the counts of bytes received and bytes sent are updated. You can click the Disconnect button to hang up or the OK button to make the dialog box go away. If you *really* want to know more, click the Details button.

Making Dial-Up Networking a Little More Convenient

Face it — clicking the Start button and choosing Programs➪Accessories➪ Comunications➪Dial-Up Networking and the connection name every time you want to connect to the Internet is not convenient. Life is way too short to issue that command more than once! You can make your Dial-Up Networking connection much easier to find by putting a shortcut to your Dial-Up Networking connection on your Windows Me desktop and on your Start menu.

You may not find this technique as useful as we do. Web browsers, such as Internet Explorer and Netscape Navigator, and mail programs, such as Outlook Express and Eudora, know how to tell Windows Me to dial up the Internet. There's still a small advantage, however, to dialing before you start the program: If you're truly impatient, you can start dialing the Internet connection and *then* start the program. That way, the program starts *while* the Internet connection is dialing: Your computer does two things at one time, and you wait only half as long.

Some programs also hang up the telephone right after they're done doing whatever it was they did. For example, if you check your mail and then send some mail and then surf the Web, the automatic-dialing procedure makes probably three telephone calls, wasting between 30 seconds and a minute of your time each time. If some of the e-mail you're reading contains Web addresses and you decide to look at those Web pages, you could be bouncing on and off the Internet any number of times. You may find it faster to dial up the Internet before you start, stay connected the whole time you're working, and then disconnect when you're all done.

Putting your connection on your desktop

Here's how to create shortcuts to your Dial-Up Networking connection. If you find that you don't use them, you can always delete the shortcuts later, with no effect on the Dial-Up Networking connection:

1. **Click the Start button and choose the Programs⇨Accessories⇨ Communications⇨Dial-Up Networking command to open the Dial-Up Networking window.**

   You see the window that was shown in Figure 4-1.

2. **Drag your favorite Dial-Up Networking connection to the Windows Me desktop.**

   That's all there is to it! Windows Me leaves your connection where it is and makes a shortcut on the desktop that runs the connection; now you have two icons for the same connection — one in the out-of-the-way Dial-Up Networking window and one right on your desktop.

3. **Leave your Dial-Up Networking window open if you want to put your Dial-Up Networking connection on your Start menu too. Otherwise, close the window.**

If you've upgraded from Windows 95, notice that this process is quite a bit simpler in Windows Me. Remember that because what's on your desktop is a *shortcut* to the actual Dial-Up Networking connection, you can delete the shortcut if you want.

Putting your connection on your Start menu

You may want to put your Dial-Up Networking connection on your Start menu. Don't bother because it's already there. Okay, do bother because you want it exactly where you want it. Then again, this ability is less important than it used to be because you can return to your desktop at any time in Windows Me by clicking the little picture of a desk blotter on the taskbar. (On ours, it's just to the right of the Internet Explorer and Outlook Explorer icons — take another look at Figure 4-5.) Still, we like to have our Dial-Up Networking connection on our Start menu so that we can get to it without messing up the desktop. Here's how:

1. **Go to Start⇨Settings⇨ and choose Dial-Up Networking.**

   Right-click and choose Open from the menu that appears. This step very conveniently opens the Dial-up Networking window.

2. **Locate and drag your connection icon to the Start menu button.**

   It's important to pause here until the Start menu opens, as shown in Figure 4-6. Don't let go, either. You have more dragging to do.

Figure 4-6:
The My
Connection
icon being
uncere-
moniously
dragged
about.

3. **After the Start menu is open, drag your connection icon into it.**

   As you move the mouse, dragging the connection icon all the while, you see black bars appear between items on the Start menu. They're telling you that if you let go, your connection icon will be placed between the two menu items it's straddling. A shortcut is automagically placed where you drop the icon.

Now you can start your Internet connection by just cruising the Start menu. Very convenient.

Canceling your Internet account

Canceling an account with an Internet Service Provider (ISP) is one of the few things you usually *can't* do over the Internet. When you sign up for an account with an ISP, you usually get a package full of stuff, including software (which we asked you to ignore), instructions (which we recommended that you ignore), and some billing information (which you probably threw away). Somewhere in there was a telephone number for account inquiries or billing questions or administrative support or something like it. That's the telephone number you want to call to cancel your account with the ISP.

If you signed up using the Internet Connection Wizard, you probably had to click OK on a confirmation screen before your credit card number went whizzing over the Internet. You may also have seen a screen full of information after your account was successfully created. We recommended that you print those screens or copy the information from them for moments just like this one.

One convenience of paying with a credit card is that your credit card company will help you with billing problems from the ISP. Usually, the credit card company counts on you to have a telephone number or contact information for the ISP, but in a pinch it can sometimes give you a contact phone number.

After you get in touch with the ISP, a short conversation is all it usually takes to get your account turned off. It wants to be able to identify you, usually by your telephone number, credit card number, and perhaps other information you gave during the sign-up. After it does, that's usually all there is to canceling your Internet account.

Fine-Tuning Your Connection

You can find out exactly what telephone number Windows Me will dial to connect to the Internet. That way, you can check yourself to see that it is local. Although you may already know this number, if you signed up with a service that created your connection automagically, you may not.

Also, Windows Me may save your Dial-Up Networking password so that you don't have to remember it. Sometimes it gets very stubborn and doesn't. We can tell you when (we think) it does and doesn't.

Making sure that the telephone number is local

If you typed the telephone number for Dial-Up Networking to use to connect to the Internet, you had a chance to look in your telephone book and see whether it's a local call for you. If you're not sure, call the telephone company. If you used an automatic sign-up wizard for an ISP, however, you may not have seen the telephone number. If that's the case, you can't be too careful: It's worth checking to make sure that your ISP is a local call before spending hours browsing the Web. We know true stories of people who signed up with what they thought was a local number until their first $500 phone bill arrived.

Follow these steps:

1. **Open the Dial-Up Networking window to look at your connection (click the Start button and choose the <u>P</u>rograms⇨Accessories⇨ Communications⇨Dial-Up Networking command) and click your connection.**

   You see the Connect To dialog box that was shown in Figure 4-2. If the telephone number in the Phone <u>n</u>umber box looks like it's been modified by Windows Me, check out the section "Location, Location, Location," later in this chapter. In any case, this telephone number is the one Windows Me will dial.

2. **Check your local telephone directory or call your telephone company's business office to make sure that you won't be paying for the Internet by the minute.**

   If the number *is* long-distance and your ISP suggests a better number to use, type the new and improved number in the Phone <u>n</u>umber box.

3. **To save any changes, you have to go ahead and connect to your Internet account by clicking <u>C</u>onnect.**

   If you make changes and then click Cancel, Windows Me throws away your changes.

"Why doesn't Windows Me save my Dial-Up Networking password?"

Suppose that you want Windows Me to save your Dial-Up Networking password. After all, it's convenient, even if it means that anyone who comes up to your computer can get on the Internet as you. (If you don't want Windows Me to save your password, you can skip to the next section.) Every once in awhile, Windows Me does not save your password; it has been one of the most vexing questions for users of previous versions of Windows.

Several possible reasons exist for why the password isn't saved, only a few of which we can help you out with. The rest get you deep into the guts of Windows Me, a place where even experienced folks have been bitten by strange and bizarre creatures occasionally and have the scars to prove it. The symptom you're most likely to see is a Connect To dialog box (like the one that was shown in Figure 4-2), where the Save password check box is grayed out and you therefore cannot check it.

The most common reason for this situation is that you didn't log on to Windows Me in the first place, so it has no idea who you are. When you started up your computer, Windows Me most likely showed you a dialog box that said Welcome to Windows or Enter Network Password or something similar. In either case, you had the option of clicking the Cancel button. If you canceled this dialog box, Windows Me still starts and you can still use it. You are not *logged in,* however. If you don't log in, Windows doesn't save passwords for you.

Luckily, you can talk Windows into saving your passwords, including your Internet password. Your best bet is to click the Start button and choose Log Off from the Start menu. Windows Me asks you to sign on again. When you enter your password this time, Windows Me should save your Dial-Up Networking password the next time you connect.

If you've forgotten your password, you can sign on with a different name, in which case Windows Me asks you for a new password. Any passwords Windows Me had saved for you are no longer available, although, as you work, Windows Me asks you for the passwords it needs. If you remember all of them, before long, Windows Me knows all the ones you need. We know of no way to get Windows Me to tell you a forgotten password.

What if Windows never asked you to sign on in the first place? When you started Windows Me for the first time, you may have pressed the Cancel button when you were asked to sign on for the first time. Windows Me figured that you didn't care about saving passwords and resolved never to bother you again. All's well and good until now, when you want it to remember a password. No problem. Click the Start button and choose Log Off, and then you see the Welcome to Windows sign-in dialog box. Enter a new username, and click OK *without* typing a password. Windows Me asks you to confirm that you don't want a password (actually, it asks you to retype your "null" password), so just click OK. From now on, whenever you start Windows, it's not supposed to ask you to sign on. If it does, you can just click OK. But now Windows saves your Dial-Up Networking passwords for you.

Windows Me may ask for your password when you start up your computer and *still* not allow you to check the Save password check box in the Connect To dialog box. If so, your password file may have gotten *messed up* (that's a technical term). It's time to call tech support, from either your computer manufacturer or Microsoft.

Location, Location, Location

If your computer moves around (as laptops typically do), you may find your-self calling the same Internet access number from places with different area codes. Dialing telephone numbers used to be so easy: If you were making a call inside your area code, you dialed seven digits; if you were making a call outside your area code, you dialed 1, the three-digit area code, and the seven-digit telephone number.

Even some local calls require that you dial 1 plus an area code. In some places, you dial the 1 only sometimes — you have to know when. If you have a desktop computer, this situation isn't so bad: After *you* figure out what to dial to get to the Internet, you can just tell Windows Me and be done with it. Because laptop computers move from place to place, however, the right way to dial a particular telephone number changes depending on where the computer is.

For laptop computer users (or anyone who moves her computer around fre-quently), Windows Me has a baroque scheme for what it calls *dialing loca-tions* that covers most, but not all, of the area code possibilities. This section first solves the most common desktop-computer dialing problems and then looks at solutions for laptop computers. In either case, you have to look at your Dial-Up Networking connections again. If you've closed the Dial-Up Networking window, click the Start button and choose the Programs⇨ Accessories⇨Communications⇨Dial-Up Networking command from the taskbar to get it back.

Dialing from your desktop computer

If your computer never moves, you only have to make sure that your Dial-Up Networking connection dials the right number when you set it up. To check which digits Windows Me dials to connect to your ISP, click the Dial-Up Networking connection you want to check out. You see the Connect To dialog box that was shown in Figure 4-2.

The digits that Windows Me dials are in the Phone number box. Windows Me may have added (or removed) the area code from the telephone number you gave it, and it may have added a prefix (like 9,) to get an outside line and a prefix (like *70) to turn off call-waiting. If Windows Me modified the telephone number you gave it, someone (you, perhaps?) told it something about its dial-ing location which made it think that it was the right thing to do.

The Dialing from box tells you where Windows Me thinks that it's dialing from. For desktop computer users, this entry almost always says New location. Windows creates this location for all computer users, and, if your computer never moves, this location should be good enough. If you want to find out more about what's in this dialog box, look in the section "Dialing from your laptop computer," just ahead.

If the telephone number Windows Me will dial is correct, you can click Cancel and skip the rest of this location business. If Windows Me has gotten smart with you and done things to your telephone number that you don't like, you can tell it to keep its hands off. After you do, it's your job to tell Windows Me about these tasks:

- ✔ Dialing 9 or something else to get an outside line
- ✔ Turning off call-waiting (call interrupt)
- ✔ Dialing an area code
- ✔ Dialing 1 before an area code

Follow these steps to tell Windows Me exactly how you want your telephone number dialed:

1. **If you're still looking at the Connect To dialog box, click Cancel to forget about dialing out right now.**

2. **In the Dial-Up Networking window, right-click the Dial-Up Networking connection you're interested in.**

   After you perform steps 3 through 6, Windows Me forgets the username and password associated with this Dial-Up Networking connection. Before you proceed, therefore, make sure that you have them written down somewhere. Windows Me tells you the username for this Dial-Up Networking connection (in the Connect To dialog box — the one you just closed in step 1 if it was still open). Windows Me does not tell you the password, however; it just indicates that it remembers the password by putting a few asterisks in the Password entry in the dialog box.

3. **Choose Properties from the pop-up menu.**

   You see a dialog box with a bunch of tabs describing the properties of your Dial-Up Networking connection. On the General tab, in the Phone Number section, you see the area code and telephone number you (or some fancy Internet setup wizard) told Windows Me to dial.

4. **Uncheck the Use area code and Dialing Properties check box.**

   By unchecking this box, you tell Windows Me that you will give it exactly the right telephone number to dial and to keep its hands off your telephone number. As a result, the area code and country code entries become unavailable: They no longer affect the number your computer dials. Also, when you see the Connect To dialog box, the Dialing from entry is not available. The reason is that Windows Me uses the location settings in the Dialing from box to decide how to mess up your telephone number; unchecking the Use area code and dialing properties check box tells Windows Me to keep its hands off your telephone number.

5. **In the Telephone number box, enter the telephone number *exactly* as Windows Me should dial it.**

   Include **9,** (a 9 with a comma) if you need to dial 9 for an outside line. Often, when you have to dial 9 to get an outside line, you have to wait until you actually get the line before you dial again. If you have to wait, you have to tell your computer to wait. Put the comma in to tell Windows Me to pause. If you have trouble connecting, try putting in a second comma to extend the pause. Include *70,, (that's star 70 with two commas) if that's what you press to disable call-waiting. (Again, the commas tell Windows Me to wait for the command to disable call-waiting to clear before it begins dialing the number.) Include the 1 and the area code if you need them.

6. **Click OK to keep your changes.**

   Presto! You're all set to dial out.

If you set up an additional Dial-Up Networking connection later, remember to uncheck the Use area code and Dialing Properties check box for that new connection, and fill in exactly what Windows Me needs to dial up the Internet.

Dialing from your laptop computer

If your computer moves around frequently, changing the area code and other dialing instructions for each Dial-Up Networking connection every time you move your computer can become tedious. Windows Me can figure out this stuff for you by defining a *dialing location,* which is basically a name and an area code. If you get fancy, a location can include things like dialing 9 to get an outside line and dialing *70 to turn off call-waiting. The simplest way to check out your locations is from the Connect To dialog box when you're about to dial.

You can get to the Dialing Properties dialog box in several different ways. Windows Me is sensitive about the order in which things happen. Make sure that you get to the Dialing Properties dialog box from the Dial-Up Networking dialog box; otherwise, some settings don't appear. Here's one way:

1. **In the Dial-Up Networking window, click the connection you want to check.**

   You see the Connect To dialog box (refer to Figure 4-2).

2. Click the Dial Properties button.

You see the Dialing Properties dialog box, as shown in Figure 4-7.

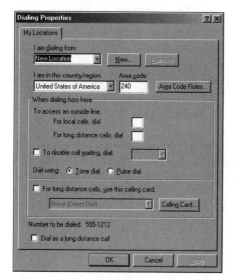

Figure 4-7:
Is this the
location
from which I
am dialing?

The following sections describe common dialing problems and ways to solve them from the Dialing Properties dialog box.

Your computer may be in one of several different places when you want it to call the Internet

Click the New button in the Dialing Properties dialog box. Windows Me creates a new dialing location with the same characteristics as the dialing location you were just looking at. Windows Me gives the new location a creative name, like New Location (2). (Click OK to acknowledge the new location.) Type a more appropriate name, like **Office** or **Home.**

You always have to dial 1 and the area code to reach this number, even though it's within your area code

If the area code you are dialing from (in the Area code box in the Dialing Properties dialog box) is the same as the area code of the number you are calling (that's the number you entered when you created the Dial-Up Networking connection you're working on), Windows Me assumes that you don't have to dial 1 and the area code. You can tell Windows Me to always dial this number as a long-distance call by checking the Dial as a long distance call check box. In the Dialing Properties dialog box is a field labeled For long distance calls, dial. Windows adds the contents of that field in addition to 1 and the area code to whatever telephone number you entered. Unlike the other settings in this dialog box, this check box applies to only the Dial-Up Networking connection you were looking at when you clicked Dial Properties in the Connect To dialog box.

You want to turn off call-waiting

Windows Me is all set for this trick: In the Dialing Properties dialog box is a check box labeled To disable call waiting, dial. Make sure that a check mark is in this box, and pick one of the call-waiting codes from the nearby list. If you dial a more creative code to disable call waiting, type what you dial.

You want to dial the area code but not a 1 in front of it

You can't dial an area code without a 1 in front of it — at least not by using the Dialing Properties and locations in Windows Me. If you need to dial the area code without the 1, you probably live in Texas or dangerously close to Washington, D.C., and the most sensible thing to do is to move. If you can't, however, look at the section "Dialing from your desktop computer," earlier in this chapter, and tell Windows Me *exactly* how you want your number dialed. You may have to define two Dial-Up Networking connections for the same telephone number. This would be the case if you called the same number from two different locations and one of them required that you dial a 1 (one) first. Location A would be *555-311-3456,* and Location B would be *1-555311-3456.* This is a great reason to use clear and concise names for your dialing locations.

You want to use a telephone calling card

We prefer to create a new dialing location for each type of calling card call we make. That way, we can select the credit card as a dialing location directly from the Connect To dialog box (refer to Figure 4-2). If you like this plan, follow the instructions in the section "Your computer may be in one of several different places when you want it to call the Internet," earlier in this chapter, to create the location. Then click the check box labeled For long-distance calls, use this calling card. Click the Calling card button to select a calling card, and enter your calling card PIN. If your calling card is not listed, you can create a new one; examine the existing ones carefully, however, so that you can figure out what your calling card should do. If you need to create a new type of card, you just wandered out of the territory covered by this book — sorry!

You're happy with your location as it now appears

Click OK to accept the dialing location you've created or modified, and get rid of the Dialing Properties dialog box. The location you've been working on now appears as the Dialing from location in the Connect To dialog box, and it's available from any other Dial-Up Networking connections you've created.

Whom to Call (and Whom Not to Call) for Support

If you're having trouble getting Dial-Up Networking to work, we can't very well tell you to go look on the World Wide Web for support, can we? This situation is a shame because delivering information is just what the World Wide Web was designed for, and it's well suited to the task. If you're having trouble getting online, however, here are some places to start looking for help.

Call your Internet Service Provider

If you use one of the national Internet Service Providers, or ISPs (such as AT&T, IBM, MCI, or Sprint or others), you most likely got a toll-free support telephone number. Despite the fact that the ISP probably didn't make your computer or your modem or the software that's trying to connect it all together, someone there will probably try to help you anyway. The reason, of course, is that the company is about to make $20 per month from you for the foreseeable future, so it wants to help you get online, and it usually does a good job. Although it may take you awhile to get through to an ISP, it's probably worth the wait, especially for the price.

On the other hand, support from local ISPs can be spotty. When you're choosing a local ISP, talk to friends about which one they use and whether they like its technical support. Although most local ISPs are technically quite competent, some are more inclined than others to do much front-line technical customer support for the technically unsophisticated (or for you, either). Some are great and go the extra mile that the nationals can't. Others get around to you eventually. Our advice? If your provider can't help you get connected, find a provider that can.

Get Windows Me help

The Windows Me help file is surprisingly complete when it comes to Dial-Up Networking. It has the added advantage that it can take you directly to some of the procedures you need to perform to get online, such as install a modem or install Dial-Up Networking. To start Windows help, click the Start button, choose the Help command, and click the Contents tab if it isn't already selected. Help for setting up Dial-Up Networking is hidden in the area of the help file called Using Windows Accessories / Connections to Other Computers. Most topics have at the bottom a link labeled Related Topics that takes you to additional pages of useful information.

A nice feature that has been improved in Windows Me is *troubleshooters,* a series of questions and recommended actions based on your answers to those questions. Because troubleshooters are integrated with Windows, they sometimes take you directly to the dialog box you need to solve your problem. They're available in Help, under "What would you like help with?", and at the bottom of the list called Troubleshooting. Dial-Up Networking help is available in the Modem area.

Although the Windows Me help file is not tremendously detailed, try it before you spend time on the telephone, because it's quick and easy.

Call Microsoft — maybe

Microsoft offers 90 days of support for your Windows Me system, starting from when you first call a support engineer. Try it, at 425-635-7000, but only if you bought your copy of Windows Me from a store. If Windows Me came pre-installed on your computer, chances are that you have an *OEM* version — a copy of Windows that was licensed by Microsoft but sold by the company that made your computer. Microsoft would much rather have you call the company that sold you the software than have you call Microsoft directly. Our experience is that Microsoft usually answers your questions, but you never know.

If you're willing to pay, Microsoft supports you after your 90 days are up, for $35 (U.S.) per incident, at 800-936-5700. Our experience with its fee-for-support has been good. Although it hurts to pay, someone there sticks with you until your problem is solved and leaves your case active for 90 days in case the problem reappears in another form. The folks there are also knowledgeable. We rate this option as a good one if you can afford it.

Call the folks who made your computer

If Windows Me came preinstalled on your computer, Microsoft requires that the computer company support the versions of Windows it sells. This requirement can be a good thing: The company that made your computer should know exactly which components it used and which combination of hardware and software went into your computer. With that knowledge, it should be able to help you zero in on the problems you're having.

In reality, as for ISPs, the quality of the support you get varies from company to company. We've found that the major brands do a surprisingly creditable job of supporting the Windows systems they sell.

Call your friends

Like playing a lifeline on "Who Wants To Be A Millionaire," if you have friends on the Internet, you're in luck, especially if they're running Windows Me (or even Windows 98, which isn't all that different). (Of course, you don't have Regis Philbin pressuring you over a 2-minute phone call.) It's even better if they're using the same ISP as you. Check out how they have their computer set up and see whether you can relate their setup to yours. You may find just the one check box or setting that's different, and that could be just what you need. If it doesn't help, at least you have someone's shoulder to cry on.

Getting your Windows Me system on the Internet shouldn't be all that difficult, although sometimes it is. Between the information in Part I of this book and a little help from your friends, however, we're confident that you're there. Now that you're dialing in and out, you're ready to get some useful (or at least some fun) work done.

Part II
Mail and Gossip

The 5th Wave   By Rich Tennant

"I don't mean to hinder your quest for knowledge,
however it's not generally a good idea to try to
download the entire Internet."

In this part . . .

*I*t seems like every day we hear about some amazing new thing that someone has figured out how to do on the Internet. Most people, however, spend most of their time on the Internet talking to other people. E-mail is the Rodney Dangerfield "I don't get no respect" use for the Internet, although it's where most of the useful work happens. We'll tell you everything you need to know to get started with e-mail on the Internet. Then you can get fancy and join mailing lists and discussion groups and watch all your free time evaporate.

Chapter 5

All about E-Mail

● ●

In This Chapter

▶ Understanding mail addresses

▶ Sending and receiving mail with Outlook Express, Netscape Messenger, Netscape 6, and Eudora

▶ Sending and receiving mail with Eudora

▶ Following mail etiquette

● ●

*E*lectronic mail, or *e-mail,* is without a doubt the most-used Internet service, even though doesn't it get as much press as the World Wide Web. E-mail is much older than the Web, and more people use it. Every system on the Net supports some sort of mail service, which means that you can send e-mail to and receive e-mail from millions of people around the world.

Because mail, much more than any other Internet service, is connected to many non-Internet systems, you can exchange mail with lots of people who don't otherwise have access to the Internet, in addition to all the people who *are* on the Net (see Chapter 10 for help in finding people's e-mail addresses).

This chapter introduces you to all the jargon-y terms and ideas around e-mail and then walks you through the use of three popular e-mail programs: Outlook Express, Netscape Messenger, and Eudora. We even take a look at the new Netscape 6.

Addresses, Domains, and Mailboxes

Everyone with e-mail access to the Net has an *e-mail address,* which is the cyberspace equivalent of a postal address or a phone number. When you send an e-mail message, you enter the address or addresses of the recipients so that the computer knows to whom to send it.

Before you do much mailing, you have to figure out your electronic-mail address so that you can give it to people who want to get in touch with you. You also have to figure out some of their addresses so that you can write to them. (If you have no friends or plan to send only anonymous hate mail, you can skip this section.)

Internet mail addresses have two parts, separated by an @ (the *at* sign). The part before the @ is the *mailbox,* which is (roughly speaking) your personal name, and the part after that is the *domain,* usually the name of your Internet provider, such as `aol.com` or `sover.net`. In other words, addresses look like this:

```
username@domain
```

What's in a username?

The mailbox is usually your *username,* the name your provider assigns to your account. If you're lucky, you get to choose your username; in other cases, providers have standardized the naming conventions, and you get what you get. Some usernames are just first names, just last names, initials, first name and last initial, first initial and last name, or anything else, including *made-up* names. Over the years, for example, John has had the usernames `john`, `john1`, `jrl`, `jlevine`, `jlevine3` (must have been at least three `jlevines` there), and even `q0246`; Carol has been `carol`, `carolb`, `cbaroudi`, and `carol377` (the provider threw in a random number); and Margy tries to stick with `margy` but has ended up with `margy1` or `73727,2305` on occasion. A few systems assign names such as `usd31516`. Ugh.

For example, you can write to the President of the United States at `president@whitehouse.gov`. The President's mailbox is `president`, and the domain that stores his mailbox is `whitehouse.gov` — reasonable enough.

Back when many fewer e-mail users were around and most users of any particular system knew each other directly, figuring out who had which username wasn't all that difficult. These days, because that process is becoming much more of a problem, many organizations are creating consistent mailbox names for all users, most often by using the user's first and last names with a dot between them. In this type of scheme, your mailbox name may be something like `elvis.presley@bluesuede.org`, even though your username is something else. (If your name isn't Elvis Presley, adjust this example suitably. On the other hand, if your name *is* Elvis Presley, please contact us immediately. We know some people who are looking for you.)

Having several names for the same mailbox is no problem, so the new, longer, consistent usernames are invariably created in addition to — rather than instead of — the traditional short nicknames.

What's in a domain name?

The domain names for Internet providers in the United States usually ends with three letters (called a *zone* or *top-level domain*) that give you a clue to what kind of place it is:

- ✔ *Commercial* organizations end with `.com`, which includes both providers such as America Online (AOL) and CompuServe and many companies that aren't public providers but that are commercial entities, such as `amrcorp.com` (AMR Corporation, better known as American Airlines), `creamery.com` (Egg Farm Dairy in New York state, which makes really good French-style soft cheeses), and `iecc.com` (the Invincible Electronic Calculator Company).

- ✔ Educational institutions end with `.edu` (such as `yale.edu`).

- ✔ Networking organizations, like ISPs, end with `.net`.

- ✔ U.S. government sites end with `.gov`.

- ✔ U.S. military sites end with `.mil`.

- ✔ Organizations that don't fall into any of those categories, like nonprofits, end with `.org`.

Outside the United States, domains often end with a country code, such as `.fr` for France or `.zm` for Zambia. See our Web site, at `http://net.gurus.com/countries`, for a listing of country codes. Just to confuse things even more, some domains in the United States end in `.us`, preceded by a town and a two-letter state code; for example, the city of Cambridge, Massachusetts, is at `ci.cambridge.ma.us`.

New domains are being registered at a ferocious rate, many thousands per month, in .com and other domains. New zones were scheduled to be added in 1998 too, as listed in Table 5-1, in an attempt to accommodate the glut, but there was this accident at the red-tape factory and — well, you can guess. It generally appears unlikely that we will see new zones any time soon.

Table 5-1	New Domains
Zone	*Description*
.firm	Business
.store	Business offering goods to purchase
.web	Organization emphasizing activities related to the World Wide Web

(continued)

Table 5-1 *(continued)*	
Zone	**Description**
.arts	Organization emphasizing cultural and entertainment activities
.rec	Organization emphasizing recreation and entertainment activities
.info	Organization providing information services
.nom	Individual or personal names

Address tips

If you're sending a message to another user in your domain (the same machine or group of machines), you can leave out the domain part altogether when you type the address. If you and a friend both use AOL, for example, you can leave out the @aol.com part of the address when you're writing to each other.

If you don't know what your e-mail address is, a good approach is to send yourself a message and use your login name as the mailbox name. Then examine the return address on the message. Or you can send a message to Internet For Dummies Mail Central, at internetme@gurus.com, and a friendly robot will send back a message with your address. (While you're at it, tell us whether you like this book, because we authors see that mail too.) Chapter 10 has more suggestions for finding e-mail addresses.

Where Mail Lives

When e-mail messages come hurtling across the Internet, they need a place to wait until someone is ready to read them. Similarly, when you write a message, you need a mailbox — not unlike the box down at the corner in which you stick your envelopes — for mailing messages. The Internet has two kinds of mail storage containers — more officially called *mail servers.*

When your mail arrives, unless you're one of the lucky (or rich) few whose computers have a permanent Internet connection, the mail doesn't get delivered to your computer automatically. Mail gets delivered instead to an *incoming mail server* (also known as a *POP server,* for Post Office Protocol, or *POP3,* for the version of that protocol), which is sort of like your local post office. To get your mail, you have to go and get it. Actually, your *mail* program has to go and get it.

For you to be able to send mail, your mail program has to take mail to the post office — your *outgoing mail server* (or *SMTP server,* for Simple Mail Transfer Protocol). It's sort of like having a post office box rather than home delivery — you have to pick it up at the post office and also deliver your outgoing mail there.

Every Internet provider runs a POP server and an SMTP server for the use of its customers. (At small ISPs, they're probably the same server, at larger ones they're separate.) When your mail program picks up the mail, it sucks your mail from your provider's POP server to your PC at top speed. After you have downloaded your mail to your own computer, you can disconnect, which is a good idea if your provider charges by the hour. Then you can read and respond to your mail while the meter isn't running — while you're *offline.* After you're ready to send your responses or new messages, you can reconnect and transmit your outgoing mail to the SMTP server, again at top network speed.

More E-Mail Programs Than You Can Shake a Stick At

Depending on what kind of account you have, you use a different program to get your mail. They all do more or less the same thing because they're all mail programs, after all — they let you read, write, reply, forward, print, and save e-mail messages.

PPP, DSL, and cable Internet accounts

You can use any Winsock-compatible e-mail program, and countless programs exist. You have your freeware, you have your shareware, and you have your commercial stuff. The good news is that Windows Me comes with a serviceable e-mail program named Outlook Express. For variety, we also describe Eudora, a solid e-mail program that many of us like. Netscape Messenger, which comes with Netscape Communicator, is okay too. Pegasus is another excellent, free e-mail program for this type of Internet account, available from the Net. Pegasus can be somewhat difficult to configure, but, after it is, you'll find it to be a most powerful e-mail client. Because Windows Me comes with Outlook Express, we concentrate on it for the remainder of this chapter, with short explanations of Eudora and Netscape Messenger.

America Online (AOL) and CompuServe

The access software you use to connect to your account includes an easy-to-use e-mail program. Most of the general information in this chapter applies also to AOL and CompuServe.

As of early 2000, neither CompuServe nor America Online has either an incoming or outgoing mail server. This omission means that you can't use an e-mail program to send or receive mail by using an AOL or CompuServe account. Instead, you have to use the AOL or CompuServe program to read and send your mail, with one important, new exception: The new Netscape 6 lets AOL users send and receive AOL mail. Forget about using Outlook Express or Eudora as your mail program. These services may install mail servers soon, however — if you have an AOL or CompuServe account, ask someone there.

On both AOL and CompuServe, go to the keyword **mail** to read and send mail. If you have an AOL account, your e-mail address is your screen name followed by @aol.com. If your screen name were SteveCase, for example, your e-mail address would be SteveCase@aol.com.

If you have a CompuServe account, you have a CompuServe ID that looks like this: 71234,567 (your numbers will differ). To turn this number into an Internet address, change the comma to a period and add @compuserve.com to the end, like this: 71234.567@compuserve.com. You can register for a name too, if you would rather have a more memorable e-mail address. Go to the keyword **register.**

Note: Both AOL and CompuServe do, however, have *Web*-based mail. This sometimes useful technology allows you to use a web browser to access your e-mail from the Web. Although the whole thing is a series of Web pages and requires you to enter your screen name and password to access it, but it can be convenient at times, like when you're at a Web kiosk at an airport or a cybercafé.

Free e-mail accounts

At least one service, Juno Online, gives you free dial-up accounts for e-mail only. The price you pay is having advertisements appear on-screen as you read your messages. (It's free, as long as the phone call your computer makes isn't a toll call, of course.) In the United States, call 800-654-JUNO to ask for a software disk, or download Juno from the Web (from http://www.juno.com), or get it from a friend. If you use Juno, you have to use its e-mail software (otherwise, the advertisements aren't displayed). You can't use the programs we describe here.

Web-based mail

Half the Web sites in the world now seem to offer free e-mail accounts you can access through the Web. The best known are Hotmail, at `http://www.hotmail.com`, and Yahoo Mail, at `http://mail.yahoo.com`, and every single portal, such as NetCenter (`http://home.netscape.com`), CⅠNet (`http://www.cnet.com`), AltaVista (`http://www.altsvista.com`), Excite (`http://www.excite.com`), and the Go Network (`http://www.go.com`). Web-based free e-mail service can be handy if you have several family members on one Internet account or if you want a separate account to get private e-mail at work. It's also an easy way to track your personal mail at work because most of them collect POP3 mail from existing accounts.

LAN and other mail

If you're connected in some other way, you probably have a different mail program. For example, you may be using a PC in your company's Local Area Network that runs cc:Mail, Lotus Notes, or Microsoft Mail and has a mail-only link to the outside world. We don't describe Local Area Network mail programs here, but don't stop reading.

Regardless of which type of mail you're using, the basics of reading, sending, addressing, and filing mail work in pretty much the same way. It's worth looking through this chapter even if you're not using any of the mail programs we describe here.

What Your E-Mail Program Needs to Know

Write your e-mail address in Table 5-2 and on the Cheat Sheet in the front of this book (then tear out the Cheat Sheet and tape it to the wall near your computer). Capitalization never matters in domains and rarely matters in mailbox names. To make it easy on your eyes, therefore, most of the domain and mailbox names in this book are shown in lowercase.

If you're using a PPP or cable account, you have to tell your e-mail program the names of your incoming (POP) and outgoing (SMTP) mail servers. Write the names of your mail servers in Table 5-2 and on the Cheat Sheet (it's hanging near your computer, right?). If you don't know what to write, ask your Internet provider.

Table 5-2	Information Your E-Mail Program Needs to Know	
Information	*Description*	*Example*
Your e-mail address	Your username followed by an @ and the domain name.	internetmeinternetme@ gurus.com
Your e-mail password	The password for your e-mail mailbox (usually the same as the password for your account). Don't write it here! It's a secret!	9tcf598
Your incoming (POP3) mail server	The name of the computer that receives your e-mail messages (get this name from your Internet provider).	mail.gurus.com
Your outgoing (SMTP) mail server	The name of the computer that distributes your outgoing mail to the rest of the Internet (often the same as the POP3 server).	mail.gurus.com

Sending and Receiving Mail with Outlook Express

Because Outlook Express comes for free with Windows Me, it's a good place to start.

Running Outlook Express the first time

The first time you run Outlook Express, it asks questions about who you are and how you want to collect your mail. Follow these steps:

1. **Start Outlook Express. You don't have to connect to your Internet provider (yet), although it's okay if you're already connected.**

   Click the Outlook Express icon, or choose it from the Start⇨Programs⇨ Internet Explorer menu. A wizard asks you where to store your

Is e-mail really private?

Relatively, but not totally. Any recipient of your mail may forward it to other people. Some mail addresses are really mailing lists that redistribute messages to many other people. In one famous case, a mistaken mail address sent a message to tens of thousands of readers. It began, "Darling, at last we have a way to send messages that is completely private."

If you send mail from work or to someone at work, your mail is not private. You and your friend may work for companies of the highest integrity whose employees would never dream of reading private e-mail. When push comes to shove, however, and someone is accusing your company of leaking confidential information and the corporate lawyer says, "Examine the e-mail," someone reads all the e-mail. (This situation happened to a friend of ours who was none too pleased to find that all his intimate correspondence with his fiancée had been read.) Some lawyers even claim that companies have a duty to read their employees' e-mail! E-mail you send and receive is stored on your disk, and most companies back up their disks regularly. Reading your e-mail is very easy for someone who really wants to, unless you encrypt it.

The usual rule of thumb is not to send anything you wouldn't want to see posted next to the water cooler or perhaps scribbled next to a pay phone. The latest e-mail systems are beginning

to include encryption features that make the privacy situation somewhat better so that anyone who doesn't know the keyword used to scramble a message can't decode it.

The most common tools for encrypted mail are known as PEM (privacy-enhanced mail) and PGP (pretty good privacy). PGP is one of the most widely used encryption programs, both in the United States and abroad. Many experts think that it's so strong that even the U.S. National Security Agency can't crack it. We don't know about that; if the NSA wants to read your mail, however, you have more complicated problems than we can help you solve.

PEM capability is included in versions of Outlook Express distributed in the United States and Canada. PEM is not as widely used as PGP, and PEM requires that you acquire something called a Digital ID from a third company.

PGP is available for free on the Net. You can buy a commercial version that has a couple more features, but the free version is very complete. The latest versions of PGP plug in to popular e-mail programs, including Outlook Express and Eudora, for easy, seamless operation. To find more information about privacy and security issues, including how to get started with PGP, point your web browser to http://net. gurus.com/pgp.

messages. It suggests the C:\Windows\Application Data\Microsoft\ Outlook Express folder.

2. **Click OK.**

The Outlook Express window appears, as shown in Figure 5-1, featuring a list of folders to the left, the contents of the current folder to the upper right, and the text of the current message to the lower right. (When you start the program, no folder or message is selected, so you don't see much.)

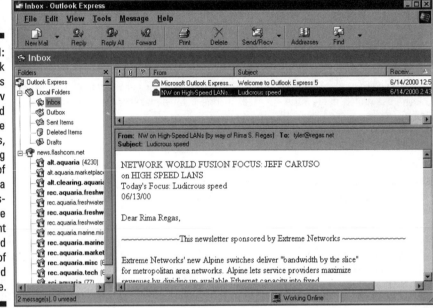

3. **Click the Inbox folder.**

   The first time you open this folder, Outlook Express may run the Internet Connection Wizard to ask you some questions about your e-mail account. If it doesn't, you can assume that it knows everything it needs to know and skip to the next section, about sending mail with Outlook Express.

4. **Type your name in the Display name box and click the Next button.**

   Type your actual name, as you want it to appear in the headers of e-mail messages you send. Don't type your e-mail address (yet).

5. **Type your e-mail address in the E-mail address box and click Next.**

   If you're an obedient reader and filled out Table 5-2 in the preceding section, you will find your e-mail address in that table and on the Cheat Sheet in the front of this book. If you're not sure of your e-mail address, ask your Internet or online service provider. Next, the Internet Connection Wizard asks about e-mail server names, as shown in Figure 5-2.

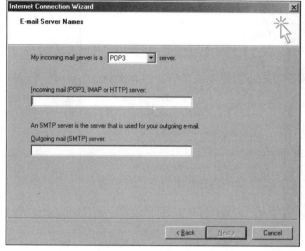

Figure 5-2:
What mail
servers do
you use for
sending and
receiving
messages?

6. **In the Incoming mail (POP3 or IMAP) server box, type the name of your POP server. In the Outgoing mail (SMTP) server box, type the name of your SMTP server. Then click Next.**

   Table 5-2 should have the names of these mail servers. The wizard asks how to log on to the account where you get your mail.

7. **In the POP account name box, type your username (the part of your e-mail address that comes before the @). In the Password box, type your account's password. Click Next again.**

   The Wizard asks for a friendly name for this account — the name *you* want to use for it in Outlook Express.

8. **In the Internet mail account name box, type the name you want to use for this account. Click Next.**

   Finally, the wizard wants to be capable of connecting to the Internet automatically when you want to get or send mail, as shown in Figure 5-3.

Figure 5-3:
How do you
connect
to the
Internet?

9. **Click the option for how you connect to the Internet, and then click Next.**

   If you dial your account by using your modem, click the option labeled Connect using my phone line. If you connect over a Local Area Network, click the option labeled Connect using my local area network (LAN). If you would rather that Outlook Express not try to connect you to the Internet and would rather do it yourself, click the option labeled I will establish my Internet connection manually.

   If you told the wizard (in Step 9) that you'll dial into the Internet (in Step 9), the wizard now wants to know which Dial-Up Networking connection to use. The window shows a list of the existing connections.

10. **If you don't yet have a Dial-Up Networking connection set up in Windows Me, click Create a new dial-up connection and flip to Chapter 3 to find out how to proceed. Otherwise, click Use an existing dial-up connection, and choose the connection from the list. Then click Next.**

    The wizard congratulates you on a job well done!

11. **Click Finish.**

    You see the Inbox window again. Now Outlook Express knows how to get some incoming mail to put in the Inbox and what to do with mail you create and put in your Outbox.

Outlook Express can send and receive mail from more than one Internet account; choose Tools⇨Accounts to tell it about other accounts.

Sending mail with Outlook Express

After Outlook Express knows all about your Internet account, here's how to send mail:

1. **Start Outlook Express by clicking the Outlook Express icon or choosing it from the Start⇨Programs⇨Internet Explorer menu.**

   You see the Outlook Express window, as shown in Figure 5-1.

2. **Click the Inbox folder.**

   Actually, you can click any of the folders on the list.

3. **Click the New Mail button (the leftmost button on the toolbar), press Ctrl+N, or choose Compose⇨New Message from the menu bar.**

   You see a New Message window, with boxes to fill in to address the message, as shown in Figure 5-4.

Figure 5-4:
Writing a
message
with Outlook
Express.

4. **In the To box, type the address to which to send the message, and then press Tab.**

   Don't press Enter unless you want to add another line to the To box so that you can type an additional address to which to send the message. If you click the little Rolodex-style card icon at the left end of the To box, you see the Select Recipients window; it's part of the Outlook Express address book, briefly described in the next chapter.

For your first e-mail message, you may want to write to us (because we will send you back a message confirming what your e-mail address is) or to yourself (if you know what your e-mail address is).

5. **If you want to send a copy of the message to someone, type that person's address in the Cc box. Another tab takes you to the Bcc box. Then press Tab again or click in the Subject line.**

Bccs, or *blind carbon copies,* are copies sent to people without putting their names on the message so that the other recipients can't tell.

6. **In the Subject box, type a succinct summary of the message. Then press Tab again.**

The cursor should be blinking in the message area, the large, empty box where the actual message goes.

7. **In the large, empty box, type the text of the message.**

When you have typed your message, you can press F7 to check its spelling or choose Tools⇨Spelling from the menu.

8. **To send the message, click the Send button (the leftmost button on the toolbar), press Alt+S (not Ctrl+S, for some strange reason), or choose File⇨Send Message from the menu.**

Outlook Express sticks the message in your Outbox folder, waiting to be sent. If you're connected to your Internet provider, Outlook Express sends the message, and you can skip Steps 9 and 10.

9. **Connect to your Internet provider if you're not already connected.**

To send the message, you have to climb on the Net.

10. **Click the Send and Receive button on the toolbar or choose Tools⇨Send and Receive from the menu.**

Your message is on its way.

After you have sent a piece of e-mail, you have no way to cancel it!

Reading mail with Outlook Express

If you begin sending e-mail (and in most cases even if you don't), you begin receiving it. The arrival of e-mail is always exciting, even when you get 200 messages a day. Here's how to get your mail:

1. **Run Outlook Express and connect to your Internet Service Provider.**

2. **Click the Send and Receive button on the toolbar or choose Tools⇨Send and Receive from the menu.**

Outlook Express downloads your incoming mail on your computer and stashes the messages in your Inbox folder. See the list of folders on the left side of the Outlook Express window? You can choose which folder full of mail to look at.

3. **Click the Inbox folder if it's not already selected.**

   The box in the upper-right part of the window lists one line for each message in your Inbox, showing the senders and subjects of each message. The box in the bottom lower-right part of the window shows the text of the message you select.

4. **Click a message on the list of messages to see the text of the message at the bottom of the Outlook Express window. Or double-click the message header to see the message in a new, big window.**

   If you see a message in its own window, click the Close button, choose File⇨Close from the menu, or press Alt+F4 to get rid of the window.

You can delete, reply to, forward, or print a message after you have seen it. (Chapter 6 tells how to do these tasks.)

If you're happy using Outlook Express, skip the section about Eudora (another e-mail program) a few paragraphs from here, and read about e-mail etiquette. If you don't find Outlook Express to your liking, read on.

Why your parents had dirty hands

The term *carbon copy* should be familiar to those of you who were born before 1960 and remember the ancient practice of putting sheets of carbon-coated paper between sheets of regular paper to make extra copies when using a typewriter. (Please don't ask us what a typewriter is.) In e-mail, a carbon copy — some people now call it a *courtesy copy* — is simply a copy of the message you send. All recipients, on both the To and Cc lines, see who's getting this message. A *blind carbon copy* (Bcc) is a copy sent to a person without putting the person's name on the message so that the other recipients can't tell.

Bccs are best avoided in most cases. The classic situation is when you mail a complaint to your boss with a Bcc to the boss's boss. The big boss, who has her secretary print all her e-mail, sends a copy to your boss and you're in hot water (assuming that your boss has a clue about Bccs). Bccs *are* handy for mailing lists, to keep everyone from getting a long list of all the recipients.

Sending and Receiving Mail with Netscape Messenger

Netscape Navigator is the second most popular Web- browsing program (you read about it in Chapter 8). The Netscape folks added a pretty good mail program named Netscape Messenger. This section describes the version of Netscape Messenger that comes with the Netscape Communicator 4.72 package. We don't think that Netscape Messenger is as good as Outlook Express or Eudora, although if you use Netscape Navigator as your web browser, you may prefer to use Netscape Messenger.

To run Netscape Messenger, click the Netscape icon on your desktop or choose Start⟹Programs⟹Netscape Communicator⟹Netscape Messenger menu. If you're already running Netscape Navigator, choose the Communicator⟹ Messenger Mail box command or click the Mailbox icon (the little picture of an inbox in the lower-right corner of the Netscape Navigator window). Either way, you see the Netscape Folder window, as shown in Figure 5-5.

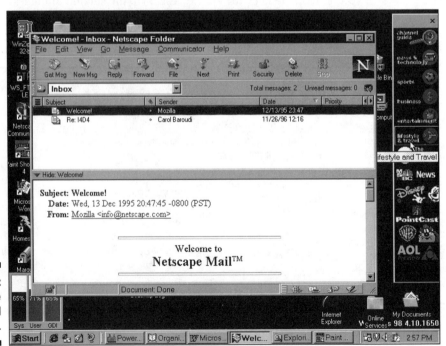

Figure 5-5: Netscape does mail too.

To tell Netscape Messenger who you are and how to get your mail, choose the Edit⇨Preferences command to display the Preferences dialog box. Click the Identity category in the Categories list to tell Netscape your name and e-mail address. Click the Mail Server category to type your POP mail server and SMTP mail server names. Click OK when you're done.

The top part of the Netscape Folder window shows a list of the messages in the folder you're looking at (you start looking at the Inbox window). The bottom part of the window shows the text of the selected message.

To get your mail, click the Get Msg icon on the toolbar. Netscape may ask you for your password.

To read your mail, make sure that the selected folder is the Inbox folder — the folder name appears in a box just below the left end of the toolbar. If it doesn't say Inbox, click the downward-pointing triangle button at the end of the box to choose the Inbox folder. Then click a message on the list of messages — the text appears in the bottom half of the window.

When you want to send a message, click the New Msg icon on the toolbar. In the Composition window that appears, fill in the To and Subject boxes, and then type the text of the message in the large box. Click the Send button when you're done.

Sending and Receiving Mail with Netscape 6

Netscape 6 is the newest Web-browsing program (you can also read about it in Chapter 8). Just like the preceding Netscape offering, Netscape version 6 includes a mail client, ingeniously named Mail. Other than its looks, one big new feature, and a few smaller additions, the program is pretty much the same. Despite the fact that it's nearly identical in operation, it has enough changes to warrant a separate section, and here it is.

To run Netscape Mail, click the Netscape icon on your desktop or choose Start⇨Programs⇨Netscape 6⇨Netscape 6 menu. If you're already running Netscape, choose the Tasks⇨ Mail command or click the Mailbox icon (the little picture of a letter in the lower-left corner of the main Netscape main window). No matter how you get there, you see the Mail window, as shown in Figure 5-6.

Figure 5-6:
The
Netscape 6
mail client.

To tell Mail who you are and how to get your mail, choose the Edit⇨ Mail/News Account Settings command (immediately above the Preferences item) command to display the Account Settings dialog box. Click the New Account button on the left side (look down), and click OK when you've finished with the wizard.

My Sidebar is quite a versatile tool. When you're in the Mail window, it shows a list of all your e-mail accounts, their associated folders, and all the Usenet servers you follow along with. The list of items that takes up most of the right side is your message list. The large, empty space below that is where selected messages appear for review.

To get your mail, click the Get Msg icon on the toolbar. Netscape will very likely ask you for your password.

To read your mail, make sure that the Inbox folder selected folder is the selected folder Inbox folder — the folder name appears in a box just below the left end of the toolbar. If it doesn't say Inbox, click the downward-pointing triangle button at the end of the box to choose the Inbox folder. Then click a message on the list of messages — the text appears in the bottom half of the window.

BTW, what does IMHO mean? RTFM!

E-mail users are often lazy typists, and many abbreviations are common. Here are some of the most widely used:

Abbreviation	*What It Means*
BTW	By the way
IANAL	I am not a lawyer, (but. . . .)
IMHO	In my humble opinion
ROFL	Rolling on floor laughing
RSN	Real soon now (vaporware)
RTFM	Read the _____ manual — you could have and should have looked it up yourself
TIA	Thanks in advance
TLA	Three-letter acronym
YMMV	Your mileage may vary

When you want to send a message, click the New Msg icon on the toolbar. In the Composition window that appears, fill in the To and Subject boxes, and then type the text of the message in the large box. Click the Send button when you're done.

Sending and Receiving Mail with Eudora

Eudora, the e-mail application formerly known as both Eudora Light and Eudora Pro, has become a single entity. That's right — to make the most popular e-mail-management application even more confusing, it now has three versions. Not confusing enough for you? Okay, all three of those versions are represented in *one application*. Now it's just called Eudora 4.3.x, and the application can be set to function in Light, Ad Supported, or Paid mode. The concept is simple. In Light mode, Eudora functions as a powerful but simple e-mail-management program that doesn't have all the features of Ad Supported and Paid modes. Ad Supported mode has all the features of Paid mode, although you have to allow your brain to be saturated with mind-numbing "adlets" that appear in the lower-left corner of the application

What's the big deal?

What's that big new feature we just mentioned in the section about sending and receiving mail with Netscape 6? AOL. America Online. Yes, you can now retrieve and respond to your AOL e-mail through Netscape 6. The only other product to ever to do that was Claris Em@iler, which is now defunct and was only on the Mac anyway. That fact alone makes it quite the

feature, considering that the AOL online service has only 45 million subscribers.

Using AOL mail is exactly the same as using Internet e-mail. All you have to do is enter the screen name for which you want to retrieve mail and enter your password. It's that simple. You can do this with all seven of your available screen names.

window. Paid mode gets rid of the ads. Qualcomm, which owns Eudora, charges $49.95 for a Paid mode license. We all agree that Eudora is a tremendous value if e-mail represents more than 20 percent or more of your morning routine or if you continually find yourself at odds with the process of managing multiple e-mail accounts.

Getting Eudora

You can buy Eudora Pro in any software store. You can also download Eudora from the Eudora Web site, at `http://www.eudora.com`. Chapter 13 tells how to download and install programs.

Setting up Eudora

The first time you run Eudora (either the Light or Pro version), you have to tell it all about yourself, your e-mail address, and your Internet account:

1. **Start Eudora.**

   Click the Eudora icon on the desktop or on the Start⇨Programs menu. You should see an introductory "splash" window that goes away after a few seconds and then an Options window. If you don't see the Options window, choose the Tools⇨Options command from the menu.

   The Options window contains all the settings that control Eudora. The left side of the window has a scroll bar with icons for the various groups of settings.

2. **Click the Getting Started icon on the left side of the Options window.**

   This step lets you enter the minimum info needed to get going.

3. **Fill in the Real name, Return address, Mail Server, and Login Name boxes with your actual name, your e-mail address, the name of your provider's mail computer, and your login name (probably the same as the part of your address before the @), respectively.**

4. **Click the Sending Mail icon.**

   You see boxes for various mail options. The Return address box already contains your e-mail address.

5. **In the SMTP server box, type the name of your SMTP mail server (refer to Table 5-2).**

   You can leave the other boxes blank.

6. **If you want Eudora to automatically connect to the Internet when you tell it to send or receive mail, scroll way down the list of icons until you find the Advanced Network icon, and click it.**

   You see a bunch of scary-looking time-out settings, which we recommend that you leave alone.

7. **Click the Automatically dial & hang up this connection check box. Choose a Dial-Up Networking connection from the Entry box, and type your username in the Username box. If you want Eudora to remember your password so that you don't have to type it each time you log in, click the Save password box too.**

   You're done — that's all that Eudora really needs to know about you.

8. **Click OK.**

   The Options box goes away.

Sending mail with Eudora

Here's how to run Eudora and send some mail:

1. **Start Eudora if it's not already running.**

   Click the Eudora icon on the desktop or on the Start⇨Programs menu. You see a window like the one shown in Figure 5-7. Exactly what's in the window varies depending on what you were looking at the last time you ran Eudora.

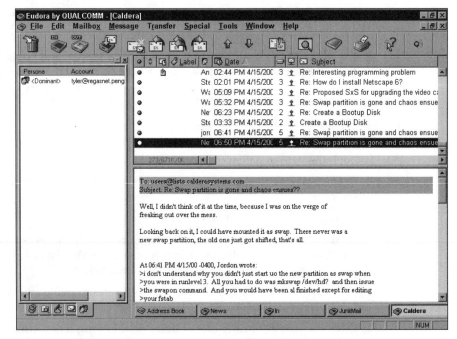

Figure 5-7:
The Eudora main window (the Eudora 4.30 paid version, in this case). Your mileage may vary!

2. **To send a message, click the New Message button (the button with the sparkly paper and pencil) on the toolbar. Or choose Message⇨New Message from the menu. (If you can remember shortcut keys, you can also press Ctrl+N).**

   Eudora pops up a new message window, with spaces in which you type the address, subject, and text of a message.

3. **On the To line, type the recipient's address** (internetme@gurus.com, **for example).**

   For your first e-mail message, you may want to write to us (because we will send you back a message confirming what your e-mail address is) or to yourself (if you know what your e-mail address is).

4. **Press Tab to skip past the From line (which is already filled in) to the Subject line and then type a subject.**

   Make the subject line short and specific.

5. **Press Tab a few more times to skip the Cc and Bcc lines (or type the addresses of people who should get carbon copies and blind carbon copies of your message).**

   Blind carbon copies are copies sent to people without Eudora putting their names on the message so that the other recipients can't tell.

6. **Press Tab to move to the large blank area, and then type your message.**

7. **To send the message, click the Send or Queue button in the upper-right corner of the message window (what the button says depends on how Eudora is set up).**

   If the button is marked Send, as soon as you click it, Eudora tries to send the message and displays a little status window that contains incomprehensible status messages. If, on the other hand, the button is marked Queue, your message is stashed in your outbox, to be sent later.

   One reason to have a Queue button is that you have a dial-up Internet connection so that your computer isn't connected to the Net all the time. Rather than dial and hang up for each message you compose, you can wait until you have queued a few messages and then send them all at one time.

8. **If your computer isn't already connected, dial up and connect to your provider.**

   If you configured Eudora in the preceding section to connect to the Internet automatically, you may be able to skip this step. Eudora tries to connect automatically when you send messages (see Step 9).

9. **Switch back to Eudora, and choose File⇨Send Queued Messages (Ctrl+T for the lazy) from the menu to transmit all the messages you have queued up.**

Even if you leave your computer connected while you write your mail messages, it's not a bad idea to set Eudora to queue the mail and not send it until you tell it to. (Choose Tools⇨Options from the Eudora menu, click the Sending Mail icon, and be sure that the Immediate Send option isn't checked.) That way, you get a few minutes after you write each message to ponder whether you really want to send it. Even though we have been using e-mail for almost 20 years, we still throw away many of the messages we have written before we send them.

After you have sent a piece of e-mail, you have no way to cancel it!

Reading mail with Eudora

One seriously cool feature of Eudora is that you can do much of what you do with mail while you're not connected to your account. On the other hand, when you really do want to check your mail, you have to be connected. Eudora can figure out that you're not connected and dial in for you (which, in our experience, doesn't always work).

If you don't have a full-time Net connection, follow these steps to get your mail:

1. **Make your Net connection, if you're not already connected.**

   If you configured Eudora in the preceding section to connect to the Internet automatically, you may be able to skip this step. Eudora tries to connect automatically when you retrieve messages (see Step 3).

2. **Start up Eudora, if she's not already running.**

3. **If Eudora doesn't retrieve mail automatically, click the Check Mail button on the toolbar (the button with the envelope and in-basket) or choose File⇨Check Mail (or press Ctrl+M) to retrieve your mail.**

   If you have a full-time Net connection, Eudora probably is set up to retrieve your mail automatically, in which case you only have to start Eudora and she gets your mail. (If you leave Eudora running, even hidden at the bottom of your screen as an icon, she automatically checks for new mail every once in a while.)

   If you have a sound card, you hear a little song (that reminds us of Mexican jumping beans) to announce new mail. If you don't have any mail, you don't get any sound effects, although you do see a nice picture of a letter with a big, red X through it. The mail appears in your inbox, in a window that Eudora labels In, listing a one-line header for each message.

4. **To see a message, double-click the line or click the line and press Enter.**

   To stop looking at a message, click the Close button for the window or press Ctrl+W or Ctrl+F4.

You can do much more to messages, which we discuss in Chapter 6.

The postmaster is in

Every Internet host that can send or receive mail has a special mail address called `postmaster` that is guaranteed to get a message to the person responsible for that host. If you send mail to someone and get back strange failure messages, you can try sending a message to the postmaster. If `king@bluesuede.org` returns an error from `bluesuede.org`, for example, you may try sending a polite question to `postmaster@bluesuede.org`. Because the postmaster is usually an overworked volunteer system administrator, it is considered poor form to ask a postmaster for favors much greater than "Does so-and-so have a mailbox on this system?"

Where Are the Etiquette Ladies?

Sadly, the Great Ladies of Etiquette, such as Emily Post and Amy Vanderbilt, died before the invention of e-mail. Here's what they may have suggested about what to say and, more important, what *not* to say in electronic mail.

E-mail is a funny hybrid, something between a phone call (or voice mail) and a letter. On one hand, it's quick and usually informal; on the other hand, because e-mail is written rather than spoken, you don't see a person's facial expressions or hear her tone of voice.

A few words of advice:

- ✔ When you send a message, watch your tone of voice.
- ✔ Don't use all capital letters — it looks like you're SHOUTING.
- ✔ If someone sends you an incredibly obnoxious and offensive message, as likely as not it's a mistake or a joke gone awry. In particular, be on the lookout for failed sarcasm.

Flame off!

Pointless and excessive outrage in electronic mail is so common that it has a name of its own: *flaming.* Don't flame. It makes you look like a jerk.

When you get a message so offensive that you just *have* to reply, stick it back in your electronic inbox for a while and wait until after lunch. Then, don't flame back. The sender probably didn't realize how the message would look. In about 20 years of using electronic mail, we can testify that we have never, ever, regretted *not* sending an angry message (although we *have* regretted sending a few — ouch).

When you're sending mail, keep in mind that someone reading it will have no idea of what you *intended* to say — just what you *did* say. Subtle sarcasm and irony are almost impossible to use in e-mail and usually come across as annoying or dumb instead. (If you're an extremely superb writer, you can disregard this advice — don't say that we didn't warn you.)

Another possibility to keep in the back of your mind is that it is technically not difficult to forge e-mail return addresses. If you get a totally off-the-wall message from someone that seems out of character for that person, somebody else may have forged it as a prank. (No, we don't tell you how to forge e-mail. How dumb do you think we are?)

Laugh and the world laughs with you

Sometimes it helps to put in a : -) (called a *smiley*), which means, "This is a joke." (Try leaning way over to the left if you don't see why it's a smile.) In some communities, notably CompuServe, <g> or <grin> serves the same purpose. Here's a typical example:

```
People who don't believe that we are all part of a warm,
        caring community who love and support each other
        are no better than rabid dogs and should be hunted
        down and shot. :-)
```

Although smileys sometimes help, if a joke needs a smiley, maybe it wasn't worth making. It may sound as though all your e-mail is supposed to be humorless. It's not that bad; until you have the hang of it, though, limit the humor. You'll be glad that you did.

What's Next?

Now that you know how to use e-mail, you will want to send some messages. See Chapter 10 to find out how to find the e-mail address of someone you know. In Chapter 6, we explain more features of e-mail. Chapter 7 tells you how to find other people to write to and how to get interesting information by e-mail.

Chapter 6

Advanced E-Mail Stuff

● ●

In This Chapter

▶ Replying to mail

▶ Using the address book

▶ Forwarding and filing mail

▶ Deleting mail

▶ Responding to mail

▶ Spotting and avoiding chain letters

▶ Sending and receiving exotic mail and mail attachments

▶ Exchanging mail with robots and fax machines

▶ Dealing with spam

▶ Using e-mail effectively

● ●

*O*kay, now you know how to send and receive mail. It's time for some tips and tricks to make you into a real mail aficionado. We tell you about Outlook Express, Netscape Messenger, and Eudora (refer to Chapter 5 for descriptions of these programs).

After you have seen an e-mail message, you can do a bunch of different things with it (much the same as with paper mail). Here are your usual choices:

✔ Throw it away.

✔ Reply to it.

✔ Forward it to other people.

✔ File it.

Unlike with paper mail, you can do any or all of these things to each message much more easily and, in most cases, automatically. Otherwise, if you don't tell your mail program what to do to a message, the message either stays in your mailbox for later perusal or gets moved to a read-messages folder, depending on which e-mail client you use.

If your mail program automatically saves messages in a read-messages, Sent, or Outbox folder, be sure to go through the folder every week or so, or else it becomes enormous and unmanageable.

Here's What We Think: Replying to Mail

You should know a few things about replying to mail. It's easy enough to do:

- ✔ In Outlook Express, click the Reply to Author button on the toolbar or choose Compose➪Reply to Author.

- ✔ In Netscape Messenger, click the Reply button on the toolbar, and then choose Reply to Send from the menu that appears. Or, choose Message➪Reply.

- ✔ In Eudora, click the Reply button on the toolbar (a left-pointing blue arrow arching over a letter) or choose Message➪Reply.

- ✔ In all three programs in this list, you can reply to a message by pressing Ctrl+R on the keyboard.

Is this the party to whom I am replying?

When you reply to a message, most mail programs address the message automagically, using the From address of the message you're replying to. They usually also fill in the Subject field with the letters _Re:_ (short for _regarding_) and the Subject field of the message to which you're replying.

Be sure to check to whom the reply is addressed. Look carefully at the To: line your mail program has filled out for you. Is that whom you thought you were addressing? If the reply is addressed to a mailing list, did you really intend to reply to the whole list, or is your message of a more personal nature and may be better addressed to the individual who sent the message? Did you mean to reply to a group? Are all the addresses you think you're replying to included on the To: list? If the To: list isn't correct, you can move the cursor to it and edit it as necessary.

Here's what you just said

Do you want to include the contents of the message to which you're replying? Most e-mail programs add the content of the message to which you're reply-ing to your reply message. If your mail program does this, be sure to edit the text to just the relevant material. If you don't give some context to people who get a great deal of e-mail, your reply makes no sense. If you're answering a question, include the question in the response. You don't have to include the entire text, although you should give your reader a break. She may have read 50 messages since she sent you mail and may not have a clue what you're talking about unless you remind her. On the other hand, it's annoying to receive a copy of the 70-line message you just sent someone, with a 1-line reply saying "I agree!" at the end.

Keeping Track of All Your New Friends

After you begin using e-mail, you quickly find that you have enough regular correspondents that it's a pain to keep track of their e-mail addresses. Fortunately, every popular e-mail program provides an *address book* in which you can save your friends' addresses so that you can send mail to `Mom`, for example, and have it automatically addressed to `chairman@exec.hq.giantcorp.com`. You can also create address lists so that you can send mail to `family`, for example, and it goes to Mom, Dad, your brother, both sisters, and your dog, all of whom have e-mail addresses.

All address books let you do the same things: save in your address book the address from a message you have just read, use addresses you have saved, and edit your address book.

The Outlook Express address book

The process of copying a correspondent's address into the address book is easy: Right-click on a message from the correspondent you want to add and choose Add Sender to Address Book (see Figure 6-1). Fill in as many of the available information fields for that individual as you need (you see lots of fields, such as name, address, phone, and work).

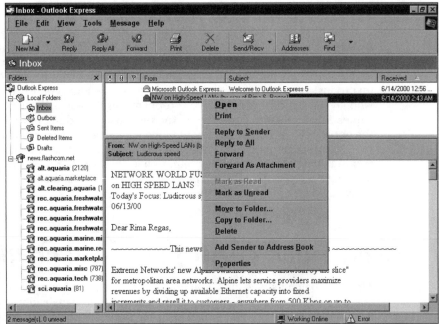

Figure 6-1:
Outlook
Express can
add the
e-mail
addresses
you want
right from
your Inbox.

To display and edit the address book, click the Address Book icon on the
Outlook Express toolbar. After you manage to get some entries into your
address book, you use them while you're creating a new message by clicking
on the To: or Cc: line the little icon that looks like a Rolodex card. In the
Select Recipients window that appears, double-click the address book entry
or entries you want to use, and then click OK. If you don't know someone's
e-mail address, use the Find button to display the Find People window; you
can search in your own address book or in various Internet directories, such
as Yahoo, Bigfoot, and WhoWhere.

The Netscape address book

You can see the Netscape Communicator 4.72 address book by choosing
Communicator➪Address Book and the one from Netscape 6 by choosing
Tasks➪Address Book (see Figure 6-2) from their respective menus. Click the
New Card icon on the toolbar to make a new entry ("card") in your address
book. If you've just gotten a message from someone whose address you want
to remember, select the message and choose the Message➪Add to Address
Book➪Sender command.

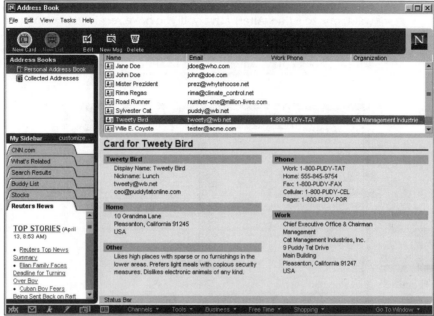

Figure 6-2:
Netscape 6
Mail has a
capable
address
book.

When you're composing a message, click the Address icon on the toolbar. Netscape lets you choose entries from the address book to use in your message.

The Eudora address book

Eudora has a good address book. If you're reading a message, choose Special⇨Make Address Book Entry (or press Ctrl+K). Eudora suggests using the person's real name as the nickname, which usually works fine. Then click OK.

To use the address book while you're composing a message, you can open the address book by choosing Tools⇨Address Book (Ctrl+L), click the nickname to use, and then click the To:, Cc:, or Bcc: button in the Address Book window (shown in Figure 6-3) to add the selected address to the message. Or use this shortcut: Type the first few letters of the nickname on the To: or Cc: line, enough to distinguish the nickname you want from other nicknames, and press Ctrl+, (the Ctrl key plus a comma). Eudora finishes the nickname for you. To make a mailing list, open the address book by choosing Tools⇨Address Book (Ctrl+L), click New to create a new nickname, and then click in the Address(es) subwindow in the address book and type the addresses you want, one to a line. Alternatively, if you have received mail in your inbox from all the people you want to put on your list, you can Ctrl+click to highlight all those messages on the inbox list and then press Ctrl+K to make a new address book entry, which is a list of all the authors of the selected messages.

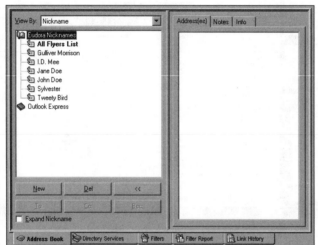

Figure 6-3:
Storing
addresses
with Eudora.

This One's for You: Forwarding Mail

You can forward e-mail along to someone else. It's easy. It's cheap. Forwarding is one of the best things about electronic mail and at the same time one of the worst. It's good because you can easily pass along messages to people who need to know about them. It's bad because you (not you personally, but, um, people around you — that's it) can just as easily send out floods of messages to recipients who would just as soon not hear *another* press release from the local Ministry of Truth. You have to think a little about whether you will enhance someone's quality of life by forwarding a message to him.

What's usually called *forwarding* a message involves wrapping the message in a new message of your own, sort of like sticking sticky notes all over a copy of it and mailing the copy and sticky notes to someone else.

TIP

Fast forward

Whenever you're forwarding mail, it's generally a good idea to get rid of uninteresting parts. All the glop in the message header is frequently included automatically in the forwarded message, and almost none of it is comprehensible, much less interesting, so get rid of it.

The tricky part is editing the text. If the message is short, a screenful or so, you probably should leave it alone:

    >Is there a lot of demand for
        fruit pizza?

    In answer to your question, I
        checked with our research
        department and found that
        the favorite pizza toppings
        in the 18-34 age group are
        pepperoni, sausage, ham,
        pineapple, olives, peppers,
        mushrooms, hamburger, and
        broccoli. I specifically
        asked about prunes, and
        they found no statistically
        significant response about
        them.

If the message is really long and only part of it is relevant, you should, as a courtesy to the reader, cut it down to the interesting part. We can tell you from experience that people pay much more attention to a concise, one-line e-mail message than they do to 12 pages of quoted stuff followed by a two-line question. Of course, all this depends on whom you're sending it to.

Sometimes it makes sense to edit material even more, particularly to emphasize one specific part. When you do so, of course, be sure not to edit to the point where you put words in the original author's mouth or garble the sense of the message, as in the following reply:

    >In answer to your question, I
        checked with

    >our research department and
        found that the

    >favorite pizza toppings ...
        and they

    >found no statistically
        significant

    >response about them.

That's an excellent way to make new enemies, especially those who like pizza. Sometimes, it makes sense to paraphrase a little — in that case, put the paraphrased part in square brackets, like this:

    >[When asked about prunes on
        pizza, research]

    >found no statistically
        significant response

    >about them.

People disagree about whether paraphrasing to shorten quotes is a good idea. On one hand, if you do it well, it saves everyone time. On the other hand, if you do it badly and someone takes offense, you're in for a week of accusations and apologies that will wipe out whatever time you may have saved. The decision is up to you.

Forwarding mail is almost as easy as replying to it:

- ✔ In Outlook Express, click the Forward message button on the toolbar or press Ctrl+F or choose Compose⇨Forward.

- ✔ In Netscape Messenger, click the Forward button on the toolbar or press Ctrl+L (since when does *L* stand for *forward?*) or choose Message⇨Forward.

- ✔ In Eudora, choose Message⇨Forward or click the icon of a blue (green or red in older versions) arrow pointing to the right. The mail program composes a message containing the text of the message you want to forward; all you have to do is address the message, optionally add a few snappy comments, and send it.

When you create a forwarded message, Eudora, Netscape Messenger, and Outlook Express provide the forwarded text in the message part of the window. Each line is commonly preceded by the greater-than sign (>). You then get to edit the message and add your own comments. See the nearby "Fast forward" sidebar for tips about pruning forwarded mail.

Sometimes, the mail you get may really have been intended for someone else. You probably will want to pass it along as is, without sticking the greater-than character at the beginning of every line, and you should leave the sender and reply-to information intact so that if the new recipient of the mail wants to respond, the response goes to the originator of the mail, not to you just because you passed it on. Some mail programs call this feature *remailing* or *bouncing,* the electronic version of scribbling another address on the outside of an envelope and dropping it back in the mailbox.

Eudora calls this process *redirecting;* you can redirect mail by choosing Message⇨Redirect from the menu or clicking the blue bouncing arrow (red-arrow-pointing-to-the-sky in older versions) icon. Eudora sticks in a polite by-way-of notice to let the new reader know how the message found her. Because neither Outlook Express nor Netscape Messenger has redirection, you have to forward messages instead.

For All You Pack Rats: Saving Mail

Saving all your e-mail for later reference is similar to filing away every piece of paper mail you get. (Who knows, the very first letter from Ed McMahon announcing that you may already be a winner could be a valuable collectible by now.) Some of your e-mail is worth saving, just as some of your paper mail is worth saving. (Lots of it *isn't,* of course, and we cover that subject next.)

You can save e-mail in a few different ways:

- ✔ Save it in a folder full of messages.
- ✔ Save it in a regular file.
- ✔ Print it and put it in a file cabinet with paper mail.

The easiest method usually is to stick messages in a folder (a folder is usually no more than a file full of messages with a separator between each message).

People use two general approaches in filing mail: by sender and by topic. Whether you use one or the other or both is mostly a matter of taste.

For filing by topic, it's entirely up to you to come up with folder names. The most difficult part is coming up with memorable names. If you're not careful, you end up with four folders with slightly different names, each with a quarter of the messages about a particular topic. Try to come up with names that are obvious, and don't abbreviate. If the topic is accounting, for example, call the folder accounting because if you abbreviate, you will never remember whether it's named acctng, acct, or acntng.

Filing with Outlook Express

To save a message in Outlook Express, you stick it in a folder. You start out with folders named Inbox, Outbox, Sent Items, Deleted Items, and Drafts. To make a new folder, choose File➪Folder➪New Folder from the menu and give the folder a name. You also have to tell Outlook Express which folder should *contain* the folder you're creating — usually you create your folders in the main the Outlook Express folder. (Make one named Personal, just to give it a try.) The new folder appears on the list of folders on the left side of the Outlook Express window. Move messages into a folder by clicking a message header and dragging it over to the folder name or choosing Edit➪Move to Folder from the menu. You can see the list of message headers for any folder by clicking the folder name.

You can save the text of a message in a text file by clicking the message and choosing File➪Save As from the menu, clicking in the Save as type box and choosing Text Files (*.txt), typing a filename, and clicking the Save button.

Filing with Netscape Messenger/Mail

To make a new folder in Netscape Messenger, choose File⇨New Folder. To move a message into a folder, select the message and choose Message⇨File Message from the menu, and then choose the folder name from the menu that appears. You may also simply drag the message until your mouse pointer is over the folder you want to file the message in and let go. To see the messages in a folder, click in the box that displays the current folder name (just below the left end of the toolbar) and choose the folder you want. You can also save a message in a text file by selecting the message and choosing File⇨Save As or pressing Ctrl+S.

Filing with Eudora

To file a message in Eudora, click the message and choose Transfer from the menu. The Transfer menu that appears lists all your mailboxes — all the choices you have for where to file your message. Choose the mailbox in which you want to stick your message. Poof — it's there. An even easier way to file a message is to highlight its line in the current menu and then drag the message into the mailbox you want in the Mailboxes window.

The first time you try to file something, you may notice that you don't have anywhere to file it. Create a new mailbox in which to stick the message by choosing New from the Transfer menu. Every time you want to create a new file, choose New. Although you eventually have enough mailboxes to handle most of your mail, for a while it may seem as though you're choosing New all the time.

You can see all the messages in a folder by choosing Mailbox from the menu — a window just like your in box appears, listing all the messages in the folder. If you have the Mailboxes window open you can just click the mailbox's icon in that window. If you want to save the message in a text file, click the message, choose File⇨Save As from the menu, move to the folder in which you want to save the message, type a filename, and click OK.

Recycle Those Electrons: Deleting Mail

When you first begin to get e-mail, the feeling is so exciting that it's difficult to imagine just throwing away the message. Eventually, however, you *have* to know how to get rid of messages, or else your computer will run out of room. Start early. Delete often.

The physical act of throwing away mail is easy enough that you probably have figured out how to do it already. In Outlook Express, click the message and then the Delete button on the toolbar or press the Del key. In Netscape Messenger, click the message and then click the Delete icon on the toolbar. In Eudora, click a message and then click the trash can icon or press Ctrl+D. If the message file is open, press @Ctrl+D or choose Message⇨Delete.

You can even delete mail without even reading it. If you subscribe to mailing lists, certain topics may not interest you. After you see the subject line, you may want to delete the message without reading it. If you're the type of person who reads every catalog and advertisement sent to you, you may have problems managing junk e-mail too. Consider getting professional help.

Fancy Mail and Getting Attached

Sooner or later, just plain, old, everyday e-mail isn't good enough for you. Someone's going to send you a picture you just have to see, or you're going to want to send something cool to your new best friend in Paris. When we talk about sending stuff other than text through the mail, we're talking about using special formats and e-mail programs or helper programs that can read them. Sometimes, the entire message is in a special format, such as HTML, which stands for HyperText Markup Language. It's the stuff Web pages are made of (visit our Web site, at `http://net.gurus.com`), although you can now use it to create mind-blowing e-mail too.

Outlook Express, Netscape Messenger, and Eudora let you select fonts; bigger and smaller font sizes; and bold, italics, and other text styles, just as you would in a word processor.

Slinky links

Outlook Express, Netscape Messenger, and Eudora all have a neat feature that turns URLs (Web site addresses) they find in e-mail messages into links to the actual Web site. You no longer have to type these addresses into your web browser. All you have to do is click or double-click the highlighted link in the e-mail message and — poof — you're at the Web site. We tell you about the Web and browsers in Chapter 8.

Mail attachments

You can *attach* almost any file stored on your computer's disks to an e-mail message. For example, when we finish writing a chapter of a book, we can attach the word-processing document to an e-mail message to our publisher. When our editor receives the file, she can save the attached file on her hard disk and then open it with her word processor.

I've been working on the chain gang

One of the most obnoxious things you can do with e-mail is to pass around chain letters. Because all mail programs have forwarding commands, with only a few keystrokes you can send a chain letter along to hundreds of other people. Don't do it. Chain letters are cute for about two seconds, and then they're just annoying. After 30 years of using e-mail, we've *never* received a chain letter worth passing along.

A few chain letters just keep coming around and around, despite our best efforts to stamp them out. Find out how to recognize them now and avoid embarrassment later:

The Good Times virus hoax: In late 1994, a chain letter appeared on America Online disguised as a warning that a horrible computer virus capable of erasing your hard disk was being spread by e-mail. The virus allegedly arrived in e-mail messages bearing the words *Good Times.* Well-intentioned individuals quickly sent it to everyone they knew. The chain letter, not the non-existent virus, spread rapidly throughout the Internet. Computer viruses are spread through infected programs that, after they are run, can have malicious effects. E-mail is stored as text — not as a program — that cannot cause damage to your disk unless you give specific commands to run a program. This chain letter shows up under various names; regardless of the title, however, viruses don't spread by e-mail.

Dying boy wants greeting (or business) cards: Not anymore, he doesn't. A decade ago, an English boy named Craig Shergold was hospitalized with a serious brain tumor. Craig wanted to set the world's record for receiving the most greeting cards. Word got out, and Craig received millions of cards and eventually got into the *Guinness Book of World Records.* Then, U.S. TV billionaire John Kluge paid for Craig to fly to the United States for a successful operation. Craig is okay now and doesn't want any more cards. (You can read all about this story on page 24 of the July 29, 1990, edition of the *The New York Times.*) Guinness is so sick of the whole business that it has closed the category — no more records for the most cards are accepted. To help dying children, give the two dollars that a card and stamp would have cost to a children's welfare organization, such as UNICEF.

The modem-tax rumor: In 1987, the U.S. Federal Communications Commission (FCC) proposed changing the rules governing the way online services are billed for their phone connections. The proposal would have had the effect of raising the prices these services charge. Online service customers made their opposition clear immediately and loudly, members of Congress made concerned inquiries, and the proposal was *dropped.* Undated notices about the proposal unfortunately have circulated ever since. If you see yet another modem-tax scare, demand the current FCC docket number because the FCC — as a government bureaucracy — can't blow its nose without making announcements, accepting comments, and so on. No docket means no action, which means that it's the same old rumor. A recent version refers to "bill 602P" by "Rep. Tony Schnell"; there's no such bill, and no such representative, in either the U.S. Congress or the Canadian parliament.

Make big bucks with a chain letter: These letters usually have the subject MAKE.MONEY.FAST, are signed by "Dave Rhodes" or "Karen Erickson," contain lots of testimonials from people who are now rolling in dough, and tell you to send $5 to the name at the top of the list, put your name at the bottom, and send the message to a zillion other suckers. Some even say, "This isn't a chain letter" (you're supposedly helping to compile a mailing list or sending reports or something — your 100 percent guaranteed tipoff that it's a chain letter). Don't even think about it. These chain letters are extremely illegal even when they say that they aren't, and, besides, they don't even work. (Why send any money? Why not just add your name and send it on? Heck, why not just replace all the names on the list with yours?) Think of them as gullibility viruses. Send a polite note to the sender's postmaster to encourage her to tell users not to send any more chain letters. If you don't believe that they're illegal, see the Postal Service Web site, at `http://www.usps.gov/websites/depart/inspect/chainlet.htm`.

Send e-mail to a publisher so that they give books to children's hospitals: This brief,

ill-considered marketing gimmick lasted for a few days in late 1996. Needless to say, they got all the mail they wanted in a few hours after word got around, and now don't want any more.

Sign the online petition about the treatment of women in Afghanistan. This one was started by a well-meaning student at Brandeis University in Massachusetts and has been going around the world for years. The petition just mail-bombs long-closed e-mail addresses. If you care about this issue, do a little online research (see Chapter 11) so that you can write well-reasoned letters to people who may be able to help.

Attachments usually come in two flavors:

✔ **MIME:** Stands for *m*ultipurpose *I*nternet *m*ail *e*xtensions

✔ **Uuencoding:** A method of including information in e-mail; invented back in the days of UNIX-to-UNIX e-mail (hence the *uu* in the name)

The technical details of these methods are totally uninteresting and irrelevant: What matters to you is that your e-mail program must be capable of attaching files by using at least one of these methods and capable of detaching incoming files that other people send you, preferably by using any of these methods.

You can generally send a file as an e-mail attachment by using your regular mail program to compose a regular message and then giving a command to attach a file to the message. You send the message by using the program's usual commands.

When you receive a file that is attached to an e-mail message, your mail program is responsible for noticing the attached file and doing something intelligent with it. Most of the time, your mail program saves the attached file as a separate file in the folder or directory you specify. After the file has been saved, you can use it just like you use any other file.

For example, you can send these types of files as attachments:

- Pictures, in image files
- Word-processing documents
- Sounds, in audio files
- Movies, in video files
- Programs, in executable files
- Compressed files, such as zip files

If you receive a message with an attachment that uses a method (MIME, uuencoding, or some other less widely used method) that your mail program doesn't know about, the attached file shows up as a large message in your mailbox. If the attached file contains text, about half the kinds of tarted-up text are readable as is, give or take some ugly punctuation. If the attached file contains sound or pictures, on the other hand, reading the message is hopeless because it just contains binary digitized versions of the images and not any sort of text approximation.

If you get a picture or sound MIME message and your mail program doesn't automatically handle it, clunky but usable methods may exist for saving the message to a file and extracting the contents with separate programs. Consult your Internet Service Provider's help desk.

Outlook Express attachments

In Outlook Express, you attach a file to a message by choosing Insert⇨File Attachment from the menu while you're composing a message or click the paper-clip icon on the toolbar. Then select the file to attach. Send the message as usual.

When an incoming message contains an attachment, a paper-clip icon appears in the message on your list of incoming messages and in the message when you view it. Click the paper clip to see the filename — double-click to see the attachment.

Netscape Messenger/Mail attachments

Click the Attach button (the fourth button on the toolbar) and then choose File from the menu that appears. Select the file you want to attach and click the Open button. (Why is the button named Open? We can only guess.) The location and filename of the attached file are displayed in the Composition window.

When you receive an attached file, you see an attachment box with information about the file. Click the link (the blue underlined text) on the left side of the box to see the attachment. If the attached file is a picture or some other type of file that Netscape can display, it does so. If Netscape doesn't know how to handle the attached file, it asks what you want to do with the file.

Eudora attachments

To attach a file to a message with Eudora, compose a message as usual. Then choose <u>M</u>essage⇨Attac<u>h</u> File from the menu or click the Attach icon (a message clipped to an envelope) or press Ctrl+H. Eudora helps you choose the document you want to attach.

If you drag a file from Windows Explorer, My Computer, or File Manager to Eudora, she attaches the file to the message you're writing. If you're not writing a message, she starts one for you.

When Eudora receives mail with attachments, she automatically saves them to your disk (in a directory you specify in the Options dialog box) and tells you where they are and what they're called.

Robot Mail

Not every mail address has an actual person behind it. Some are mailing lists (which we talk about in Chapter 7), and some are *robots,* programs that automatically reply to messages. Mail robots have become popular as a way to query databases and retrieve files because setting up a connection for electronic mail is much easier than setting up one that handles the more standard file transfer. You send a message to the robot (usually referred to as a *mailbot* or *mail server*), it takes some action based on the contents of your message, and then the robot sends back a response. If you send a message to internetme@gurus.com, for example, you receive a response telling you your e-mail address.

The most common use for mail robots is to get on and off mailing lists. Companies also often use the robots to send back canned responses to requests for information sent to info@whatever.com.

Your Own Personal Mail Manager

After you begin sending e-mail, you probably will find that you receive quite a bit of it, particularly if you put yourself on some mailing lists (see Chapter 7). Your incoming mail soon becomes a trickle, and then a stream, and then a torrent, and pretty soon you can't walk past your keyboard without getting soaking wet, metaphorically speaking.

Fortunately, most mail systems provide ways for you to manage the flow and avoid ruining your clothes (enough of this metaphor already). Here are some tips for handling the deluge:

✔ If most of your messages come from mailing lists, you should check to see whether the lists are available instead as *Usenet* newsgroups. (Visit our Web site, at `http://net.gurus.com` for information about newsgroups.) Usenet newsreading programs (including Outlook Express and Netscape Messenger, conveniently enough) generally enable you to look through messages and find the interesting ones more quickly than your mail program does and to automatically sort the messages so that you can quickly read or ignore an entire *thread* (conversation) of messages about a particular topic. Your system manager can usually arrange to make particularly chatty mailing lists look like Usenet newsgroups. At our site, we handle about 40 mailing lists that way.

✔ Eudora users can create *filters* that can automatically check incoming messages against a list of senders and subjects and file them in appropriate folders. Outlook Express has the Inbox Assistant, which can sort your mail automatically. Even Netscape Communicator 4.72 and later and Netscape 6 filter mail. Some other mail programs have similar filtering features.

For example, you can create filters that tell your mail program, "Any message that comes from the POULTRY-L mailing list should be automatically filed in the Chickens folder." In Outlook Express, tell the Inbox Assistant how to sort your mail into folders by choosing Tools⇨Inbox Assistant from the menu. In Netscape Messenger, choose Edit⇨Mail Filters to display the Mail Filters window, where you can create, edit, and delete filters. In Eudora, choose Tools⇨Filters to see a similar window. (Eudora Pro has even more flexible filters, so use Eudora Pro if you use filters frequently.)

All this automatic-sorting nonsense may seem like overkill, and if you get only five or ten messages a day, it is. After the mail really gets flowing, however, dealing with it takes much more of your time than it used to. Keep those automated tools in mind — if not for now, for later.

Can the Spam

Pink tender morsel,

Glistening with salty gel.

What the hell is it?

— Spam haiku, found on the Internet

More and more often, it seems, we get unsolicited e-mail from some organization or person we don't know. The word *spam* (the brand name of that tasty pork product from Hormel) on the Internet now means thousands (or millions) of copies of the same piece of unwanted e-mail, sent to either individual e-mail accounts or Internet newsgroups. It's also known as *junk e-mail* or *unsolicited commercial e-mail* (UCE). The message usually consists of unsavory advertising for get-rich-quick schemes or pornographic Web sites — something you may not want to see and something you definitely don't want your children to see. The message is *spam,* the practice is *spamming,* and the person sending the spam is a *spammer.*

Spam is, unfortunately, becoming a major problem on the Internet because both sleazy business entrepreneurs and political lowlifes have decided that it's the ideal way to advertise. Unfortunately, e-mail spam has become an increasing problem, with no end in sight.

Why call it spam?

The meat? Nobody knows. Oh, you mean the unwanted e-mail? It came from the Monty Python skit in which a group of Vikings sing "Spammity-Spam, wonderful Spam" repeatedly in a march tempo, drowning out all other discourse.

Is it so bad?

You may think that spam, like junk mail, is just a nuisance we have to live with. It's different from junk mail, however, in several ways. First is the cost factor. Unlike receiving junk mail, you, the recipient, pay much more than the sender does to deliver the message. Paper junk mail costs 25 to 50 cents an envelope to mail, and nothing to receive. Sending e-mail is cheap: A spammer can send thousands of messages an hour from a PC and a dial-up connection, so it costs the mailer just a tiny fraction of a cent to mail. The time and disk space you use to download e-mail from spammers, though, is costing you money. After that, it costs you time to read (at least the subject line) and dispose of the mail. If spam volume continues to grow at its alarming pace, pretty soon e-mail will prove to be useless because the real e-mail is buried under the junk.

Not only do all of us as e-mail users have to bear a cost, but this volume of e-mail also strains the resources of mail servers and the entire Internet. Think of all the disk space and communication capacity occupied by millions of useless e-mail messages! Internet Service Providers have to pass along the added costs to its users. America Online has been reported to estimate that of the 20 million pieces of e-mail its mail servers handle daily, about one-third is spam.

Then you have to consider the issue of content. The stuff these spams advertise is generally fraudulent, dishonest, or pornographic. Many offers are for get-rich-quick schemes. No honest business would attempt to advertise by broadcasting on the Internet because of the immense bad publicity it would bring on itself.

Many spams include a line that instructs you how to get off their lists, something like "Send us a message with the word REMOVE in it." Why should you have to waste your time to get off the list? In addition, doing so usually doesn't work — some people report getting *more* spam after responding to a removal address. By responding, you've confirmed that you are a warm body who reads your e-mail.

Can I do something?

The Internet tries to be self policing; the community of people who make up the users and inventors of this marvelous medium don't want the Internet to fall under the control of the government, commercial interests, or gangsters. The Internet grew from a need for the easy and free flow of information, and everyone using it should strive to keep it that way.

Check out these Web sites for information about spam and how to fight it, both technically and legally:

```
http://www.cauce.org
http://spam.abuse.net
```

"Is There a Trick to Using E-Mail Effectively?"

Not really, except to always pace yourself and hold on to messages before sending them. It's much easier to send e-mail than it is to send paper mail, and e-mail doesn't carry the burden of having to know the individuals or ever needing to meet them in public (or in a darkened alleyway). Always treat people with respect, even if they are disrespectful. Never use questionable language unless it has been established as acceptable by unanimous consent. Brush your teeth twice a day, and that sort of thing.

Last, but by far not the least, don't beat people over the head with your e-mail. What we mean is that if someone on a mailing list or newsgroup or other community discussion arena says something stupid, don't make that person feel even more stupid after the fact. We each have sent e-mail that was gravely regretted immediately after sending it, and we always appreciated the tolerance of our peers when we did.

You may think that this advice is patronizing, but from our experience (we've been using e-mail for more than 30 years), we still take time out on occasion to utter something completely uncalled for. Take our word for it: It can happen, and it does.

Chapter 7

The World According to E-Mail: Electronic Mailing Lists

In This Chapter

▶ Subscribing and unsubscribing to mailing lists

▶ Getting more or less junk mail

▶ Finding mailing lists that interest you

▶ Checking out a few interesting mailing lists

▶ Running your own mailing list

*N*ow that you know all about how to send and receive mail, only one thing stands between you and a rich, fulfilling, mail-blessed life: You may not know many people with whom you can exchange mail. Fortunately, you can get yourself on lots of mailing lists, which ensures that you arrive every morning to a mailbox with 400 new messages. (Maybe you should start out with only one or two lists.)

You Say You Never Get Any Mail?

Mailing lists are simple. The list has its own special e-mail address, and anything someone sends to that address is re-sent to all the people on the list. Because these people in turn often respond to the messages, the result is a running conversation among a large group of people.

Different lists have different styles. Some are relatively formal, hewing closely to the official topic of the list. Others tend to go flying off into outer space, topicwise. You have to read them for a while to be able to tell which list works which way.

Mailing lists fall into three categories:

- ✔ **Discussion:** Every subscriber can post a message. These lists lead to freewheeling discussions and can include a certain number of off-topic messages.

- ✔ **Moderated:** A moderator reviews each message before it gets distributed. The moderator can stop unrelated, redundant, or clueless postings from wasting everyone's time.

- ✔ **Announcement-only:** Only the moderator posts messages. Announcement mailing lists work well for publishing an online newsletter, for example.

Signing On to and Getting Off Mailing Lists

The way you get on or off a mailing list is also simple: You send a mail message. Two general schools of mailing-list management exist: the *manual* and the *automatic*. Manual management is the more traditional way: Your message is read by a human being who updates the files to put people on or take them off the list. The advantage of manual management is that you get personal service; the disadvantage is that the list maintainer may not get around to servicing you for quite a while if more pressing business (such as her real job) intervenes.

These days, lists are commonly maintained automatically, which saves human attention for times when things are fouled up. The most widely used automatic mailing managers are families of programs known as LISTSERV, Majordomo, and ListProc, which get their own sections later in this chapter.

The human touch

To get on or off a manually managed list, you send a nice note to the human being who manages the list. Manual lists follow a widely observed convention regarding list manager addresses. Suppose that you want to join a list for fans of James Buchanan (the 15th President of the United States and the only one who never married, in case you slept through that part of history class), and the list's name is buchanan-lovers@gurus.com. The list manager's address is almost certainly buchanan-lovers-request@gurus.com. In other words, just add -request to the list's address to get the manager's address. Because the list is maintained by hand, your request to be added or dropped doesn't have to take any particular form, as long as it's polite. Please add me to the buchanan-lovers list does quite well. When you decide that you have had all the Buchanan you can stand, another message saying Please remove me from the buchanan-lovers list works equally well.

Look before you leap

Here's a handy tip: After you subscribe to a list, don't send anything to it until you have been reading it for a week. Trust us — the list has been getting along without your insights since it began, and it can get along without them for one more week.

This method gives you a chance to learn the sorts of topics that people really discuss, the tone of the list, and so on. It also gives you a fair idea about which topics people are tired of. The classic newcomer gaffe is to subscribe to a list and immediately send a message asking a dumb question that isn't really germane to the topic and that was beaten to death three days earlier. Bide your time, and don't let this situation happen to you.

The number-two newcomer gaffe is to send a message directly to the list asking to subscribe or unsubscribe. This type of message should go to the list manager or to a LISTSERV, Majordomo, or ListProc address, where the list maintainer (human or robotic) can handle it, *not* to the list itself, where all the other subscribers can see that you screwed up.

To summarize: The first message you send, to join a list, should go to a *something*-request or LISTSERV or majordomo or listproc address, *not* to the list itself. After you have joined the list and read it for a while, *then* you can send messages to the list.

Here's another thing not to do: Unless you're expressly invited to do so, don't send attach-ments to mailing lists. Many people don't have the program they would need to open the attachment anyway. If you have a file you want to distribute on a mailing list, send a message inviting people interested in getting the file to e-mail you privately.

One last thing not to do: If you don't like what another person is posting (for example, some newbie is posting blank messages or "unsub-scribe me" messages or is ranting interminably about a topic), don't waste everyone's time by posting a response on the list. The only thing stupider than a stupid posting is a response complaining about it. Instead, e-mail the person *privately* and tell him to stop, or e-mail the list manager and ask that person to intervene.

The preceding advice does have one exception (as in all things). Certain products, typically shareware and freeware, host lists specifically for their users so that they have a place to go to ask for assistance. The reason that these lists exist in the first place is to provide support and community, so the members already there likely understand this and will not be miffed that you posted immediately upon subscription. Do, how-ever, pay attention to the existence of other help materials, such as a Frequently Asked Questions (FAQ) list that is often generated by the questions on the list or other materials.

If you're sure that you have exhausted all other prescribed avenues, post to the list immediately. You're likely to get an immediate and helpful response.

Messages to -request addresses are read and handled by human beings who sometimes eat, sleep, and work regular jobs as well as maintain mailing lists. Therefore, these people don't necessarily read your request the moment it arrives. It can take a day or so to be added to or removed from a list, and, after you ask to be removed, you usually get a few more messages before they remove you. If it takes longer than you want, be patient. *Don't* send cranky follow-ups — they just cheese off the list maintainer. It's not nice to cheese off the list maintainer.

LISTSERV, the tyrannosaur of mail managers

Because maintaining lots of mailing lists is a great deal of work, people who used an older network named BITNET came up with a program to automate the process. They named their program *LISTSERV,* and it originally ran on great big IBM mainframe computers. (The IBM mainframe types have an inordinate fondness for eight-letter uppercase names, EVEN THOUGH TO MOST OF US IT SEEMS LIKE SHOUTING.) BITNET is history now, and anyone with an Internet address can use LISTSERV, which these days has grown to the point that it is an all-singing, all-dancing mailing-list program with about 15 zillion features and options, almost none of which you care about.

Although LISTSERV is a little clunky to use, it has the huge advantage of being able to easily handle enormous mailing lists that contain thousands of members, something that makes many of the regular Internet mail programs choke. (LISTSERV can send mail to 1,000 addresses in about five minutes, for example, whereas that task would take the regular Internet `sendmail` program more than an hour.)

You put yourself on and off a LISTSERV mailing list by sending mail to `LIST-SERV@some.machine.or.other`, where `some.machine.or.other` is the name of the particular machine on which the mailing list lives. This address — the address that includes "LISTSERV" as the username — is called the *administrative* address for the list. You send all administrative commands, such as commands to get on or off the list, to the administrative address.

Because LISTSERV list managers are computer programs, they're rather simpleminded, and you have to speak to them clearly and distinctly, using standardized commands.

Suppose that you want to join a list named `SNUFLE-L` (LISTSERV mailing lists usually end with `-L`), which lives at `bluesuede.org`. To join, send to `LIST-SERV@bluesuede.org` (the administrative address) a message that contains this line in the text of the message (not the subject line):

```
SUB SNUFLE-L Roger Sherman
```

You don't have to add a subject line or anything else to this message — it's better not to, so as not to confuse the LISTSERV program. SUB is short for subscribe, `SNUFLE-L` is the name of the list, and anything after that is supposed to be your real name. (You can put whatever you want there, but keep in mind that it shows up in the return address of anything you send to the list.) You don't have to tell LISTSERV your e-mail address, which it can read from the automatically generated headers at the top of your message.

Shortly afterward, you should get back two messages:

- ✔ A chatty, machine-generated welcoming message telling you that you have joined the list, along with a description of some commands you can use to fiddle with your mailing-list membership. Sometimes, this message includes a request to confirm that you received this message. Follow the instructions by replying to this message with the single word *OK* in the body of the message. This trick helps lists ensure that they aren't mailing into the void and that it was indeed you who asked to put your name on that list. If you don't provide this confirmation, you don't get on the list.

- ✔ An incredibly boring message telling you that the IBM mainframe ran a program to handle your request and reporting the exact number of milliseconds of computer time and number of disk operations the request took. Whoopee. (It's sobering to think that somewhere there are people who find these messages interesting.)

Keep the chatty, informative welcome message that tells you about all the commands you can use when you're dealing with the list. For one thing, it tells you how to get *off* the mailing list if it's not to your liking. We have in our mail program a folder named Mailing Lists in which we store the welcome messages from all the mailing lists we join.

After you've subscribed, to send a message to this list, mail to the list name at the same machine — in this case, `SNUFLE-L@bluesuede.org`. This address is called the *list address* (creatively enough), and it's *only* for messages to be distributed to the entire list. Be sure to provide something descriptive on the Subject line for the multitudes who will benefit from your pearls of wisdom. Within a matter of minutes, people from all over the world will read your message.

To get off a list, you again write to `LISTSERV@some.machine.or.other`, this time typing in the body of the message (not on the subject line) the following command followed by whatever the list name is:

```
SIGNOFF SNUFLE-L
```

You don't have to give your name again because after you're off the list, LISTSERV has no more interest in you and forgets that you ever existed.

Some lists are more difficult than others to get on and off. Usually, you ask to get on a list, and you're on the list. In some cases, however, the list isn't open to all comers, and the human list owner screens requests to join the list, in which case you may get some messages from the list owner to discuss your request to join.

TIP

Too many messages give computers heartburn!

Some mailing lists are *digested*. No, they're not dripping with digital gastric juices — they're digested more in the sense of *Reader's Digest*. All the messages over a particular period (usually a day or two) are gathered into one big message with a table of contents added at the front. Many people find this method more convenient than getting messages separately, because you can easily look at all the messages on the topic at one time.

Some mail and newsreading programs give you the option of dividing digests back into the individual messages so that you can see them one at a time yet still grouped together. This option is sometimes known as *undigestifying*, or *exploding*, a digest. (First, it's digested, and then it explodes, sort of like a burrito.) Check the specifics of your particular mail program to see whether it has an option for digest-exploding.

To contact the actual human being who runs a particular list, the mail address is OWNER- followed by the list name (OWNER-SNUFLE-L, for example). The owner can do all sorts of things to lists that mere mortals can't do. In particular, the owner can fix messed-up names on the list or add a name that for some reason the automatic method doesn't handle. You have to appeal for manual intervention if your mail system doesn't put your correct network mail address on the From: line of your messages, as sometimes happens when your local mail system isn't set up quite right or if you no longer use the address from which you subscribed.

Make LISTSERV do stuff

The people who maintain the LISTSERV program have added so many bells and whistles to it that it would take an entire book to describe them all, and, frankly, they're not that interesting. Here are a few stupid LISTSERV tricks. For each of them, you send a message to LISTSERV@some.machine.or.other to talk to the LISTSERV program. You can send several commands in the same message if you want to do two or three tricks at one time:

✔ **Temporarily stop mail:** Sometimes, you're going to be away for a week or two, and you don't want to get a bunch of mailing-list mail in the meantime. Because you're planning to come back, though, you don't want to take yourself off all the lists either. To stop mail temporarily from the SNUFLE-L mailing list, send this message:

```
SET SNUFLE-L NOMAIL
```

The list stops sending you messages. To turn the mail back on, send this message:

```
SET SNUFLE-L MAIL
```

✔ **Get messages as a digest:** If you're getting a large number of messages from a list and would rather get them all at one time as a daily digest, send this message:

```
SET SNUFLE-L DIGEST
```

Although not all lists can be digested (again, if you've read the sidebars earlier in this chapter, think of burritos), the indigestible ones let you know and don't take offense. If you later want individual messages again:

```
SET SNUFLE-L NODIGEST
```

✔ **Find out who's on a list:** To find out who subscribes to a list, send this message:

```
REVIEW SNUFLE-L
```

Some lists can be reviewed only by people on the list and others not at all. Because some lists are enormous, be prepared to get back an enormous message listing thousands of subscribers.

✔ **Get or not get your own mail:** When you send mail to a LISTSERV list of which you're a member, the list usually sends you a copy of your own message to confirm that it got there okay. Some people find this process needlessly redundant. ("Your message has been sent. You will be receiving it shortly." Huh?) To avoid getting copies of your own messages, send this message:

```
SET SNUFLE-L NOACK
```

To resume getting copies of your own messages, send this one:

```
SET SNUFLE-L ACK
```

✔ **Get files:** Most LISTSERV servers have a library of files available, usually documents contributed by the mailing-list members. To find out which files are available, send

```
INDEX
```

To have LISTSERV send you a particular file by e-mail, send this message:

```
GET listname filename
```

where *listname* is the name of the list and *filename* is the name of a file from the INDEX command. For example, to get the article about Social Security number security from the LISTSERV that hosts the privacy forum, send this message:

```
GET privacy prc.ssn-10 to LISTSERV@vortex.com
```

✔ **Find out which lists are available:** To find out which LISTSERV mailing lists are available on a particular host, send this message:

```
LIST
```

Note: Keep in mind that just because a list exists doesn't necessarily mean that you can subscribe to it. It never hurts to try.

✔ **Get LISTSERV to do other things:** Lots of other commands lurk in LISTSERV, most of which apply only to people on IBM mainframes. If you're one of these people or if you're just nosy, send a message containing this line:

```
HELP
```

You receive a helpful response that lists other commands.

Majordomo at your service, madam

Another widely used mailing-list manager is *Majordomo* and its Macintosh counterpart, the appropriately named *Macjordomo*. (We stick to Majordomo for this section, although it would be unlikely that you would note the difference between the two.) It started out as a LISTSERV wannabe for UNIX workstations but has evolved into a system that works quite well. Because of its wannabe origins, Majordomo commands are almost but (pretend to be surprised now) not quite the same as their LISTSERV equivalents.

The administrative address for Majordomo lists (the address to which you send commands), as you may expect, is majordomo@some.machine.or. other. Majordomo lists tend to have long and expressive names. One of our favorites is named explosive-cargo, a funny weekly column written by a guy in Boston who is in real life a computer technical writer. To subscribe, because the list is maintained on host world.std.com, send this message to Majordomo@world.std.com:

```
subscribe explosive-cargo
```

Note: Unlike with LISTSERV, you *don't* put your real name in the subscribe command. Like LISTSERV, Majordomo may send back a confirmation question to make sure that it was you who wanted to subscribe.

To unsubscribe:

```
unsubscribe explosive-cargo
```

After you have subscribed, you can send a message to everyone on the mailing list by addressing it to the list address — `listname@some.machine.or.other`. (You can't post messages to `explosive-cargo` because it's an announcements-only list: Only the guy in Boston who runs it is allowed to post messages.)

Majordomo does stuff too

Not to be outdone by LISTSERV, Majordomo has its own set of not particularly useful commands (as with LISTSERV, you can send in a single message as many of these as you want):

- ✔ To find out which lists at a Majordomo system you're subscribed to:

  ```
  which
  ```

- ✔ To find all the lists managed by a Majordomo system:

  ```
  lists
  ```

- ✔ Majordomo also can keep files related to its lists. To find the names of the files for a particular list:

  ```
  index name-of-list
  ```

- ✔ To tell Majordomo to send you one of the files by e-mail:

  ```
  get name-of-list name-of-file
  ```

- ✔ To find out the rest of the goofy things Majordomo can do:

  ```
  help
  ```

- ✔ If you want to contact the human manager of a Majordomo system because you can't get off a list you want to leave or otherwise have an insoluble problem, send a polite message to `owner-majordomo@host-name`. Remember that because humans eat, sleep, and have real jobs, you may not get an answer for a day or two.

They made them different just to annoy you!

Because LISTSERV, ListProc, and Majordomo work in sort of the same way, even experienced mailing-list mavens get their commands confused. Here are the important differences:

✔ The address for LISTSERV is LISTSERV@*hostname*, the address for Majordomo is majordomo@*hostname*, and the address for ListProc is listproc@*hostname*.

✔ To subscribe to a LISTSERV or ListProc list, send sub or subscribe followed by the list name followed by your real name. To subscribe to a Majordomo list, just send subscribe and the list name.

ListProc — yet another list manager

Although ListProc is not as widely used as LISTSERV and Majordomo, its popularity is increasing because it is cheaper, easier to install than LISTSERV, and almost as powerful.

To subscribe to a ListProc mailing list, you send this message to the administrative address for the list, listproc@some-computer:

```
subscribe listname yourname
```

To subscribe to the (hypothetical) chickens mailing list at gurus.com, for example, you send this message to listproc@gurus.com:

```
subscribe chickens George Washington
```

(assuming that you were named after the same person that the first President of the United States was).

To get off the mailing list, send this message to the same address:

```
signoff listname
```

You don't have to provide your name — the ListProc program should already know it.

After you have subscribed to the list, you can send messages to everyone on the list by addressing e-mail to the list address, listname@some-computer — chickens@gurus.com, for example. (Don't try it — no such mailing list exists!)

If you want to get your messages in daily or weekly groups rather than one at a time, send this message:

```
set listname mail digest
```

To switch back to getting messages one at a time, send this command:

```
set listname mail ack
```

To find out other things ListProc can do, send the message `help` to `lisproc@whatever,` where `whatever` is the name of the computer on which the ListProc mailing list lives.

Sending your first message

Okay, you're signed up on a mailing list. Now what? First, as we say a few pages back, wait a week or so to see what sort of messages arrive from the list — that way, you can get an idea of what you should or should not send to it. When you think that you have seen enough to avoid embarrassing yourself, try sending something in. That's easy: You mail a message to the list address, which is the same as the name of the list — `buchanan-lovers@gurus.com` or `snufle-l@bluesuede.org` or whatever. Keep in mind that because hundreds or thousands of people will be reading your pearls of wisdom, you should at least try to spell things correctly. (You may have thought that this advice is obvious, but you would be sadly mistaken.) On popular lists, you may begin to get back responses within a few minutes of sending a message.

Some lists encourage new subscribers to send in a message introducing themselves and saying briefly what their interests are. Others don't. Don't send anything until you have something to say.

After you watch the flow of messages on a list for a while, all this stuff becomes obvious.

Some mailing lists have rules about who is allowed to send messages, meaning that just because you're on the list doesn't automatically mean that any messages you send appear on the list. Some lists are *moderated:* Any message you send in gets sent to a human *moderator,* who decides what goes to the list and what doesn't. Although this process may sound sort of fascist, in practice the arrangement makes a list about 50 times more interesting than it would be otherwise because a good moderator can filter out the boring and irrelevant messages and keep the list on track. Indeed, the people who complain the loudest about moderator censorship are usually the ones whose messages most deserve to be filtered out.

Follow the bouncing message

Computer accounts are created and deleted often enough and mail addresses change often enough that a large list always contains, at any given moment, some addresses that are no longer valid. If you send a message to the list, your message is forwarded to these invalid addresses, and a return message reporting the bad addresses is generated for each of them.

Mailing-list managers (both human and computer) normally try to deflect the error messages so that they go to the list owner, who can do something about them, rather than to you. As often as not, however, a persistently dumb mail system sends one of these failure messages directly to you. Just ignore it because you can't do anything about it.

Another rule that sometimes causes trouble is that many lists allow messages to be sent only from people whose addresses appear on the list. This rule becomes a pain if your mailing address changes. Suppose that you get a well-organized new mail administrator and that your official e-mail address changes from jj@shamu.pol.bluesuede.org to John.Jay@bluesuede.org, although your old address still works. You may find that some lists begin *bouncing* your messages (sending them back to you rather than to the list) because they don't understand that John.Jay@bluesuede.org, the name under which you now send messages, is the same as jj@shamu.pol.bluesuede.org, the name under which you originally subscribed to the list. Worse, LISTSERV doesn't let you take yourself off the list, for the same reason. To resolve this mess, you have to write to the human list managers of any lists in which this problem arises and ask them to fix the problem by hand.

Reply Like a Pro

Often, you receive an interesting message from a list and want to respond to it. When you send your answer, does it go *just* to the person who sent the original message, or does it go to the *entire list?* It depends, mostly on how the list owner set up the software that handles the list. About half the list owners set things up so that replies automatically go to just the person who sent the original message, on the theory that your response is likely to be of interest only to the original author. The other half set things up so that replies go to the entire list, on the theory that the list is a running public discussion. In messages coming from the list, the mailing-list software automatically sets the Reply-To header line to the address to which replies should be sent.

Mailing lists versus Usenet news versus Web pages

Some mailing lists are *gatewayed* to Usenet newsgroups (visit our Web site, at http://net.gurus.com), which means that all the messages you would receive if you subscribed to the mailing list appear as items in the newsgroup and vice versa. Most gateways are two-way: Anything you mail to the list shows up also in the newsgroup, and anything you post as a news item also goes to the list. A few are one-way, usually because of sloppy gateway management, and many of them are moderated, which means that you have to mail any items to the human moderator, who filters out inappropriate messages. An increasing number of mailing lists are also available as Web pages, where you can search through both current messages and the list's archives of old messages.

Whether you get a particular list as mail or news is largely a matter of personal taste. The advantages of receiving lists as mail are that mail items tend to arrive faster than news items do (usually by only a few hours); mail items stick around until you explicitly delete them, whereas newsgroup articles are deleted automatically after a few days; and some mail programs are more flexible than the newsreading programs. The advantages of receiving news are that items are collected in a newsgroup rather than mixed in with your mail; items are automatically deleted unless you save them, avoiding mailbox bloat if you don't read and clean up your mail every day; and news programs usually do a better job than mail programs of collecting threads of related messages so that you can read them in order.

Fortunately, you're in charge. When you start to create a reply, your mail program should show you the address to which it's replying. If you don't like the address it's using, change the address. Check the To: and Cc: fields to make sure that you're sending your message where you want.

While you're fixing the recipient's address, you may also want to fix the Subject line. After a few rounds of replies to replies to replies, the topic of discussion often wanders away from the original topic, and it's a good idea to change the subject to better describe what is really under discussion.

Some Lists to Whet Your Appetite

Thousands of lists reside on the Internet — so many, in fact, that entire *books* have been written that just enumerate all the *lists*. To get you started, this section presents some lists we find interesting in addition to short descriptions of what they are. These addresses change relatively frequently, and we keep finding new and interesting lists. For our latest list of lists, check out our Web update, at http://net.gurus.com/lists. For a complete list of lists —

thousands exist — check out one of the mailing-list directory sites, such as the Liszt (bad pun) site, at `http://www.liszt.com`.

If you don't have access to the Web, send e-mail to `lists@gurus.com`, and we'll send you back our current list of recommended lists. If you have a favorite list you want to share, send us mail at `listsuggestions@gurus.com`.

Each list in our list of lists is accompanied by at least one of the following codes, describing what kind of list it is:

- ✔ **Manual:** Manually maintained list. To get on or off or to contact the human who maintains the list, write to `whatever-request@sitename`. In the text of your e-mail, state what you want. A human being handles these requests.

- ✔ **LISTSERV:** A LISTSERV-type list. To get on or off, send e-mail to `listserv@sitename`. In the body of the message, use the LISTSERV commands detailed earlier in this chapter, as shown in this example:

  ```
  sub LISTNAME yourname
  signoff LISTNAME
  ```

  To contact the relevant human, send mail to `owner-whatever@sitname`.

- ✔ **Majordomo:** A Majordomo list. To get on or off, send a "subscribe" or "unsubscribe" message to `Majordomo@sitename` asking to subscribe to the list name we give, as shown in this example:

  ```
  subscribe listname
  unsubscribe listname
  ```

- ✔ **ListProc:** A ListProc list. To get on or off, send a "subscribe" or "signoff" message to `listproc@sitename` asking to subscribe to the list name we give. Put your name after the list name, as shown in this example:

  ```
  sub listname yourname
  signoff listname
  ```

- ✔ **Moderated:** Moderated list. Messages are filtered by the human list owner (moderator).

- ✔ **News:** The list is also available as Usenet news, which is usually the better way to receive it (see the preceding sidebar, "Mailing lists versus Usenet news versus Web pages"). Although nearly all BITNET lists are also available as a special type of newsgroup, this list marks only lists available as regular news.

- ✔ **Digest:** Messages normally arrive as a digest rather than one at a time.

Net-Happenings Digest
LISTSERV@hypatia.cs.wisc.edu
LISTSERV (list name NET-HAPPENINGS) moderated, digest

This list, moderated by Gleason Sackman, announces new Web sites, mailing lists, and other new items of interest on the Internet.

TipWorld
`http://www.tipworld.com`
Web-based list, moderated

To subscribe to the TipWorld lists, go to its Web site, at `http://www.tipworld.com`, and fill out an online form. (See Chapter 8 if you don't know how to go to a Web site.) TipWorld, which is run by PC World Communications, offers daily tips by e-mail about Windows, the Internet, and other computer-related topics.

InfoBeat
`http://www.infobeat.com`
Web-based list, moderated

InfoBeat is another announcement mailing list (newsletter, really) that you subscribe to on a Web site, in this case at `http://www.infobeat.com`. InfoBeat can mail you a free daily newspaper by e-mail with information from the major news organizations — what a deal!

Risks Digest
Majordomo¢l.sri.com
Majordomo (list name risks) moderated, news, digest

This forum discusses risks to the public in computers and related systems. It covers the risks of modern technology, particularly of computer technology (lots of great war stories).

Privacy Forum Digest
LISTSERV@vortex.com
LISTSERV (list name PRIVACY) moderated

This running discussion of privacy in the computer age has lots of creepy reports about people and organizations you would never expect were snooping on you (ambulance drivers, for example).

Travel-L
LISTSERV@vm.ege.edu.tr
LISTSERV (list name TRAVEL-L)

The TRAVEL-L list covers travel and tourism, airlines, guidebooks, places to stay — you name it. Because participants come from all over the world (the host system is in Europe), you get lots of tips you would never get locally.

The Jazz Lover's List
LISTSERV@brownvm.brown.edu
LISTSERV (list name JAZZ-L)

This friendly, laid-back, ongoing discussion makes no claim to staying on-topic but rather to creating a salon-type atmosphere in which "like-minded, intelligent people from diverse backgrounds" can make real connections.

Liberal Judaism
Listproc@shamash.org
Listproc (list name MLJ) moderated, digest

Nonjudgmental discussions of liberal Judaism (including Reform, Reconstructionist, conservative, and secular humanist), issues, practices, opinions, and beliefs take place here. Include your real first and last name in your request — such as `subscribe MLJ yourfirstname yourlastname`.

Running Your Own List (?!)

We apologize if we scared you with this one. We honestly hope that we didn't turn you off to this idea by describing exactly the list-management software you will *not* be using. Fortunately, it's far easier than all that technical mess, and you can choose from plenty of services. Some new alternatives are also now available because of the booming broadband market.

A number of Web sites provide e-mail list hosting and management. First, here's a list of some popular services, and then we get into more detailed stuff:

CoolList: `http://www.coollist.com`

eGroups: `http://www.egroups.com` or `http://www.onelist.com`

Topica: `http://www.topica.com`

Each of these services allows you to create, manage, and moderate e-mail-based discussion lists for free. All they ask in return is that a small advertisement be placed at the bottom of every message, which is really not very noticeable, with the exception of Topica. Topica, in a turn-around from the ethic it initially followed, places large (7- to 9-line) ads at the top of most messages filtered through its system, a practice that is obnoxious, conflicting, and just plain rude. But we digress because this is not a review (although that information will likely help you decide which service *not* to patronize).

CoolList, the simplest of these services, has few administrative functions and options and no extras like the ones eGroups provides. CoolList is probably the best solution if all you want to do is host a simple list or keep a group of friends or family members in touch. It offers *only* lists. You can set up any number of lists, to be categorized under whatever topic you deem appropriate. With any list you create, it's up to you to promote the list. Don't think that immediately after you create it, users magically subscribe. You must let people know that your list exists.

eGroups, on the other hand, offers a wide range of services that revolve around group communication. It was so eager to add functionality, in fact, that it bought out its main competitor, OneList, and integrated the OneList lists and information into its own system. Setting up an account with eGroups is simple and quick, so do that first:

1. **Open your web browser and go to** `http://www.egroups.com`.

   In the leftmost column on the page is a short list of links with the title New Member.

2. **Click the Sign-up today for free! link at the top.**

3. **Enter the e-mail address you want to use to administer your lists, enter a password, and fill out the other requested (mostly demographic) information.**

   Wouldn't it be nice to be able to have more than one home address? That way, you could always hand out one address to the people and services you believe will send you junk and the other, "real," address to those you want to receive mail from. You can get a P.O. box, but it costs money and many places refuse to accept that type of address because they don't want their junk mail to end up in the trash. With e-mail, you have lots of options, and they're all free! First, check with your ISP to see whether you can get more than one e-mail address for your account. Some ISPs allow more than one e-mail address at no extra charge or for a nominal additional charge. AOL and CompuServe give you as many as seven, and MindSpring allows you to set up four additional mailboxes at no additional charge. Most ISPs allow you to have more than one e-mail address, although you have to ask. A large number of free, Web-based e-mail services also exist, such as HotMail and Yahoo! Most of them automatically forward mail received at that account to another account — your ISP account, for example. Just having another account that you can give out when you fill in online forms is a lifesaver because it can always be used to catch, and then filter, any resulting spam.

4. **Click the I Accept, Continue button if you've read the license agreement and agree, or even if you didn't read it or care.**

   Most of these license agreements simply absolve the service provider of any fault, make explicit statements about the service's functionality, and other typically legal stuff. You just click through most of them, although if the service is for a fee, you should read it from top to bottom because you never know what loathsome conditions some marketing whiz may have sneaked in there.

All the chapters in this part of the book deal with the e-mail address you entered in the preceding step. eGroups sends a confirmation message to that address, and you need to respond to it to activate your new account.

5. **The message should already be in your Inbox, so you can click a link in the message if your e-mail application supports that feature; otherwise, just click Reply and send it right back.**

   Seconds later, you receive a confirmation message telling you that you can get started.

6. **Click the Continue Registration button, and you're all finished — at least with registering.**

As you can see, registration is quite easy. However, it has nothing to do (yet) with actually setting up a mailing list! That's next. First, though, is the matter of eGroups eLerts, a collection of "free" newsletters you can sign up for. Our personal opinion is that you should skip them. For the most part, they are merely an additional means to display more advertising, without having much in the way of real content. Just look at all the topics covered! Now, on to the list-creation stuff:

1. **Click the Start A Group button in the upper-right corner of the page. A 3-step form, similar to the one you just filled out, appears.**

2. **Give your list an e-mail address.**

   The address is just like a personal e-mail address, but it's for a list. If, for example, you want to host a list for people interested in underwater basket weaving, you could name it

   ```
   underwater-basket-weavers@egroups.com
   ```

3. **Choose whether subscribers can post freely to your list (unmoderated), whether messages require your approval (moderated), or whether your list will only send out messages, like a newsletter or an announcement list.**

4. **Decide whether you want people to be able to find the list through the eGroups directory.**

   It's generally a good idea to *not* publicize a list if you plan on having only friends and family.

5. **Choose whether to allow people to join freely. (If not, you must approve every request personally.)**

6. **The next two choices are easy: Fill out a short and a long description of your list's *raison d'etre.***

7. Select a primary language for the list.

eGroups smartly does *not* assume that everyone is from America. This assumption is a good one because a large number of lists hosted by eGroups are *not* in the English language.

8. Click the I Accept, Continue button to create your list.

9. Select the category for your list.

Select carefully because the category helps or hinders people looking for lists concerning your chosen topic. A list dedicated to Underwater Basket Weaving should not be listed under the Computers category, for example, simply because the list is managed and read on computers. UBWeaving is a sport!

10. When you have located the category in which you want to place your list, click the Place my group here button that has appeared near the top.

11. You may enter the e-mail addresses of people whom you know to have shown an interest in subscribing to your list or whom you want to invite to join.

You can either ask people whether they want to subscribe or simply add them to the list without asking. Use your common sense here because this issue skims the border between spamming and listing.

12. Click the I Accept, Continue button.

You're done. From the final screen, you can head off in other directions and modify this and that. Take the time to read the instructions and, if something's unclear, ask. Lots of people on the lists are happy, of course, to help you make the most of the service.

Finally, we have just a few notes you may want to absorb. They can help foster a better, more productive list, even if it's just for fun. First of all, define a *list charter.* A clear, concise charter spells out exactly why the list was formed and which discussions it should foster. Moving off the topic may not be strictly forbidden, but it should be enforced to a good degree. Regardless, it's bad policy to let discussions of religion, politics, and sex go *anywhere.* Although every topic can inflame emotions, these three topics seem to take the cake, by sparking immense flame wars. If off-topic discussions are damaging, these three are downright catastrophic. Approach them with extreme prejudice.

Try to limit the distribution of personal information as much as possible. Names and e-mail addresses are okay, but addresses, phone numbers, and other very personal information is bad form. General-purpose lists can have any number of rather "interesting" individuals, if you get our drift. Sure, anyone can look up anyone else, but don't hand out this kind of information freely.

Take the time to compose a monthly Help message that you distribute to everyone, well, monthly. The general idea is to include information on how to subscribe, unsubscribe, change to digest mode (where the subscriber receives a compilation of all messages sent to the list over a specified period, typically once a day, in a single large message), how to get to the eGroups home page, how to get to other sites that relate to the lists charter, and whatever else you deem important or helpful. Urge them to retain the message so that they know how to work with the list, not against it.

The ubiquitous FAQ (Frequently Asked Questions) document helps reduce redundant activity on the list by providing a central place where all charter-related questions are answered. It also helps reduce the frequency of sarcastic and caustic messages from old-timers. It's best to start compiling the data for a FAQ as soon as the list starts up. If you wait and have to parse through thousands of messages, you'll know what we mean.

Maintain a presence on the list as its owner and moderator. Let your subscribers know that someone is at the helm. Make yourself available for questions, and never be afraid to ask them yourself. People join lists so that they can converse with their peers on a common interest. As such, nobody can know everything, so share and learn. That's what lists are all about.

Last, but far from least, have fun. If it's a chore or job, then close it or hand the responsibility to someone else who may have an interest. If you aren't having fun, neither is the list. Enjoy.

For lots more advice about running lists, see *Poor Richard's Building Online Communities* (Top Floor Publishing), written by some authors whose names you may recognize.

Part III
Windows Me
Web-Whacking

The 5th Wave   By Rich Tennant

IT'S FRICASSEE OF PYTHON WITH FRIED ANTS AND CRISPY GRASSHOPPERS.

YOU'RE GETTING RECIPES OFF THE INTERNET AGAIN, AREN'T YOU?

In this part . . .

The World Wide Web is the part of the Internet that gets all the publicity. The Web is so popular that more and more of what people do nowadays on the Internet, they're doing through the World Wide Web. In this part, we give you everything you need to know to surf the Web. Because so much stuff is out there, finding what you're looking for can be a real trick, so we've included a chapter about how to do that.

Chapter 8

Windows Me Meets the World Wide Web

• •

In This Chapter

▶ Hyper who?

▶ Understanding URLs

▶ An introduction to Netscape and Internet Explorer

▶ The basics of Web surfing

• •

*P*eople are talking about *the Web* today at least as much as they're talking about *the Net*. Although the World Wide Web and the Internet are not the same thing, they are related. The World Wide Web (which we call the Web because we're lazy typists) lives "on top of" the Internet. The Internet's network is at the core of the Web, although the Web itself is something different.

So what is it already? The Web is in some ways sort of a cross between libraries, television, computer networks, and telephones — it's all of the above and none of the above.

The Web is a huge collection of "pages" of information connected to each other around the globe. Each page can be a combination of text, pictures, audio clips, video clips, animations, and other stuff. (We're vague about naming the other stuff because they add new types of other stuff every day.) What makes Web pages interesting is that they contain *hyperlinks* (usually called just *links* because the Net already has plenty of hype). Each link points to another Web page, and, when you click a link, your browser program fetches the page the link connects to. (Your *browser* is the program that lets you view the Web — we talk about browsers in a couple of pages.)

Each page your browser displays for you can have more links that take you to other places. Web pages can be linked to other pages anywhere in the world so that when you browse the Web, you can look at pages from Singapore to Calgary, from Sydney to Buenos Aires — you're only seconds away from any site, anywhere in the world.

Where did the Web come from?

The World Wide Web was invented in 1989 at the European Particle Physics Lab in Geneva, Switzerland, an unlikely spot for a revolution in computing. The inventor is a British researcher named Tim Berners-Lee, who is now the director of the World Wide Web Consortium (W3), the organization that sets standards and loosely oversees the development of the Web. Tim is terrifically smart and hard-working and is the nicest guy you would ever want to meet. (Margy met him through Sunday school — is that wholesome or what?)

Tim invented *HTTP (Hypertext Transport Protocol)*, the way web browsers communicate with web servers; *HTML (HyperText Markup Language)*, the language in which Web pages are written; and *URLs (Uniform Resource Locators)*, the codes used to identify Web pages and most other information on the Net. He envisioned the Web as a way for everyone to both publish and read information on the Net, and early web browsers had editors that enabled you to create Web pages almost as easily as you could read them, a feature that has recently come back into vogue. (To find out more about this subject, visit our Web site, at `http://net.gurus.com`).

For more information about the development of the Web and the work of the World Wide Web Consortium, visit its Web site, at `http://www.w3.org`.

This system of interlinked documents is known as *hypertext*. Figure 8-1 shows a Web page: Each underlined phrase is a link to another Web page. Hypertext is one of those simple ideas that turns out to have a much bigger effect than you would think.

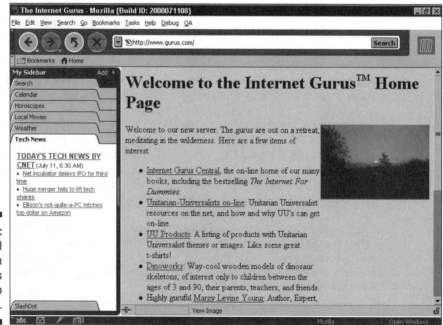

Figure 8-1: Underlined phrases on Web pages are links to other pages.

All Hyped Up and Someplace to Go

If you can get a handle on the fundamental structure of the Web, you can use it better and think about all the other ways it can be used. Linked pages of information — hypertext — connect information in ways that make it easy to find — in theory. In traditional libraries (both the kinds with books and the kinds in computers), information is organized in a relatively arbitrary way, such as alphabetical order or the Dewey decimal system. This order reflects nothing about the relationships among different pieces of information. In the world of hypertext, information is organized in relationship to other information. The relationships between different pieces of information are, in fact, often much more valuable than the pieces themselves.

Hypertext also enables the same set of information to be arranged in multiple ways at the same time. In a conventional library, a book can be on only one shelf at a time; a book about mental health, for example, is shelved under medicine or psychology, and it can't be in both places at one time. Hypertext is not as limited, and it's no problem to have links to the same document from both medical topics and psychological topics, for example.

Suppose that you're interested in what influenced a particular historical person. You can begin by looking at her basic biographical information: where and when she was born, the names of her parents, her religion, and other basic stuff like that. Then you can expand on each fact by finding out what else was happening at that time in her part of the world, what was happening in other parts of the world, and what influence her religion may have had on her. You draw a picture by pulling together all these aspects and understanding their connections — a picture that's hard to draw from just lists of names and dates.

A hypertext system allows people to create connections between pieces of information that enable you to find related information easily. As you draw connections between the pieces of information, you can begin to envision the Web created by the links between the pieces. What's so remarkable about the Web is that it connects pieces of information from all around the *planet,* on different machines and in different databases, all pretty much seamlessly (a feat you would be hard pressed to match with a card catalog). You may think of it as an extremely large but friendly alien centipede made of information.

The other important thing about the Web is that the information in it is searchable. In about ten seconds, for example, you can get a list of all the Web pages that contain the words *domestic poultry* or your name or the name of a book you want to find out about. You can follow links to see each page on the list, to see which pages contain the information you want.

The father of hypertext

John writes:

The term and concept of hypertext were invented around 1969 by Ted Nelson, a famous computer visionary who has been thinking about the relationship between computers and literature for at least 30 years now — starting back when most people would have considered it silly to think that such a relationship could exist. Twenty years ago, he claimed that people would have computers in their pockets with leatherette cases and racing stripes. (I haven't seen any racing stripes yet, but otherwise he was dead-on.)

Back in 1970, Ted told me that we all would have little computers with inexpensive screens on our desks with superwhizzo graphical hypertext systems. "Naah," I said. "For hypertext, you want a mainframe with gobs of memory and a high-resolution screen." We were both right, of course, because what we have on our desks in 2000 are little computers that are faster than 1970s mainframes and that have more memory and better screens.

Various hypertext projects have come and gone over the years, including one at Brown University (of which Ted was a part) and one at the Stanford Research Institute (which was arguably the most influential project in computing history because it invented screen windows and mice).

Ted's own hypertext system, Project Xanadu, which can be found on (of all things) the Web, is at http://www.xanadu.com. It has been in the works for about 20 years, under a variety of financing and management setups, with many of the same people slogging along and making it work. The project addresses many issues that other systems don't. In particular, Ted figured out how to pay authors for their work in a hypertext system, even when one document has pieces linked from others and the ensuing document consists almost entirely of a compendium of pieces of other documents. For a decade, I have been hearing every year that Xanadu (and, last I'd heard, a smaller Xanadu Light — which was supposed to take advantage of a great deal of existing software) was slated to hit the streets last year.

Of course, because I had troubled myself to make a prediction, it turned out to be incorrect. Alas, what *did* happen was that the project was made *Open Source,* which means that anyone who wants to can modify, improve, and add programming code. We certainly hope that it goes somewhere now.

What's in a Name?

You have to know about one more basic concept before hitting the Web. Every Web page has an *address,* a code by which it can be found and the name that gets attached to it so that browsers can find it. Great figures in the world of software engineering (Tim again) named this name *URL,* or *Uniform Resource Locator.* Every Web page has a URL. Strings of characters that begin with http:// or www. are URLs. Some people pronounce each letter ("U-R-L,"), and some think that it's a word (pronounced "earl") — it's your choice. Now you know enough to go browsing.

Browsing Around

To check out the Web for yourself, you need a *browser,* the software that gets Web pages and displays them on your screen. Fortunately, you already have one — Windows Me usually comes with a copy of Internet Explorer, or IE (although, if the U.S. Justice Department has its way, you may have a choice of other browsers). If you want to get a copy of Netscape Communicator, see the section "Getting and Installing Internet Explorer or Navigator or Communicator," near the end of this chapter.

If you use America Online or CompuServe software, almost everything we say about Internet Explorer also applies.

So where is this browser we've been talking about so much? If you're using Internet Explorer, you find it in several places on your computer. From the Start menu, you can choose Programs➪Internet Explorer. On the taskbar, just beside the Start button is a little area with some icons in it, including the Microsoft Internet Explorer *e* — clicking it starts Internet Explorer. On your desktop, near the upper-left corner, is probably a larger Internet Explorer *e.* Clicking that starts Internet Explorer too.

If Netscape Navigator or Communicator is installed on your computer, it shows up in almost as many places. Try choosing Start➪Programs➪Netscape➪ Navigator or looking for a Netscape Navigator or Communicator icon on your desktop.

However you got there, and whichever browser you're using, as soon as you get your computer connected to the Internet, you're ready to surf the Web. If you follow our recommendations in Chapter 4, your computer dials out whenever it needs to. If not, you may have put your Dial-Up Networking connection on your desktop or on your Start menu. Now would be a good time to start it up. If you still can't find it, try choosing Start➪Programs➪Internet Explorer➪Dial-Up Networking. You see a window that should contain your Dial-Up Networking connection.

Surfing the Web with Windows Me

When you start Netscape, you see a screen similar to the one that was shown in Figure 8-1. The Internet Explorer window looks like the one shown in Figure 8-2. Which Web page your browser displays depends on how the browser is set up; many providers arrange to have a browser display their home page. Because Microsoft and Netscape have a fondness for displaying their own Web pages when your browser starts up, you may find yourself looking at them. Netscape is even working at making its page a Web "destination," with news summaries and links to other interesting places.

The master plan for the 21st century

The 20th century was when the Scientific Revolution came of age, for better or worse. The 21st century will be about the Information Revolution — led by the World Wide Web. The Web will link together all the information in the known universe, starting with all the stuff on the Internet and heading up from there. (This statement may be a slight exaggeration, although we don't think so.)

One of the keys to global domination is to give everything (at least everything that could be available on the Web) a name, and in particular a consistent name so that no matter what kind of thing a hypertext link refers to, a web browser can find it and know what to do with it.

Look at this typical URL, the one for the Web page that was shown in Figure 8-1:

```
http://net.gurus.com/index.phtml
```

The first thing in a URL, the word before the colon, is the *scheme,* which describes the way a browser can get to the resource. Although ten schemes are defined, the most common by far is *HTTP,* the *Hypertext Transfer Protocol* that is the Web's native transfer technique. (Don't confuse HTTP, which is the way pages are sent over the Net, with *HTML,* which is the way the pages are coded internally.)

Although the details of the rest of the URL depend on the scheme, most schemes use a consistent syntax. Following the colon are two slashes (always forward slashes, never reverse slashes) and the name of the host computer on which the resource lives; in this case, `net.gurus.com`. Often, the host name starts with www. Can you guess what www stands for? (No fair peeking at the chapter title.) Next comes another slash and a *path,* which gives the name of the resource on that host; in this case, a file named `index.phtml`.

Web URLs allow a few other optional parts. They can include a *port number,* which specifies, roughly speaking, which of several programs running on that host computer should handle the request. The port number goes after a colon after the host name, like this:

```
http://net.gurus.com:80/index.
   phtml
```

Because the standard `http` port number is 80, if that's the port you want (it usually is), you can leave it out. Finally, a Web URL can have a *search part* at the end, following a question mark, like this:

```
http://net.gurus.com:80/
   index.phtml?chickens
```

Although not all pages can have search parts, in those that do, they tell the host, uh, what to search for. (You almost never type a search part yourself — it's usually constructed for you from fill-in fields on Web pages.)

Three other useful URL schemes are `mailto`, `ftp`, and `file`. A `mailto` URL looks like this:

```
mailto:internet98@gurus.com
```

That is, it's an e-mail address. Clicking a `mailto` URL runs the Outlook Express program or whatever you've designated as your default mail program. (Outlook Express is described in Chapters 5 and 6.) Mailto URLs are most commonly used for sending comments to the owner of a page.

A URL that starts with `ftp` lets you download files from an FTP server on the Internet (see Chapter 13 for information about FTP servers). An `ftp` URL looks like this:

```
ftp://ftp.loc.gov/pub/thomas/
   c104/s652.enr.txt
```

The part after the two slashes is the name of the FTP server (`ftp.loc.gov`, in this case). The rest of the URL is the pathname of the file you want to download.

The `file` URL specifies a file on your computer. The URL looks like this:

```
file:///C|/www/index.htm
```

On a Windows computer, this line indicates a Web page stored in the file C:\www\index.htm. The colon turns into a vertical bar (because colons in URLs mean something else), and the reverse slashes turn into forward slashes. File URLs are useful mostly for looking at graphics files with gif and jpg filename extensions and for looking at a Web page you just wrote and stuck in a file on your disk.

Figure 8-2: Your typical Web page, using Internet Explorer.

Anatomy of a browser window

Figure 8-3 illustrates the Internet Explorer browser window, indicating the important parts you really should know about. Here's the rundown:

Figure 8-3:
The
Microsoft
Internet
Explorer
window.

✔ **Address line:** The Address line contains the *Uniform Resource Locator,* or *URL,* for the current page. (Netscape labels this box Location.) Remember that URLs are an important part of Web lore because they're the secret codes that name all the pages on the Web. For details, see the sidebar "The master plan for the 21st century," earlier in this chapter. *Remember:* To type a URL in the Address or Location box, you first must click in the box so that either the address is highlighted (white text on a dark background) or a blinking cursor indicates where your typed characters will go. This process is not as obvious as it may seem. Figure 8-4 shows a browser that's ready to listen to the address you type.

Figure 8-4:
Browsers
listen to an
address you
type only
if they're
focused on
the Address
line.

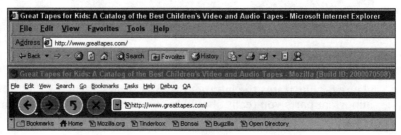

✔ **Back button:** Web browsers remember pages you visited recently, so if you click a link and decide that you're not so crazy about the new page, you can easily go back to the preceding one. To go back, click the Back button (its icon is an arrow pointing to the left) or press Alt+←. If the Back button is gray, you've gone all the way back to where you began your wandering since you ran your browser today.

✔ **Forward button:** If you've used the Back button to look at a Web page recently on your wanderings around the Web, you can use the Forward button to move forward along that path. Similar to the Back button, if the Forward button is gray, it means that you're as far along your path as you've ever been and you have to tell your browser where you want to go next.

✔ **Refresh/Reload button:** We talk about this button a little later in this chapter, in the section "If at first you don't succeed." In short, it goes out to the Web and asks for a fresh copy of the Web page you're looking at.

✔ **Stop button:** This button represents the alternative to the saying "If at first you don't succeed." In other words, give up. If you're tired of waiting for something to arrive from the World Wide Web, you can tell your web browser to give up waiting and go on and do something else.

✔ **Favorites and Bookmarks:** These two deserve a section all to themselves, and that's what they get in Chapter 9.

✔ **Fullscreen:** Only in Internet Explorer, this button removes most of the "Window dressing" from your Internet browser window, leaving only a small version of the toolbar. The rest of your screen is available for the Web page itself.

Microsoft added the full-screen option because it envisioned a world that would use the Web for everything, and so it gave us channels. Channels that were designed to take advantage of Fullscreen mode were to be animated, lively, interactive, and not the least bit entertaining. Well, channels no longer exist, the last vestige of which, Mobile Channels for Windows CE devices, has recently been wiped away as Microsoft has adopted the AvantGo service for its channels. Phew! All of this is really unimportant — just remember that you can turn Fullscreen mode on and off by pressing the F11 key.

✔ **The Status area:** Web pages are made up of many different pieces. When you're in the process of receiving a Web page, the status area tells you what it is that your browser is receiving and perhaps also how far along it is. (Navigator is better about this stuff than Internet Explorer is; the latter tends to make unwarrantedly optimistic reports.) After you've received a page, you may wonder where the links go. Before you actually click a link, the status area tells you where you would go.

> ✔ **The browser's logo:** The only reason you care about this thing is because it's your indication that your browser thinks that more information is coming. If the little comets are still streaking by the Netscape *N* or the world is still revolving around the Internet Explorer *e,* your browser has not received the "all clear, everything's here." Check out the section "If at first you don't succeed," later in this chapter, if you think that your browser is confused.

Click when ready

The primary skill you need (if we can call something as basic as a single mouse-click a skill) is moving from page to page on the Web.

It's easy: You just click any link that looks interesting. Underlined blue text and blue-bordered pictures are links. (Although links may be a color other than blue, depending on the look the Web page designer is going for, they're always underlined unless the page is the victim of a truly awful designer.) You can tell when you're pointing to a link because the mouse pointer changes to a little hand. In fact, if you selected the Web style when you configured your Windows Me desktop (See Chapter 3), opening a Web link is just like opening any icon on your Windows Me desktop.

If you're not sure whether something is a link, click it anyway because, if it's not, it doesn't hurt anything. Clicking outside a link selects the text you click or does nothing.

Do you know where your browser has been?

Web browsers not only remember pages you visited recently, but Internet Explorer also keeps track of all the places you visited in the past 20 days. For a recap of your surfing experiences, click the History button on the Internet Explorer button bar. We believe that you should be able to surf with privacy. To change the number of days history information is kept (you can set it to zero) or to just clear out the history file, choose Tools➪Internet Options to display the Internet Options dialog box. Click the General tab and look at the settings in the History section, near the bottom of the dialog box. Click OK when you're done.

Picture this

Some picture links are *image maps,* such as the big picture shown in the middle of Figure 8-5. In a regular link, it doesn't matter where you click; on an image map, it does. The image map in this figure is typical and has a bunch of obvious places you click for various types of information. (All the 1990 census data except private individual info is online on the Net, by the way, at `http://www.census.gov`.) Some image maps are actual maps — a map of the United States at the Census Bureau, for example, that shows you information about the state you click.

As you move the mouse cursor around a Web page, whenever you're pointing at a link, the place you have linked to appears in small type at the bottom of the window. If the link is an image map, you may see the link followed by a question mark and two numbers that are the X and Y positions of where you are on the map. The numbers don't matter to you (it's up to the web server to make sense of them); if you see a pair of numbers counting up and down when you move the mouse, however, you know that you're on an image map.

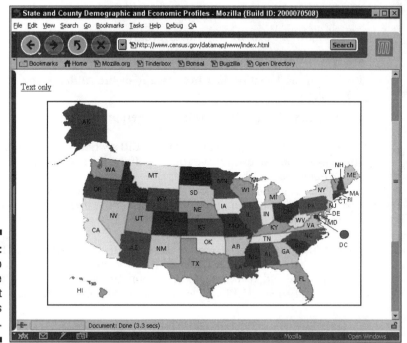

Figure 8-5:
Stand up and be counted at the Census Bureau.

There's no place like home

These days, everyone and his dog has a home page. (Check out `http://users.aimnet.com/~carver/cindy.html`.) A *home page* is the main Web page for a person or organization. To find out how to make one for yourself and your dog, visit our Web site, at `http://net.gurus.com`. Companies are advertising their home pages, and people are sending e-mail talking about cool sites. Whenever you see a URL you want to check out, here's what you do:

1. **Click in the Location or Address box, near the top of the Netscape or Internet Explorer window.**

2. **Type the URL in the box.**

   The URL is something like `http://net.gurus.com/`.

3. **Press Enter.**

Many programs, such as Outlook Express and Eudora, automagically highlight any URL they see so that you can click it to send your browser there. If you see a URL in a document that isn't highlighted, however, you can use standard cut-and-paste techniques and avoid retyping:

1. **Highlight the URL in whichever program is showing it.**

2. **Press Ctrl+C to copy the info to the Clipboard.**

3. **Click in the Location box in Netscape or the Address box in Internet Explorer.**

4. **Press Ctrl+V to paste the URL, and then press Enter.**

You can leave the `http://` off the front of URLs when you type them in the Address box. You can even leave the `www` off the front and the `com` off the back — that is, rather than type `http://www.idgbooks.com`, you can just type `idgbooks`. If you don't know a company's URL, it is usually worth typing the company or product name in your browser's Address box before you try other search methods.

One last tip: URLs appear in ads, on the sides of cereal boxes, and in sentences throughout this book. When a URL appears in a sentence, it may be followed by a period, a comma, or other punctuation. Don't type the punctuation into your browser! URLs never end with periods or commas.

A few good links to start with

You find out more in Chapter 10 about how to find things on the Net; for now, here's a good way to get started: Go to the Yahoo! page. (Yes, the name of the Web page includes an exclamation point — it's very excitable. But we leave it out throughout this book because we find it annoying.) That is, type this URL in the Location or Address box and then press Enter:

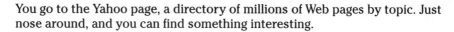
```
http://www.yahoo.com
```

You go to the Yahoo page, a directory of millions of Web pages by topic. Just nose around, and you can find something interesting.

For updates to the very book you're holding, go to this URL:

```
http://net.gurus.com
```

Follow the links to the page about our books, and then select the pages for readers of *The Internet For Microsoft Windows Millennium Edition For Dummies*. If we have any late-breaking news about the Internet or updates and corrections to this book, you can find them there. If you find mistakes in this book or have other comments, by the way, please send e-mail to us at internetme@ gurus.com.

If at first you don't succeed

Sometimes a Web page gets garbled on the way in or you interrupt it (by clicking the Stop button on the toolbar). Sometimes you receive half a Web page and the rest never shows up. Sometimes you receive the whole thing except for a picture. The Internet is like that: If you've read Chapter 1, you know that the Internet was designed to fail by giving you as much of what you want as it can instead of cutting you off completely. That's what the Stop button and the Refresh/Reload buttons are for: You can tell your browser to get the information on the page again. If your browser still thinks that it's waiting for information (and you disagree), click the Stop button. You know that your browser thinks that more information is out there if the browser's logo in the upper-right corner is still swirling around. After you've clicked the Stop button to tell your browser to give up, in Internet Explorer, click the Refresh button or press F5; in Netscape, click the Reload button or press Ctrl+R. Hope for better luck this time.

Time to quit

Sooner or later, even the most dedicated Web surfer has to stop to eat or attend to other bodily needs. You leave Netscape or Internet Explorer in the same way as you leave any other Windows Me program: by choosing File⇨Close. You can also click the Close button in the upper-right corner of the window.

Getting and Installing Internet Explorer or Navigator or Communicator

If all goes according to the Microsoft plan, Internet Explorer is already installed on your Windows Me computer. If all goes according to the Department of Justice plan, your computer manufacturer will have decided for you whether to include Netscape Navigator or Microsoft Internet Explorer. Whatever they choose, you may want to try out the competition. Here's how to exercise your choice and get the browser you want. One of the nicest aspects of this choice is that it doesn't cost you any money. Microsoft has been giving away copies of Internet Explorer since the original version came out. Netscape, which had an on-again-off-again policy about giving away copies of its full-blown product, decided once and for all in early 1998 to give away the whole browser. If you're looking at Netscape, you see references to a suite of programs named Netscape Communicator, which includes Navigator (the web browser) in addition to a mail program and a Web page editor, in case you want to create your own Web pages. (Visit our Web site, at `http://net.gurus.com`, to find out how to create Web pages.)

Even if you already have a copy of Navigator or Internet Explorer, new versions come out every 20 minutes or so, and it's worth knowing how to upgrade because occasionally the new versions fix some bugs — that's what's supposed to make them better than the old versions. The steps are relatively simple:

1. **Get a copy of the Navigator or Internet Explorer installation package on your computer.**

2. **Unpack the installation package.**

3. **Install the software.**

Because computers are involved, each of these steps is, naturally, a little more difficult than necessary.

About downloading a browser: Who, what, where

You can download both Netscape Navigator (and its big brother, Communicator) and Microsoft Internet Explorer from the Net. If you have access to any web browser, try the manufacturers' Web sites:

✔ **Netscape home page (for Navigator or Communicator):**
   `http://home.netscape.com`

✔ **Microsoft home page (for Internet Explorer):**
   `http://www.microsoft.com/ie`

Because both companies are eager to have you try their product, they make it easy to find the Download link for their newest product. At the time we write this chapter, Netscape has a link labeled Download on its home page (it's a round button at the top with a downward-pointing arrow that says, of course, *Download* under it). This link takes you directly to a page that enables you to choose the Netscape product you want (Navigator or Communicator) and download it. At the same time, the Microsoft home page has a link to `http://www.microsoft.com/windows/ie`.

Several other sites not affiliated with the manufacturers also enable you to download the browser software. The advantage is that the sites are some-times not as crowded as the manufacturers' sites and therefore download more quickly. Their disadvantage is that they may not have absolutely the latest version, and they probably don't have the selection of download options that the manufacturers do. Still, if you can't get through to Netscape or Microsoft, you can try

✔ **TUCOWS (The Ultimate Collection of Internet Software):**
   `http://www.tucows.com`

   TUCOWS sites are distributed all over the United States (and the world), so you have to pick one that's close to you (of course, that means more reliable downloads). After you do, look for a category of software named Windows 98 or, if they're quick about it, Windows Me, and then look for Browsers and Accessories.

✔ **The Consummate Winsock Applications page:**
   `http://cws.internet.com`

   You can probably find Internet browsers by browsing The Consummate Winsock's 32-bit programs and then looking for web browsers. You may be able to get directly there by going to `http://cws.internet.com/web.html`. (Hey, this is the Internet — things change every day — but we're trying to help out here.)

After you get to any of these sites, you notice that each of these browsers comes in a dizzying number of versions. We can help you make some sense of them all: Basically, each browser comes in about four (count 'em — four) flavors:

- ✔ The latest and greatest, with all the trimmings. This is probably version 4.something, and is more than 10 megabytes of program to download.

- ✔ The latest and greatest, "lite." Also version 4.something, but they left out some things that really aren't that essential for most people. The advantage is that your download takes less time.

- ✔ The previous version, with all the trimmings. This is probably version 3.something. It's also probably pretty big (but not as big as the latest version). It may be more reliable, at the expense of not doing some of the latest whiz-bang browser tricks.

- ✔ The previous version, "lite." Relatively small and relatively reliable, but at the shallow end of the feature pool.

Which do you pick? Because you're running Windows Me, you can probably skip the previous versions. After all, they were engineered to run well on Windows 9x. As far as whether you want the "lite" version or the full version, the answer depends on how patient you can be and how good your modem connection is. If you have the time (and the space on your hard drive), you may as well go for the whole thing. If you have any trouble with the download, you may want to consult Chapter 13 for more information about downloading files from the Internet.

You have another option than downloading the latest version, and it's worth considering. Both Netscape and Microsoft (and a number of computer stores) will sell you a CD with the complete browser on it. Now that the browsers have gotten so big, this option can be attractive. You don't tie up your computer for three or more hours downloading software, you have an actual physical CD in case you have to reinstall the software, and Netscape even gives you a discount on Netscape stuff (T-shirts and the like) if you buy its CD. Although the CDs also come in a zillion versions, the basic ones with the software on them are all about $20 — not free, but a good deal for all that software.

The CDs also come with two valuable features: installation instructions and a technical-support telephone number. Although we give you as much detail as we can regarding installation, because everything we're talking about is coming from the World Wide Web, it could change between today, when you're reading this chapter, and tomorrow, when you go to try it out. By the way, both Netscape and Internet Explorer are also available in versions for Windows 9x, Windows 3.1, the Macintosh, and most versions of UNIX (except Internet Explorer, which is available for only HP-UX and Solaris. You're unlikely to be using either, so ignore it). So everyone in your home or organization can use the same browser, if you want.

Downloading your browser

You've found a Web page that has the version of Microsoft Internet Explorer, Netscape Navigator, or Netscape Communicator that you want. You've answered questions (maybe many questions, maybe just one), and your browser has asked whether and where you want to save the distribution file you're about to download. We suggest a folder with a devilishly hip and cool name like, well, Download. That keeps all the browser distribution and installation files separate from whatever other work you've been doing and proves to be a nicely convenient place to later store other downloaded items. Now, you're probably looking at a dialog box like the one shown in Figure 8-6 or Figure 8-7. Here's what to do:

Figure 8-6:
Put your downloaded files where you want them.

Figure 8-7:
The message may also look like this.

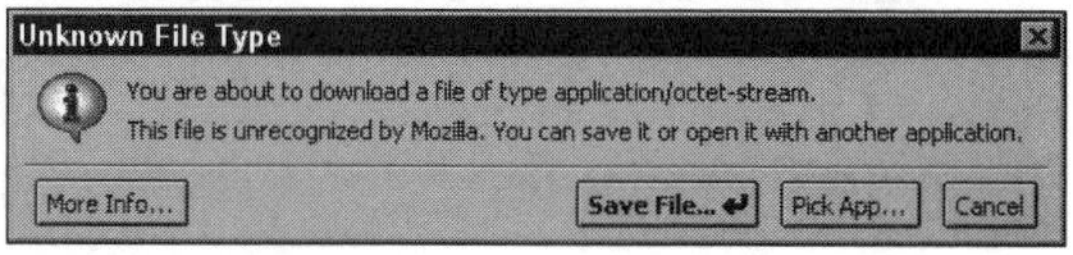

1. **The dialog box asks whether you would rather save it to disk or run it from where it is.**

   We shy away from the latter because it can cause all kinds of problems, not the least of which is not being able to find what you downloaded.

2. **Click OK.**

   Another dialog box appears, wanting to know *where* you want to save the file. You find yourself in a place named My Documents. This cleverly monikered locale is sort of a catchall for pretty much anything. There's even an icon for it on the desktop. Right now, your computer thinks that you want to save the file in My Documents. Rein it in by moving to the next step.

3. Click the new-folder button.

It's the one to the right of the Save in drop-down list, with the picture of the folder with the sparkle on it. Windows obliges and creates a new folder for you, with the inspired name of New Folder. You're also set to rename this folder.

4. Type the aforementioned fiendishly creative name Download **(or what-ever you choose) and press Enter.**

Your folder is renamed, although your download hasn't started yet. Your browser should still be suggesting a more or less cryptic name for the distribution file you're about to download.

5. Double-click the folder you just created.

Your browser is now ready to save the distribution file you're download-ing into your new folder.

6. Click the Save button.

The download begins.

Finished downloading so soon? If you downloaded Microsoft Internet Explorer and your download finished in less than an hour (perhaps in just several minutes), you're in for a surprise: The file you just downloaded isn't really Internet Explorer. It's an installation program that goes out to the Internet and fetches the rest of the program.

If you downloaded from TUCOWS, you probably got all of Internet Explorer and you can skip to the following section. If you downloaded from The Consummate Winsock page or the Microsoft page, you probably got the installation program. Here's how to get the whole thing:

1. Switch to the desktop.

If you're not already there, click the little green icon on the Quick Launch bar or minimize any windows you may have open so that you can see the desktop and double-click on My Documents. Here's another easy way to get there: Click the Start button, choose Documents⇨My Documents, and, while your mouse pointer is on the My Documents menu item, double-click it.

2. Find the folder you just created with the name Download.

If you already have lots of items in your My Documents folder, you may have to look for it, although you can always press the D key repeatedly until the Download folder is highlighted. (Neat-o trick, eh? Just don't do it too fast, or you'll miss it.)

3. Double-click the Download folder.

A new window opens with the contents of the Download folder inside, including the file you just downloaded, probably named ie5setup.

4. Double-click the file you just downloaded.

Wouldn't you know it: another wizard — in this case, the Internet Explorer Active Setup Wizard.

5. Click Next.

The program license agreement appears.

6. If you can tolerate the license terms, click the I accept option, and then click Next.

Like you have any choice. Download options appear.

7. Click the Download only option, and then click Next.

We *strongly* recommend this option. That way, if you have to install the program again, you already have the files you need.

8. Select the flavor of Internet Explorer you want, and then click Next.

The Browser only option is enough for most people; if you have time to burn or a fast connection, however, by all means go for Full installation.

10. Just make sure that the United States is clicked (unless you're on another continent), and click Next.

The wizard suggests saving the Internet Explorer files in a folder named Internet Explorer 5.0 Setup. We like it.

11. Click Next.

You're asked from which location you want to download. This list should look familiar — it's the same list of places from which you got to download the setup program.

12. Select a site from the list of download sites and click Next.

You can select pretty much at random, as long as it's on the same continent you are, although choosing something close to you is a good bet.

13. Go out for pizza (lots of pizza).

Congratulations: You've downloaded the installation program for Netscape Navigator (or Communicator) or for Microsoft Internet Explorer. Oh, and you've had some pizza. That's always cause for celebration.

Got it! Now what? (The installation)

After you have the program, you have to unpack it and install it. If you got Navigator or Internet Explorer on CD-ROM, follow the instructions that come with it. They vary depending on the version of the software you have but are generally along the lines of "Put the CD into your CD-ROM drive and press the Install button when the CD's Welcome screen appears." After you get past the startup screen, the process to install software from the CD is exactly the same as to install the downloaded version. (It's the same program, after all.)

If you downloaded the Netscape Navigator (or Communicator) or Microsoft Internet Explorer distribution file on your hard disk, follow these instructions:

1. **Switch to Windows Explorer.**

   If you already have a copy of Windows Explorer running, click its icon on the taskbar. If you don't, use the Start⇨Programs⇨Window Explorer command to start one.

2. **Find the folder you just created, probably in disk drive C.**

   If you were following along, it's in a folder named either C:\Download or C:\Internet Explorer 5.0 Setup. You may have to scroll up or down the Windows Explorer window to find it. If the C: disk drive has a plus sign in front of it, you may have to click the plus sign.

3. **Click the appropriate folder.**

   The contents of the folder appear, including the file you just down-loaded. If you downloaded Navigator, the file is probably named some-thing like c32e473; if you downloaded Explorer, it has a zillion files, including one named something like ie5setup. In either case, you're look-ing for a file that Windows Me tells you is an application. If you ended up with a file that Windows Explorer tells you is a zip file or a WinZip file or an archive file, your file has been freeze-dried before it arrived on your computer. Chapter 13 contains complete instructions on how to add water to zip files so that you can use what's in them.

4. **After you've found the appropriate application file, double-click it.**

   The installation process begins.

After you've found your new browser, installing it is easy. When you start the application file you just found, you're asked a bunch of questions, all of which have answers like Yes, Accept, Next, or Install. You get the idea: The Microsoft and Netscape folks have made a bunch of perfectly reasonable choices you can deviate from if you're feeling perverse, although we recom-mend just going with the flow here. For basic browser installations, that method has always worked well for us. (Microsoft Internet Explorer may rec-ommend only updating newer components, and we think that's a good recommendation.)

When the installation is complete and you've given the obvious answer to a few more questions ("No, don't read the Readme file" is the only one that may trip you up), the installation program asks whether it can restart your computer. Click Yes unless you're in the middle of other work — in that case, finish your work and restart your computer yourself.

You're ready to try out your shiny, new Internet browser. If you didn't set up your Internet connection to automatically dial the phone, as explained in Chapter 3, you may want to connect to your Internet provider or online service because the first thing your new browser wants to do is to display a Web page.

Click your new browser's artistically crafted icon. The first time you run Netscape, you see a bunch of legal boilerplate stuff describing the license conditions for Netscape. If you can stand the conditions (many people can), click to indicate your acceptance. Netscape then starts up. It may want to connect to the Netscape Web page so that you can register your copy of Netscape — follow its instructions.

One point of note here is the Netscape Net Center. You no longer have to pay for Communicator, although they still want you to register. When you finish your installation, you're whisked away to register for a Net Center account.

The first time you run Internet Explorer, it may run the Internet Connection Wizard, which offers to help you get connected to the Internet. If so, check out Chapter 3, where we explain the wizard in excruciating detail. Don't worry: If you already have an Internet connection that works, you don't have to create a new one. You have a chance to tell the wizard about your existing connection.

Unless you need the disk space, we recommend keeping the files in the C:\My Documents\Download or C:\Internet Explorer 5 Setup folders, in case you have to reinstall your web browser. If you have a tape backup or one of the newer, large "floppy" drives (from Iomega, SyQuest, Imation, and others) that hold 100 or 250 megabytes or more, you may want to copy the files you downloaded to someplace where you can keep them. It's probably not worth a great deal of effort, however, to copy them to regular old floppy disks.

If you're upgrading from an older version of Netscape to a newer one, you can install the new version to replace the old one. The newer version of the Netscape browsers offers what Netscape calls Profiles. Each unique user can have his own shiny set of personalized bookmarks and browser settings. Neat-o torpedo! Don't worry about your old settings. They're rolled into the new installation.

Chapter 9

Working Web Wonders

In This Chapter

▶ Keeping track of your favorite sites

▶ Making your Web journey faster

▶ Clearing some room on your screen

▶ Filling in Web forms

▶ Saving pages for posterity

▶ Doing more than one thing at a time

▶ Printing pages from the Web

▶ Getting plugged in with plug-ins

*I*f you know how to find your way around the Web, you are ready for to some comparatively advanced features so that you can start to feel like a Web pro in no time. Try poking around. The best way to find out what you can do is by trying everything. You have this book, so you could resort to reading it, of course, but why spoil all the fun?

Where Did I See That?

You really want to show a friend that exotic cooking page you found with the recipe for chilled snail on crabgrass, but you lost the slip of paper on which you wrote the URL. Fortunately, browsers provide a handy way for you to remember sites and not have to write down those nasty URLs just to have to type them again later.

Although the name varies, the idea is simple: You tell your browser to add to a list the URL of the Web page now displayed. Later, when you want to go back, you just go to your list and pick out that cool site. Internet Explorer calls these hot spots *favorites;* Netscape calls them *bookmarks.*

Playing Favorites in Internet Explorer

Internet Explorer lets you add the current page to your Windows Me Favorites folder. This Favorites folder is shared, however, with other programs on your computer. Because Microsoft preloads *its* favorites to your Favorites folder, it's a jumble (in our opinion) of Web pages, files, and other things.

To add the current page to your Favorites folder, choose Favorites⇨Add to Favorites from the menu. To see your Favorites folder, choose Favorites from the menu bar; your favorite Web pages appear right on the menu. Another way to take a look at your favorite sites is to click the Favorites button on the toolbar. The list of Web sites appears on the left side of your Internet Explorer window. To display one of these Web pages, just click the item on the Favorites list. When you want to make the Favorites list go away, click the Favorites button again.

To organize your Favorites folder, choose Favorites⇨Organize Favorites. You see the Organize Favorites dialog box, as shown in Figure 9-1.

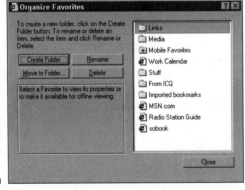

Figure 9-1:
Your favorite
Web pages
appear in
the Organize
Favorites
window.

Here are things you can do to organize your favorite Web sites:

✔ Change the order of the list by dragging items up or down the list.

✔ Get rid of them by selecting a Web page and clicking the Delete button.

✔ Change the names of the Web page on the list by selecting the Web page and clicking the Rename button. You can't change the Web page's name on the Web, of course, but you can change the name that appears on your Favorites list.

✔ Create subfolders in the Favorites folder so that you can store different
   types of files in different folders. To create a folder, click the Create New
   Folder button (the button with the yellow folder with a little sparkle,
   near the upper-right corner of the window). To move an item in the
   Favorites window into a folder, click the item, click the Move button, and
   select the folder to move it to. You can see the contents of a folder by
   double-clicking it.

When you're done organizing your favorite items, click the Close button.

The folders you create in the Organize Favorites window appear on your
Favorites menu, and the items you put in the folders appear on submenus. To
return to a Web page you've added to your Favorites folder, just choose it
from the Favorites menu.

In Windows Me, the Favorites folder usually appears on your Start menu. You
can double-click the folder to open it and double-click an item to return to
that item. If the item is a Web page, your browser fires up and (if you're connected to the Internet) displays the Web page.

Bookmarking Netscape

The Netscape version of favorites lurks under the Bookmarks menu. To add a
bookmark for a Web page displayed in Netscape 4.0, choose Communicator⇨
Bookmarks⇨Add Bookmark or press Ctrl+D. You can see your bookmarks as
entries on the menu that appears when you click the Bookmarks Quick File
button, to the left of the Location box. To go to one of the pages on your
bookmark list, just choose its entry from this menu.

If you're like most users, your bookmark menu gets bigger and bigger and
crawls down your screen and eventually ends up flopping down on the floor,
which is both unattractive and unsanitary. Fortunately, you can smoosh (technical term) your menu into a more tractable form. Choose Communicator⇨
Bookmarks⇨Edit Bookmarks or press Ctrl+B to display your Bookmarks
window, as shown in Figure 9-2.

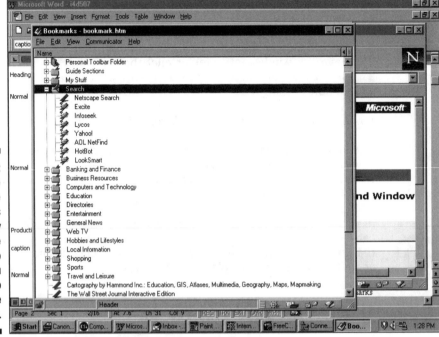

Figure 9-2:
The
Netscape
Bookmarks
window
shows the
list of Web
pages you
want to
come
back to.

Here are things you can do with the Bookmarks window:

- Because all these bookmarks are "live," you can go to any of them by clicking them. (You can leave this window open while you move around the Web in your main Netscape window.)

- Delete a bookmark by selecting it and pressing the Del key.

- Change the order of the bookmarks by dragging them up and down the list.

- Rename a bookmark by clicking it and choosing Edit⇨Bookmark Properties from the Bookmarks window menu bar. You can type a comment about the Web page too, if you want.

- If your list gets really long and you can't find the Web page you're looking for, choose Edit⇨Find in Bookmarks to search for a word or phrase that appears in a bookmark title, URL, or comment.

- You can also add separator lines and submenus to organize your bookmarks and make the individual menus less unwieldy. Submenus look like folders in the Bookmarks window. Choose File⇨New Separator from the Bookmarks window's menu bar to add a separator line. Choose File⇨New Folder to add a new submenu. (Netscape asks you to type the name of the submenu before it creates the folder.) You can then drag the bookmarks, separators, and folders up and down to where you want them in the Bookmarks window. Drag an item to a folder to put it in that folder's submenu, and double-click a folder to display or hide that submenu.

Because any changes you make in the Bookmarks window are reflected immediately on the Bookmarks menu, it's easy to fiddle with the bookmarks until you get something you like.

When you're done fooling with your bookmarks, choose File⇨Close or press Ctrl+W to close the Bookmarks window.

Netscape 4.x also has a cool feature that enables you to see which of the items on your bookmark list have been updated since you last looked at them. Open the Bookmarks window as described earlier in this section and then choose View⇨Update Bookmarks from the menu bar in the Bookmarks window. A dialog box asks which bookmarks you want to check: all your bookmarks, or just the one (or ones) you selected. Click the Start Checking button. Netscape checks the contents of all Web pages on your bookmarks list to check whether the page has changed since you last looked at it! When Netscape is done checking the Web pages on your bookmarks list, it displays a message telling you how many have changed. The icons in the Bookmarks window reveal which pages have changed: The ones with little sparkles have new material, the ones with question marks are the ones Netscape isn't sure about, and the ones that look normal haven't changed.

Making the Paint Dry Faster

Unless you have a cable modem or a high-speed dedicated connection rather than an ordinary dial-up account, you probably spend a great deal of time wishing that the process of getting to stuff on the Web were much faster. Some people compare Web browsing over a slow modem to watching paint dry. (John has a high-speed dedicated connection, and Carol has a cable modem, and they spend a certain amount of time waiting for the Web anyway. Margy, who has a slow modem, has taken up knitting.) This section shows you a handful of tricks you can use to try to speed things up.

Pick a faster place to start

In Internet Explorer: Internet Explorer starts by displaying the Microsoft home page. You can change that start page, or you can tell Internet Explorer to use a blank page. Follow these steps to change your start page:

1. **Display the Web page you want to use as your start page.**

   For example, you may want to start at the Yahoo page, as described in Chapter 10, or Internet Gurus Central, at `http://net.gurus.com`.

2. **Choose Tools⇨Internet Options from the menu.**

   You see the Internet Options dialog box.

3. Find the General tab along the top of the dialog box and click it.

If you click the Use Current button, the URL of the current page appears in the Address box. You can also type in the Address box the address of the home page you want Internet Explorer to use or click the Use Blank page option.

Choose to start with a blank page or a start page that doesn't have many pictures: By starting with a Web page that loads faster or with no page, you don't have to wait long to start browsing.

In Netscape: When Netscape starts up, it loads the large and attractive Netscape home page. After one or two times, beautiful as the home page is, you may find that you can do without it. You can tell Netscape which Web page to display when you start the program:

1. Choose Edit⇨Preferences.

You see the Preferences dialog box.

2. Click the Navigator category.

You see a setting labeled Navigator starts with.

3. If you want to start with no Web page, click Blank Page. If you want to start with a page you specify, click Home Page, click in the box below it, and type the name of a page you would rather see (your Internet Service Provider's home page, for example).

You also have the option of starting where you left off last time, by clicking Last page visited.

4. Click OK.

Skip the pix

You can save a great deal of time by skipping the pictures when you're browsing the Web. True, the pages don't look as snazzy, but they load like the wind. If you decide that you want to see the missing pictures after all, you can still do so.

In Internet Explorer: You can tell Internet Explorer not to bother loading images by choosing Tools⇨Internet Options from the menu, clicking the Advanced tab, and scrolling down to the Multimedia section. If a check mark appears in the Show pictures box, click the box to remove the check mark. Then click OK. Where pictures usually appear, you see a little box with three shapes in it. If you want to see a particular picture, right-click the little box and choose Show Picture from the menu that appears.

In Netscape: Choose Edit⇨Preferences from the menu and then click the Advanced category. Uncheck Auto Load Images. At every place on the page where an image should go, Netscape displays a box with three colored shapes. To see a particular image, right-click the three-shape box and choose Load Image from the menu that appears.

Catch up with your cache

When Internet Explorer or Netscape retrieves a page you have asked to see, it stores the page on your disk. If you ask for the same page again five minutes later, the program doesn't have to retrieve the page again — it can reuse the copy it already has. If you tell the program not to load images, for example, you get a fair number of them anyway because they have already been downloaded.

The space your browser uses to store pages is its *cache* (pronounced "cash" because it's French and gives your cache more *cachet*). The more space you tell your browser to use for its cache, the more likely it is that a page will appear more quickly the second time you look at it.

In Internet Explorer: To set the size of the Internet Explorer cache, follow these steps:

1. **Choose Tools⇨Internet Options from the menu.**

   You see the Internet Options dialog box.

2. **Click the General tab.**

3. **Click the Settings button in the Temporary Internet files box.**

   You see the Settings dialog box, with information about the cache. (Many versions of Internet Explorer never call it a cache — guess they don't speak French.)

4. **Click the slider on the Amount of disk space to use or Maximum size line and move it to about 40 MB or 10 percent, whichever is less.**

   If you have tons of empty disk space, you can slide it rightward to 80 MB. If you're short on disk space, move it leftward to 1 percent or 2 percent.

5. **Click OK twice.**

In Netscape: To set the size of the Netscape cache, follow these steps:

1. **Choose Edit⇨Preferences from the menu.**

   You see the Preferences dialog box.

2. Double-click the Advanced category and click the Cache category.

The Disk Cache box shows the maximum size of the cache in kilobytes (KB): We like to set Disk Cache to at least 10,000 KB (10 MB). Set it to a higher number if you have a large hard disk with loads of free space — the more space your cache can occupy, the more often you can load a Web page quickly from the cache rather than slowly from the Net.

3. Click OK.

Some of us hardly ever exit from our browsers, which is probably not a good idea for our long-term mental stability. If you are one of us, however, remember that the pages your browser has cached aren't reloaded from the Web (they're taken from your disk) until you reload them. If you want to make sure that you're getting fresh pages, reload pages that you think may have changed since you last visited. Your browser is supposed to check whether a saved page has changed, but because the check sometimes doesn't work perfectly, an occasional Reload command for pages that change frequently, such as stock prices or the weather report, is advisable.

Clear the Deck

Netscape and Internet Explorer have so many buttons, icons, and boxes near the top of the window that not much space is left to display the Web page.

In Internet Explorer: Those folks at Microsoft noticed this problem and, taking a cue from some old word-processing programs, came up with a toolbar button to deal with it. On the Internet Explorer toolbar is a button named Fullscreen. When you press this button, everything on your screen disappears, and the whole thing becomes the browser's playground, with the exception of a small toolbar at the top of the screen. This technique is very useful if you're doing some serious surfing for a while and don't want to think about what else might be going on in your computer. Naturally, because the Fullscreen button is one of those on the small toolbar that remains, you can go back to a regular Internet Explorer window.

If that's a little drastic for your tastes, you can selectively remove things from the Internet Explorer window:

- ✔ To get rid of the toolbar (the row of buttons just below the menu), choose View➪Toolbars➪Standard Buttons. Most buttons on the toolbar have keyboard equivalents, some of which we describe in this chapter.

- ✔ To suppress the Address bar and the Address box, choose View➪ Toolbars➪Address Bar. This action isn't such a great idea because you need that Address box for typing URLs.

- ✔ To get rid of the status bar (the gray bar at the bottom of the Internet Explorer window), choose View➪Status Bar.

Give the same command again to restore the item you got rid of. Although we prefer to keep these items on-screen most of the time, your tastes may differ, and we have pretty big screens.

In Netscape: You can clear off a little more space in the Netscape window by using commands from the Options or View menu:

- ✔ To clear off the Location box, choose View⇨Hide Location Toolbar. This action isn't such a good idea most of the time because the Location box shows you the URL of the page you're looking at and lets you type a new URL to go to.

- ✔ To say sayonara to the toolbar (the row of buttons just below the menu), choose View⇨Hide Navigation Toolbar. Most people use the Back button all the time, but you won't miss it if you remember that pressing Alt+← does the same thing.

To restore any of the things you just blew away, give the same command again.

Forms, Forms, Forms

Back in the Dark Ages of the Web (that is, in 1993), Web pages were just pages to look at. Because that wasn't anywhere near enough fun nor complicated enough, Web forms were invented. A *form* is sort of like a paper form, with boxes you can fill out and then send in. Techies call the boxes *fields.* Figure 9-3 shows a typical form.

The top two lines in the form are fill-in text boxes in which you type, in this case, your name and e-mail address. Under that is a set of *check boxes,* in which you check whichever ones apply (all of them, we hope), and a set of *radio buttons,* which are similar to check boxes except that you can choose only one of them. Under that is a *list box,* in which you can choose one of the possibilities in the box. In most cases, you see more entries than can fit in the box, so you scroll them up and down. Although you can usually choose only one entry, some list boxes let you choose more.

At the bottom of the form are two buttons. The one on the left clears the form fields to their initial state and sends nothing, and the one on the right, known as the *Submit* button, sends the filled-out form back to the web server for processing.

After the data is sent from the form back to the web server, it's entirely up to the server how to interpret it.

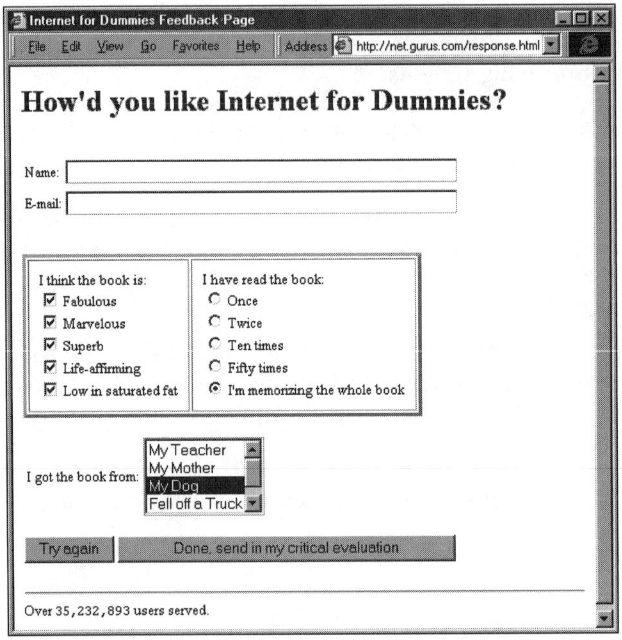

Internet for Dummies Feedback Page

File Edit View Go Favorites Help | Address http://net.gurus.com/response.html

How'd you like Internet for Dummies?

Name:

E-mail:

I think the book is:
☑ Fabulous
☑ Marvelous
☑ Superb
☑ Life-affirming
☑ Low in saturated fat

I have read the book:
○ Once
○ Twice
○ Ten times
○ Fifty times
◉ I'm memorizing the whole book

I got the book from:
My Teacher
My Mother
My Dog
Fell off a Truck

[Try again] [Done, send in my critical evaluation]

Over 35,232,893 users served.

Figure 9-3:
A Web form.
(Oh, wow!)

Save It for a Rainy Day

Frequently, you see something on a Web page that's worth saving for later. Sometimes it's a Web page full of interesting information or a picture or some other type of file. Fortunately, saving stuff is easy.

When you save a Web page, you have to decide whether to save only the text that appears or the entire HTML version of the page, with the format codes. (To find out all about HTML, visit our Web site, at http://net.gurus.com. You can also save the pictures that appear on Web pages.

In either Netscape or Internet Explorer, choose File➪Save As to save the current Web page in a file. You see the standard Save As dialog box, in which you specify the name to save the incoming file. Click in the Save as type box to determine how to save the page: Choose Plain Text to save only the text of the page, with little notes where pictures occur. Choose HTML or HTML Files to save the entire HTML file. Then click the Save or OK button.

To save an image you see on a Web page, right-click the image (click the image with your right mouse button). Choose Save Image As or Save Picture As from the menu that appears. When you see the Save As dialog box, move to the folder or directory in which you want to save the graphics file, type a filename in the File name box, and click the Save or OK button.

A note about copyright: Contrary to popular belief, almost all Web pages, along with almost everything else on the Internet, are copyrighted by their authors. If you save a Web page or a picture from a Web page, you don't necessarily have permission to use it any way you want. Before you reuse the text or pictures in any way, send an e-mail message to the owner of the site. If an address doesn't appear on the page, write to webmaster@domain.com, replacing domain.com with the domain name part of the URL of the Web page. For permission to use information on the http://net.gurus.com/books.html page, for example, write to webmaster@gurus.com.

Touch Your Nose and Rub Your Belly

Netscape and Internet Explorer are known in the trade as *multithreaded* programs. What this term means in practice is that the program can do several things at a time.

If you ask Netscape or Internet Explorer to begin downloading a big file, it displays a small window. The Netscape version of this window displays a "thermometer" showing the download progress; Internet Explorer shows tiny pages flying from one folder to another. Although some people consider watching the thermometer grow or the pages fly entertainment (we do when we're tired enough), you can click back to the main Netscape or Internet Explorer window and continue surfing. You can also have several web browser windows open at a time. Press Ctrl+N or choose File⇨New⇨Window (in Internet Explorer) or File⇨New⇨Navigator Window (in Netscape 4.0) to create a new window. We find this technique the most useful way to look at two related pages side by side (or overlapping) on-screen.

Doing two or three things at a time in your browser when you have a dial-up Net connection is not unlike squeezing blood from a turnip — there's only so much blood there, no matter how hard you squeeze. In this case, the blood is the amount of data your Internet Service Provider (ISP) can pump through your modem. A single download task can keep your modem close to 100 percent busy *if* (and that's a big *if*) the data you're downloading arrives at your ISP faster than your modem can handle it. Even if it does, if you're viewing a Web page while you're doing a big download, things usually work okay because you spend a fair amount of time looking at what the web browser is displaying; the download can then run while you think.

What happens more often in this age of Internet traffic jams is that you, your modem, and your ISP are all waiting around for data to trickle its way across the Internet. When that happens, browsing Web pages doesn't make your downloads take any longer. At times like these, the fact that Netscape and Internet Explorer let you start two (or more) download tasks at one time can be handy. Until you're using up the whole capacity of the line between your modem and your ISP, requesting more Web pages or downloads at the same time doesn't slow you down. (Asking for multiple things at one time creates more load on your ISP and on the high-capacity lines that form the major arteries of the Internet, but not by so much as to make too much difference for anyone.)

So how do you find out whether your modem is waiting around for data to arrive from the Internet? If you have an external modem, it's easy. The modem probably has a light labeled RD (for Receive Data), or perhaps just Receive. When you're downloading information from the Internet, it should be on almost steadily. If it is, your modem is running at full speed. If it isn't, you have joined what has come to be called the World Wide Wait. If you have an internal modem or a PC Card modem, determining how fast data is arriving at your PC can be a little more difficult. You can get a rough idea by double-clicking the dial-up icon (the one with the two little computer screens) near the right end of your taskbar. (We introduce this icon in Chapter 4, in the section about monitoring your Dial-Up Networking connection.)

Double-clicking this icon displays the Communications Statistics dialog box, as shown over in Figure 4-5. If the number of bytes received is counting up in fits and starts, you're probably waiting for the Internet, not for your modem.

Making Treeware (Printing)

To print a page from Internet Explorer or Netscape, just click the Print button on the toolbar, press Ctrl+P, or choose File⇨Print. Reformatting the page to print it can take awhile, so patience is a virtue. Fortunately, Netscape and Internet Explorer each display a progress window to keep you apprised of how they're doing.

Keep Your Cookie Crumbs Off My Computer

In Chapter 1, we mention cookies — not the kind you eat, but the kind Web sites put on your computer so that they can identify you and remember something about you. We also mention there that many of us have different feelings about cookies. Some of us don't care about them, and some of us view them as an unconscionable invasion of privacy. You get to decide for yourself. Both Internet Explorer and Netscape Navigator let you control whether and when cookies are stored on your computer.

In Internet Explorer, use the Tools⇨Internet Options command to display the Internet Options dialog box. The Advanced tab in this dialog box contains a *long* list of settings that control how Internet Explorer works. It's such a long list, in fact, that we could write a whole chapter about it. But we don't. Just scroll about halfway down the list (using the scrollbar). You see a heading with a little lock on it labeled Security; it has a subsection with a little Caution symbol labeled Cookies: In that subsection, you see these options:

- ✔ **Always accept cookies:** This option is for those of us who don't care what computers remember about us. It makes for the least amount of nagging from Web sites and from the browser, and we like that.

- ✔ **Prompt before accepting cookies:** For the truly discriminating, you get to decide on a case-by-case basis whether the site you're looking at gets to put a cookie on your computer.

- ✔ **Disable all cookie use:** Most Web sites still work if you disable cookies, although they may spend a certain amount of time nagging you about who you are and asking whether they've ever heard of you.

Choose whichever one you're comfortable with.

The situation is similar in Netscape Navigator. The command is Edit⇨ Preferences Advanced, and it shows a Preferences dialog box with a list of option categories on the left and settings associated with those options on the right. The last of the major headings is Advanced. Click on it and you see some settings on the right side of the dialog box, including settings for cookies. The options are similar to those in Internet Explorer:

- ✔ Accept all cookies.

- ✔ Accept only cookies that get sent back to the originating server. Unlike Internet Explorer, Navigator is willing to keep track of which cookie belongs to which Web site. Even those of us concerned about privacy like this option.

- ✔ Disable cookies.

Additionally, Navigator is willing to warn you whenever it's about to accept a cookie, no matter where it gets sent back. Check the Warn me before accepting a cookie option if you want to know.

Figure 9-4 shows the dialog boxes that help you control cookie behavior.

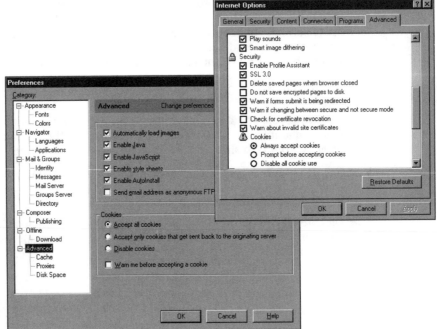

Figure 9-4:
Your web
browser,
cookies,
and you.

Plug In to What's Happening

As Netscape has evolved from an unknown newcomer in the Web biz to the big gorilla on the block, it has gained a few new features. Lots and lots of features. Lots and lots and lots of features. Netscape already had about as many features as any single human could comprehend, but just in case someone somewhere understood the whole thing, you can now extend Netscape capabilities with *plug-ins*, or add-on programs that glue themselves to Netscape and add even more features.

Not to be outdone, each version of Internet Explorer tries to match the Netscape features. In addition to using plug-ins, you can also extend the already excessive Internet Explorer capabilities by using *ActiveX* controls (formerly called OCX controls, formerly called VBX controls, but they keep changing the name as soon as people start to figure out what they are).

Web pages with pictures are old hat. Now, Web pages have to have pictures that sing and dance or ticker-style messages that move across the page or video clips. Every month, new types of information delivery appear on the Web.

What's a web browser to do with all these new kinds of information? Get the plug-in program that handles that kind of information and glue it onto Netscape or Internet Explorer. You *Star Trek* fans can think of plug-ins as parasitic life-forms that attach themselves to your browser and enhance its intelligence.

This section is just an introduction to the vastly complex and mind-boggling array of plug-ins, helper applications, and viewers available for Netscape, Internet Explorer, and Opera. For more information about the exciting world of plug-ins and their ilk, head over to Chapter 11.

Popular plug-ins

Here are some useful plug-ins:

- **RealPlayer:** Plays sound files as you download them. (Other programs have to wait until the entire file has downloaded before beginning to play.) Microsoft NetShow does much the same thing.
- **QuickTime:** Plays video files and VDOLive, which plays video files as you download them.
- **Shockwave:** Plays both audio and video files in addition to other types of animation.
- **iChat:** Lets you use your web browser to participate in online chats.
- **Netscape Live3D, WIRL, Liquid Reality, and other VR plug-ins:** Let you move around inside 3-D "virtual reality" worlds on Web pages.

Using plug-ins

Some of us try to ignore plug-ins as much as possible. It's not that we have anything against them — it's just that we don't particularly care whose bits of computer code are running in our browser to make someone else's Web site look right. Most Web sites that require a plug-in or ActiveX control either automatically download it for you or provide a link close at hand that will download it for you. Your browser may try to let you know that you're about to run someone else's computer code and advise that you engage in safe computing; as long as you stay in the nice neighborhoods on the Web, how-ever, you shouldn't have to worry too much.

If you want to make sure that your browser is fully equipped with plug-ins from reputable sources, you can find Netscape plug-ins and Internet Explorer ActiveX controls at TUCOWS (http://www.tucows.com), the Consummate Winsock Applications page (http://cws.internet.com), the Netscape Web site (http://home.netscape.com), and other reputable sources of software on the Web. That way, when you're surfing an unknown Web site, your browser doesn't have to download any new computer code.

After you have downloaded a plug-in from the Net, run it (double-click its file-name in My Computer or Windows Explorer) to install it. Depending on what the plug-in does, you follow different steps to try it out. Here are some examples:

- **RealPlayer:** Go to the `http://www.realaudio.com` Web page for a list of sites that handle RealAudio sound files. Our favorite site is the National Public Radio Web site (`http://www.npr.org`), where you can hear recent NPR radio stories, and John's site, at `http://iecc.com`, where you can listen to his radio show.

- **iChat:** Go to the iChat Web site, at `http://www.ichat.com`, to join chats with other iChat users or to participate in Internet Relay Chat (IRC) conversations. (See Chapter 14 for more information about IRC and Chapter 11 for more about plug-ins.)

Chapter 10

Finding Stuff on the Net

In This Chapter

▶ Basic search strategies

▶ Finding stuff on the Web

▶ Finding companies on the Web

▶ Finding people on the Web

▶ Online shopping

"**O**kay, all this great stuff is out there on the Net. How do I find it?" That's an excellent question. Thanks for asking that question. Questions like that are what makes this country strong and vibrant. We salute you and say, "Keep asking questions!" Next question, please.

Oh, you want an *answer* to your question. Fortunately, quite a bit of (technical term follows) stuff-finding stuff is on the Net. More particularly, indexes and directories of much of the interesting material are available on the Net.

The Net has different types of indexes and directories for different types of material. Because the indexes tend to be organized, unfortunately, by the type of Internet service they provide rather than by the nature of the material, you find Web resources in one place, e-mail resources in another place, and so on. You can search in dozens of hundreds of different ways, depending on what you're looking for and how you prefer to search. (John has remarked that his ideal restaurant has only one item on the menu, but that it's just what he wants. The Internet is about as far from that ideal as you can possibly imagine.)

To provide a smidgen of structure to this discussion, we describe several different sorts of searches:

✓ **Topics:** Places, things, ideas — anything you want to find out more about

✓ **Companies:** Organizations that you think have a Web site or other Net presence

✓ **People:** Actual human beings whom you want to contact or spy on

✓ **Goods and services:** Stuff to buy, from mortgages to mouthwash

Index, directory — what's the difference?

When we talk about a *directory,* we mean a listing that's divided into named categories and the entries assigned to categories partly or entirely by humans. You look things up by finding a category you want and seeing what it contains. In this book, we would think of the table of contents as a directory.

An *index,* on the other hand, simply collects all the items, extracts keywords from them (by taking all the words except for *the, and,* and the like), and makes a big list. You search the index by specifying some words that seem likely, and it finds all the entries which contain that word. The index in the back of this book is more like an index.

Each has its advantages and disadvantages. Directories are organized so that when you find a category of interest, all items in that category are likely to be related to what you want. Indexes, on the other hand, don't know what the words mean. If you look for program, for example, an index finds computer programs, educational programs, theater programs, and anything else that contains the word. Because indexes can be created largely or completely automatically, indexes on the Net tend to contain many more entries and to be updated more often than directories, which need human catalogers.

Some overlap exists between indexes and directories — Yahoo, the best-known Web page directory, lets you search by keyword, and many indexes divide their entries into general categories that let you limit the search.

To find topics, we use the various online indexes and directories, such as Yahoo and AltaVista. To find companies, we also use *WHOIS,* the main directory of Internet domains. To find people, however, we use directories of people, which are (fortunately) different from directories of Web pages. Wondering what we're talking about? Read on for an explanation!

The Five-Minute Guide to Searching

When we're looking for topics on the Net, we always begin with one of the Web guides (indexes and directories) discussed in this section.

You use them all in more or less the same way:

1. **Start your web browser, such as Netscape or Internet Explorer.**
2. **Pick a directory or index you like, and tell your browser to go to the index or directory's home page.**

    We list the URLs (page names) of the home pages later in this section.

    After you get there, you can choose between two approaches.

Just for you: The Gurus search page

You may feel a wee bit overwhelmed with all the search directories and indexes we discuss in this chapter. If it makes you feel any better, so do we.

To make a little sense of all this stuff, we made ourselves a search page that connects to all the directories and indexes we use so that we get one-stop searching. You can use it too. Give it a try, at

`http://net.gurus.com/search/`

In the not unlikely event that new search systems are created or some of the existing ones have moved or died, this page gives you our latest greatest list.

> **3. a. If a Search box is available, type some keywords in the box and click Search.**
>
> This is the index approach, to look for topic areas that match your keywords.
>
> After a perhaps long delay (the Web is big), an index page is returned with links to pages that match your keywords. The list of links may be way too long to deal with — like 300,000 of them.
>
> **b. If you see a list of links to topic areas, click a topic area of interest.**
>
> In the directory approach, you begin at a general topic and get more and more specific. Each page has links to pages that get more and more specific until they link to actual pages that are likely to be of interest.

After some clicking around to get the hang of it, you find all sorts of good stuff.

Don't be fooled! Some directories masquerade as indexes and some indexes (like Moose) trick people by looking like directories. These are not Acme Disguise Kits in action, but rather something more insidious: enhanced functionality! Egads! Melodramatics aside, most indexes (indexen?) and directories (directoren?) allow you to do the same things their cousins do. Now you get to pick the one or ones you like best!

You hear a great deal of talk around the Web about *search engines*. That's a fancy way to say stuff-finding stuff. All the directories and indexes we're about to describe are in the broad category called search engines, so don't get upset by some high-falutin'-sounding terms.

Searching in Depth

So much for the theory of searching for stuff on the Net. Now for some practice. (Theory and practice are much further apart in practice than they are in theory.) We use our two favorite search systems for examples: Yahoo, a directory, and AltaVista, an index.

Yahoo!

You can find stuff in Yahoo in two ways. The easier way is just to click from category to category until you find something you like.

We start our Yahoo visit at its home page, `http://www.yahoo.com` (at least the page name doesn't use an exclamation point), which looks like Figure 10-1. A whole bunch of categories and subcategories are listed. You can click any of them to see another page that has yet more subcategories and links to actual Web pages. You can click a link to a page if you see one you like or on a subsubcategory, and so on.

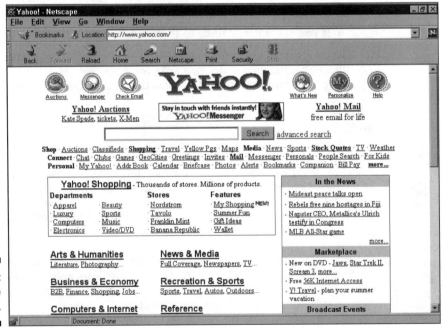

Figure 10-1:
Ready to
Yahoo.

At the top of each Yahoo page is the list of categories, subcategories, and so on, separated by colons, that lead to that page. If you want to back up a few levels and look at different subcategories, just click the place on that list to which you want to back up. After a little clicking up and down, it's second nature. Many pages appear in more than one place in the directory because they fall into more than one category. An advantage of a Web page directory over a card catalog in a library is that although a book can be in only one place on the shelf in the library, Web pages can have as many links referring to them as they want.

Although all the categories in the Yahoo list have plenty of subcategories under them, some have many more than others. If you're looking for a business-related page, it helps to know that Yahoo sticks just about everything commercial under the category Business and Economy, as shown in Figure 10-2. If you were looking for Internet for Dummies Central, for example (which we think people should look for several times a day, at least), you could click your way to it from the Yahoo home page by clicking Business and Economy, clicking Shopping and Services on that page, and then clicking Books and then Booksellers and, finally, Computers (phew!); on that page, you link to three pages, including ours.

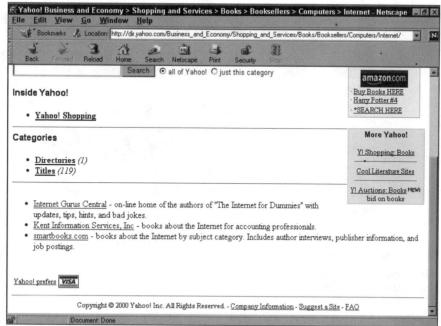

Figure 10-2:
A store-house of commercial information at Yahoo.

If you know in general but not in detail what you're looking for, clicking up and down through the Yahoo directory pages is a good way to narrow your search and find pages of interest.

More Yahoo

"Click Business and Economy, click Shopping and Services on that page, and then click Books and then Booksellers and, finally, Computers." "How the heck did they know which categories to click?" you're doubtless asking. We admit it. We cheated.

Yahoo also lets you search its index by keyword, which is the best way to use it if you have some idea of the title of the page you're looking for. Every Yahoo screen has near the top a search box in which you can type words you want to find in the Yahoo entry for pages of interest. For example, we typed `internet dummies books`, clicked the Search button next to the type-in box, and got the answer shown in Figure 10-3, with one entry for our Web site and one book by Dan Gookin, who also has written the occasional *...For Dummies* book.

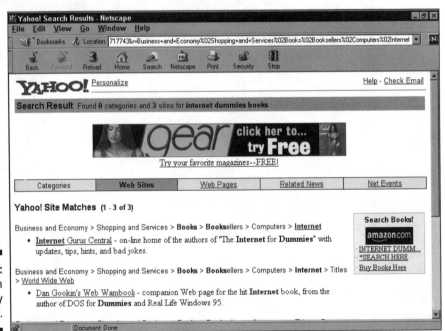

Figure 10-3:
Zeroing in
on quality
literature.

Above each entry Yahoo finds, it reports the category in which it found the entry. Even if the entry isn't quite right, if you click the category, you find other related titles, and some of them may well do the trick.

If Yahoo finds hundreds of pages or categories, you should refine your search. One way to do that is to add extra words to make more specific what you're looking for. If you're looking for a key lime pie recipe (John sent out a good one on the Net about ten years ago) and you search for baking, you get 71 fairly random pages; if you search for key lime pie, however, you get 3 pages, one of which is on the Entertainment:Food and Eating:Recipes:Pie page, which has links to lots of tasty pie recipes.

You can click Advanced Search, next to the Search button, to get to the slightly more advanced Yahoo search page. It lets you limit how far back you want to see pages (three years is the default), and you can tell it to look for either all the words or any of the words you typed.

It's also a cheese grater

Although Yahoo is primarily a directory of resources available on the Web, it has other databases available, each with a link you can click just under the box in which you would enter search terms:

- ✔ **Shopping:** A very good directory of online merchants.
- ✔ **Auctions:** A directory of online auctions. (eBay isn't the only one!)
- ✔ **Yellow Pages:** A business directory (but not our favorite — see the section "Looking for Businesses," later in this chapter).
- ✔ **People Search:** Finds addresses and phone numbers, like a white pages directory (see the "Person to Person" section, later in this chapter).
- ✔ **Maps:** Gets a more or less accurate map of a street address you type.
- ✔ **Travel:** Find rates and other travel-related information.
- ✔ **Classifieds:** Lets you read and submit ads for automobiles, apartments, computers, and jobs.
- ✔ **Personals:** Lets you read and submit ads for dates in all combinations.
- ✔ **Games:** Online entertainment and other time wasters all in one convenient location!
- ✔ **Chat:** Gets you into online chat through the Web.
- ✔ **Clubs:** A sort of digital, online high school reunion.
- ✔ **Mail:** Free, Web-based e-mail service.

✓ **Calendar:** A wall calendar on the Web without any pretty pictures (oh, well).

✓ **Messenger:** The obligatory Yahoo entry into the bursting-at-the-seams instant-messaging arena.

✓ **Companion:** Very cool and highly recommended. Attaches an additional toolbar to your browser that is fully customizable *and has no advertising*. Of course, it gives you so-called one-click access to all the Yahoo services, but it doesn't ask for much personal information and certainly not your name and address.

✓ **My Yahoo:** A customized starting page just for you, with headlines, sports scores, and other news based on your preferences.

✓ **Today's News, Sports, Weather, TV, Stock Quotes, and more:** News from Reuters and other sources.

AltaVista

AltaVista is an index, not a directory. The good news is that it has about ten times as many pages as Yahoo; the bad news is that finding the one you want can be difficult. Regardless of what you ask for, you probably will get 15,000 pages on your first try. After you refine your request a little, however, you can usually get the number of pages down to a somewhat more manageable number.

Using AltaVista, or any index, effectively is an exercise in remote-control mind reading because you have to guess words that will appear on the pages you're looking for. Sometimes, that's easy — if you're looking for recipes for key lime pie, `key lime pie` is a good set of search words because you know the name of what you're looking for. On the other hand, if you have forgotten that the capital of Germany is Berlin, it's hard to tease a useful page out of AltaVista because you don't know what words to look for. (If you try `Germany capital`, you find stuff about investment banking.)

Now that we have you all discouraged, try some AltaVista searches. Direct your browser to `http://www.altavista.com`. You see a screen like the one shown in Figure 10-4.

Note: AltaVista has a little robot named Scooter that spends its time merrily visiting Web pages all over the Net and reporting back what she saw. AltaVista makes a humongous index of which words occurred in which pages; when you search AltaVista, it picks pages from the index that contain the words you asked for.

Figure 10-4:
AltaVista,
ready to roll.

(Reproduced with the permission of © 2000 AltaVista Company. AltaVista(r) is a registered trademark and Smart is Beautiful and the AltaVista logo are trademarks of AltaVista Company.)

Type some search terms, and AltaVista finds the pages that best match your terms. That's *best match,* not *match* — if it can't match all the terms, it finds pages that match as well as possible. AltaVista ignores words that occur too often to be usable as index terms, both the obvious ones such as `and`, `the`, and `of` and terms such as `internet` and `mail`. These rules can sound somewhat discouraging, but in fact it's still not hard to tease useful results out of AltaVista. You just have to think up good search terms. Try that key lime pie example, by typing **key lime pie** and pressing the Search button. You get the response shown in Figure 10-5.

Figure 10-5:
A plethora
of pages
of pie.

(Reproduced with the permission of © 2000 AltaVista Company. AltaVista(r) is a registered trademark and Smart is Beautiful and the AltaVista logo are trademarks of AltaVista Company.)

Your results may not look exactly like Figure 10-5 because we told AltaVista to display the results in Compact form rather than in Standard form (by clicking the Preferences button before searching) so that the example would fit on this page. All the pages it found do, in fact, have something to do with key lime pie, and the first page on that list has a pretty good recipe. Notice that it found about 7,605 matches. Although that's probably more than you wanted to look at, you should at least look at the next couple of screens of matches if the first screen doesn't have what you want. At the bottom of the AltaVista screen are page numbers; click Next to go to the next page.

Speling counts

A major reason that searches fail is that one of the search words is spelled wrong. Check carefully. We once did a search on an embarrassing disease and found the three sites in the world that had misspelled it the same way we did. (Thanks to our friend Jean Armour Polly, for reminding us about this problem.)

404, why oh why?

More often than we want to admit, when you click a link that Yahoo or one of its competitors found, you get, rather than the promised page, a message such as 404 Not Found. What did you do wrong? Nothing. Web pages come and go and move around with great velocity, and the various search systems do a lousy job, frankly, of cleaning out links to old, dead pages that have gone away.

The automated indexes, such as AltaVista and Lycos, are better in this regard than the manual directories, such as Yahoo. The automated ones have software robots that revisit all the indexed pages every once in a while and note whether they still exist; even so, many lonely months can pass between robot visits, and a great deal can happen to a page in the meantime.

It's just part of life on the online frontier — the high-tech equivalent of riding your horse along the trail in the old West and noticing that there sure are lots of bleached-white cattle skulls lying around.

AltaVista hints

AltaVista, unlike Yahoo, makes it easy to refine your search more exactly to target the pages you want to find. After each search, your search terms appear in a box at the top of the page so that you can change them and try again. Here are some tips on how you may want to change your terms:

- ✔ Type most search words in lowercase. Type proper names with a single capital letter, such as Elvis. Don't type any words in all capital letters. It's about as effective as "pushing the button *harder.*"

- ✔ If two or more words should appear together, put quotes around them, as in "Elvis Presley". As a matter of fact, if you do that with the pie search ("key lime pie") because, after all, that is what the pie is called, you get a nice 3,000 matches rather than more than 7,000.

- ✔ Use + and - to indicate words that must either appear or not appear, such as +Elvis +Costello -Presley if you're looking for the modern Elvis, not the classic one.

Yahoo and AltaVista — what a pair!

It occurs to us that a rather effective way to search the Web is to look in the Yahoo directory and then, if you don't find what you want, try AltaVista. Because great minds (or maybe tiny minds) think alike, the Yahoo and AltaVista people got together to make it easy to do just that.

It's all free — just like TV

You may be wondering who pays for all these wonderful search systems. All are supported by advertising. On every page of Yahoo, Lycos, and most other search systems, you see lots and lots of ads. In theory, the advertising pays the costs; in reality, the independent advertising-supported search systems Excite, the GO Network (formerly Infoseek), Lycos, and Yahoo have all lost pots of money. (In this case, a pot is sized in millions of bucks.) Fortunately for all of them, because they issued stock to the public at the height of the 1996 Internet investment craze, each has plenty of cash to burn up while they try to figure out how to turn a profit.

The exception used to be AltaVista, originally a research project to see just how fast the Alpha line of workstations at Digital Equipment Corporation were. The new line turned out to be extremely fast, blowing the socks off most of the competition. Because DEC knew a good thing when it saw it, it turned AltaVista into a product line that it licenses to other search systems (such as Yahoo and CNET, Inc.) and that companies can use to create their own internal indexes. Some folks thought that DEC might issue stock in its AltaVista Internet Software division as well (if the Excite, GO Network, Lycos, and Yahoo guys can raise all that money, you may as well get in on the party).

Some people think that a big "bubble" is occurring in the search biz and that we can expect some search systems to run out of money and shut down or merge with others. Visit `http://net.gurus.com/search/` for the latest up- or down-dates.

AltaVista away

AltaVista has a few other options that can be handy:

- ✔ Rather than search Web pages, you can search Usenet, the giant collection of Internet newsgroups (online discussion groups). Simply select the results you want next to the item that says Find Result On under the blank space where you type. Notice the four check boxes: For the Web, News, Discussion Groups, and Products. If a topic has been discussed recently on Usenet, this technique is the best way to find the messages about that topic. To find out all about Usenet, visit our Web site, at `http://net.gurus.com`.

- ✔ You can choose how detailed a report you want to get, in Compact or Detailed form, on the Preferences page. The Compact option gives you a single line per item found; Detailed, about three lines per item. AltaVista normally uses Standard form, which tells it to use Compact if you're doing a Usenet search or Detailed if you're doing a Web search.

Because the compact report is much smaller, it loads faster. If you have a slow dial-up Net connection, Compact form makes searching much snappier, at the cost of not being able to tell quite so easily what's in each item found. If you're searching for a particular page or Usenet item that you will recognize when you see it, Compact form is definitely quicker.

✔ You can limit your search to documents in a specific language. No sense in finding pages in a language you can't read.

But Wait — There's More

After you have surfed around Yahoo and AltaVista for a while, you may want to check out the competition.

AskJeeves

`http://www.ask.com`

Using a unique butler theme, AskJeeves is even more unique in that you actually ask it questions. Not cheesy half questions like "where cheese?" or "cooking chicken?" but rather full-fledged questions like "Where can I find some good English Camembert?" Try it — just don't forget to click the Ask button to the *left* side of the window.

Google

`http://www.google.com`

It's the funny name with a killer search engine attached. If we didn't like Yahoo and AltaVista as much as we do, Google would be numero uno. (Maybe it is, anyway.) Using an innovative scoring system, it defines keywords for sites based on which sites link to it. This previously unused method makes it more likely that the pages at the top of a search are interesting and topical *and* have the words you asked for.

WebCrawler

`http://www.webcrawler.com`

WebCrawler is an automated indexer that crawls around the Web, cataloging and indexing every page it comes across — again, sort of like AltaVista. Although America Online (AOL) owns WebCrawler, anyone can use it. It's a reasonable alternative to AltaVista.

The GO Network

`http://www.go.com`

Infoseek is an index similar to AltaVista rather than a directory: You give it some keywords to look for, and it finds the pages that match the best. It also has a directory of useful Web pages. It can search the Web, Usenet, Reuters news, and a few other odds and ends.

Excite

`http://www.excite.com`

Excite is primarily an index, like AltaVista, with a "concept search," which is supposed to find relevant pages even if you don't type exactly the same words the pages use. We don't find that the Excite concept search helps much, but perhaps we were too wordy to start with. Excite also has sections with reviews of Web pages, city directories, white pages, and more.

HotBot

`http://www.hotbot.com`

HotBot is yet another index, like AltaVista. It used to be affiliated with *Wired* magazine and still uses — in classic *Wired* style — bright, clashing colors that make your head hurt. Lycos, the new owners, haven't changed anything, so there's no accounting for taste. If you can deal with the bright, obnoxious, neon-ish colors (try sunglasses), it's not a bad index.

Lycos

`http://www.lycos.com`

Lycos is a largely automated index, sort of like AltaVista. It began as a project at Carnegie-Mellon University and has also gone commercial. It also has a directory named Top 5% of Web Sites. Although Lycos was one of the earliest Web search systems, AltaVista has, at this point, honestly, a better index, and Yahoo has a better directory. Lycos also has headline news and local pages for some cities around the United States.

Northern Light

`http://www.northernlight.com`

This site contains an automated index of both the Web and its Special Collection, articles from various sources for which you must pay, usually a dollar or two, if you decide to read them. If you would rather stick with the (free) Web, you can choose to do so. The Northern Light searches also automatically categorize the pages they find, displaying a listing of "folders" you can choose among. We have found, on occasion, useful information in Northern Light and nowhere else. We have also found its folder arrangement to be uniquely functional.

Other Web guides

Lots of other Web guides are available, including many specialized guides put together for particular interests. (Femina, for example, is a feminist guide, at `http://www.femina.com`.)

Yahoo has a directory of other guides: Starting at the Yahoo page (`http://www.yahoo.com`), choose WWW (which appears under Computers) and then Searching the Web.

Looking for Businesses

If you are looking for the Web site of a company or organization, try typing its name in the address box of your browser. Many firms have a URL that looks like `www.companyname.com`, and your browser fills in the `www.` and `.com` parts.

The second way to search for companies is to search for the company name as a topic. If you're looking for the Egg Farm Dairy, for example, search for `Egg Farm Dairy` in Yahoo, AltaVista, or any of the other search systems. (You'll find it, too. We like the Muscoot cheese.)

After you have done that, a few other places are worth checking for business-related info.

WHOIS is a wiz

```
http://www.allwhois.com
http://www.geektools.com (click the whois button)
```

Every registered Internet domain has a listed owner and contacts. The WHOIS facility lets you look up domains and contacts. Although some separate WHOIS programs exist, you can do just as well for most purposes by visiting the Geektools or AllWhois.com WHOIS Web page. Geektools isn't as pretty, but does a better job of finding every scrap of whois info.

On those pages, you get to choose which WHOIS server to use and what to search for. Dozens of WHOIS servers exist, for all the different domains on the Net. These two services try to guess, usually correctly, the best server to use for any particular query.

In the Search strings box, enter the name of the company or contact person or network in which you're interested and click Search. With luck, you get back one entry that matches. More likely, you get back a list of all the matches. When we searched for IBM.COM, here's part of what we got:

```
International Business Machines (IBM-DOM)  IBM.COM
International Business Machines (IBM4-HST) IBM.COM
129.34.139.30
To single out one record, look it up with "!xxx", where xxx
        is the handle, shown in parenthesis following the
        name, which comes first.
```

Two possible matches are listed: the IBM.COM domain and the single computer that happens to be named IBM.COM. Each has a code in parentheses, which is a link to more information about that match. The *DOM* in *IBM-DOM* suggests that this might be the official IBM domain, so click it to get a more concrete answer with the full name of the company and the e-mail address of the person responsible for the domain.

In a company as large as IBM, the domain contact is doubtless a technical network specialist; in small companies, however, it's usually someone who can answer short, polite questions, such as "What's the e-mail address of your sales department?" or "Does Jim Smith still work there?"

Hoover is not a vacuum cleaner

http://www.hoovers.com

Although WHOIS tells you about a company's connection to the Internet, it doesn't tell you much about the company itself. Hoover's is a business information company that has been publishing paper business directories for quite a while. Now it's on the Net. Its Web site offers free company capsules, stock prices, and other company info. If you sign up for its paid service, it offers considerably more. Even the free stuff is quite useful.

Your tax dollars at work — EDGAR

http://edgar.sec.gov *(government)*
http://www.edgar-online.com *(private)*

The U.S. Securities and Exchange Commission (SEC), the agency that regulates stock and bond markets, has a system named EDGAR that collects all the financial material that publicly traded companies have to file with the government. Although most of this stuff is dry and financial, if you can read financial statements, you can find all sorts of interesting information, such as Bill Gates' salary.

The government EDGAR site is run directly by the SEC, and the private site, EDGAR ONLINE, is run by an independent company, Cybernet Data Systems, Inc. Although the two sites have pretty much the same information, the private site offers free, limited access and charges a modest price (about $5 per month) for more complete access and automatic e-mail updates when a company in which you're interested files EDGAR documents. Because EDGAR ONLINE has partner arrangements with several other companies, including Hoover's, if you check on a company in Hoover's and then click the EDGAR link to get to EDGAR ONLINE, you can often get documents not directly available from the EDGAR ONLINE home page. If you use EDGAR ONLINE often, however, pay the five bucks.

A bounty of business directories

Tons of business information is available on the Net. Here are a few places to begin.

Companies Online

```
http://www.CompaniesOnline.com
```

Companies Online is a joint project between Dun & Bradstreet and Lycos. You enter the name of a company in which you're interested, and this site tells you about it.

Inc. magazine

```
http://www.inc.com
http://www.inc.com/500
```

Inc. magazine concentrates on small, fast-growing companies. Each year, its Inc. 500 features the 500 companies it likes the best. Many hot little companies are listed here, with contact information.

Yellow Pages

```
http://www.bigyellow.com
http://yp.gte.net
http://www.switchboard.com
http://www.abii.com (use Fast Search under the InfoUSA logo)
```

Quite a few yellow pages business directories, both national and local, are on the Net. The directories on this list are some of the national ones. We like Big Yellow the best (even though it's run by Bell Atlantic, which is otherwise not our favorite telephone company), although they're all worth a look. InfoUSA also offers reverse lookup, in case you have a number without a name.

·Person to Person

Finding people on the Net is surprisingly easy. It's so easy that, indeed, sometimes it's creepy. Two overlapping categories of people finders are available: those that look for people on the Net with e-mail and Web addresses and those that look for people in real life with phone numbers and street addresses.

The hard-boiled egg test

Our friend Doug Hacker claims to be able to find the answer to any factual query on the Net in less time than it takes to hard-boil an egg — about ten minutes. Carol challenged him to find a quote she vaguely knew from the liner notes of a Duke Ellington album, whose title she couldn't remember. He had the complete quote in about an hour but spent less than five minutes himself. How? He found a mailing list about Duke Ellington, subscribed, and asked the question. Several members replied in short order. The more time you spend finding your way around the Net, the more you know where to go for the information you need.

Call me

A number of directories feature information compiled from telephone white pages all over the world. You don't even have to know what city the person you are seeking lives in (unless he has a common surname like Smith or Jones). Track down that long-lost high school sweetheart! If he hasn't had a listed phone number in the past few years, though, you probably won't find an entry in any of these directories.

On the Net

The process of finding e-mail and Web addresses is somewhat hit-and-miss. Because no online equivalent to the official phone book the telephone company produces has ever existed, directories of e-mail addresses are collected from addresses used in Usenet messages, mailing lists, and other more or less public places on the Net. Because the different directories use different sources, if you don't find someone in one directory, you can try another. Remember that because the e-mail directories are incomplete, there's no substitute for calling someone up and asking, "What's your e-mail address?"

If you're wondering whether someone has a Web page, use AltaVista to search for her name. If you're wondering whether you're famous, use AltaVista to search for your own name and see how many people mention you or link to your Web pages.

Yahoo People Search

http://people.yahoo.com/

Yahoo has a useful directory that looks up people by name and optionally their address and gives you the full address and phone number.

WhoWhere

http://www.whowhere.com

WhoWhere is another e-mail address directory. Some people are listed in WhoWhere who aren't listed in other places.

Canada 411

http://www.canada411.sympatico.ca

Canada 411 is a Canadian telephone book that is complete except for the boring provinces of Alberta and Saskatchewan. Canada 411 is sponsored by most of the major Canadian telephone companies. Aussi disponsible en français, eh? (*Note to residents of Alberta and Saskatchewan:* Advise Telus and Saskatel to prove that you're not boring by joining up and adding their listings. Saskatel has a separate directory, at http://www.saskyellowpages.com/, that is still pretty boring but better than nothing.)

Bigfoot

http://www.bigfoot.com

Bigfoot provides a way to search for people in addition to permanent, free e-mail addresses for life. ***Warning:*** After you're listed at Bigfoot, either voluntarily or if it found your name some other way, you have no way to remove the listing, either automatically or manually. We find this situation obnoxious. When those folks say for life, they mean it. We wonder whether they read the obituaries to keep up on which usernames they should recycle.

Mail, one more time

Mailing lists are another important resource. Most lists (but not all — check before you ask) welcome concrete, politely phrased questions related to the list's topic. See Chapter 7 to find more information about mailing lists, including how to look for lists of particular topics of interest to you.

Where do I buy an aardvark?

All the serious directories and indices now put shopping information somewhere on their home page to help get your credit card closer to the Web faster. Some are even sponsored by VISA. You can find department stores and catalogs from all over, offering every conceivable item (and some inconceivable items). Give it a try.

Chapter 11

Unlikely Ways to Use and See the Web

. . . .

In This Chapter

▶ Multimedia and other Web(by) gizmos

▶ RealPlayer, QuickTime, Shockwave, and other neat product names with arbitrarily located capital letters

▶ Displaying Web pages by using the Active Desktop

▶ Using Web pages as window backgrounds

▶ Getting help on the Web

▶ Updating Windows via the Web

. . . .

*M*uch of the appeal of Windows Me is its integration with the Internet (and that it holds 80 percent of overall market share, but that's another story entirely). You can look at that integration, however, in another way: From the Internet's point of view, or, more to the point, from the view afforded companies driving the Internet. All these smart folks are scrambling around, doing this and selling that and trying to find something that nobody else has done with the Internet. Some companies (Real, Apple, Macromedia, and Sun Microsystems, for example) came across the Internet early enough to establish a comfortable lead or had enough clout so that arriving late was not a problem; many others (PointCast, NetCaster, Sizzler, Envoy) missed the boat entirely, working hard to establish a brand and a following but failing against harsh competition.

So where does all this leave you? You end up in a good place because such a competitive marketplace is a thriving cauldron of innovation and advancement. Several leaders have emerged, and you just may know their names. Companies such as Real Networks, Apple Computer, Macromedia, and Microsoft have carved out markets that support millions of users. Not surprisingly, they all have to do with entertainment and how to get it to you as easily and conveniently as possible.

Because media on the Web is so hip, cool, and starch free, we cover it in reasonable detail in this chapter. You find out about the four most popular plugins that make the Web much cooler. To that end, we talk about QuickTime (from Apple), RealPlayer 8 (Real), Flash and Shockwave (Macromedia), and the new Windows Media Player (Microsoft), which, coincidentally and conveniently, comes with Windows Me.

Not to be undersold, we also talk about some other Windows Internet integration features, like the seemingly defunct Active Desktop, which allows the following cool activities:

- You can replace that boring blue-ish screen (or that exciting picture of an eclipse you use as wallpaper on your Windows Me desktop) with a Web page.

- Perhaps a more interesting feature is that you can display a site subscription on your PC, either in an Internet Explorer window or on your desktop. A *subscription* is a collection of Web pages your PC goes out and gets on whatever schedule you specify. That way, whenever you want to look at those Web pages, the interruptions, the inconvenience, and the slow speed are all out of the way, and you can see just the content you're interested in.

- Another means of delivery to your PC uses live data feeds, in which information flows automatically to your screen. One example is a stock market ticker: You can have the current price of your favorite stock in your face all the time. For live data feeds to work, however, you have to be online all the time.

Windows Me comes with several Internet-related "convenience" features because Microsoft wants you to get as much help as possible from the Web rather than bother its living, breathing support engineers. The Internet is also a great mechanism for distributing software updates — improvements to Windows Me. We talk in this chapter about the pros and cons of this approach. First, though, let's dive right into the nifty stuff.

Multimedia and Other Web (by) Gizmoids

You may have heard the term *streaming*. You likely visualized a nice, flowing body of water into which you flip a fly caster back and forth, vying for river trout. Pop that bubble because we're talking about Party A (the media people) getting cool-looking stuff that wiggles and sings to Party B (you). The big thing right now is music on the Web. Practically any kind of media is available online, though, if you have a fast enough connection (such as DSL and cable access). Hundreds of American and international radio stations simulcast their signal over the Web, allowing people thousands of miles away to listen. Dozens of television stations are broadcasting their local newscasts live over the Internet. Several cable networks, including CourtTV and Bloomberg, point their live feed at the Internet. Macromedia, which makes the Flash and Shockwave plug-ins, has enabled a vast array of original animations and other multimedia content to be published and viewed by anyone around the world. We also talk about some cool sites that even 56K modem users can easily enjoy. To use any of these features, however, you need special software — the aforementioned plug-ins (or helper applications, in this case).

We know that you've heard of MP3 (pronounced "emm-pee-three") and have seen all the legal hoopla over it in the news. Regardless of the legalese, MP3 files are remarkably popular because they're relatively small and sound about as good as a CD. Unfortunately, nearly every MP3 file available on the Net is pirated without the permission of the copyright owner, which has provoked lots of lawsuits. Our advice is to stick to the handful of secure and sanctioned digital music services until MP3 settles down.

RealPlayer 8

Possibly the most popular, downloaded, and used multimedia enhancement to one's Web experience, the RealPlayer has been maturing for some time. RealPlayer 8, the latest version as of this writing, is a significant improvement over previous versions. If you're not familiar with this product, you need some background. RealPlayer began its days as a simple Netscape browser plug-in, named RealAudio, that played voice or music. At that time, Internet media was practically unknown and only whispered about among the supernerds.

Now, however, dozens of services show full-length feature films, animated shorts (not the cloth kind), and everything in between at speeds of as much as 1.5 megabits per second, which is almost like watching TV (that's *really* fast). If you want this application, first find out whether you already have it. Click the Start button, choose Programs, and look on the menu for an item named Real. If it's on there, a version of RealPlayer is already installed, although it's probably an older one.

Follow these steps to get RealPlayer or to upgrade the version you already have:

1. **Start up your favorite web browser, go to** http://www.real.com/, **and click Download.**

2. **Click on the link near the bottom, labeled something like RealPlayer 8 Basic is our free player. Fill out the form and select the items underneath that indicate what kind of computer and connection you have.**

   Because this book is about Windows Me, you can feel safe picking Windows 98 or Windows Me (if they've updated it) and Pentium-class Computer.

3. **You have to select your language and connection (we're smart but not psychic). When you finish, click the large Download FREE RealPlayer 8 Basic button.**

   It's your option whether you accept the silly online phone deal or too-frequent-for-our-tastes newsletter.

4. **Peruse the chart that lists the packages you can download and what each package includes, as shown in Figure 11-1.**

   Although the "recommended" option is the middle one with more stuff tacked on, we prefer the Standalone version. Feel free to select any one you like.

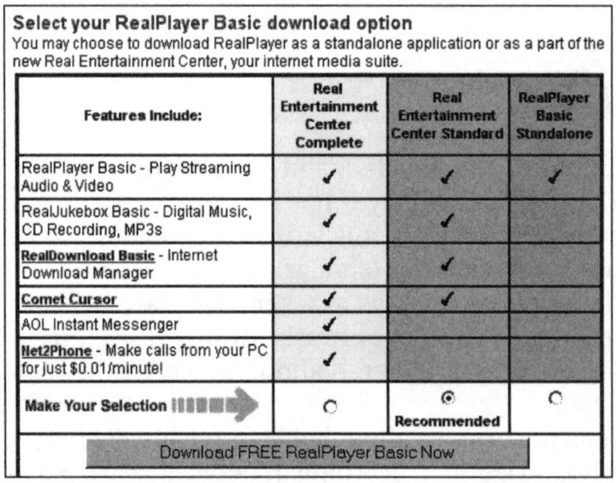

Figure 11-1:
Your
RealPlayer
download
options.
Choose
wisely, O
reader.

Select your RealPlayer Basic download option
You may choose to download RealPlayer as a standalone application or as a part of the new Real Entertainment Center, your internet media suite.

Features Include:	Real Entertainment Center Complete	Real Entertainment Center Standard	RealPlayer Basic Standalone
RealPlayer Basic - Play Streaming Audio & Video	✓	✓	✓
RealJukebox Basic - Digital Music, CD Recording, MP3s	✓	✓	
RealDownload Basic - Internet Download Manager	✓	✓	
Comet Cursor	✓	✓	
AOL Instant Messenger	✓		
Net2Phone - Make calls from your PC for just $0.01/minute!	✓		
Make Your Selection ▶	○	◉ Recommended	○

Download FREE RealPlayer Basic Now

5. **Click the Download FREE RealPlayer 8 Basic NOW button.**

   Of course, you realize that it's fibbing — one more step.

6. **Lots of links on the next page indicate the physical locations of the computers from which you can download RealPlayer. Click to select one that is reasonably close to you.**

   The (hopefully) familiar File Download dialog box appears, asking whether you want to save the file to disk or open it from where it is.

Selecting the option labeled Open it from where it is really just down-loads it to a temporary folder on your hard drive, gives it an indecipher-able name so that you can't find it later, and then runs it. Saving it to disk does the same thing but puts it where you tell it and gives it a name that's easy to read. Then you have to run the program. Oh, well.

After the file has finished downloading, go to where you saved it. (Saving it to the desktop is easiest. You can move it somewhere else or throw it away later). Click the file to run the installer program, and then follow the instructions.

If you stick to the defaults, and after having endured a number of seem-ingly identical pages, you will have completed the installation of RealPlayer. During that process, it will also have installed a plug-in for your browser. If you come across any RealPlayer content on the Web, it automatically either plays it on the Web page or opens the RealPlayer application. In Figure 11-2, you can see a clip of *Little Shop of Horrors* from liketelevision.com.

Figure 11-2:
Screening that classic *Little Shop of Horrors.*

You may have noted that Real offered you numerous occasions to actually pay for RealPlayer 8. Believe it or not, when you pay, you *do* get an enhanced version. How enhanced is debatable, but because everyone expects every-thing on the Internet to be free, we suggest that you fiddle with the free ver-sion before coughing up any dough.

QuickTime 4

Apple has been in the multimedia game longer than anyone else — it invented all the underlying concepts of multimedia (the convergence of video, sound, and interactivity) before it was even called multimedia. QuickTime 4, the latest iteration of the player, has had the capability to receive streaming "broadcasts" since 1999, something that was missing in earlier versions.

QuickTime 4 is significantly easier to retrieve and install:

1. **Point your browser to** `http://www.apple.com/quicktime/download`.

2. **Fill out the short form (as shown in Figure 11-3), select your options, change the version to Windows, and select your language.**

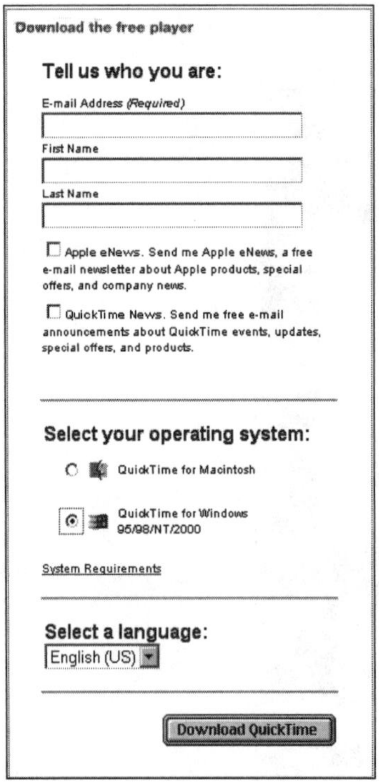

Figure 11-3: Apple doesn't ask for your children's dietary patterns.

Download the free player

Tell us who you are:

E-mail Address *(Required)*

First Name

Last Name

☐ Apple eNews. Send me Apple eNews, a free e-mail newsletter about Apple products, special offers, and company news.

☐ QuickTime News. Send me free e-mail announcements about QuickTime events, updates, special offers, and products.

Select your operating system:

○ QuickTime for Macintosh

⦿ QuickTime for Windows 95/98/NT/2000

System Requirements

Select a language:
English (US) ▼

[Download QuickTime]

3. **Click the Download QuickTime button.**

4. **Select the Save To Disk option and click OK, and then indicate in the Save File dialog box where you want the installer to be downloaded. Click OK again.**

   Note that the download seems inordinately short. It is. In fact, the file that's being downloaded is a "remote" installer. (QuickTime weighs in at nearly 7MB of squished files.)

5. **When the file is done, go to where you saved it (to whatever folder you told your browser to save downloads in) and run the program. Follow the easy instructions, agree to the license agreement that nobody ever reads, and click Next until you run out of Next buttons.**

   The installer then downloads all the files you need for running QuickTime and automatically installs them when it's finished.

The last thing the installer asks is whether you want to see a sample movie. Do so. This response not only lets you see whether the installation works (failure can happen anywhere, at any time), it also lets you see a nifty, red Apple thing. Very neat-o. Apple has been able to get lots of heavy content hitters to jump on the bandwagon, including Disney.

Flash and Shockwave

Several years ago, when Macromedia was trying to figure out how to become a hot Internet commodity, some bright person figured that the company would make its premier multimedia authoring software available via the ether. That software was Director, and the Internet version was dubbed Shockwave. It was a shock, all right! It was huge and slow, and it didn't look all that great. Its creators kept working at it and bought another company for their animation technology, which they named Flash. Now, they're able to get the power of both Flash and Shockwave into a smallish 2MB download.

So what does Shockwave do, historians? Simple. It plays files that can display moving pictures and sound and be *interactive* — you can click on links that let you do things or take you to other parts of the presentation or a web page. Think of Flash and Shockwave as a way of putting great-looking Saturday-morning cartoons on the Internet without the process taking so long. Video is huge. Flash and Shockwave files, by contrast, are tiny. It's something that you have to see for yourself:

1. **Point your web browser to** `http://www.shockwave.com.`

   If you already have Flash and Shockwave installed, you see some neat-looking animations. If not, a small dialog box appears, telling you that you need an update. Why? Because Windows ships with Flash and

Shockwave already installed in Internet Explorer. Explorer and newer versions will have invariably become available since it was added to Windows.

2. **Click OK.**

The Security Warning dialog box appears, probably telling you that it can't validate the Shockwave 8 player.

3. **Click Yes at the bottom of the page.**

After another short wait, another dialog box appears telling you that the download is in progress. The little progress bar at the bottom tells you whether you get to make that sandwich. Some of us prefer toasted bologna, although a decent ham and cheese on rye will do. Easy on the mayo — we still have a few productive years ahead of us.

4. **Enter your name and e-mail address, and, after making sure that the AutoUpdate feature is turned on, click Finish.**

You see a neat animation sequence in the blue box.

5. **Click the Go to shockwave.com link under the movie and enjoy.**

It's a great deal!

Shockwave and Flash media sites are often very rich in content and quality. The Shockwave.com site features a wide array of shows, games, music, and some inexplicable content from some people who seem somewhat offbeat but who have true artistic talent. One of the coolest games at the site is Tank Wars in 3-D.

Windows Media Player

You already have it. The new Windows Media Player is quite a change over the previous version, which was mostly just a glorified transistor radio, as Web media players go. The new and improved Windows Media Player (WMP) is a VCR, CD player, media storage system, jukebox, radio, portable media-management system, and psycho-funk-a-delic disco machine, all rolled into one snazzy interface intended to make sure that you never — ever — want to use anyone else's media software.

Because it's Microsoft software we're talking about, it's way more than just a new version of software. The company has also created a completely new Web site to kick it off. To gain access to all sorts of interesting and new media-related thingies, point your web browser to `http://www.windowsmedia.com` and get ready. New content is provided daily, and it's usually quite entertaining. Figure 11-4 shows the Windows Media Player radio tuner.

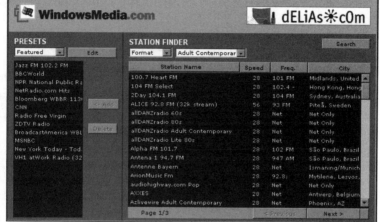

Figure 11-4:
Many
available
stations
aren't even
in the United
States!

Watch Out for Flying Protocol Handlers!

So you've decided to install all four media players, and you're all set to experience the Web in all its multimedia glory — except that you're looking at an error you can't quite understand. We sympathize with you because this is not solely a newcomer's affliction. This situation is known to some as protocol juggling, to others as file-type rustling, and to the rest of us as a royal pain. Both RealPlayer and the Windows Media Player can play MP3 and other MPEG audio formats. Whenever you run one of these applications, it checks to see whether it still retains ownership of those types of files. Each one thinks that *it* should be the one to handle all of these files for you. Whenever it finds that it's not, it usually automatically reclaims the file type for itself. This travesty happens every time, with all these applications.

Suppose that you've settled on WinAmp (a slick MP3 file player, at `http://www.winamp.com`) to handle a type of file and you start Yahoo! Player (based on Windows Media Player technology, at `http://digital.broadcast.com`). The Yahoo! Player promptly complains that WinAmp has "thieved" its settings and informs you that this nasty misdeed has occurred and that it will fix it. Unfortunately, because WinAmp never complains about the swipe, you don't know about it until you click on an MP3 file in your web browser and it opens in Yahoo! Player.

Real, Apple, Macromedia, Microsoft — they all want to be your only choice. With that in mind, they do their best to make their software do what everyone else's can, and more. To make matters worse, they all try to make exclusive deals with the numerous content sites out there (such as Like Television, at http://www.liketelevision.com, and Broadcast.com, from Yahoo, at http://www.broadcast.com), which usually end up taking on several protocols. In the end, it means that you need more than one player application.

So now you know the dirty little details and you want to be able to stop it. Sadly, it's not all that easy, although it can be done. Every time you install one of these applications, it usually asks which file types you want to *associate* with it. If you don't answer, you discover that the application has opted to be associated with all the file types it can handle (and in some cases, a few that it can't). Shockwave is the only player in this group that does not steal file types and is not stolen from, so you can ignore it for now.

Pay close attention to what the other three player programs do. When you start RealPlayer, for example, and some of its file types have been usurped by Windows Media Player or QuickTime, a small dialog box pops up, telling you that some of your player's file types have been thieved. Click on the Details button to see a list of oddly named items that have check marks next to them. Don't worry about exactly what they mean; just know that they're file types — whenever a checkmark appears next to one, it means that the software "catches" them and plays them back. Easy enough, right?

The general rule here is to turn *off* the items that you would rather have opened by other applications. RealPlayer should open only RealMedia files and not MP3s. Windows Media Player should not try to open QuickTime movies because it can't (except for some very old versions). QuickTime should not bother with Windows AVI files any more because it can no longer read them correctly. You get the idea.

The (Hyper-)Active Desktop

It used to be (before Windows 98) that a real desktop was a good analogy for your Windows desktop. The desktop was just that: a desktop, on top of which you put things, usually icons that ran programs or windows through which programs communicated to you. Microsoft decided to change your boring, old, regular desktop into a desktop covered with a mixture of information from your hard disk and from the Internet. To distinguish this new look from the old Internet-free Windows, Microsoft named it the *Active Desktop* — "Active" because it can feed you information from the Internet at any time.

The latest and greatest (not really)

When Windows 98 first came out, this newfangled *push* technology was the latest and greatest thing. Microsoft dived in whole-hog and invented the Active Desktop. Not all that different from an inactive desktop, this new miracle would lead the masses to a new hope and a new generation of technology-savvy global citizens with screens full of swell content pushed from vendors all over the world. Posh. None of that happened, and Microsoft is somewhat embarrassed that Active Desktop and its channels even existed. (Ever heard of B.O.B.? Didn't think so). The only problem was that Microsoft was in the early stages of its latest troubles with the Department of Justice over a matter of antitrust law. Because Active Desktop was a component of Internet Explorer and Microsoft had argued that Internet Explorer was as much a part of the operating system as anything else and that it couldn't be removed or the whole thing would blow up, Internet Explorer couldn't be taken out. That would risk invalidating the company's own argument.

So it stays.

This is why you find these push components still in Windows Me. Mind you, only a small percentage of users ever use anything other than the single-click option because it makes navigating the interface easier. We never found the prospect (or even the reality) of sinking Web pages into our desktops very appealing because most of the things you could sink look an awful lot like ads — not to mention that when you click a link in one of these things, it opens Internet Explorer! Anyway, if you find yourself interested in looking up some channels or other Active Desktop add-ons and such, you find very little available. Microsoft does have a Web site for it, at http://www.microsoft.com/windows/ie/ie40/gallery/.

But we strongly suggest that you do *not* use anything at the site. All tests with these applications and Windows Me proved fatal to our computers. The other components work just fine. We just hope that you don't get hooked on them because very few remain.

After you clear away all the hype, however, the new Active Desktop is just like the old inactive desktop, except for these two features:

 ✔ **Web style:** To complete the mixture (confusion?) of your system with the Internet, Microsoft lets you make your Active Desktop act more like a Web page. You can set your desktop to run programs by single-clicking instead rather than double-clicking and to underline icon names so that they look like the links on Web pages. Both these changes make the Active Desktop feel more like a Web page than the old inactive desktop did.

Many people who were used to previous versions of Windows, however, don't like the changes, so Microsoft lets you have it your way: You can turn the features of the Active Desktop on or off individually. That's why Chapter 3 has a sidebar titled "With a double-click here and a single-click there." We refer to this sidebar in each of the succeeding chapters in this book, to make sure that your Windows Me desktop is set up the same way ours was when we wrote the instructions. If you've chosen the Web-style desktop (by single-clicking), the way we suggest in Chapter 3, the icon names on your desktop are underlined, as though they were links on a Web page.

✔ **Putting Web pages on the desktop:** Active Desktop lets you display a whole list of items (usually Web pages) on your desktop; read the next two sections to find out how.

Putting a tiger in your tank and a Web page on your desktop

Although we whisk you past it rather quickly in Chapter 3, the Display Properties dialog box is the key to seeing Web pages on your desktop. Why would you want to do that? We can think of only two reasons. One is to display live feeds, such as stock market prices, which requires that you be connected to the Internet all the time. The other is to alert you to changes in Web sites that change every so often and whose content is extremely important to you. Our favorite example is that of our local performing arts center. Every week or so, it updates its Web site with new performances, and we always forget to check it. With the Active Desktop, the up-to-date Web site can always appear in one corner of our screen and we can browse more deeply if we see something that looks interesting.

Here's the simple way to display a Web page on your desktop:

1. *Right*-click a blank portion of your desktop.

   Depending on how many Web pages and icons you have on your desk, this step can be a difficult trick. For most of us, however, some space on the desktop shows. You know that you're in the right place when nothing is highlighted under your mouse pointer and you're not on top of a Web page. When you right-click the desktop itself, you see a pop-up menu; the first pick on this menu is Active Desktop.

2. **Choose A̲ctive Desktop➪C̲ustomize my Desktop from the pop-up menu.**

   You see the Display Properties dialog box with a number of tabs in it. Although the Web tab should be selected, if it's not, click the word *Web* to bring it to your screen. The box labeled View my Active Desktop as a Web page should have a check mark in it; if it doesn't, you haven't followed the instructions in Chapter 3 (shame on you!). This check box controls whether Active Desktop is working on your computer. Turn it on now because you won't be able to see Web pages on your desktop unless this box has a check mark in it.

The box below this check box lists the Web pages to display on your Active Desktop.

Right now, ignore the entire thing and tell Windows Me that you want to display on your desktop a Web page of your own choosing.

3. Click the New button.

You are greeted by the New Active Desktop Item dialog box. Microsoft has correctly determined that putting a boring old Web page on your desktop may not make you immediately appreciate all the time and effort you may have taken to upgrade to Windows Me. It keeps the Active Desktop Gallery (a page full of widgets you may want to add to your desktop) on the Microsoft Web site, just to give you a sense of what's possible. Right now, skip the gallery and concentrate on putting a simple Web page on the desktop.

4. Click No to tell Microsoft that you're going it alone.

You see a New Active Desktop Item dialog box with the Location box, in which you can type the address of the Web page you want to put on your desktop. You may find it useful to press the Browse button *if* you have bookmarked the page you want to add to your desktop (in that case, you may find the page somewhere in your Favorites folder). Otherwise, warm up those fingers and type the Web address yourself.

5. Click OK when you have the address you want.

Congratulations — you're probably finished. Click OK. The Web page you specified should appear on your desktop. (Don't worry if it doesn't; the rest of this chapter contains lots more information about getting Web pages to appear!)

What exactly have you accomplished? You've taken a Web page (the same kind of Web page you're used to seeing in Internet Explorer or Netscape Navigator) and placed it on your desktop, behind any icons or windows that may be floating there. Windows has gone out to the Internet and gotten a copy of the Web page and stashed it somewhere on your computer so that it can redisplay it without having to connect to the Internet again (avoiding the interruption, inconvenience, and slowness of getting things from the Net directly).

You can display more than one Web page on your Active Desktop. In fact, the Display Properties dialog box has space for a whole list of Web pages. After you have some Web pages on the desktop, you can drag them around and put each one exactly where you want it (see the section "Moving an Active Desktop item," just ahead).

Care and feeding of your Active Desktop items

So just what is on the Active Desktop, anyway? *Active Desktop items* can be Web pages or widgets from the Microsoft Active Desktop Gallery. Each Active Desktop item appears in a little box: These items aren't traditional windows because everything else on your computer screen (including icons on your desktop) appears on top of them. Desktop items aren't programs either because they don't appear on the taskbar.

Active Desktop items are in very special windows, but windows nonetheless, which act similarly to other windows on your computer. This section tells you how to do windows-ish things to the Web pages and widgets on your Active Desktop.

Changing the size of an Active Desktop item

As you glide your mouse pointer over the edges of an Active Desktop item, two things happen. First, a gray border appears around the Active Desktop item. This *window border* shows where the edge of the Active Desktop item is. (It may not be obvious if the background of the desktop item is the same color as your desktop.) Second (and you may have to move your mouse pointer slowly over the gray border to see it), the mouse pointer turns into a double-headed arrow. Clicking and dragging the double-headed arrow moves the window border, which changes the size of the Active Desktop item.

Your Active Desktop items may have scroll bars in them if they're too small to display their contents. Although these scroll bars work like regular scroll bars, we find them kind of annoying. Try resizing your Active Desktop windows until they go away.

Moving an Active Desktop item

When your mouse pointer gets near the top of an Active Desktop item, a fat, gray bar appears, similar to the title bar in a regular window. By clicking the bar and dragging it around, you can move the Active Desktop item around on your screen.

Remember that if you move the Active Desktop item over an icon on your desktop, the icons float *over* the desktop item. If you drag one Active Desktop item on top of another, Windows decides which one stays on top (usually the one you're dragging, so if you cover up an item, you have a tricky time finding the buried one).

Hiding an Active Desktop item

On that title bar at the top of the Active Desktop item window, at the right end, you see a familiar X, like the one in a normal window. This X does just what you would expect: It closes the Active Desktop item (the item disappears). You can display it again from the Web tab in the Display Properties dialog box.

You can also hide an Active Desktop item by clicking the little down arrow at the left end of the title bar and choosing Close from the menu that appears.

I want what I want the way I want it when I want it

A couple of tricks can help you get the Active Desktop to display what you really want when you really want it. Here are a few reasons you may want to know about these tricks:

✔ You can control how often the Active Desktop goes out and gets a fresh copy of your Web pages. *Channels* (Web pages that expect to be picked up this way) can tell the desktop how often they want to be updated; regular Web pages get updated just once a day. You can change that frequency, though. If you have DSL or a cable modem, you can even set it to check for updates every five minutes, although we think that's a bit loopy. Once an hour often does well enough unless you live life at a truly frightening speed.

✔ You can control the fine points of whether the Active Desktop connects to the Internet just to retrieve your page and whether it does so while you're working.

✔ Your Web page may require that you log on with a username and password.

As usual with Windows, you can do most of this stuff in two ways: the Wizard way and the cast-your-own-spell way. The Subscription Wizard can be hard to find when you need it, though, and really isn't much simpler than doing it yourself. We show you how to do it yourself.

All the do-it-yourself incantations for Active Desktop Web pages start from the Display Properties dialog box. Display the dialog box by right-clicking the desktop and choosing <u>A</u>ctive Desktop⇨<u>C</u>ustomize My Desktop from the pop-up menu; then click the Web tab. (You can also click the Windows Me Start button, choose <u>S</u>ettings⇨<u>C</u>ontrol Panel, and select the Display item.)

You can also display the properties for an Active Desktop item by displaying its title bar (cruise your mouse pointer over the top of the item and wait for the title bar to appear), clicking the down arrow at the left end of the title bar, and choosing Properties from the menu that appears.

The wizard of subscriptions

You can start the Subscription Wizard in two ways. One is from the Add Item to Active Desktop dialog box — that's what you see when you're at the end of the process of adding an item to your Active Desktop. The other way is from Internet Explorer. If you're looking at a Web page and choose Favorites⇨Add to Favorites, the dialog box you see contains a Customize button that starts the Subscription Wizard.

The Subscription Wizard is one of the more simple-minded wizards in Windows Me. If you start the wizard, look through the instructions there; they should contain all the information you need to make it through the wizard.

Hiding and exposing a page you've subscribed to

Each of the Web pages you've put on your desktop has a check box in front of it. You can remove the Web page from your desktop by clearing the check box. You are still subscribed to the Web page; that is, Windows Me continues to go out and download updates to the Web site according to the schedule you've given it. To be able to see it, however, you have to come back to this dialog box and fill in the check box again.

Providing a password for a Web page on your active desktop

Click the Receiving tab of the Desktop Item Properties dialog box, and then click the Login button. Windows asks you to enter your username and password for the Web pages you want to retrieve. Click OK after you've typed them, and click OK after you're done with the Desktop Item Properties dialog box.

Getting several pages from the same Web site

Click the Receiving tab of the Desktop Item Properties dialog box, and then click the Advanced button. The setting labeled Download linked pages within a depth of in the Advanced Download Options dialog box is the one you're looking for. Translated into English, it says "Download all the pages within so many clicks of the home page." Setting this number to two, for example, means that you can follow a link from the home page and again to a third page, all without connecting to the Internet.

It is probably important that you uncheck the check box labeled Follow links outside this page's Web site. Otherwise, you could end up downloading a tremendous amount of information from the Internet.

The Active Desktop is designed (in our opinion) for people whose computers are permanently connected to the Internet, usually at a company or school. These people don't really care how often their computers zip out to the

Internet to update information. At the other extreme, those people who have only one telephone line they share with their computer probably care a great deal about when their computer picks up the telephone. In consideration of those folks, Windows Me enables you to update your Web pages only when you want.

On the Schedule tab of the Desktop Item Properties dialog box is the Manually setting. Click this setting if you want the whole dialing and updating process to happen only when you tell it to, with no automatic updates. To update the Web pages on your desktop, you have to run Internet Explorer and then choose Favorites➪Update All Subscriptions. Although that command connects to the Internet just as though you wanted to see the Web page in the Internet Explorer web browser, it runs down the list of Web pages on your desktop and updates all of them.

Getting pages daily, weekly, or monthly

Click the Schedule tab of the Desktop Item Properties dialog box to show when Windows thinks that it should go get the Web pages you just said you were interested in. The exact schedule appears under the Manually setting (which can be a little confusing). You can click in the Scheduled box to choose Daily, Weekly, or Monthly.

If the Windows schedules are not to your liking, you can click the Edit button and look at the Custom Schedule dialog box to set up your own schedule. Or you can click the New button to create and name your own schedule and get different options depending on whether you click Daily, Weekly, or Monthly first.

We want to point out that the check box labeled Varies exact time of next update to improve performance is present not so much to help you as to help the Internet. Imagine the traffic jam at 4:30 a.m. if all 100 million Windows computers got on the Internet to update their Web pages. Unless the exact time of your update really matters to you, do the rest of us a favor and leave this box checked.

If you're in a hotel room somewhere, the answer to this question is probably No. If you're at home and the only way your computer *ever* connected to the Internet is over the phone, the answer is probably Yes. That's what the Dial as needed check box is for (it's on the Schedule tab in the Desktop Item Properties dialog box). Those of us who use only dial-up connections to the Internet should make sure that this box is checked, to enable Windows Me to make a phone call whenever necessary. Otherwise, all this scheduling stuff is to no avail because Windows Me tries to update your Web pages and won't be able to find the Internet. You may see a dialog box from Windows asking whether you're really sure that you want to let Windows dial at will. You are.

Help on the Web

Microsoft started working to integrate its resources with the software running on your computer, connecting the two pieces through the World Wide Web, back in Windows 98. Windows Me has closed the functionality gap by vastly improving the System Information application with nearly ubiquitous access to the Microsoft Internet-based resources. The part you see most often, though, is the Windows Update option, at the top of the Start menu. That option starts up Internet Explorer and takes you to a page at the Microsoft Web site where you can ask a technical question or get your system software upgraded. We talk about upgrades in the following section. First, what about getting questions answered online?

Before Microsoft gives you any information, you have to tell it who you are. You have to register your copy of Windows Me, if you haven't already done so. The questions Microsoft asks aren't much different from the questions Netscape asks when you go to subscribe to one of its channels: your name and address, telephone number, e-mail address, and, in the case of Microsoft, where you got Windows Me. Who knows what it does with this information? You can at least ask that it not rent your name to the direct-mail people.

After you've convinced Microsoft that you're on the up-and-up, you can start looking for information from it. Microsoft answers many questions from many people about its software. You can get through to the company on the telephone, and the person you talk to will, in all likelihood, be able to answer your question. If your question has been answered before, however, chances are good that Microsoft has put it in its *Knowledge Base,* a large database of questions and answers Microsoft has put together to avoid figuring out the same stuff over and over and over again.

We always find that it's worth searching the Knowledge Base before we go on infinite hold to wait for a human being. The search itself is straightforward: You pick from a list the product you're interested in and then type the keywords that you think may get you to your question. About half the time, we find something useful.

Updates on the Web

Getting software updates is the other option you have when you choose the Windows Update command from the Start menu. Microsoft has prepared some software at its Web site that tries to look around your computer to see what new system software it needs.

This idea is pretty cool. New *drivers* (the little bits and pieces of software that talk to different parts of the hardware in your computer) come out practically every day. By the time you install Windows Me on your computer, some piece of it is almost bound to be out of date. If you buy an add-on component for your computer, it most likely comes with a software driver, which is almost inevitably out of date. It had to be manufactured, integrated with the hardware package, sent to the retailer, and then sent on to you, a process that can take months!

The Update Wizard aims to fix all that by looking around your computer system and finding the out-of-date software. We can tell you that this process works well because it was thoroughly tested in Windows 98, in which people discovered horrible new security flaws about twice a month, with frequent updates from Microsoft to fix them. On one hand, we've always been fans of the "If it ain't broke, don't fix it" school of software updates. On the other hand, with Windows being so complicated, some things may fail only once or twice a week, and an update you didn't know you needed may just fix it.

We tested these hi-falutin', fancy-pants features using a 56K modem, usually at connection speeds of 38K or 40K bits per second. At that speed, the response ranged from acceptable to slow. At slower speeds, our guess is that some of them would tax your patience so much that you wouldn't want to bother with them. On the other hand, using subscriptions to load Web information in the middle of the night may be particularly attractive if your modem is slow. Just make sure that it gets done by the time you arrive in the morning with your coffee. If, of course, you have DSL or a cable modem, you shouldn't have to worry.

The other component of the Windows Me file updating thing-a-ma-jig (a very technical term used only by trained computational experts) is the new AutoUpdater. This little gadget sits in the background and periodically checks to see whether updates are available for your system. Sounds good, doesn't it? No? You must have a 56K modem and not warp-speed DSL or cable access. Sure, it's nice to have something always looking out for you, but it really depends, doesn't it?

Fortunately, you can set rules for how AutoUpdate treats the process of checking for updates and even how it treats those updates when it receives them. You can tell it to check only when you're already online. It can check when you aren't online. It can check using a schedule you define. It can be forced to ask you whether you want to be notified before downloading an update. It can download it and then ask whether you want it. It can just fetch the files and do it without even notifying you. You can even turn the thingy off completely.

If you have a fast, permanent connection, you can turn on all the gizmos and thing-a-ma-bobs and never really have to worry about much. Most of us prefer to require AutoUpdate to notify us whenever updates are ready to be installed so that we can inspect them. That's our advice to you: Don't let anything that installs what-zits and chatchkis (no comment) put anything on your computer without your knowing what it is and when it was done. Period.

Part IV
Other Stuff You Can Do on the Internet

The 5th Wave   By Rich Tennant

"It's a letter from the company that installed our in-ground sprinkler system. They're offering Internet access now."

In this part . . .

Computer geeks enjoy collecting software from the Net. Photographers enjoy collecting pictures from the Net. Collectors enjoy getting catalogs from the Net. No matter what you get from the Net, however, you need to know how to get it on your computer. That's what downloading is all about. You can also waste (or invest) a tremendous amount of time chatting with people on the Internet. And nobody should be without a home page on the World Wide Web. We'll show you how to make your own.

Chapter 12

More Shopping, Less Dropping

● ●

In This Chapter

▶ Why shop online?

▶ To charge it or not to charge it

▶ Step-by-step shopping

▶ Where to find tickets, mutual funds, books, clothes, computers, food, and pretty much everything else online

● ●

*I*f, because of severe insomnia, you follow the computer trade press, you have heard far, far too much about online commerce (or *e-commerce*). Surprisingly, much of the hype turns out to be true, and you can quite reasonably buy all sorts of stuff over the Net. We have bought lots of things online, from books to pants to plane tickets to stocks and mutual funds to computer parts to, uh, specialized personal products (don't read too much into that) and lived to tell the tale.

Shopping Online: Pros and Cons

Here are some reasons that we shop on the Net:

✔ Online stores are convenient, open all night, and don't mind if you window-shop for a week before you buy something.

✔ Online stores can sometimes offer great prices and better selection than brick-and-mortar stores.

✔ Two of the three authors of this book live in small rural towns; lots of stuff just isn't available locally. (Although Trumansburg, New York, is a wonderful place, you can't get a decent cup of coffee.)

✔ Unlike malls, online stores don't have Muzak (well, some do, but that's another matter entirely).

Net shopping's greatest hits

What should you buy online? Here are some good bets:

✔ **Books and CDs:** Online stores are fiercely competitive, and the prices can be impressively cheap. Browsing is harder, though, and you usually can't read the first chapter before you choose. Music, on the other hand, is often represented by short clips or even complete versions of some songs from the CD.

✔ **Airplane tickets and other travel arrangements:** You can do better than all except the best travel agents. We go online to find great fares and then challenge our local agent to match or beat it.

✔ **Computers:** If you know what you want, online is usually cheaper and less hassle than a big computer store.

✔ **Stocks and mutual funds:** If you make your own investment decisions, online brokerage is much, much cheaper than a regular broker — $8 to $20 per trade rather than as much as $50 for discount or $100 for a full-service broker. Also, online brokers don't get annoyed if you check stock prices 47 times a day.

✔ **Anything you'd buy from a mail-order catalog:** Most catalog merchants have Web sites, usually with special offers not in the paper catalog. (They really want you to order over the Net rather than talk to an expensive, live operator at a toll-free number.)

On the other hand, here are some reasons that we don't buy everything on the Net:

✔ You can't physically look at stuff before you buy it, and, in most cases, you have to wait for it to be shipped to you. (We don't expect to buy milk and bananas online any time soon, although services named Peapod and Netgrocer offer them.)

✔ We like our local stores and prefer to support them whenever we can.

✔ You can't flirt with the staff at a Web store, or find out about the latest town gossip.

The Credit Card Question

How do you pay for stuff you buy online? Most often, with a credit card, the same way you pay for anything else. What? Isn't that response nonchalant on our part? Isn't it incredibly, awfully dangerous to give out your credit card number online? Well, no.

After several years of asking for reports of card numbers being stolen from the Net, we have yet to hear of one. It doesn't happen. For one thing, most online stores encrypt the message between your computer and the store's server (indicated in your web browser by a closed lock icon in the lower-left corner of the window); for another, plucking the occasional credit card number from the gigabytes of traffic that flows every minute on the Net would be extremely difficult even without encryption.

When you use your plastic at a restaurant, you give your physical card with your physical signature to the physical waiter who takes it to the physical back room, does something physical with it out of your sight, and then physically brings it back (oddly, can you hear the Olivia Newton-John Muzak in the background?). Compared to that, the risk of sending your number to an online store is remote. A friend of ours who used to run a restaurant and later ran an online store assures us that there's no comparison — the online store had none of the plastic problems that the restaurant did.

If, after this harangue, you still don't want to send your plastic over the Net or you're one of the fiscally responsible holdouts who doesn't do plastic, most online stores are happy to have you call in your card number over the phone or send them a check.

A word about the Trust logos (they read "Trust-E" or "BBB Online") you may see somewhere near the bottom of Web pages. Although the logos may *seem* to give the site you are visiting some sort of trustworthiness sanction, or blessing, all the Web site is required to do in order to be able to sport the logo is publish its privacy policy somewhere on the site. Whether that policy is consumer friendly is immaterial — the site doesn't have to conform to any rules regarding privacy issues.

Let's Go to the Store

Stores on the Web work in two general ways: with and without virtual "shopping carts." In stores without carts, you either order one item at a time or fill out a big order form with a check box for everything the store offers. In stores with carts, as you look at the items the store has for sale, you can add items to your cart and then visit the virtual checkout line when you're done and then provide your payment and delivery information. Until you check out, you can add and remove items whenever you want, just like in the real world — except that you don't have to actually traipse around a store to put unwanted items back on the shelf.

Simple shopping

For a simple example, we lead you through a shopping trip at the Great Tapes for Kids Web site, a small online store for children's videotapes, audiotapes, and books, run by one of us authors. (Us? Venal? Naah.) Start at the home page, `http://www.greattapes.com`, as shown in Figure 12-1. It shows a featured item and has links to pages listing all other available books and tapes.

When you know what you want, you click the Order Form icon on one of the Web pages to see a giant order form with a box for everything you could possibly want to order, as shown in Figure 12-2. (At large online stores, this method gets a little unwieldy.) As you continue through the form by pressing the cursor keys or clicking the scroll bar, you mark whatever it is that you want to buy. At the bottom of the form, as shown in Figure 12-3, you enter the same stuff you would put on a paper order form. Most forms have a place for typing a credit card number; if you're not comfortable entering it there (we are, as we describe in the section "The Credit Card Question," earlier in this chapter), leave it blank — the store invariably has a way you can call the number in. Click the Send Order button, and your order is on its way.

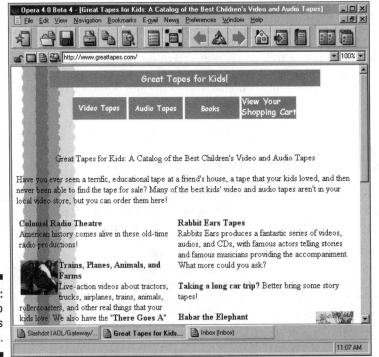

Figure 12-1:
Welcome to
Great Tapes
for Kids.

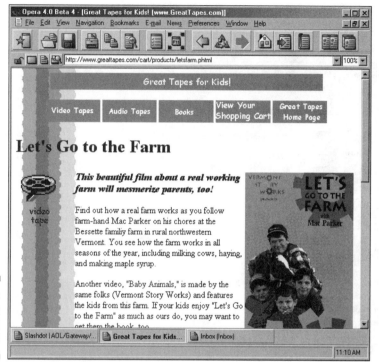

Figure 12-2:
Let's order
some animal
movies!

You generally get an e-mail message confirming the details of your order and, frequently, e-mail updates if any problems or delays occur.

TIP

Cookie alert

You may have heard horrible stories about things called *cookies* that Web sites reputedly use to spy on you, steal your data, ravage your computer, inject cellulite into your hips while you sleep, and otherwise make your life miserable. After extensive investigation, we have found that most cookies aren't all that bad; when you're shopping online, they can even be quite helpful.

A *cookie* is no more than a little chunk of text a Web site sends to a PC with a request (not a command) to send the cookie back during future visits to the same Web site. The cookie is stored on your computer in the form of a tiny (as much as 4 kilobytes) text file. That's all it is. You can see the cookies now on file on your PC in a file named something like Cookies.txt. (If you use Netscape, it's probably in your C:\Program Files\Netscape\Users*name* folder. If you use Internet Explorer, your cookies are in the C:\Windows\Cookies folder.) For online shopping, cookies let the web server track your "shopping cart" of items you have selected but not yet bought, even if you log out and turn off your computer in the interim.

Figure 12-3:
Have you finished your holiday shopping?

Fancy shopping

Although a simple store with a giant order form works okay for stores that don't have many different items in a catalog or businesses where you buy one thing at a time, this method is hopeless for stores with large catalogs. While writing this chapter, we (John, actually) decided that the Great Tapes order form had gotten hopelessly large, so we reprogrammed the Web site to provide a *shopping cart* to help track the items people order. (John would do practically anything to avoid writing.)

As you click your way around a site, you can toss items into your cart, adding and removing them as you want, by clicking a button labeled something like Add Item to Your Shopping Cart. Then, when you have the items you want, you visit the virtual checkout line and buy the items in your cart. Until you visit the checkout, you can always put back the items in your cart if you decide that you don't want them.

The shopping-cart-ized version of Great Tapes for Kids looks just like the old version, until you click the Order button on one of its pages. The giant order form is gone, and in its place is the shopping cart page, the interesting part of which is shown in Figure 12-3.

Suppose that one tape isn't enough for you because you have two nephews, so you click the Resume Shopping button, find another tape, and click Order again. Now both tapes are in your cart. (Although this process looks totally obvious, the programming required to make it work correctly on a web server is kind of tricky. Much as we would love to share the technical details, our editor regretfully informs us that we're short of space. Phoo.)

At this point, you can continue shopping, adjust the quantities (including adjusting down to zero anything you don't want), or go to the checkout to finish your order. When you have selected the items you want to buy, you click the Proceed to Checkout button. You see a page with areas to put your name, address, and payment details and a button you click to confirm your order.

Most virtual stores use a cookie (we talk about them in the "Cookie alert" sidebar, earlier in this chapter) to identify your personal shopping cart. The cookie lets you log out from the Internet, return to the Great Tapes Web site a day or two later, and find your shopping cart still there with your stuff in it. We find this process particularly handy for book shopping — every few days, we hear about a book we want and virtually throw it into our cart. (Throwing is okay because in cyberspace nothing gets dented.) Then, when we have enough books to make a decent order, we submit the order and pay a single shipping charge for the whole bunch rather than order them one at a time.

Up, Up, and Away

We buy lots of airline tickets online. Although the online travel sites aren't as good as really good travel agents, the sites are much better than bad travel agents. Even if you have a good agent, online sites let you look around to see what your options are before you get on the phone. We have also found some good travel agents who work via Web sites and e-mail.

The general theory of airline tickets

Four giant airline computer systems in the United States handle nearly all the airline reservations in the country. (The systems are known as *CRS*s for computer reservations systems or *GDS* for Global Distribution System.) Although each airline has a "home" CRS, the systems are all interlinked so that you can, with few exceptions, buy tickets for any airline from any CRS. The systems are Sabre (home to American and US Airways), Apollo (home to United), Worldspan (home to Delta, Northwest, and TWA), and Amadeus (home to Continental.) Many low-price start-up airlines don't participate in any of these systems, but have their own Web sites where you can check flights and buy tickets. Southwest, the largest and oldest of the low-price airlines, doesn't participate but has an arrangement with Sabre, so Sabre shows Southwest flights even though none of the other three does.

In theory, all the systems show the same data; in practice, however, they get a little out of sync with each other. If you're looking for seats on a sold-out flight, an airline's home system is most likely to have that last, elusive seat. If you're looking for the lowest fare to somewhere, check all four systems (Web sites) because a fare that's marked as sold out on one system often mysteriously reappears on another system. Some categories of fares are visible only to travel agents and don't appear on any of the Web sites, particularly if you aren't staying over a weekend, so check with a good agent before buying. On the other hand, many airlines have available some special deals that are *only* on their Web sites and that agents often don't know about. Confused? You should be. We were.

The confusion is even worse if you want to fly internationally. Official fares to most countries are set via a treaty organization called the IATA, so computer systems usually list only IATA fares for international flights. It's easy to find entirely legal "consolidator" tickets sold for considerably less than the official price, however, so an online or offline agent is extremely useful for getting the best price. The airlines also have some impressive online offers, most notably from Cathay Pacific and Lufthansa, which once or twice a year runs online auctions for a plane full of tickets from the United States to Hong Kong and Europe, respectively, with the lowest winning bids often less than half the normal fare.

Here's our distilled wisdom about buying tickets online:

- Check the online systems to see what flights are available and for an idea of the price ranges. Check more than one CRS.

- After you have found a likely airline, check that airline's site to see whether it has any special Web-only deals. If a low-fare airline flies the route, be sure to check that one too.

- Check with a travel agent to see whether he can beat the online price, and buy your tickets from the agent unless the online deal is better. Some agents give you a small discount if you make your reservations yourself because the agent only has to issue the ticket and mail the receipt to you.

- For international tickets, do everything in this list, and check both online and with your agent for consolidator tickets, particularly if you don't qualify for the lowest published fare.

- If you bid on airline tickets at a travel auction Web site, make sure that you already know the price at which you could buy the ticket, so you don't bid more. Remember to add in the taxes and fees, which can often be $50 or more.

More about online airlines

Because the online airline situation changes weekly, anything we print here would be out of date before you read it. One of the authors of this book is a plane nerd in his spare time; to get a current list of online CRSs, airline Web sites, Web specials, and online travel agents, visit his Web site, at `http://www.iecc.com/airline`.

Taking It to the Bank

As though everything else weren't enough, you can also perform all your banking online. Most banks, in order to remain banks, have to offer some sort of online access to their customers, but some smart people have seen it another way. The deal now is Internet-*only* banks. That's right — no branches, no ATMs, no nothing — just bank. One of the first to enter this fray was Wingspan (`http://www.wingspan.com`) which offers all the things a real brick-and-mortar bank offers, with the exception that you have to mail in your deposits. Of course, that's true for all online banks, of which there are a few to choose from.

Two more are Wachovia (`http://www.wachovia.com`) and USAccess (`http://www.usaccess.com`). USAccess has a helpful link to a free ATM finder hosted by the Independent Bankers Association of America (IABB, at `http://www.jabb.org`). This service is important in online banking because all transactions occur either via mail or via ATM; having access to one that does *not* add surcharges to every transaction is a godsend, to say the least.

Before committing to a long-term online banking arrangement, check to see whether your employer supports direct deposit. This feature is critical because you're likely to spend more on postage per month than you would on checking account fees (if you keep your balance up, that is).

Here are two pieces of advice that should apply pretty much anywhere: Never accept a reduction of services just because the bank is online. Expect the opposite. You should get more because these people don't have to maintain branches in local areas. Branches suck up funds faster then a warthog can nuzzle truffles. Also, never — *ever* — send your money to anyone unless you can verify, without a shadow of a doubt, that they are who they say they are.

Moving Money Around

Sure, old standards such as Western Union can still shuttle cash back and forth between persons, but much niftier (that's our word) services are available than those old-schoolers offer. PayPal is the latest in convenience-oriented services. It owes its very existence to the Internet. Backed by the well-funded online bank X.com, there's little chance that PayPal will go belly-up.

The premise is simple. Suppose that you go online, get drawn into an auction, and become the proud owner of a naked hula dancer lamp/mirror from 1939. Now you have to pay the kind person for your new possession. Use PayPal! Simply log on, indicate to whom you want to transfer money, click Submit, and you're golden, baby. The previous owner receives an e-mail message and can then go and collect.

The nice thing about PayPal is that no cash needs to be involved. In fact, not even any paper is involved. The money comes from your PayPal account, which, if it's empty, can be topped up at your option from your credit card or checking account. PayPal claims greater security than personal transactions because it uses top-notch encryption and no account information is ever revealed to third parties.

Finally, PayPal is free. How? That's simple — it hopes that your funds stay in its system for a while. Because millions of monetary units remain in the PayPal system for a couple of days (bankers call it *float*), PayPal gets cash from which it can earn interest. (Now you know why American Express wants you to save that last traveler's cheque — same idea.)

Pure Money

If you invest in mutual funds or the stock market (something that's difficult to avoid these days unless you anticipate dying at an early age), you can find a remarkable range of resources online. An enormous amount of stock information is also available, providing Net users with research resources as good as professional analysts had a few years ago.

The most important thing to remember about all the online financial resources is that everyone has an ax to grind and wants to get paid somehow. In most cases, the situation is straightforward; for example, a mutual fund manager wants you to invest with her funds, and a stockbroker wants you to buy and sell stocks with him. Some other sites are less obvious: Some are supported by advertising, and others push other kinds of investments. Just keep a source's interests in mind when you're considering that source's advice.

Mutual funds

Mutual funds are definitely the investment of the Baby Boomer generation. The world now has more mutual funds than it has stocks for the funds to buy. (Kind of makes you wonder, doesn't it?) Most fund managers have at least descriptions of the funds and prospectuses online, and many now provide online access so that you can check your account and move money from one fund to another within a fund group.

Well-known fund groups include

- ✔ **Fidelity Investments:** The 500-pound gorilla of mutual funds; specializes in actively managed funds (`http://www.fidelity.com`)
- ✔ **Vanguard Group:** Specializes in low-cost and index funds (`http://www.vanguard.com`)
- ✔ **American Century:** Another broad group of funds (`http://www.americancentury.com`)

Many of the online brokers listed in the following section also let you buy and sell mutual funds, although it almost always costs less if you deal directly with a fund manager. Yahoo! (`http://www.yahoo.com`) has a long list of funds and fund groups; click the Business and Economy option and then Finance and Investment and then Mutual Funds.

Stockbrokers

Most of the well-known full-service brokerage firms have jumped on the Web, along with a new generation of low-cost online brokers offering remarkably cheap stock trading. A trade that may cost $100 with a full-service firm can cost as little as $8 with a low-cost broker. The main difference is that the cheap firms don't offer investment advice and don't assign you to a specific broker. For people who do their own research and don't want advice from a broker, low-cost firms work well. For people who do need some advice, the partial- or full-service firms often offer lower-cost trades online, and they let you get a complete view of your account whenever you want. The number of extra services the brokerages offer (such as retirement accounts, dividend reinvestment, and automatic transfers to and from your checking account) varies widely.

Online brokers include

- ✔ **Charles Schwab:** One of the oldest discount brokers (`http://www.schwab.com`)
- ✔ **Morgan Stanley Dean Witter Online:** A medium-cost, limited-advice broker (`online.msdw.com`)

- ✔ **Ameritrade:** A very low-cost, no-advice broker (http://www.ameritrade.com)

- ✔ **Salomon Smith Barney:** A full-service broker with online access to accounts and research info (http://www.smithbarney.com)

Most fund groups, including the ones in this list, have brokerage departments, which can be a good choice if you want to hold both individual stocks and funds.

Tracking your portfolio

Several services let you track your portfolio online. You enter the number of shares of each fund and stock you own, and at any time they tell you exactly how much they're worth and how much money you have lost today. Some of them send by e-mail a daily portfolio report, if you want. These reports are handy if you have mutual funds from more than one group or both funds and stocks. All the tracking services are either supported by advertising or run by a brokerage that hopes to get your trading business:

- ✔ **My Yahoo:** (my.yahoo.com) You can enter multiple portfolios and customize your screens with related company and general news reports. You can also get lots of company and industry news, including some access to sites that otherwise requires paid subscriptions. It's advertiser-supported and very comprehensive and easy to use.

- ✔ **My Snap:** (my.snap.com) Snap is a clone of Yahoo!. Its portfolio features are similar to and arguably better than Yahoo's.

- ✔ **Reuters Moneynet:** (http://www.moneynet.com) Track portfolios and read Reuters news stories. Although a variety of premium services, such as real-time stock quotes, cost money, the free portfolio tracker isn't bad.

- ✔ **MoneyCentral Investor:** (investor.msn.com) Also has portfolios and lots of information, although we find it a pain to use.

Even More Places to Shop

Here are a few other places to shop that we have visited on the Web. We have even bought stuff from most of them.

Books and such

Although you can't (yet) flip through the books in an online bookstore, if you know what you want, you can get good deals.

✔ **Amazon.com** (`http://www.amazon.com`): Amazon.com is one of online commerce's great success stories, springing up from nothing (if you call several million dollars of seed money nothing) to one of the Net's biggest online stores. Amazon has an enormous catalog of books, music, and a growing variety of other junk, much of which it can get to you in a few days. It also has an "affiliates" program in which other Web sites can refer you to their favorite books for sale at Amazon, creating sort of a virtual virtual bookstore. For an example, see our Web site, at `net.gurus.com`, where we venally have links to Amazon for every book we have written in case, because of an oversight, you don't already have them all. Amazon sells most books at less than list price; for users outside the United States, the prices are low enough that even with shipping they're usually cheaper than buying locally.

✔ **BarnesandNoble.Com** (`http://www.bn.com`): Barnes and Noble is one of the biggest bookstore chains, and their online bookstore is also big, complete, and well done.

✔ **Borders.com:** (`http://www.borders.com`): Borders is another excellent book chain with an excellent Web-based bookstore and extremely fast delivery.

✔ **Fatbrain** (`http://www.fatbrain.com`): An online bookstore specializing in computer books. It stocks many technical titles and can often get books to you the next day.

✔ **CDNow** (`http://www.cdnow.com`): It has a huge selection of music CDs. You can even listen to some tracks if you have RealPlayer installed (see Chapter 11).

Clothes

This section points out a few familiar merchants with online stores. Directories such as Yahoo! have hundreds of other stores, both familiar and obscure:

✔ **Lands End** (`http://www.landsend.com`): Most of this catalog is online, and you can order anything you find in any of its individual printed catalogs, along with online-only discounted overstocks. It also has plenty of the folksy blather that encourages you to think of the company in terms of a few folks in the cornfields of Wisconsin rather than a corporate mail-order colossus. (It's both, actually.) Moderately cool 3-D virtual models attempt to show what the clothes you're ordering look like on a cyborg with a body shaped like yours.

- ✔ **REI** (http://www.rei.com): This large, sports equipment and outdoor-wear co-op is headquartered in Seattle. (Members get a small rebate on purchases.) The whole catalog is online, and online orders get discounted shipping.

- ✔ **The Gap** (http://www.gap.com): Although this site doesn't yet have the full line of stuff in the stores, for those of us who are of unusual vertical or horizontal dimension, it has jeans in sizes the stores don't stock, and the View As Images option is super cool.

Computers

When you're shopping for computer hardware online, be sure that a vendor you're considering has both a good return policy, in case you don't want the computer when it arrives, and a long warranty.

- ✔ **Dell Computers** (http://www.dell.com): This site has an extensive catalog with online ordering and custom computer system configurations.

- ✔ **IBM** (http://www.ibm.com): The world's largest computer company has what feels like the world's largest Web site with a great deal of information about both IBM products and more general computing topics. IBM sells stuff online at commerce.www.ibm.com. The online store sells everything from home PCs to printed manuals to midrange business systems. We got as far as putting a $1.1 million AS/400 9406-650 in our cart, but then we chickened out. We did buy a nice manual for the 1965-era 360/67 for our historical collection. (At IBM, nothing seems to go out of print.)

- ✔ **Apple Computer** (store.apple.com): The Apple site has lots of information about Apple products and has online purchasing of systems and upgrades too.

- ✔ **PC Connection** (http://www.pcconnection.com): For computer hardware, software, and accessories, PC Connection is one of the oldest and most reliable online sources. And you can get overnight delivery within the continental United States, even if you order as late as 2 a.m.!

- ✔ **Computer Discount Warehouse** (http://www.cdw.com): CDW does a terrific job of letting you compare the prices and technical specs of various computer systems.

Auctions and used stuff

You can participate in online auctions of everything from computers and computer parts to antiques to vacation packages. Online auctions are like any other kind of auction in at least one respect: If you know what you're looking for and know what it's worth, you can get some great values; if you don't, you can easily overpay for junk. When someone swiped our car phone handset, we found at eBay an exact replacement phone for $31, rather than the $150 the manufacturer charged for just the handset.

Many auctions, notably eBay, also allow you to list your own stuff for sale, which can be a way to get rid of some of your household clutter a little more discreetly than in a tag sale:

- ✔ **eBay** (`http://www.ebay.com`): The most popular auction site on the Web, it sells all sorts of stuff (see Figure 12-4). *You* can sell stuff, too, by registering as a seller.

- ✔ **Yahoo! Auctions** (`http://auctions.yahoo.com`): eBay was such a big hit that Yahoo decided to hold auctions too.

- ✔ **Priceline.com** (`http://www.priceline.com`): This site sells airline tickets, hotel rooms, new cars, and even groceries. It's not really an auction; you specify a price for what you want and Priceline accepts or rejects it.

- ✔ **United Computer Exchange** (`http://www.uce.com`): UCE is "a global clearinghouse for buyers and sellers of new and used computer equipment."

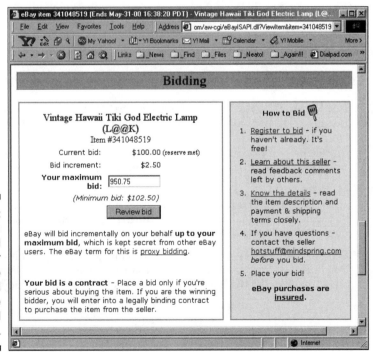

Figure 12-4:
To place a bid, scroll down, enter your top price, and click the Review Bid button.

Food

Here are our two favorite online dairies, along with a recipe site and two grocery-delivery services.

- ✔ **Egg Farm Dairy** (http://www.creamery.com): This site offers the best cheese in New York — better than much of the cheese from France. Try their new Lake Tear of the Clouds semisoft, or just order its excellent butter (which arrives in one-pound sticks, frozen solid). The site sells ice cream too, at http://www.cybericecream.com (and you don't have to pick transistors out of your teeth, either!).

- ✔ **Cabot Creamery** (http://www.cabotcheese.com): This site sells the best cheese in Vermont. Good bovine sound effects on the Web site, too.

- ✔ **The Kitchen Link** (http://www.kitchenlink.com): Search this site for the perfect recipe, and then shop for the ingredients.

- ✔ **Peapod** (http://www.peapod.com): Peapod lets you shop for groceries online and then delivers them to your home. Of course, you have to live in a major metropolitan area where the site has an agreement with a supermarket that will provide the groceries. If you live in the Boston area, try HomeRuns (http://www.homeruns.com), too.

All-In-One

Here is a limited list of familiar department store and cable shopping outlets:

- ✔ **Nordstrom** (http://www.nordstrom.com): This site offers a good portion of, but not all, the merchandise you would find at an actual Nordstrom's. Unlike an actual Nordstrom's, the Web site always has items on sale in every category, and it has no annoyingly cheerful sales clerks to annoy you! Unfortunately, the shopping experience is still pricey.

- ✔ **JC Penney** (http://www.jcpenney.com): It's basically the same JC Penney we all know. This site is great if you hate mall shopping, or if you don't have a mall nearby. Like Nordstrom's, Penney's has quite a large sale and clearance section.

- ✔ **QVC** (http://www.qvc.com): It's the same QVC of cable television fame. You find the same great prices and abundance of merchandise on this well-organized Web site. The no-questions-asked return policy applies here as well.

An online shopper's checklist

Here are some questions to keep in mind when you're shopping online. An astute shopper will notice that these are the same questions you keep in mind when you're shopping anywhere else:

✔ Are the descriptions clear enough to know what you're ordering?

✔ Are the prices competitive, both with other online stores and with mail-order and regular retail?

✔ Does the store have the products in stock, or does it offer a firm shipping date?

✔ Are different shipping options offered (FedEx, UPS, USPS, or alien spacecraft, for example)?

✔ Does the store have a good reputation?

✔ Can you return unsatisfactory goods?

The Shopping Update

Like everything else on the Net, shopping changes day by day as new businesses appear and old ones change. For the latest updates, see our update pages, at `net.gurus.com/shopping`.

Chapter 13

Downloading, Uploading, and Other File-Flinging Fun

● ●

In This Chapter

▶ Why download files from the Net?

▶ Why upload files to the Net?

▶ Downloading using your web browser

▶ File-transfer basics

▶ Giving your web browser FTP URLs to swipe files

▶ Using better file-transfer programs (WS_FTP)

▶ Uploading files to the Net

▶ Installing software you've grabbed from the Net

▶ Getting WinZip to handle zip files

● ●

*F*irst, the fancy terminology: *Downloading* means copying files from a computer that's Up There on the Internet "down" to the computer you're using. Because the Internet has an amazing number of cool files available, lots of stuff is available to download. *Uploading* is the reverse — copying a file from your computer "up" to a computer on the Internet. If your Internet Service Provider (ISP) lets you "publish" Web pages, you upload your Web pages to your provider's computer to do the publishing. *File transfer* means to copy files from one system to another — downloading or uploading. *FTP* stands for File Transfer Protocol, one way that computers transfer files across the Internet.

In this chapter, we tell you about two ways to download files: using a web browser and using an FTP program. The Web is the easiest way to download files, although you usually can't upload. FTP programs can both download and upload.

Why Download Files?

Because lots of cool stuff is available out there for free. You can download programs, pictures, sounds, and text to your computer — the process is relatively quick, and the price is right. Much of the Internet software we use with PPP accounts, for example, you can download right from the Internet, and you can also get nice clip art, recipes — you name it!

Why Upload Files?

You may be a crackerjack programmer who has written a wonderful program you want to contribute to one of the many libraries of shareware and freeware on the Internet. The most common reason to upload files, however, is to create or update a Web site; you create the Web pages for your Web site on your computer and then upload them to a Web server, as described at our Web site, at `http://net.gurus.com`.

Downloading Web Pages

Getting files over the Web is simplicity itself. You probably have been doing it for ages and didn't even know. Every Web page, every icon or image on a Web page, every ornate Web background is a file. Every time you click a link or type a URL to go to a Web page, you're getting at least one file. (If it's a page with a large number of graphics, you're getting a large number of files, one per picture.)

The technical term for the way that files are transferred by using the Web is *HTTP*, or *Hypertext Transport Protocol*. In English, this term means that your browser sends a command across the Internet to the Web server on which a file is stored, asking for the file to be sent to your computer. All you have to do to trigger this type of command is to know where to click. (We crabby old nerds feel that this stuff makes life much too simple, but such is the price of progress.)

Downloading pictures

To download a picture over the Web, first display the picture in your web browser. When you see on a Web page a picture you want to save on your hard disk, right-click the picture. From the menu that appears, choose Save Image As or Save Picture As. Tell your browser where to save the picture. That's all it takes!

Graphics files have filename extensions that identify what graphics format the file is in. When you download a picture, you can change the name of the file, but *don't* change its extension. Most graphics files on Web pages have the extension GIF or JPEG or JPG because these are the types of graphics files that most web browsers can display.

Just because a picture is now stored on your hard disk doesn't mean that you own it. Most pictures on Web pages are copyrighted. Unless a picture comes from a site that specifically offers pictures as reusable "clip art," you have to get permission to use the picture for commercial purposes or even to upload it to your own noncommercial Web page.

Downloading programs

Downloading a program file over the Web is also easy — you click a link to it, frequently a link that says either Download or the name of the program. Your web browser stops and asks what to do with the file. If it's a program (an EXE or COM file) or a zip file, the most reasonable thing for your browser to do is to save it to disk so that you can run it or unzip it later. If it's a zip file and you have WinZip (mentioned later in this chapter) installed, you can also tell the browser to run WinZip directly, by making it the handler program for zip files; we find that method less handy than you may think.

If you're interested in downloading an Internet program, for example, you may go to TUCOWS, at http://www.tucows.com. After you're at the site, click a link to choose a site near you, choose one of the Windows options , and choose the type of program you want to download. TUCOWS displays a Web page like the one shown in Figure 13-1, with a list of programs available for downloading. To download a program file, just click the name of the program, the Download button (if you see one), or any other link that looks like it may download something.

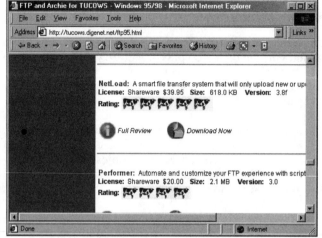

Figure 13-1:
Click the
program
name to
download
the program
file.

To make absolutely sure that your browser downloads a file for which you have a Web link to the disk, rather than try to run it, display it, or otherwise get clever, hold down the Shift key while you click the link.

Downloading other files

To download other types of files — sound files, video files, whatever — you follow the same steps as for downloading a program. Find a Web page that contains a link to the file you want. For sound clips of news stories, for example, you can try the National Public Radio Web site, at `http://www.npr.org`. Then click the link for the file you want, and tell your browser where to store it.

Some files, however, get handed off to another application, like RealPlayer, QuickTime, or Windows Media Player. What are those? Well, they play those music and video files that clog the Internet these days. You may have heard the term *MP3* (pronounced "em-pee-three"), especially in relation to another strangely named program, Napster. MP3 files are songs taken from CDs and turned into small files that can be stored and played on your computer.

We don't bore you with the details here; those are in Chapter 11. Suffice it to say that not all things you download appear as a file. Sometimes you click on a link and another program opens up to handle it. It's better to be prepared, we always say.

File Transfer in Theory and in Practice

Being able to download files from the Web is great, although not all files are *available* over the Web. And what if you want to upload a file? You need FTP — File Transfer Protocol.

Transferring a file via FTP requires two participants: an FTP client program and an FTP server program. The FTP *client* is the program that we, the Joe Six-Pack Users of the world, run on our computers. The FTP *server* is the program that runs on the huge mainframe somewhere (or, these days, likely as not, on a PC under someone's desk) and stores tens of thousands of files. The FTP server is similar to an online library of files. The FTP client can *upload* (send) files to the FTP server or, more commonly, *download* (receive) files from the FTP server.

Thousands of publicly accessible FTP servers exist, and they store hundreds of thousands of files. Many files are freeware or shareware programs. Some FTP servers are so popular that they can't handle the number of file requests they receive. When FTP servers are inundated, other FTP servers, called *mirrors,* which have copies of the same files, are set up to handle the overflow traffic.

Anonymous downloads

To use an FTP server, you have to log in with a username and password. What happens if you don't have an account on the FTP server machine? No problem, if it's a publicly accessible FTP server. You log in as `anonymous` and type your e-mail address as your password. Voilà! You have access to lots of files! This method of using public FTP servers is called *anonymous FTP.* There's nothing sleazy about it; public FTP sites expect you to use anonymous FTP to download files.

A few anonymous FTP tips

Some FTP servers limit the number of anonymous users or the times of day that anonymous FTP is allowed. Although you may be refused access, don't gripe about it — no law says that the owner of the system has to provide any access.

Don't store (*upload*) files on the FTP server unless the owner invites you to do so. A directory named INCOMING or something similar is usually available in which you can put stuff.

Some FTP servers allow anonymous FTP only from host computers that have names. That is, if you try to FTP anonymously from a host that has a number but no name, these hosts don't let you in. This problem occurs most often with PPP dial-up accounts, which, because they generally offer no services that are useful to other people, don't always have names assigned. If you have this problem, complain to your Internet Service Provider, who can fix it easily.

Text files versus everything else

FTP puts files into two different categories: ASCII and binary. An *ASCII* file is a text file; a *binary* file is anything else. FTP has two modes — ASCII and binary (also called *image* mode) — to transfer the two types of files. When you transfer an ASCII file between different types of computers that store text files differently, ASCII mode automatically adjusts the file during the transfer so that the file is a valid text file when it's stored on the receiving end. (Because Macs, Windows, and UNIX all have slightly different conventions for storing text files, this automatic conversion can save a great deal of hassle.) A binary file is left alone and transferred verbatim.

Choosing an FTP client program

If you want to get files by FTP, you need an FTP client program. Luckily, you have several excellent ways to do so:

- ✔ **Use your web browser.** Most browsers can handle anonymous FTP for downloading files (no anonymous uploading — you probably didn't want to do that anyway). See the next section, "Downloading Files By Using Your Web Browser."

- ✔ **If you have a PPP account, you can use a Winsock program.** The most popular freeware Windows FTP program is WS_FTP, and you find out how to use it in this chapter (in the section "Downloading with WS_FTP"). WS_FTP can handle both uploading and downloading files by using both anonymous FTP or private accounts on an FTP server.

- ✔ **Use the Windows Me built-in Ftp program.** Yes, Windows 98 comes with an FTP client program, but it's so old-fashioned that we don't suggest you use it. If you are desperate, see the sidebar "FTP-ing the old-fashioned way," later in this chapter.

- ✔ **If you use America Online (AOL) or CompuServe, it's easy to get files via anonymous FTP. On both services, use the keyword** ftp.

Downloading Files By Using Your Web Browser

To get your web browser to transfer files by using FTP, you use a special kind of URL: an FTP URL. (Don'tcha love these acronyms!) Interestingly, browsers are smart enough to tell which files are ASCII and which are binary. You don't have to worry about it.

The URL of FTP

When you've used your web browser as a web browser, you have probably typed URLs that begin with *http,* the abbreviation for the way browsers talk with Web servers (Hypertext Transport Protocol, if you must know). To tell your web browser to log in to an FTP server, you tell it a different kind of URL — an FTP URL. An FTP server's URL looks like this:

```
ftp://servername/directoryname/filename
```

You can leave out the directory name and filename, if you like, to get the top-level directory of that FTP server. For example, the URL of the Microsoft FTP server (at ftp.microsoft.com) is

```
ftp://ftp.microsoft.com/
```

This URL has no filename part: If you omit the filename, the server displays the top-level directory to which you have access.

Giving your browser an FTP URL

No matter which web browser you use, you follow the same general steps to retrieve files via FTP:

1. **Run the web browser as usual.**

2. **To tell your browser to load the URL of the FTP server, type the FTP URL in the Address, URL, or Netsite box just below the toolbar, and then press Enter.**

Downloading from your own private account

Some web browsers — Netscape Navigator, in particular — can handle more than just anonymous FTP; they can FTP files from sites on which you have to have an account. To download a file from a password-protected FTP server, assuming that you have an account on the server, you can include your account name by typing the account name followed by an at-sign immediately before the FTP server name. If your account name is zac, for example, and your password is framistan, you type a URL like this:

```
ftp://zac:framistan@ftp.gurus.com
```

Because this line puts your otherwise secret password on-screen for everyone to see, don't type this line whenever untrustworthy folk are present or if other people use your computer. Netscape, but not Internet Explorer, lets you leave the password off the URL and lets you type it instead in a box where it's displayed as asterisks, as a password should.

If you use a browser in which you can't type a URL in that box, you must give a command to tell it which URL to go to. Internet Explorer and Netscape Navigator let you choose File⇨Open (or press Ctrl+O) and then type the URL in the dialog box that's displayed.

The browser logs in to the FTP server and displays its home directory, as shown in Figure 13-2. Each file and directory in the current directory appears as a link. Depending on the web browser you use, the format may differ from the one shown in this figure.

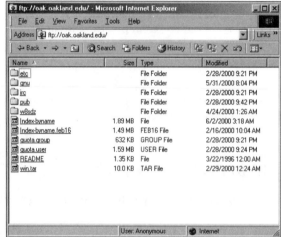

Figure 13-2: Internet Explorer can act as your FTP program.

3. **Click the directory name to move to the directory that contains the file you want.**

When you click a directory name, you move to that directory and your browser displays its contents.

4. **Click a filename to download the file.**

If you download a text file or another file your browser knows how to display, the browser displays it after it downloads. If you click the filename Readme.txt, for example, the browser displays the text file. If you want to save the file after you look at it, choose File⇨Save As from the menu and tell your browser the filename to use.

If you download a file your browser doesn't know how to display, such as a program, it usually asks what to do. (Figure 13-3 shows the message Internet Explorer displays.)

5. **If your browser asks what to do with the file, tell it to save the file and choose the directory and filename in which to save it.**

Your browser downloads the file.

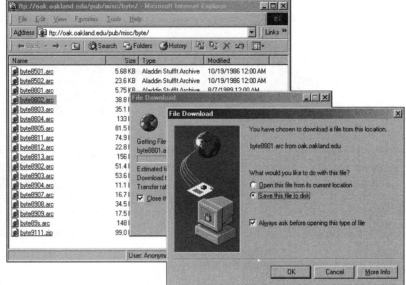

Figure 13-3:
Internet
Explorer
doesn't
know what
to do with
the file you
want to
download.

Real FTP with WS_FTP

What if you want to upload files? Or what if you want to be able to transfer groups of files or rename files after you transfer them or see the files that are on the FTP server? Your web browser just doesn't cut the mustard. Face it — you need a *real* FTP program.

If you use a PPP Internet account, you can use any Winsock FTP client program. Many good freeware and shareware FTP programs are available right off the Internet. This section describes how to use our favorite, WS_FTP. Technically it's WS_FTP 5.0.8 LE, but we avoid that messiness. We don't think that Ipswitch will mind terribly. Oh, it's at http://www.ipswitch.com. Tasty features of WS_FTP include

🖙 Scrollable and selectable windows for the names of local and remote files and directories

🖙 Clickable buttons for such common operations as connecting and setting binary mode

🖙 Connection profiles, which save the hostname, login name, password, and remote host directory of your favorite FTP sites; comes with a bunch of useful profiles already set

FTP-ing Web pages

If you maintain a Web site, you use FTP to transfer from your computer to the Web server the Web pages you create or edit. You can use WS_FTP or another FTP program to transfer the pages, although you have to keep track of which Web pages you created, changed, or deleted on your computer and remember to do the same on the Web server computer. The larger your Web site grows, the bigger headache you have.

There's a better way: Use an FTP program designed just for maintaining Web sites. Margy uses NetLoad, a nifty program that can compare the files (by checking file sizes and dates) on your computer and on your Web site to see which files need to be uploaded or deleted. One click of a button, and NetLoad transfers all the necessary files. You can get NetLoad, or one of a number of similar programs, from TUCOWS (at http://www.tucows.com) on the Net.

Downloading WS_FTP

The freeware version of our favorite FTP program, WS_FTP LE (the LE is for Limited Edition), is available by (what else!) FTP from a variety of places, including its "home," the United States Military Academy. (And you thought that they were only trained how to fight wars!) You can also download the program from the Web; follow these steps:

1. **In My Computer or Windows Explorer, make a folder in which to put WS_FTP.**

2. **Use your web browser to go to TUCOWS, at http://www.tucows.com. Choose the Windows 95/98 link, click the mirror site closest to you, and then find the link for FTP in the Network Utilities section.**

   You see a long list of freeware and shareware FTP clients. Cool!

3. **Scroll down to WS_FTP LE and click the program name. Tell your browser to store the file in the folder you created in Step 1.**

   Your browser downloads the file. It's time to install it.

4. **Unzip the Wsftp32.zip file.**

   We give you instructions later in this chapter for unzipping a file. You end up with a bunch of files, including the install program, which is named Inst32.exe.

5. **Run the installation program.**

   It asks a bunch of questions, such as whether you agree to the terms for noncommercial use (if you're a home user, you probably do), which directories to use, and which version of the program to use. In each case, the suggested answer is fine.

You're ready to FTP by using WS_FTP!

The big WS_FTP picture

The steps you follow to use WS_FTP (or any other FTP client program) are more complicated than using a browser:

1. **Connect to the Internet.**
2. **Log in to the FTP server by using WS_FTP.**
3. **Move to the directory on the server that contains the files you want to download, or move to the directory to which you want to upload files.**

   FTP servers have the same kinds of tree-structured directory structure as Windows. Most FTP servers use pathnames similar to the ones Windows uses, except for forward slashes (/) rather than backslashes (\ ).

4. **Move to the folder on your own computer in which you want to download files or from which you want to upload files.**
5. **Tell the program which type of files (ASCII or binary) you are moving.**
6. **Download or upload the files.**
7. **Log off the FTP server.**

Connecting to an FTP server

Here's how to use the WS_FTP program to connect to an FTP server:

1. **Run the WS_FTP program by double-clicking its icon.**

   You see the Session Properties dialog box, as shown in Figure 13-4. This dialog box lets you enter information about the FTP server you want to connect to. After you have entered this information, WS_FTP saves it so that you can easily connect to the saved FTP server again.

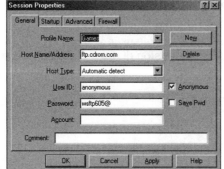

Figure 13-4:
Which FTP
server do
you want to
talk to?

2. **In the Profile Name box, enter the name you want to use for this FTP server.**

   If you want to FTP to `rtfm.mit.edu`, for example, which contains FAQs for all the Usenet newsgroups, you may enter **Usenet FAQ Central**.

3. **In the Host Name box/Address, enter the name of the FTP server.**

   This name can be a regular Internet name (such as `oak.oakland.edu`, another useful FTP server) or a numeric address.

4. **Leave the Host Type box set to auto-detect.**

   This step tells WS_FTP to guess which operating system the FTP server is using. It usually guesses right.

5. **If you really have a username on the FTP server, enter your username and password in the User ID and Password boxes.**

   Otherwise, click the Anonymous Login box. WS_FTP asks for your e-mail address, which it uses as your password (the usual thing to do when you FTP anonymously).

6. **Enter your address and click OK.**

   WS_FTP fills in the User ID and Password boxes for you.

   If you want WS_FTP to store the password in the Password box rather than ask you for it every time you connect to the FTP server, click the Save Password box so that it contains an X.

   Leave the Account box blank, unless you have your own account on the FTP server and you know what account name to enter.

7. **Switch to the Startup tab and, in the Initial Directories Remote Host box, enter the directory in which you want to look on the FTP server.**

   Alternatively, you can leave this box blank and look around on your own.

8. **In the Initial Directories Local PC box, enter the folder on your own PC in which you want to store downloaded files.**

   Clicking the OK button saves the information and opens the connection; clicking Apply just saves this information and leaves the Properties dialog box open.

   If you clicked OK, WS_FTP tries to connect to the FTP server.

"It won't speak to me!"

If you have a problem connecting to the FTP server, messages appear in the two-line box at the bottom of the WS_FTP window. You can scroll the little window up and down to see what happened. For example, rtfm.mit.edu is frequently overloaded and doesn't let you log on. When this situation happens, some helpful messages are displayed about other FTP sites that may have the information you want. You can see these messages in this box.

To see the messages the FTP server sent, double-click them. WS_FTP opens a big window so that you can see them better. These messages can be helpful if something isn't working the way you hoped. To close the window, click the Close button.

Local and remote

After you're connected to the FTP server, you see the WS_FTP window, as shown in Figure 13-5. (Some versions of WS_FTP arrange the window a little differently and you can arrange the panes in an alternative fashion in WS_FTP LE. WS_FTP Pro 6.5 even has a mode that looks like a regular Windows directory view.) WS_FTP displays information about the files on your own computer on the left side of the window (labeled Local System) and the directories and files on the FTP server on the right side (labeled Remote System). On each side are buttons that enable you to change directories (ChgDir), make directories (MkDir), delete directories (RmDir), view files, and so on. Naturally, you don't have permission to delete or change anything on most FTP servers, so don't even try.

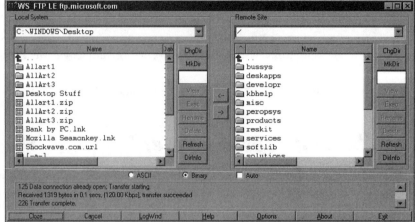

Figure 13-5:
Prepare to
receive
some files!

To move from directory to directory on the FTP server, choose directory
names from the list box on the Remote side. Or you can click the ChDir
button and enter the full pathname of the directory to go to.

Here's how to download a file:

1. **Choose ASCII or Binary by clicking the buttons at the bottom of the**
window.

   For files that consist entirely of text (like HTML files), choose ASCII. For
   anything else (like graphics files), choose Binary. You also have the
   option of allowing WS_FTP to determine what the file is by checking the
   Auto box. This option is typically quite reliable, but be aware that if
   something comes through jumbled, you may have to set it manually.

2. **On the Remote System side, move to the directory that contains the**
file you want to download, and then select the file.

3. **On the Local System side, move to the folder on your own computer in**
which you want to store the downloaded file.

4. **Click the left-pointing arrow button in the middle of the window.**

   The arrow points from the Remote side to the Local side, and WS_FTP
   downloads the file. For large files, this step can take some time; WS_FTP
   displays your progress as a percentage completed.

If you want to download several files from the same directory (and all the
files are the same type — either text or binary), you can select all the filenames and download them at the same time. Click the first filename. Then
Shift+click the last filename to select it and all the filenames in between. Or
Ctrl+click to select one additional filename.

Why is it called FTP?

We could say that FTP is short for *file-transfer program* and you probably would believe us, but that would be wrong. It really stands for *File Transfer Protocol*. Way back in 1971, the Internet Powers That Be decided on a *protocol,* a set of conventions for copying files from one place to another on the Net. Then many people wrote programs that implemented the protocol and called them all FTP. Is this clear? Never mind. The geeks among us also use FTP as a verb. The megageeks try to pronounce FTP as a word.

I am outta here!

To disconnect from the FTP server after you're finished, click the Close button in the bottom-left corner of the WS_FTP window.

Connecting again

To call someone else, click the Connect button. You see the Session Profile window again. Fill in different information and click OK to make the connection.

To call an FTP server you have called before, click Connect. In the FTP Client Connect To window, click the arrow button to the right of the Config name box. You see a list of the configurations you've entered — choose one and click OK.

FTP-ing wrong

The most common error that inexperienced Internet users make (and *experienced* users, for that matter) is transferring a file in the wrong mode. If you transfer a text file in binary mode from a UNIX system to your Windows Me system, the file looks something like this:

```
This file
        should have been
                      copied in
                             ASCII mode.
```

Hurry up and wait

The Internet is pretty fast, although not infinitely so. When you're copying stuff between two computers on the same local network, information can move at about 200,000 characters per second. When the two machines are separated by a great deal of intervening Internet, the speed drops — often to 1,000 characters per second or fewer. If you're copying a file that's 500,000 characters long (the size of your typical inspirational GIF image), it takes only a few seconds over a local network, although it can take several minutes over a long-haul connection.

It's often comforting to look at the directory listing before retrieving a file so that you know how big the file is and can have an idea of how long the copy will take. Because programs get inexorably larger, even with faster modems, patience remains as the key to successful downloading.

If, on the other hand, you copy something in ASCII mode that isn't a text file, it gets scrambled. Compressed files don't decompress; executable files don't execute (or they crash or hang the machine); images look unimaginably bad if they even appear at all. When a file is corrupted, the first thing you should suspect is the wrong mode in FTP.

If you're FTP-ing (Is that a verb? It is now!) files between two computers of the same type, such as from one Windows system to another, you can and should make all your transfers in binary mode. Because a text file or a non-text file doesn't require any conversion, binary mode does the right thing.

Uploading Is Cool Too

Okay, now you know how to retrieve files from other computers. How about copying the other way? If you write your own Web pages and want to upload them to your Internet provider's computer, here's how you do it: FTP them to the provider's Web server.

Internet Explorer doesn't handle uploading. You have to use a real FTP program, like WS_FTP or Netscape Navigator, if you want to use FTP to upload files to your server.

Uploading with Netscape

In Netscape Navigator, you can log in to the Web server as yourself by using an FTP URL that includes your username, like this:

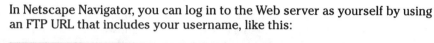

```
ftp://yourid@www.yourprovider.com/
```

Type your login ID in place of `yourid`. (It pops up a box asking for your password when needed.) Rather than type `www.provider.com`, type the name of your provider's Web server, which most likely is `www` followed by the provider's domain name but may also be something like `ftp.www.fargle.net`. (Ask your provider if this info isn't in the sign-up packet it gave you.)

When you connect to an FTP server by using this method, you see your home Web directory listed on-screen. If you want to upload files to a different directory, click that directory's name so that you see that directory.

After you have the directory you want on-screen, just drag the file to upload it from any other program (such as Windows Explorer or My Computer) into the browser window. Way cool. Netscape Navigator asks whether you really want to upload the file. You can also choose File⇨Upload File from the menu if you find dragging to be a drag.

Uploading with WS_FTP

In WS_FTP, log in as we just described in the preceding section, using your login ID and password. After you have the local and remote directories you want in their respective windows in WS_FTP, just click the local file you want to upload, and then click the right-pointing arrow button pointing to the Remote window.

Some FTP servers are cool enough to send you to your directory automatically, just by recognizing your username. It saves lots of trouble and time, not to mention that it's a great stress reliever.

If you're uploading a Web page to a Web server, be sure to upload the page itself (in ASCII mode because the HTML file that contains the Web page is a text file) along with any graphics files that contain pictures which appear on the page (in binary mode).

After You Download a Program

Using FTP, you can download freeware and shareware programs and install and use them. You need a few well-chosen software tools, including a program to uncompress compressed files. (Useful little programs like this one are called *utilities* in the jargon.)

Installing FTP'd software usually requires three steps:

1. **Using FTP, download the file that contains the software.**

2. **If the software isn't in a self-installing file, it's usually in a compressed format, so uncompress it.**

3. **Run the installation program that comes with it, or at least create an icon for the program.**

By now, you know how to do Step 1, the FTP part. The rest of this chapter describes Steps 2 and 3: uncompressing and installing. Here goes!

Getting WinZip for unzipping

Most software on FTP servers is in a compressed format, to save both storage space on the server and transmission time when you download the file. An increasing amount of software is *self installing* — the file is a program that does the necessary uncompressing and installing. Self-installing files end with EXE, and non-self-installing compressed files end with ZIP (and are called *zip files*). To uncompress a self-installing EXE file, just run it — lots of files pop out.

If you download a zip file, you need a program to unzip with it. A guy named Nico Mak wrote a nice little Windows program called WinZip that can both unzip and zip things for you. Other programs work too, like PKZIP and PKUNZIP.

If you already have WinZip (which is also available through the mail or from various shareware outlets), skip ahead to the following section, "Running WinZip." If you have and love PKZIP and PKUNZIP or UNZIP and don't mind running them from an MS-DOS window, you too can skip this section. You can get a Windows version of PKUNZIP, which isn't as nice as WinZip, although some people like it. It works fine.

To get WinZip on the Web, go to `http://www.winzip.com`, a page full of pictures of outer-space-type blobs. Click the blob marked Download Evaluation to get to the download page. On that page, download the Windows 95, Windows 98, Windows NT, or Windows 2000 version.

To install WinZip:

1. **Run Winzip95.exe or Winzip98.exe (or whatever the name of the file is that you downloaded).**
2. **Follow the installation instructions WinZip gives you.**

   Although you have a bunch of options, you can accept the suggested defaults for all of them. WinZip installs itself and makes a WinZip icon on your desktop. We prefer the WinZip Classic to the WinZip Wizard interface, so that's what we describe here.

Running WinZip

Give it a try! Click that icon! WinZip looks like Figure 13-6.

WinZip - teragen.zip
File Actions Options Help
New Open Favorites Add Extract View Install Wizard
Name Modified Size Ratio Packed Path
Setup.ins 1/10/1998 4:22 PM 68,987 1% 68,181
Setup.exe 1/18/1997 10:53 AM 45,312 46% 24,437
Setup.pkg 2/3/2000 8:16 PM 1,004 48% 520
Setup.ini 2/3/2000 8:16 PM 29 0% 29
inst32i.ex_ 1/18/1997 11:04 AM 320,411 0% 319,668
isdel.exe 9/7/1995 7:22 PM 8,192 54% 3,783
setup.dll 12/19/1996 4:03 PM 6,128 51% 3,033
setup.lib 2/3/2000 8:16 PM 194,799 1% 193,010
setup.1 2/3/2000 8:16 PM 2,115,339 3% 2,056,507
Disk1.id 2/3/2000 8:16 PM 5 0% 5
Selected 0 files, 0 bytes
Total 10 files, 2,696KB

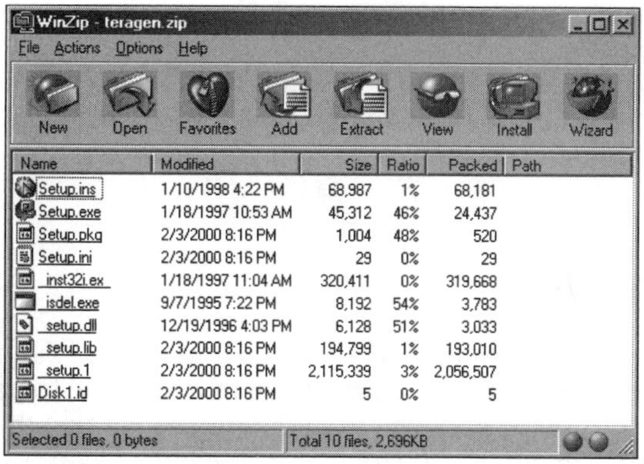

Figure 13-6: WinZip is ready to deal with your zip files.

To open a zip file (which the WinZip folks call an *archive*), click the Open button on the toolbar and choose the directory and filename for the zip file. Poof! WinZip displays a list of the files in the archive, with their dates and sizes.

Unzipping files

Sounds suggestive, we know, although it's not as much fun as it sounds. If you want to use a file from a zip file, after you have opened the zip file, you *extract* it — that is, you ask WinZip to uncompress it and store it in a new file.

To extract a file:

1. **Choose it from the list of files.**

   You can choose a group of files that are listed together by clicking the first one and then Shift+clicking the last one. To select an additional file, Ctrl+click it.

2. **Click the Extract button.**

   A dialog box asks in which directory you want to put the file and whether you want to extract all the files in the archive or just the one you selected.

3. **Select the directory in which to store the unzipped files.**

4. **Click OK.**

   WinZip unzips the file. The zip file is unchanged, and now you have the uncompressed file (or files) also.

Another way to unzip files is to select them in the WinZip window and drag them to a Windows Explorer or My Computer window. (Drag-and-drop can be so convenient sometimes.)

Zipping around

Although WinZip can do a bunch of other things too, such as add files to a zip file and create your own zip file, you don't have to know how to perform these tasks in order to swipe software from the Net, so we skip them. (We bet that you can figure them out, just by looking at the buttons on the WinZip toolbar.)

Easy? Windows? Hurray for Aladdin Expander!

An alternative to the shareware WinZip utility is Aladdin Expander for Windows, a free micro application. It may not have all those nifty GUI gizmos that WinZip has, but we bet that you'll use it more often. First, go get it from Aladdin Systems and install it (we beg your forgiveness because this procedure is unduly long — blame Aladdin Systems):

1. **Direct your browser to the Aladdin Systems Web site.**

   Open your web browser and enter **www.aladdinsys.com** on the address line. Press Return or click Go.

2. **Look under the Product Index list for Expander. You can find it in the left column, a little below Quick Links. Click the link.**

3. **Look near the top of the page for the word *Windows* in bold. Click the link next to it to go to another page. Scroll to the bottom, where you see a short form. Fill it out, and uncheck the obnoxious Notify me option.**

   If you don't, you get an ad mailer about every week or two. Don't check any of the other options, either.

   You're taken to another page.

4. **Scroll about halfway down and you see some yellow fields with text in them. Below the first field is a link to Aladdin Expander 5.0 for Windows 95/98/NT (.exe) (DS3 California). Click on it.**

   We realize that this may be excessive, but you go to another page.

5. **If you're using Internet Explorer or Netscape Navigator or Communicator, the Save As dialog box appears and you can save the installation file anywhere you want. If you're using Opera, the dialog box doesn't automatically appear, so just click on the Download Expander 5.0 (.exe) link and you're prompted to save the program.**

6. **Locate the installation file you just downloaded and double-click it.**

7. **Click Next until you can't click Next any more.**

   In a moment, Aladdin Expander is installed.

   You're asked whether you want to view the Read Me file and whether you want to run Expander immediately.

8. **Say no to both questions.**

   There are no surprises, and the default settings are more than sufficient. As part of the installation process, a small icon is placed on your desktop (we suspect that you already have many icons there).

Now that you have Expander installed and ready to go with an icon on your desktop, you're ready to drop items on it. "Drop?" you ask. Yes, drop. The point of the icon is to drop archives "into" it, and out comes expanded files, neatly tucked away in a new folder. To test this procedure, locate a handy zip file and drop it on the Expander icon. Be careful to ensure that a small plus (+) sign appears next to your mouse pointer before releasing the mouse button. The (+) indicates that the icon is placed over the Expander icon. After you drop the item, you hear some grinding from the hard disk and a little progress bar briefly appears in the middle of the screen.

After Expander is done, you have a new folder named the same as the zip file and that now holds whatever was in the zip file. If you have more than one item, you can select them all and drag them to the Expander icon, where they all are extracted in sequence — and where they all get their own neat little folders. Nifty, eh? That little "dropping" gizmo started life on the Macintosh, where drag-and-drop is an everyday matter.

Now that you know how to unzip software you get from the Internet, you're ready for our next topic: safe software.

Scanning for viruses

We all know that you practice safe software: You check every new program you get to make sure that it doesn't contain any hidden software viruses that may display obnoxious messages or trash your hard disk. If that's true of you, you can skip this section.

For the rest of you, it's a good idea to run a virus-scanning program. You never know what naughty piece of code you may otherwise unwittingly download to your defenseless computer!

Run a virus checker after you have obtained and run any new piece of software. Although the FTP servers on the Internet make every effort to keep their software archives virus-free, nobody is perfect. Don't get caught by some prankster's idea of a joke!

If you use WinZip, you can configure it to run your virus checker before you even unzip the zip file containing a program. Choose Options⇨Program Locations from the menu and type in the Scan program box the pathname of your virus checker program. Although Aladdin Expander does not have the same functionality, all virus checkers that we are aware of are either capable of checking files as they arrive, checking the files that appear in a certain folder, or allowing you to at least right-click the file and select Scan or something similar. After the file gets a clean bill of health, you can drop it on Expander.

Although Windows Me doesn't come with a virus checker, several commercial ones are available, including the McAfee VirusScan program, which you can download from the McAfee Web site, at http://www.mcafee.com. Lots of other virus scanners are available at TUCOWS (http://www.tucows.com). Most of them give you 30 days free before you have to pay to unlock them for permanent use.

FTP-ing the old-fashioned way

Why download WS_FTP when Windows Me comes with a perfectly good FTP program? Because the FTP program that comes with Windows Me is an old-fashioned command-line program that requires you to type DOS-like commands carefully at a DOS-like prompt. Yuck!

If you are stuck for an FTP program, however, and you really, really need to download or upload just one little file, here's a quick lesson.

To run FTP, click the Start button and choose the Run command, type **ftp** followed by a space and the hostname of the FTP server. Then click OK. If you're not connected to the Internet, you see the Dial-Up Networking window; click Connect. The Ftp program tries to connect to the FTP server. If it succeeds, the FTP server asks for a username and password. If you have an account on the server, type your username and password when it asks. If you don't have an account on the server, type **anonymous** for the username and your e-mail address as the password. Press Enter after typing each entry command in FTP.

To move to a different directory on the FTP server, use the **cd** command followed by the name of the directory to which you want to move. For example, most public FTP servers put all their good stuff in a subdirectory of the /pub directory, so type **cd /pub** to move there. To move up one directory (that is, to move to the parent directory of where you are now), type **cd** followed by a space and two dots.

To see a list of the files in current directory, type **dir**. To find out what directory you're in, type **pwd**.

To change the current folder on your own computer, type **lcd** (local directory) followed by the name of the folder. If the pathname of the folder contains spaces, enclose the pathname in quotes.

To tell FTP whether to transfer files as text or binary, type **ascii** (for text) or **binary**.

After you find the file you want to download, type **get** followed by a space and the filename. To upload a file, type **put** and the filename. You can tell FTP to rename the uploaded or downloaded file by adding a second filename to the command. For example, to download the f12nm45.exe file and name it fractals.exe on your computer, you would type

```
get f12nm45.exe fractals.exe
```

To disconnect from the server and exit the FTP program, type **quit** or **bye**.

Installing the program you downloaded — finally!

After you have downloaded the software and unzipped it (if it's a zip file), the program is ready to install. To install the program, click its name in Windows Explorer or My Computer. If it's an installation file, it installs the program. In the process, the installation program usually creates an icon for the program. It may also add the program to your Start menu or Programs menu.

Some programs don't come with an installation program — you just get the program itself. To make the program easy to run, you need an icon for it. Here's how to make one:

1. **Run either My Computer or Windows Explorer, and select the program file (the file with the extension EXE or, occasionally, COM).**

2. **Use your right mouse button to drag the filename out on the desktop or into an open folder on the desktop.**

   An icon for the program appears. (Technically, this icon is a *shortcut,* and it works great for running a program.)

Configuring the program

Now you can run the program by double-clicking its icon. Hooray!

You may have to tell the program, however, about your Internet address or your computer or who knows what before it can do its job. Refer to the text files, if any, that came with the program or choose Help from the program's menu bar to get more information about how to configure and run your new program.

Finding the Good Stuff

"The world of FTP sounds fine and dandy," you may say, "but what's out there, and where can I find it?" One of the best places to find software is to look at `http://www.tucows.com`. It has a great collection of FTP sites grouped by platform and category of program.

Also visit our online favorite software page, with our current updated list of greatest hits:

`http://net.gurus.com/software`

Chapter 14

Online Chatting: How to Make Friends and Influence People

● ●

In This Chapter

▶ Getting involved in online chat

▶ Understanding chat culture, etiquette, and safety

▶ Chatting on America Online

▶ Participating in Internet Relay Chat (IRC)

▶ Voice chat and instant messaging

▶ Chatting in 3-D worlds

● ●

*I*f you like e-mail but get irritated when people don't answer for hours or maybe even days (what? — they have something better to do?) while you sit around looking at your empty mailbox, maybe online chat is for you. *Online chat* lets you communicate instantly with another person who is logged on to the Net anywhere, by typing messages back and forth to each other. It's much faster than regular mail and considerably faster than e-mail. You can chat with several people at one time. And Windows Me comes with an unbearably cute chat program that even displays your conversation as a comic strip — what more could you ask?

What's Chatting All About?

Online chat is similar to talking on an old-fashioned party line or CB radio. Although you're probably too young to remember, in the infancy of the telephone system, people often didn't have private phone lines; instead, they shared their line with one or more other families, especially in rural America, where stringing telephone lines was expensive. Everyone on the party line could join in any conversation, although they weren't always welcome to do so, of course. Now, people often arrange conference calls to have several people all talk together.

Chatting is similar to a conference call except that rather than talk, you type on your keyboard what you want to say and read on-screen what other people are saying. Although all the people participating in the chat can be typing at one time, each person's contribution is presented on-screen in order of its receipt, identified by the name of the person who typed it. After you type what you want to say, it appears on the screen of general conversation and is identified by your screen name.

You can chat in two main ways:

- **Channels or rooms:** Resemble an ongoing conference call with a bunch of people. After you join a channel, you can read on-screen what people are saying and then add your own comments just by typing them and pressing Enter.

- **Direct connection:** A private conversation between you and another person connected to the chat portion of the Internet.

"Is there a room for me?"

Which groups are available when you begin to chat depends on how you're connected to the Internet. If you use America Online (AOL), where the groups are called *rooms,* you chat with other AOL users. If you access the Internet, you talk to other people by using the Internet's IRC (Internet Relay Chat) capability — see the section "Cruising IRC with Microsoft Chat," near the end of this chapter. Some Web sites let you chat by using your browser.

Each room or channel has a name; with luck, the name is an indication of what the chatters there are talking about or what they have in common. Here's a sample chat room conversation:

```
FJD718: Hi everyone
Buline596: Hi DavQC
Draw7card: HIya FJD
Pezaz: a man that other men don't like LOL
ORNOT2B: not discussing me...pez
Mostlyfun: {{{{{{{{{{dav}}}}}}}}}}}] thanks he is hopeless
DavQC: anyone catch clintons speech?
Draw7card:: Hiya Pez
Snowball133: Hi FJD
FJD718: hi Draw
Mostlyfun: Davvvvvvvvvvvvvvvvvvvvvvvv ;-)
DavQC: FJD whats with debra
ORNOT2B: hi paige
Paige282: Hi everyone
Snowball133: sorry dav
Harddisc3: anyone from atlanta area ?
Mostlyfun: Paige hiya
LadyA3826: snooooooo Queen
Draw7card: HIya SNO
DavQC: Paigeee
```

"I didn't catch your name"

No matter which chat facility you're using, you should know that most people select a *screen name, handle,* or *nickname* to use before they join a group. Other members of the group know you by your screen name, a temporary name often chosen to be unique, colorful, or clever and used as a mask. The choice of a screen name may be good for only the duration of a chat session. If you join a group and have a nice chat with someone named ObiWan, the next time you see that name, you have no guarantee that it's the same person. This anonymity can make chatting a place to be careful. On the other hand, one of the attractions of chatting is meeting new and interesting people. Many warm and wonderful friendships have evolved from a chance meeting in a chat room.

IRC (Internet Relay Chat) servers, on the other hand, typically offer a way to preserve your chosen alternative moniker, and you can be booted and even forced to change your "/nick" to something else because someone has already claimed it and saved it to the chat server.

When you join a group and begin chatting, you see the screen names of the people who are already there and a window in which the current conversation goes flying by. If the group is friendly, somebody usually sends you a welcome message because everyone is notified when you join the group.

As in real life, a room full of strangers may include people you don't like much. Because it's possible to be somewhat anonymous on the Internet, some people take advantage of the situation to act boorish, vulgar, crude, or worse. For that reason, don't let your children chat unsupervised. While you're new to chat, you may accidentally visit a number of disgusting places, although you can find out how to avoid them and find rooms that have useful, friendly, and supportive conversations.

Getting Ready to Chat

Your first time in a chat room can seem stupid or daunting. Here are some of the things you can do to get through your first encounters:

- ✔ Remember that when you enter a chat room, a conversation is probably already in progress. You don't know what went on before you entered.

- ✔ Wait a minute or two for a page full of exchanges to appear on-screen so that you can understand some of the context before you start writing.

- ✔ Start by following the comments of a single screen name. Then follow the people that the person mentions or who reply to that person.

- ✔ After you can follow one thread, try picking up another. It takes practice to get the hang of it.

✔ Some services, such as AOL, let you highlight the messages from one or more screen names. This technique can make things easier to follow.

✔ You can also indicate screen names to ignore. Messages from these chatters no longer appear on-screen, though other members' replies to them do appear.

✔ Scroll up to see older messages if you have to, and remember that after you have scrolled up, no new messages appear until you scroll back down.

✔ If you find one chat room uninteresting, leave it and try another.

Chat etiquette

Chatting etiquette is not that much different from e-mail etiquette, and common sense is your best online guide. Here are some additional chatting tips:

✔ The first rule of chatting is not to hurt anyone. A real person with real feelings is at the other end of the computer chat connection.

✔ The second rule is to be cautious. You really have no idea who that other person is. See the next section, "A serious chat about safe chatting."

✔ Read messages for a while to figure out what is happening before sending a message to a chat group. (Reading what's happening in a chat room or mailing list without saying anything is known as *lurking,* and, contrary to what that word may imply, it's perfectly good manners in a chat or e-mail list. When you finally venture to say something, you're *de-lurking.* People de-lurking for the first time often mention that in their message. It tells others that you've been following the conversation and may actually know what's been going on.)

✔ Keep your messages short and to the point.

✔ Don't insult people, and don't use foul language.

✔ Create a profile with information about yourself. Most chat systems have provisions for creating profiles (personal information) that other members can access. We caution people never to give out their last name, phone number, or address. We think that the extra caution is necessary for kids: Insist that kids *not* enter their age, hometown, or school nor their last name, phone number, or address.

✔ Although you don't have to tell everything about yourself in your profile, what you do say should be truthful.

✔ If you want to talk to someone in private, send that person a message saying hi, who you are, and what you want.

✔ If the tone of conversation in one chat room offends you, you can always leave. As in real life, you may run into more people out there whom you *don't* want to meet than people you *do*.

A serious chat about safe chatting

Here are some guidelines for conducting safe and healthy chats:

✔ Many people in chat groups lie about their occupation, age, locality, and, yes, even gender. Some think that they're just being cute, some are exploring their own fantasies, and some are really sick.

✔ Be careful about revealing information that enables someone to find you personally — such as where you live or work or your phone number. This information includes your last name, phone number, mailing address, and schools your kids attend.

✔ Never give out your password to anyone. No one should ever ask you for it. (We once received a message saying, "There's been a serious threat to security, and we need your password to help determine the problem.") If you ever get a message like that — whenever you're online, in a chat room or anywhere else, inform your Internet provider's staff. No legitimate person will ever ask you for your password.

✔ If your chat service offers profiles and a person without a profile wants to chat with you, be extra cautious.

✔ If you're a child, never, ever meet someone without your parents. Do not give out personal information about yourself or any member of your family, even when you're offered some sort of prize for filling out a form.

✔ If your children use chat, realize that others may try to meet them. Review the guidelines in this list with your kids before they log on.

If you choose to meet an online friend in person, use at least the same caution you would use in meeting someone through a newspaper ad:

✔ Don't arrange a meeting until you have talked to a person a number of times, including conversations at length by telephone over the course of days or weeks. (If you think that someone's single and he won't let you call him at home, think again.)

✔ Meet in a well-lit public place.

✔ Bring a friend along, if you can. If not, at least let someone know what you're doing and agree to call that person at a certain time (for example, a half-hour) after the planned meeting time.

✔ Arrange to stay in a hotel if you travel a long distance to meet someone. Don't commit yourself to staying at that person's home.

Abbreviations, emoticons, and smileys

Many chat abbreviations are the same as those used in e-mail, as described in Chapter 5. Because chat is live, however, some are unique. We've also listed some common *emoticons* (sometimes called *smileys*) — funky combinations of punctuation used to depict the emotional inflection of the sender. If at first you don't see what they are, try tilting your head down to the left.) Table 14-1 shows you a short list of chat abbreviations and emoticons.

Table 14-1	Chat Shorthand
Abbreviation	*What It Means*
AFK	Away from keyboard
A/S/L	Age/sex/location (response may be 35 / f / LA)
BAK	Back at keyboard
BBIAF	Be back in a flash
BBL	Be back later
BRB	Be right back
BTW	By the way
GMTA	Great minds think alike
IM	Instant message
IMHO	In my humble opinion
IMNSHO	In my not-so-humble opinion
J/K	Just kidding
LTNS	Long time no see
LOL	Laughing out loud
M4M	Men seeking other men
NP	No problem
ROTFL	Rolling on the floor laughing
RTFM	Read the fine manual
TOS	Terms of service (the AOL member contract)
TTFN	Ta-ta for now!
WAV	A sound file
WB	Welcome back

WTG	Way to go!
:D	A smile or big grin
:) or :-)	A smile
;)	A wink
{{{{bob}}}}	A hug for Bob
:(or :-(	Frown
:'(	Crying
:~~(	Crying
0:)	Angel
}:>	Devil
:P	Sticking out tongue
:P~~	Drooling
***	Kisses
<-----	Action marker (`<----eating pizza`, for example,)

In addition to the abbreviations shown in Table 14-1, chatters sometimes use simple shorthand abbreviations, as in "`If u cn rd ths u r rdy 4 chat.`"

There is always some jerk

Some people act badly online while hiding behind the anonymity that chat provides. You have four good options and one bad option when this situation happens:

- ✔ Go to another chat room. Some rooms are just nasty. You don't have to hang around.

- ✔ Pay no attention to the troublemaker, and just converse with the other folks.

- ✔ Make offenders disappear from your screen. On AOL, double-click the jerk's screen name on the room list and then click the Ignore box.

- ✔ Complain to the individual's Internet Service Provider. This technique is most effective on the value-added services. See the section "The chat police at your service," later in this chapter, if you use AOL.

- ✔ (The bad option.) Respond in kind, which just gives the offender the attention he (it's usually a he) wants and may get *you* kicked off your service.

Ways to chat

The rest of this chapter describes chatting on America Online (AOL) and Internet Relay Chat (IRC) — the Internet's original chat service — and the use of Web-based chat services.

Chatting on AOL

Although many online service providers have their own chat services, the AOL service is unique. Its large membership means that thousands of potential chatters are always online. The AOL chat rooms, even the specialized ones, are lively most of the time. Also, because chat is a major AOL attraction, AOL has staff members who check on its chat rooms to prevent the boorish, outlandish, and sometimes dangerous behavior that is too often common on unsupervised services like IRC. Although this supervision is by no means perfect, it makes AOL a top choice if you're planning to let your kids chat online.

AOL users can participate in IRC too. AOL has a built-in IRC program (go to keyword **irc**).

Only AOL members can participate in the AOL chat rooms. If you have Internet access through a different service, you can join AOL at a reduced rate. Go to `http://www.aol.com/info/pricing.html` and look for the Bring Your Own Access membership item.

Walk on in

You get started chatting in America Online 5.0 by clicking the People icon on the toolbar and choosing People Connection or by typing the keyword **chat**. Then click the Chat Now icon.

You're now in an AOL "lobby room." You see two windows — a larger one in which conversation is taking place and a smaller one that lists the people (screen names) in this room. If you're one of those people who just has to say something when you enter a crowded room, type something in the bottom area of the conversation window and click Send. In a few seconds, your comment is displayed in the window.

AOL limits the number of people in most public rooms to 23 (though you'll probably see several oddly named rooms with more), so when a room is full and a new user wants to join in, a new (similar) room is automatically created.

Rooms with a view

You probably won't find much conversation of interest in the lobby room you were thrown into when you joined the chatters. Pressing the Find a Chat button shows you the Find a Chat window with a list of public chat rooms that are available. Two windows are displayed; the left one shows the room categories. When you double-click a category, the right window shows the room names in that category along with the number of current occupants in that room.

The room categories are mostly self explanatory:

✔ **Town Square:** Rooms with a restaurant, bar, or coffeehouse flavor

✔ **Art & Entertainment:** Hollywood, music, book, and trivia themes

✔ **Friends:** People who like to talk

✔ **Life:** All sorts of lifestyles and age groups

✔ **News, Sports, Finance:** What you would expect

✔ **Places:** Major metropolitan areas

✔ **Romance:** Boy meets girl, in all combinations

✔ **Special Interests:** Hobbies, pets, cars, and religion

✔ **Countries:** Germany, United Kingdom, Canada, France, and Japan

Figure 14-1 shows a chat taking place in the Boston room (it's room number 4 because the first three Boston rooms already had 23 participants). Everything you type in the little box at the bottom, next to the Send button, is part of the conversation. You can either press the Enter key after typing your message or click Send. Whenever you want to leave a room, click List Chats, find another room, and join it. Or you can close the window of the chat room to get out of the AOL People Connection.

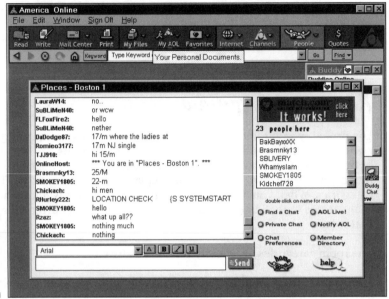

Figure 14-1:
Chatting in
the Boston
room.

People power

If you want to know something about the other occupants of the room, double-click one of their names in the window labeled People Here. A little box pops up that enables you to do one of several things:

- ✔ **Ignore:** If you check this box, no messages from this user are displayed on-screen. This technique is one way to stop receiving messages from annoying people.

- ✔ **Get Profile:** Click this button to retrieve the profile of this user. A *profile* is a list of information a user has supplied about herself. You have no guarantee that a profile has any true facts in it.

- ✔ **Send Message:** Click to send an instant mail message to this user. It's sort of like whispering in his ear. If someone sends you this type of message (an Instant Message, or IM), that message appears in a small window. You can ignore it or respond with a message of your own. The two of you can keep a running conversation going as long as you want.

Several AOL chat rooms are technically oriented and the people in them are often happy to offer technical assistance, which comes in handy when something particularly frustrating happens. If you engage one of these kind and knowledgeable persons and the room happens to be full, what do you do? Send him an instant message and kindly ask whether he would mind answering a few questions. It's easier to chat quietly in a private room than it is to shout over the deafening noise of a crowded room.

"Who am I now?"

You're identified by your screen name, the name you used when you signed on to the service. For privacy reasons, many people use a different screen name when they're chatting. AOL lets each account use as many as seven different screen names. One of the screen names is the *master* screen name, which can never be changed. If you want to add or change other screen names, you must log on to AOL under the master screen name. After you've established other screen names and passwords, you can log on to AOL by using the alternative name. Each screen name has a separate mailbox. You can use screen names for either different family members or different personalities: for example, your business self and your private self.

To set your *profile,* the information that other users can see about you when you're chatting, click the Member Directory button under the People Here window or go to keyword **profile.** A box is displayed in which you can search the AOL membership list for names you may know. In this window is a button labeled My Profile. If you click this button, you can set or modify all your own profile settings.

For members only

In addition to the chat rooms AOL sets up, members can create rooms. Click the Find a Chat button in the lower-right part of the chat window. In the Find a Chat window that appears, click the button labeled Member Chats, and the list of rooms switches over to the member rooms. Anyone can create a member room, and so can you, by clicking the Start Your Own Chat button. These rooms have the same categories as the public rooms — they're usually silly, serious, or kinky.

So how weird can it get?

You asked for it. Here's a short transcript from an AOL chat room named *Abducted by UFOs*. It's apparently quite full of alien life-forms:

OnlineHost:	*** You are in "Special Interests - Abducted by UFOs". ***
UDONLIKEITGETOUT:	SO DANNY BOY
DonR305:	better be 100% pure woman
DBibbsufo1953628:	where are you Don?
UDONLIKEITGETOUT:	I
UDONLIKEITGETOUT:	LOVE
UDONLIKEITGETOUT:	YOU
UDONLIKEITGETOUT:	ALL
DBibbsufo1953628:	i am sugar

DonR305:	<-- right here
Ford man 7362:	WHAT
LGuzick:	is any one a alien in here besides me?
DBibbsufo1953628:	1000 real woman
SandiPrzy1:	i was born a 100% female..

Generally, ambiguity and lack of clarity are bad and avoiding contact with chat room individuals is good. If you've forged a number of friendships, however, in a particular group where you all share the same interests, it's not such a bad idea to set up a little get-together named "Get me away from this computer and out of the house after three weeks, although I should take a bath first."

Meet me under the sign of the rose

The names of private rooms, unlike public or member rooms, are not revealed. To join one, you have to know its name; that is, someone must invite you to join. When you click the Enter a Private Chat button in the Find a Chat window, you're asked to name the room you want to join. If it doesn't exist, one is created and you're the sole occupant.

Private rooms enable people to talk more intimately — you face little danger of a stranger's popping in. Two (or more) people can agree to create a private room and meet there. Private rooms have a somewhat sleazy reputation: If you get invited to one, you should be careful about guarding your privacy — anyone in a room can save the conversation to a file. Just take a look at the nearby sidebar, "So how weird can it get?" Would you like to be known to have said some of those things in public?

The chat police at your service

Another button under the People Here window is labeled Notify AOL. If you think that someone is violating the AOL terms of service (TOS) by asking you for your password or credit card number, using abusive language, or otherwise behaving badly, you can and should report that person to AOL. When you press the Notify AOL button, a window pops up to help you gather all the information you want to report: the chat category and room you were in, the offensive chat dialog pasted into a window, and the offender's screen name, for example.

Because of this policing and the power of AOL to terminate (permanently) the accounts of people who play without the rules, the AOL chat rooms have a deserved reputation for safety and for being a good place to play.

Cruising IRC with Microsoft Chat

IRC (Internet Relay Chat) is available from most Internet providers. To use IRC, you need an IRC client program on your computer. An IRC *client program* (or just *IRC program* or *chat program*) is another Internet program, like your web browser or e-mail program; freeware and shareware IRC programs are available for you to download from the Net. Windows Me comes with an IRC program named Microsoft Chat, although you can use other chat programs (see the sidebar "Alternatives to Microsoft Chat," later in this chapter).

If you would rather avoid the messiness of installing another application on top of the vast number that are already splitting the seams of your hard drive, Microsoft has recently revealed MSN Chat, the follow-up to Microsoft Chat. We discuss the Web-based MSN Chat a little later in this chapter; for now, we start with Microsoft Chat.

"Serve me some chat"

Microsoft Chat (or any chat program) has to connect to an *IRC server* — an Internet host computer that serves as a switchboard for IRC conversations. Although dozens of IRC servers are available, many are full most of the time and may refuse your connection. You may have to try several servers, or the same one dozens of times, before you can connect.

IRC servers are organized into networks. Although servers within each network talk to each other, servers on one IRC network don't connect to servers on other networks. Someone on EFnet can't talk to someone on Undernet, for example.

The four biggest networks and their home pages are shown in this list (in descending order):

- **EFnet:** `http://www.irchelp.org` (This original network of servers has the largest number of users. Oh, and it's pronounced "eff net.")
- **Undernet:** `http://www.undernet.org`
- **IRCnet:** `http://www.funet.fi/~irc`
- **DALNet:** `http://www.dal.net`

Most people on IRC eventually develop a preference for one network — usually the one where their friends hang out.

Lots of smaller IRC networks exist. Microsoft has its own that appears automatically in the Chat Connection window. Here are some, with the addresses of Web pages that have more information about them:

- **Microsoft:** `http://mschat.msn.com`
- **Kidsworld:** `http://www.kidsworld.org`
- **StarLink:** `http://www.starlink.org`

When you're choosing a server, pick one that's geographically close to you (to minimize response lag, as explained in the following sidebar, "Splits and lags") and on the IRC network you want. Because each server entry notes its network and location, you can easily choose one near you.

Roaming the channels

The most popular way to use IRC is through *channels*. Most channels have names that start with the # character. Channel names are not case sensitive. Numbered channels also exist. (When you type a channel number, you don't use the # character.)

In Microsoft Chat, channels are called *rooms*. Why? Because Microsoft can do anything it wants, that's why.

Thousands of IRC channels are available. Different channels are available on different IRC networks. You can find an annotated list of some of the best by visiting `http://www.funet.fi/~irc/channels.html`. Each channel listed there has its own linked home page that tells you much more about what that channel offers.

Good channels to know about include

> ✔ **#irchelp:** A place to ask questions about IRC
>
> (You can also check out our Web page, at `http://net.gurus.com/.irc/tips.html`, for some tips and tricks and some links to more information about IRC.)
>
> ✔ **#newbies:** All your IRC questions answered
>
> ✔ **#21plus: and #30plus:** Age-appropriate meeting places
>
> ✔ **#41plus:** A more mature channel (with many people on it younger than 41)
>
> ✔ **#teens:** For teenagers — chill and chat
>
> ✔ **#hottub:** A "rougher" meeting place
>
> ✔ **#collective:** The place to report problems on the Microsoft IRC server
>
> ✔ **#windows98:** A meeting place for Windows 98 users
>
> ✔ **#chat:** A friendly chat channel
>
> ✔ **#mirc:** A help channel for mIRC users

You can also try typing **#** followed by the name of a country or major city.

Splits and lags

Two phenomena, lags and netsplits, are the bane of an IRCer's existence. A *lag* is the delay between the time you type a message and when it appears on other people's screens. Lags foul up conversations. Sometimes, one group of people on a channel are lagged while another group is not, and the first group's messages appear after delays of several minutes. You can check on the amount of time a message takes to get from you to another person and back again by clicking on a nickname on the members list and choosing Member⇨Lag Time.

A *netsplit* breaks the connection between IRC servers — the network of connected IRC servers gets split into two smaller networks. A netsplit looks like a bunch of people suddenly leaving your channel and then reappearing en masse sometime later. Although all the people who are connected to the IRC servers in one half of the network can chat among themselves, they can't communicate with the people connected to the IRC servers in the other half. Eventually (after minutes or hours), the two networks reconnect and the netsplit is over.

Every rule has an exception

You probably think that the discussion about nicknames and all that in the nearby section "You too can be jolly Saint Nick" is true because we've included it in our book. Although we would love the recognition that ubiquitous acceptance of all we've said affords, the DALnet IRC network provides what it calls NickServ. If you register with NickServ, you can be the sole owner of that nickname for as long as you patronize the network (you need to show up only every 20 days). When someone else tries to use your nickname, you can kick that out or you can instruct NickServ to do the dirty work for you. Of course, if your nickname is relatively obscure, nobody will steal it anyway, so — oh, never mind.

You too can be jolly Saint Nick

Everyone using IRC needs a *nickname*. This name is unique within the network: No two people connected to the same IRC network can use the same nickname at the same time. If you attempt to connect to a network and your chosen nickname is already in use, you cannot join a channel. The name can be the same as the username in your e-mail address, although most people pick a different name.

Nicknames can be as long as nine characters. Because common names are usually already in use, choose something distinctive.

Unlike e-mail addresses, nicknames can change from day to day. Whoever claims a nickname first on an IRC server gets to keep it for as long as she is logged in. Nicknames are good for only a single session on IRC. If you chatted with someone named AlGore yesterday and then run into someone named AlGore today, you have no guarantee that it's the same person. To find out more about the person behind a nickname, double-click his entry on the list of room members.

Installing Microsoft Chat

Because Microsoft Chat is an optional part of Windows Me, it may not be installed on your computer. Try running Chat by clicking the Start button and choosing Programs➪Internet Explorer➪Microsoft Chat. If no such command exists, you have to install Chat from your Windows Me CD-ROM or disks. If the program runs, skip this section — you're ready to chat.

To install Chat, follow these steps:

1. **Close all your other programs, and then click the Start button and choose Settings⇨Control Panel.**

   You see the Windows Me Control Panel window.

2. **Click or double-click the Add/Remove Programs icon — whatever it takes to display the Add/Remove Programs Properties window.**

3. **Click the Windows Setup tab.**

   Windows Me thinks for a few minutes while it checks to see which programs you've already installed. You see a list of the types of programs that come with Windows Me.

4. **Click Communications on the list of components because Chat is all about communications! Click the Details button to see the list of programs of that type.**

5. **Click the Microsoft Chat program so that a check mark appears in its box, and then click the OK button to return to the Add/Remove Programs Properties Windows Setup dialog box.**

6. **Click the OK button.**

   Windows Me determines which programs to install and then installs them. If Windows says that you have to restart your computer when the installation is complete, click Yes to do so.

Check with your Internet provider for any additional information you may need in order to use IRC. If you have a direct link to the Internet, ask your system administrator whether the link supports IRC. Many companies block it.

Alternatives to Microsoft Chat

Another good shareware Windows IRC program is mIRC. You can find mIRC, along with others, at shareware Web sites, such as TUCOWS (http://www.tucows.com), or at the mIRC home page (http://www.mirc.co.uk).

For more detailed information about setting up mIRC, point your browser to http://www.mirc.com. You can also find a great deal of useful information about IRC there.

If you want to chat with a friend who does not have Windows Me, she can probably get a suitable IRC client. Microsoft Chat and mIRC also work on older versions of Windows, *Ircle* is a good choice for Macintosh users, and most UNIX systems feature a built-in client, which you start by typing the command **irc** or **ircii**.

Connecting on chat

Start the Microsoft Chat program by clicking the Start button and choosing Programs⇨Internet Explorer⇨Microsoft Chat. You see the Connect dialog box, as shown in Figure 14-2. Click the Server box and click a server on the list that appears. You can also choose the channel you want to join. Click OK to attempt to connect to the server.

Figure 14-2: Which IRC server do you want to connect to?

When you get connected, you see the Microsoft Chat window, as shown in Figure 14-3. If you're not in comic strip view (we are not making this up), you can choose View⇨Comic Strip to make your window look more like the one shown in Figure 14-3. The conversation, in comic strip form, appears in the left part of the window. In the upper-right corner is a list of the people in the chat room with their comic strip characters (you can't tell the players without a scorecard!). Scroll this list up and down to see everyone. In the lower-right corner is a gizmo that lets you choose the facial expression of your own character.

At peak times, the servers can be extremely busy. If at first you don't connect, try, try again. If you don't see the Connect dialog box or you want to reconnect later, click the Connect button on the toolbar (the fourth button from the left).

Figure 14-3:
Microsoft
Chat in
comic strip
view.

"What's on the channels tonight?"

In Microsoft Chat, the name of the channel (room) you're in appears on the title bar for the window, so you can always tell where you are. To see a list of available channels on the IRC server to which you're connected, click the Chat Room List button on the toolbar (the 11th button from the left) or choose Room⇨Room List from the menu bar. You see the Chat Room List window, as shown in Figure 14-4.

If you're looking for a particular channel name, type in the Match text box the text you're looking for. If you want to see channels with at least several people on them (rather than the hundreds of channels with one bored, lonely, or lascivious person waiting), type a number in the Min box. Then click Update List. Because the list of channels can be extremely long, you may have to wait a few minutes for the list to be displayed. If you want to see the channels listed in your Channels folder (the list of channels you visit frequently), click the Channels folder icon instead.

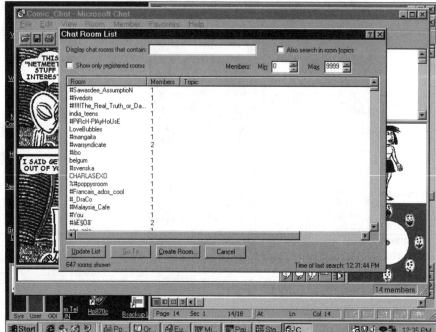

Figure 14-4:
A long list of
available
rooms
(channels).

"Join me"

If you're looking at the Chat Room List window, join a channel by double-clicking its name. Otherwise, you can join a channel by clicking the Enter Room button on the toolbar (the sixth button from the left) or by choosing Room⇨Enter Room from the menu bar. Then type the name of the channel in the box provided. Don't forget the # before the channel name.

In some chat programs, you can join several channels at a time; Microsoft Chat doesn't let you — although you can fire up several copies of the program and use different channels with each one. You leave a channel by clicking the Leave Room icon on the toolbar (the seventh from the left) or by choosing Room⇨Leave Room.

Telling chat who you are

You can tell Microsoft Chat your preferred nickname so that it doesn't ask you every time you run it. Choose View⇨Options, click the Personal Info tab, and enter your chosen name in the Nickname box.

See ya in the funnies

Plain old text as a conversation tool isn't good enough for Microsoft, which likes to "embrace and extend" existing Internet standards. Microsoft Chat can display a chat room's conversation as panels in a comic strip that your computer draws on the fly. Click the Comics View button on the toolbar (the one with the face) or choose View⇨Comic Strip to try it. You select the character that will represent you by choosing View⇨Options and clicking the Character tab. You can also select one of several emotions your character will display by using a little wheel in the bottom-right corner of the chat window.

Comic displays are well realized and fun to watch, although they can get confusing when a number of people are in the room. Click the Text View icon or choose View⇨Plain Text if you yearn for a conventional text display of the conversation.

"Whisper in my ear"

To send a private message to someone in on a channel, click her name on the members list and click the Whisper Box icon or choose Member⇨Whisper Box from the menu bar.

You can set up private conversations with more than one room member. Right-click a person's name on the member list and then click the Whisper Box icon. Repeat this process for each person you want to engage in private chat. If you want several members in the same conversation, select each name and click the Whisper Box icon.

Trying to manage too many conversations at one time can get you into a heap of trouble.

Own your own channel

Each channel has its own channel operator, or *chanop,* who can control, to some extent, what happens on that channel. In the list of nicknames on a channel, operators' nicknames are preceded by a gavel icon. You can start your own channel and automatically become its chanop by choosing Room⇨Create Room or clicking the Create Room button on the toolbar (the eighth one from the left).

As with nicknames, whoever asks for a channel name first gets it. You can keep the name for as long as you're logged on as the chanop. You can let other people be chanops for your channel — just make sure that they're people you can trust. A channel exists as long as anyone is on it; when the last person leaves, the channel winks out of existence.

As chanop, you get to use special commands, like setting the room properties by using the Room⇨Room Properties command. The main one is Member⇨Host⇨Kick, which kicks someone off your channel, at least for the three seconds until he rejoins the channel. Kicking someone off is a thrill (although a rather small one), sort of like finding a penny on the sidewalk. People usually get kicked off channels for being rude or by sending so many garbage messages that they make the channel unusable. To kick people out and keep them out, choose Member⇨Host⇨Ban.

Server operators manage entire servers and can kick unruly users off a server permanently.

By invitation only

Three types of channels are available in IRC:

- ✔ **Public:** Everyone can see them, and everyone can join.
- ✔ **Private:** Although everyone can see them, you can join them only by invitation.
- ✔ **Secret:** They don't show up on the usual list of channels, and you can join them only by invitation.

If you're on a private or secret channel, you can invite someone else to join by choosing Member⇨Invite from the menu.

Command performance

You can also control what is happening during your chat session by typing IRC commands. All IRC commands start with the slash character (/). You can type IRC commands in upper- or lowercase or a mixture — IRC doesn't care. If you use Microsoft Chat, many commands are available directly from the toolbar. Other commands don't work at all — Microsoft Chat just displays an error message.

If anyone ever tells you to type in IRC any commands you don't understand, *don't do it — ever.* You can unwittingly give away control of your IRC program and even your computer account to another person. (No, we don't tell you the commands!)

The most important command for you to know gets you out of IRC:

```
/quit
```

The second most important command gives you an online summary of the various IRC commands:

```
/help
```

Here are a few more useful IRC commands:

- ✔ **/admin** *server:* Displays information about a server.

- ✔ **/away:** Tells IRC that you will be away for a while. You don't have to leave this type of message; if you do, however, it's displayed to anyone who wants to talk to you.

- ✔ **/clear:** Clears your screen.

- ✔ **/join:** *channel:* Joins a channel. The old-fashioned way of doing the things, which we describe in the "Join me" section, earlier in this chapter.

- ✔ **/leave:** Leaves a channel. Typing /part does the same thing.

- ✔ **/me:** Sends a message that describes what you're doing and is used to punctuate your conversation with a description of gestures. If you're Mandrake, for example, and type /me gestures hypnotically, other users see *Mandrake gestures hypnotically on-screen.

- ✔ **/topic** *whatwearetalkingabout:* Sets the topic message for the current channel.

- ✔ **/who** *channel:* Lists all the people on *channel*. If you type /who *, you see displayed the names of the people on the channel you're on.

- ✔ **/whois** *name:* Lists some information about the user name. You can use your own name to see what other users can see about you.

- ✔ **/nick** *newname:* Changes your name to *newname*.

- ✔ **/ping** *#channelname:* Gives information about the lag (delay) between you and everyone on that channel.

- ✔ **/msg** *name message:* Sends a private message to *name* (only *name* can see it).

Before typing **/list** to see all the available channels, type

```
/set hold_mode on
```

This phrase keeps the names from flying by so fast on-screen that you can't read them. Don't forget to type /set hold_mode off after you finish reading the list.

You can also limit the number of channels listed by typing

```
/list -min 8
```

Only channels with at least eight people on them are listed when you type this phrase.

Remember: Lines that start with a slash are commands to the IRC program; everything else you type is conversation and gets put in the chat box. You may be a tad embarrassed if you're in #cleanliving and type join #hottub, forgetting the slash.

You're not in Kansas anymore

Compared to AOL, IRC is a lawless frontier. Few rules, if any, exist. If things get really bad, you can try to find out an offender's e-mail address by choosing Member⇨Get Identity from the menu or clicking the Get identity button on the toolbar. You receive some information about that person, including, perhaps, his e-mail address — badguy@jclt.com, for example. You can then send an e-mail complaint to postmaster at the same hostname; in this example, postmaster@jclt.com. Don't expect much help, however.

Microsoft is making some attempt to control its own IRC server. You can report problems to the channel #collective.

Web-Based Chat

Although IRC is still the most popular chat service on the Internet, some sites on the Web let you chat by using the web browser — Internet Explorer or Netscape — you already have. You don't have to download and install any software or learn any arcane commands. The good news is that new Web-based chat sites are appearing all the time. The bad news is that having so many chat sites to choose from may not be such a good thing because each site has relatively few members at any given time, particularly compared to AOL and IRC.

Here are a few Web sites with chat service you may want to try:

Geocities: http://www.geocities.com

WBS: http://pages.wbs.com

Parent's Place: http://www.parentsplace.com

You can find more Web-based chat sites listed by starting at Yahoo (http://www.yahoo.com) and choosing Computers and Internet, and then Internet, and then World Wide Web, and then Chat.

MSN Chat

The older, IRC-based Microsoft Chat and the newer MSN Chat have two primary differences between them: Comic Chat is gone, and the servers are now proprietary (how surprising). Oh, and it's all run in your web browser, although that's no big deal. It depends on what you think of chat overall, but if you just know that going a day without chatting about *something* would nearly kill you, then MSN Chat is for you. Amazingly, you do *not* have to be an MSN member to use the service. Even more amazingly, you don't have to use Internet Explorer, either.

How does this happen? Very painfully. A Microsoft-made file named NpWrap.exe enables you to chat in Netscape while using its Chat program, by letting you "glue" into Netscape an ActiveX program you need for Chat. The NpWrap.exe gizmo doesn't yet work in Opera, although it does work well in Navigator 4.08 and Communicator 4.73.

Follow these steps:

1. **Open Internet Explorer or Netscape Navigator and enter the URL** chat.msn.com. **(It's the MSN Chat Web site.)**

2. **Click on any interesting-looking chat room link listed underneath the Chat Categories heading.**

   If you selected a chat room that involves adult issues, or even just adults, you're first asked to verify your age by — get this — selecting your age range and clicking a button. (We all know that no 14-year-old would ever lie about his age.)

3. **After you click the age button, either the installation page loads or you're told that you're too young.**

   If the latter is true, choose another room. Emoticon Lobby is a popular place to learn all the new automatic Chat emoticons. A dialog box is likely to appear, asking whether it should install the MSN Chat software.

4. **Click Yes, and then click Yes a second time.**

After a few minutes, the chat room you chose appears in a chat window in your browser.

We think that you need to pay close attention to two things. Although ActiveX programs are promoted as alternatives to Java programs, these full-fledged Windows programs are (unlike Java programs) loaded into and running on your computer; a prime example is MSN Chat. The problem is that these are *real* Windows applications, not safe, pleasant Java applications that can't really damage your computer.

Our advice is that whenever a dialog box pops up and asks whether you want to allow it to install something, ask yourself whether you knew that the question was going to be asked and whether you trust this company, organization, or group. Also, never, *ever,* allow any company — not even Microsoft — to be trusted. Leave unchecked the check box labeled Always trust content from. You download few enough of these ActiveX gizmos that it's quite reasonable to check each one yourself.

The other thing you have to pay attention to is the content of some of the chat rooms. One contributor to this book reported hate groups hosting obviously anti-racial rooms. Although the rooms are usually removed relatively quickly, the damage usually is already done. If you have children, spend time with them when they're chatting so that you can step in when needed or to answer any difficult questions.

About the MSN Chat interface. If you've used Microsoft Chat, you're taking a step or two back. Take a look at Figure 14-5. The large pane that dominates the window is where all the chatting occurs. The list of current participants is to the right. Along the bottom, you type your comments. If you're interested in fiddling with the options (there are only a few), you can click the Options button along the top edge of the main chat pane.

When you sign on to MSN Chat, you get a permanent name, which is nice. Also, don't be turned off by offensive rooms. They're typically removed, and, after awhile, the bozos behind them drift off in search of easier targets.

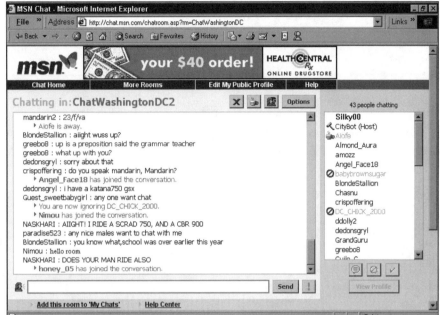

Figure 14-5:
MSN Chat in
the room.
Spooky!

Chatting in 3-D Worlds

People are now building three-dimensional (3-D) worlds on the Internet. In these virtual reality worlds, you see a 3-D landscape on-screen, and your character and others are represented by figures *(avatars)* that walk, talk, and gesture. A prime example of this type of environment is AlphaWorld (http://www.worlds.net/alphaworld). Microsoft used to have its own 3-D chat technology, called *V-chat* (the *V* stands for *virtual*), but it has "divested" itself of it.

Chapter 15

Getting Together with NetMeeting

• •

In This Chapter

▶ Calling people and receiving calls

▶ Videoconferencing with another person

▶ Chatting with a bunch of people

▶ Drawing on the whiteboard to make your point

▶ Co-authoring a document

• •

*W*hen you use IRC as explained in Chapter 14, you probably think to yourself, "This would be a great way for me to meet with my business associates without having to fly to Cleveland (or Dallas or Chicago or Toronto)." Okay, maybe you don't think that. Using the Internet to improve communication among individuals, however, is what the Internet is all about.

How do you make the jump from social chatting with IRC to an online business meeting? By using NetMeeting, of course. NetMeeting is an audio- and videoconferencing program. It allows you to

✔ Talk to another person through your computer's microphone and hear the person speaking through your computer's speakers.

✔ Meet face-to-face with another person (if both of you have cameras connected to your PCs). Even if you don't have a camera, you can still receive video and see the other person. She just can't see you.

✔ Hold a chat session where a number of people can type messages on the screen.

✔ Send files to other meeting participants, a handy way to distribute agendas for the meeting.

✔ Create and edit drawings by using a draw program and an online whiteboard that everyone can see.

✔ Share an application with others and see immediately the editing changes your collaborators make online.

This chapter explains how to do all these things in NetMeeting Version 3.01. We also describe the technical stuff you need to know to get NetMeeting up and running on your PC.

Setting Up NetMeeting

NetMeeting has many features; to use most of them, all you need is your Internet connection. To use audio- or videoconferencing, however, you need some extra hardware on your PC:

- **Audioconferencing:** To talk to another person and hear responses, you need a microphone and speakers connected to your PC. You also need a sound card — a full-duplex sound card works best. Because most newer computers have a full-duplex sound card, you probably don't have to worry about it. If you have an older computer, however, or if you want to see what kind of sound card you have, check the owner's manual for your PC. If you can't locate the sound card information, just go ahead and set up NetMeeting — it won't hurt anything. The worst that happens is that you can't send or receive audio.

- **Videoconferencing:** If you want to transmit your picture to another person, you need a camera installed on your PC. What happens if you don't have a camera? You still see the other person, assuming that a camera is attached to his PC, although he doesn't see you.

 Whenever you change or upgrade your sound card or drivers, you have to run the Audio Tuning Wizard in NetMeeting. You can access it by choosing Tools⇨Audio Tuning Wizard from the NetMeeting toolbar.

When you've checked out your hardware, you're ready to start NetMeeting. The first time you start NetMeeting, you're asked to fill out some personal information to identify yourself.

To start NetMeeting, click the Start button and choose Programs⇨ Internet Explorer⇨Microsoft NetMeeting. (In addition to using the version of NetMeeting that comes with Windows Me, you can get NetMeeting by downloading it from the Microsoft Web site, at http://www.microsoft.com/windows/netmeeting. To start your downloaded version of NetMeeting, click the Start button and choose Programs⇨Accessories⇨ Communications⇨NetMeeting.)

Your ID, please

When you run NetMeeting, you do not log on to a server right away. Many servers are available; some are hosted by Microsoft, although most are at other companies.

Each server has a directory that shows who is logged on to the server. To call someone, you can either select her name from the directory list or type her e-mail address. Of course, other people can also select your name and call you from the directory list. (To keep yourself from being pestered by people you don't want to talk to, a Do Not Disturb option is available. We go over all this a little later when we tell you how to make calls.)

As part of your setup process for getting NetMeeting up and running, you have to supply the personal information (such as your name, e-mail address, and location) that other people see in the directory. You can also add comments to help people locate you or to indicate what you want to talk about.

NetMeeting is a great tool to use to meet with people you know, although you can also call strangers from the directory list. Even though we focus on using NetMeeting for business meetings, you can also put it to use in your personal life — maybe you want to start an online book discussion club or use it for a brainstorming session while writing song lyrics.

Get started by filling out the NetMeeting start-up screens. (If NetMeeting is already set up on your computer, skip this section.) To fill out the start-up screens, follow these steps:

1. **Read the introductory remarks on the first screen, and click** <u>N</u>**ext.**

2. **Make sure that the** <u>L</u>**og on to a directory server when NetMeeting starts check box is selected. Leave the directory server at** `ils.microsoft.com` **for now.**

   After you see the NetMeeting window, you can view directory lists from different servers to see who is logged on or log on to a different server. Because `ils.microsoft.com` is the default server, it gets quite busy. If you have trouble logging on to the server, you can always change this setting later from the NetMeeting window.

3. **Fill in your name, e-mail address, location, and comments you want to show in the directory, as shown in Figure 15-1.**

   The directory is like the server's phone book — your listing in the directory identifies you to everyone else on the server. Although comments are optional, they do help identify you and what you're going to talk about in the meeting. Don't worry if you can't think of any pithy comments right now. You can always modify these settings at another time from the NetMeeting Options dialog box (by choosing <u>C</u>all⇨ <u>C</u>hange My Information).

   Wondering where the nickname goes? If you would rather use a nickname than your real name, enter the nickname in the First name and Last name fields (you must have something in both fields). The information from the First name and Last name fields is displayed on the call recipient's screen when you make a call.

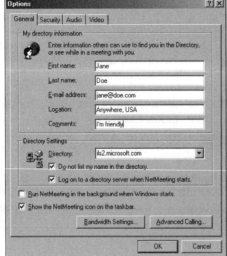

Figure 15-1:
Filling in
personal
information
for the
directory.

4. **Select the For business use category.**

   Again, you can select any category you want; for the purposes of this chapter, we concentrate on business meetings.

5. **Select the option that matches your modem speed or connection method.**

   If you're not sure which option to select, accept the default selection for now and go to the next screen. If you're keen to choose anyway, here are some simple guidelines. If you're in an office and you don't have to wait to get on the Internet, select LAN. If you're at home and you don't occupy any phone lines or you don't hear strange beeping or screeching noises immediately before using the Internet, select DSL or Cable. If you do hear funny noises before connecting to the Internet and you do lose a phone line while surfing, you have a couple of options. If the computer is brand-spanking new, select 56K. If it's a couple of years old, select 33.6K. If it's been around for more than three years and you know that nobody's ever crawled around inside there, use 28.8K. If, on the other hand, you're uncomfortable selecting, rest assured that your settings, even if you guess wrong, will not hurt your system.

6. **Click the down arrow and select the video-capture device your computer uses.**

   Again, if you're not sure what to select, leave the default selection as is and go to the next screen.

7. **Verify that you don't have any other programs running on your computer that use audio or video and click Next.**

8. **Click the down arrow and select the Recording device used on your computer. Do the same for the Playback device.**

   You can probably guess what to do if you're not sure what to select. That's right! Leave the default selections and go to the next screen.

9. **Click the Test button to fine-tune your audio.**

   You should hear a drumming noise coming from your speakers. Move the slider bar to adjust the volume.

10. **Click Stop to stop the drumming noise, and click Next.**

11. **Click Finish.**

    The NetMeeting window opens and you're finished with the start-up screens!

Getting connected

Depending on how you set up your Internet connection in Chapter 4, you're connected automatically to the Internet when you start NetMeeting, or else you have to log on manually. *Hint:* If you see a Dial-Up Connection dialog box prompting you for your username and password, you have to log on manually.

When you get connected to the Internet, you're logged on to the default server you selected on the start-up screen and the directory is displayed, as shown in Figure 15-2. (If you don't see the directory, click the Directory button.)

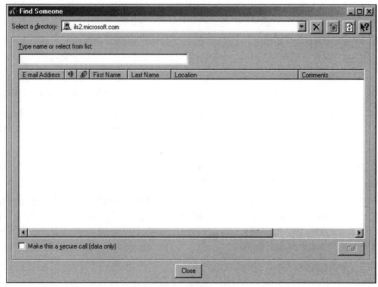

Figure 15-2:
This is it! The NetMeeting window — your base of operations for all things NetMeeting.

Anatomy of the NetMeeting window

The NetMeeting window contains the usual menu bar, although the toolbar you're accustomed to seeing has been replaced by some neat-looking buttons arrayed around the reduced interface. (The old version, 2.1, had a big, clunky interface.) You see how to use these menu options and buttons as you progress through this chapter. What's unusual about the NetMeeting window are the buttons arrayed in the window and the audio controls.

The buttons on the right side and below the video frame of the window control what information you see in the rest of the NetMeeting window and other windows. When you click a button, depending on which function you choose, another window opens or the view of something changes in the NetMeeting window. Here's what the buttons do:

- **Place Call:** Opens the Place A Call dialog box, where you can enter the address of the person to call and require that it be or not be a secured call; you can open the Directory window by clicking the Directory button in the lower-left corner of the dialog box.

- **End Call:** The equivalent of hanging up the phone. The unfortunate part is that you cannot derive satisfaction from slamming the mouse button really, really hard. Oh, well!

- **Directory:** Shows the Directory list — the list of people logged on to the server. A speaker icon next to a name indicates that the person has audio capabilities; a camera icon indicates that the person has video capabilities (the person's computer does, anyway). Your name should appear on the list too.

- **Start Video:** Turns on and off your video feed, which is convenient for when you'd rather not let everyone know what was for lunch.

- **Picture-in-Picture:** Produces another video feed in a small window in the corner of your main video feed.

- **Adjust Audio Volume/View Participant List:** Switches back and forth between the two views that appear just below the buttons on this row.

- **Share Program:** Launches a program that all participants have so that you can share documents; excellent for Word documents that need lots of work from lots of people.

- **Chat:** Opens a text-based chat window that can be used for the meeting or for separate, private meetings between select attendees.

- **Whiteboard:** Opens a slightly modified version of Microsoft Paint on all participants' screens and allows all participants to scribble. This button is great if you need to illustrate something that just doesn't seem to get across any other way.

- **Transfer Files:** Allows participants to move files between computers; a great way to distribute meeting notes or agendas.

Near the top of the window are audio buttons. You see two sections of audio controls — one for your microphone and one for your speakers. When the check boxes next to the microphone icon and the speaker icon are selected, you have full audio capabilities. You should be able to carry on a conversation with the person you've called by speaking into the microphone and listening to the speakers.

If the volume isn't quite right, move the slider bar until the volume levels are acceptable. If the person you're talking to has trouble hearing you, for example, increase the volume on your microphone. If you hear only faint sounds from your speakers, increase the volume on your speakers.

NetMeeting has a "hold" button of sorts. If you want to stop sending audio and video feeds momentarily, you can click the Start Video button. This feature is handy if you want to confer with someone in your office without the person in NetMeeting hearing you or if you suddenly need to sneeze. When you're ready to resume the conversation in NetMeeting, click the button again to enable your microphone.

Trying another server

Occasionally, you may get an error message saying that the server is busy, or you may want to look at the directory list for a different server.

Why would you want to do that?

- ✔ If the default server is too busy, you can't use NetMeeting until you log on to a server that's *not* too busy.
- ✔ If you can't find the person you want to call on one directory, you can view another server's directory and then call the person.

To log on to a different server if your default server is busy:

1. **Click the Directory button to access the directory screen.**

2. **Choose Tools⇨Options.**

3. **Click the General tab. Click the down-arrow button at the right end of the Directory name box and select a different server from the list that appears.**

    When you click OK to exit the Options dialog box, you log on to the new server. If you get disconnected for some reason, reconnect by choosing Call⇨Log On To. You can always tell which server you're logged on to — the server name is displayed on the right side of the status bar at the bottom of the window.

The new server you've selected stays in effect until you go back in and change it on the My Information tab. The next time you start NetMeeting, your default server is the new server you selected.

You're not limited to calling people who are on your server. You can be logged on to one server and call someone on a different server. Your name is listed in only one directory, however, and that's the directory of the server you're logged on to. (Or, as your high school English teacher would make you say, the server on to which you're logged. Hmmm, sometimes computerese doesn't fit in well with proper English.)

Suppose that you want to call some people whose names don't appear in your directory. They may be logged on to a different server or in a different category. Using the Server and Category fields on the directory screen, you can locate them without logging off your current server.

Here's how to find people on different servers:

1. **Click the Directory button, and then click the down-arrow button at the right end of the Directory box. Select a new server from the list that appears.**

   The status bar at the bottom of your Find Someone window relays everything that's happening. The left side of the status bar shows the directory you've chosen to look at, and the right side of the bar shows the server to which you're connected. The names of the people logged on to the new server are displayed on the screen.

2. **If you still can't find the person you're looking for, repeat Step 1.**

   You can keep trying different servers until you find the person or people you want to call.

   You can also try looking in a different category. Click the down arrow next to the Category box, and select a new category. Options on the category list also enable you to limit the number of names you see in the directory. You can elect to see only people with videocameras, for example, or only people in your country.

To see whether any new people have logged on while you were messing around, click the Refresh button on the toolbar to update the directory list.

Making a Call

To make calling people as convenient as possible, you can use one of many methods because Microsoft couldn't make up its mind about how the NetMeeting program should work. All the methods work the same way and accomplish the same task. Try each method to find the one that's most comfortable for you.

Because audio- and videoconferencing work with you and just one other person, start off by calling one other person. (Whether you're calling one person or ten people, the methods you use to place the call are the same.) In the "Let's Chat" section, later in this chapter, we talk about including lots of people in a meeting.

To call another person in NetMeeting, use one of these methods:

- ✔ Locate in the directory the person you want to call and double-click his name.
- ✔ Click the Call button on the toolbar and type the e-mail address of the person you want to call.
- ✔ Choose Call⇨New Call (or press Ctrl+N) and type the e-mail address of the person you want to call.
- ✔ Click the down arrow to the right of the black text field at the top of the NetMeeting window and click a name on your SpeedDial list.

If you watch the status bar, you see the message Waiting for response followed by the name of the person you called. A dialog box appears on the recipient's screen, telling her that you're calling and asking whether she wants to accept the call or ignore it. When she decides what she wants to do with your call, you're notified. If the recipient accepts your call, you see the Current Call list, and you're ready to start your conversation.

Whenever you want to terminate a call, click the Hang Up button on the toolbar. In most cases, if you placed the call, the other person is also disconnected when you use the Hang Up button.

Talk to me

Assuming that both you and the person you called have microphones and speakers hooked up to your computers, you can start talking as soon as the call is connected. (Remember to look for the speaker icon next to the person's name to check for audio capabilities.)

After your call is accepted, all you have to do to talk to the other person is speak into the microphone! (Think about this: Thousands of dollars' worth of computer hardware and software, and you've re-created the functions of a $19 telephone! But wait; it does get better if you start using some other NetMeeting features.) The other person's voice is relayed to you through your computer's speakers. During the conversation, you can move the slider bars in the Audio section to adjust the volume.

If you're going to play around with your microphone or speaker volume during a conversation, tell the other person what you're doing before you start experimenting with the volume controls. It's only polite!

Watch what you say

You've probably noticed the small box in the middle of the NetMeeting window. This box is your video connection. The box shows the other person's name and picture. It's video, not a still picture; when you move, the other caller sees your movements and vice versa.

To start sending video, click the Start button (the gray triangle) at the bottom of the video box.

If you want to stop sending video, click the stop button (which is the same button) at the bottom of the video box.

You can still keep talking to the other person, whether or not you're sending or receiving video.

The videocamera captures, roughly, your head and shoulders and whatever is in the background. It may be necessary to reposition your camera to hide a messy office. Also, if you got up in the morning and put on only the top half of your business suit (knowing that the camera could not see below your shoulders), remember not to stand up during your conversation. You don't want your colleague to see you in your jammies. *A tip within a tip:* You may want to check your video image *before* you call anybody. To do so, make sure that you're not on a call, and then click the Start button. This button puts you in Preview mode, as shown in Figure 15-3, and you can fiddle around with the camera placement and the placement of your chair, for example, before anybody else sees the video. If you work in your bedroom, consider putting a poster of something impressive on the wall behind you.

Figure 15-3:
Previewing
your out-
going video
before
anyone else
sees it.

I see you!

Video options are available that let you control whether images are sent and received automatically at the beginning of a call. The default video options are set to start receiving video immediately at the beginning of a call and to wait until you click the Start button before sending your video to the other person. These settings mean that all you have to do to see the other person is just look in the video box on the Current Call screen. Figure 15-4 shows a Current Call list when both parties are using video. (Don't worry — he's not *really* angry. He's just reminding the girl about keeping personal information personal when she's on the Web.)

Figure 15-4:
A conversation in which both people are using video.

If the other person's video is not coming through on your screen, click the Start button that's at the bottom of his video box or ask the person (via the microphone) whether the camera is working.

You can change the video options by choosing Tools⇨Options, clicking the Video tab and selecting or unselecting the options in the Sending and receiving video area.

Answering a Call

When someone calls you, a dialog box like the one shown in Figure 15-5 pops up on your screen. All you have to do to answer the call is click the Accept button. If you don't recognize the caller's name or if you don't want to take the call, click the Ignore button.

Figure 15-5:
Deciding whether to accept or ignore an incoming call.

A list of all incoming calls is kept on the History list. To view the list, click the History button. You can call a person on the history list by double-clicking the name.

It's possible to be too popular. If you don't want calls to come through, choose Call⇨Do Not Disturb. This command stops the dialog box from popping up on your screen. People who try to call you are still listed on the history screen. When you're ready to remove the Do Not Disturb sign, choose Call⇨Do Not Disturb to remove the check mark.

Let's Chat

One-to-one communication seems pretty easy, but how do you get a group of people together? Suppose that you need to meet with four business associates on Monday morning. All five of you are in different cities. You contact the people before the meeting by phone, e-mail, or postal mail and schedule the meeting for 11 a.m. on Monday. At 11 a.m., each person starts NetMeeting. Because you're the person organizing the meeting, you volunteer to call the others. You call them by locating their names on a directory list or by typing their e-mail addresses in the New Call box. As each person accepts your call, the meeting is formed. When everyone is assembled, you start the discussion in the Chat window.

That's really all there is to it. Although you can do additional things — like send a file, have a private side meeting with one person, or draw on a whiteboard — holding a meeting online takes just a little organization and the hardware and software to make the connection.

We hate to give you warnings because communicating on the Internet is such a convenient and easy way to get people together, but you should know that you probably shouldn't discuss company secrets over the Internet. With the vast amount of information flowing across the Internet these days, it's unlikely that someone would pick up on your conversation; if you need to discuss supersensitive topics, however, it's probably better to round up everybody in one geographical location, behind closed doors.

Whenever your meeting includes more than two people, you communicate with each other by typing messages in the Chat window. (During the meeting, you can have a one-to-one audio- or videoconference with one participant, if you want.)

To conduct a meeting by using the Chat window, follow these steps:

1. **Call each meeting participant.**

2. **Verify that all the participants are listed on the Participant list (that little white box below the video box. If there are audio controls down there, click the button with the head on it). Click the Chat button at the bottom of the NetMeeting window.**

   (Or choose Tools⇨Chat or press Ctrl+T.) When one person opens the Chat window, the Chat window opens on everybody's screen and all participants can start typing messages. Everyone can see the messages instantly, as the messages are entered.

3. **Type the message you want to send and press Enter.**

   Your message is displayed in the Chat window for everyone to see. The default setting places your name before your message.

4. **If you want to add the date or time to your message, choose Tools⇨ Options and select the items you want to display in the Information Display area.**

5. **Messages can be saved to a file for future reference. To save the messages in the Chat window, choose File⇨Save and type a filename.**

   If you've already saved the messages once and you want to save them under a new filename, choose File⇨Save As and type the filename.

6. **Messages in the Chat window can be your printed minutes of the meeting. To print a copy, choose File⇨Print.**

7. **When the meeting is over, close the Chat window. Click the Hang Up button to the right of the video box.**

One benefit an online meeting has over an in-person meeting is your ability to easily remove someone from the meeting. Unless you have the Do Not Disturb option selected, you can still receive incoming calls. If someone in your meeting accidentally accepts a call from a person who should not be in the meeting, you (as the person who originated the meeting calls) can remove the errant party by right-clicking the party's name on the Current Call list and clicking Remove.

Sending a file

While you're in your meeting, you can do things other than type and read messages. At some point, you probably need to send a file to one or all of the participants. Sending a file is a good way to distribute an agenda or topic list to participants.

To send a file to everyone listed on the Current Call screen, choose Tools⇨File Transfer (or press Ctrl+F). Select the file or type the filename (if you know the exact name of the file and you're already in the directory that said file resides in).

To send a file to one person listed on the Current Call list, right-click the person's name, and then choose Send File from the menu that appears. Select the file or type the filename.

On the receiving end, the person you sent the file to sees a Transfer dialog box. She can choose to open the file or save it to disk.

Although sending a file is most common when you're meeting with a group of people, you can also send a file to the other person during a one-to-one audio- or videoconference.

Talking privately

Another thing you may want to do during a meeting is talk privately with one meeting participant. You can either send a private, typed message or initiate an audio and video connection so that you and the other person can talk to and see each other.

To send a private, typed message to another person in the meeting:

1. **In the Chat window, click the down-arrow button at the right end of the Send to box. From the list that appears, select the person to whom you want to send the message.**

2. **Type your message in the Message box and press Enter.**

   Make sure that you don't type the message first and press Enter while the Everyone in Chat destination is listed in the Send To box. If you do, everyone sees your message that was intended for one person. That could be embarrassing.

To start a private audio or video conversation with another person in the meeting, click their Name in the Participant list. When you're finished with the private conversation, click the Switch button again and click the person's name again to remove the check mark. (You can also right-click the person's name on the Current Call list to start and stop the connection.)

You Gotta Have Art

Some people just can't say it all in words. They have to be able to create pictures and illustrations to present their ideas. If you're one of these people (or if you know someone like this), the whiteboard in NetMeeting is for you. With the whiteboard, you can draw as much as you want just as though you were in your company's meeting room. (Well, give or take your skill with paint programs, which is what the whiteboard resembles.) Doing a presentation? Because multiple pages are available on the whiteboard, you can use it to simulate a flip chart.

Whether you're meeting with one person or with many people, everyone can see the whiteboard as soon as you open it. In fact, if you let them, other people can even contribute to your drawing.

Here's how you open the whiteboard and start drawing:

1. **Click the Whiteboard button at the bottom of the NetMeeting window.**

   (Or choose Tools⇨Whiteboard or press Ctrl+W.) The whiteboard window opens on your screen and on all other meeting participants' screens.

2. **Using the drawing tools on the left side of the whiteboard, create your drawing.**

   Figure 15-6 shows an organizational chart drawn on the whiteboard.

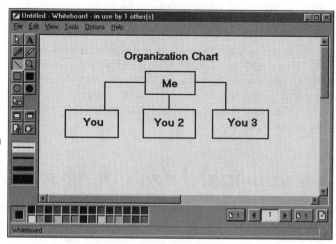

Figure 15-6:
A basic
drawing
on the
whiteboard.

3. **To start a new, blank page, click the Insert New Page button located in the lower-right corner of the whiteboard (the white sheet of paper with a plus sign on it).**

   A new, blank whiteboard appears. Your first page is still on the board. To move backward and forward through the pages, click the Next Page and Previous Page buttons at the bottom of the whiteboard. If the other people who are viewing the whiteboard feel like it, they can add items to the drawing or edit the drawing. You see their changes instantly, as they are entered.

4. **If you create something too precious to throw away, choose File➪Save and give it a filename.**

   Whiteboard files are saved with the extension .wht.

5. **Need a printout? Choose File➪Print, and select the print options you want.**

6. **When you're finished using the whiteboard, close the whiteboard window.**

   Participants have to close their own whiteboard window on their computers.

Tempted to change the drawing?

Watching someone else create a drawing on the whiteboard is fun. You see each stroke and item as it is entered. If you have a number of people participating in your meeting, the whiteboard can be a place for brainstorming ideas and mapping out thoughts.

As you watch, you may want to jump in and add your own two cents to the drawing. Feel free to do that! (If this action causes pain to the originator of the drawing, he can always lock the whiteboard.) Whenever you see something that should be moved or one little thing that's not quite right, go ahead and change it. The same drawing tools that are available to the originator of the drawing are available to you.

Edit my drawing? I don't think so

Free expression is one thing, but what if you've created a masterpiece and other people are trying to change it? Fear not, for you can lock the whiteboard and keep all other participants from altering your drawing.

To lock the whiteboard, click the Lock Contents button in the drawing tools area. When you're ready to grant dispensation and reopen the drawing to the masses, click the Lock Contents button again. The drawing is once again available to all other meeting participants.

Sharing with Your Friends and Associates

As we all learned in kindergarten, sharing is good. Whether it's your toys or your computer programs, sharing something with others is a nice thing to do. In NetMeeting, you can open a file in its original application and let other people in your meeting see it. Although they can't change it (we discuss that topic in the section "Collaborating with Your Partners," later in this chapter), they can see it in its original format. It's a good way to relay information without having to retype data in the Chat window or read information to another person.

Here's how to share an application with the other people in your meeting:

1. **Open the application you want to share.**

2. **In the application window, open the file you want everyone to see.**

3. **On the taskbar, click Microsoft NetMeeting to return to the NetMeeting window.**

   Make sure that you see the Current Call list. (To get back to it, click the Current Call button on the left side of the NetMeeting window.)

4. **Click the Share button on the toolbar, and select the program from the drop-down menu.**

   The document is visible to everyone in the meeting. You may have to minimize the NetMeeting window to see the entire document.

To stop sharing, click the Share button on the toolbar. Click the application you want to stop sharing to remove the check mark.

To collaborate on a document with other people, you must first share the application in which the document is written. If you're collaborating on a Word document, for example, you have to share Word before others can collaborate on the document.

Collaborating with Your Partners

If you've ever tried to co-author a document by exchanging e-mail messages, letters, or faxes, you know how time consuming that process can be. What if you and your co-author could view the document and see editing changes as they're made? Life would be grand.

Get out of the past and fast-forward to the present — now, you and your co-author can access the same document at the same time online. By sharing the document in its original application and electing to collaborate on the document, you can exchange control of it. One person takes control and makes editing changes, and then the other person takes control and makes changes. All changes are visible to both parties.

While you're sharing a document, the program you're sharing runs on only one person's computer. For example, if you and a coworker are sharing a Word document and you started Word and shared it with your coworker, then Word is running on your computer and the document is stored on your computer. Although your coworker sees an image of Microsoft Word and the document on her screen and can type commands to edit the document, the document is still stored on your computer. When you are done collaborating on the document, you can send the finished file to your coworker.

Before you can collaborate on a document, you must share the application in which the document is written. After you complete the steps to share the application, follow these steps to collaborate on a document:

1. **Switch to the NetMeeting window, and then click the Share Program button at the bottom of the window.**

2. **To gain control of the document, click the mouse button anywhere in the document.**

   Only one person at a time can be in control of the document. You can tell who is in control of the document because the user's initials are displayed on your screen. When you're not in control of the document, you cannot move your cursor, and you see a message telling you to click the mouse button to regain control (see Figure 15-7).

3. **When you're finished collaborating, click the mouse button to regain control of the document. Click the Share Program button to turn off the collaboration feature.**

   If clicking the mouse button doesn't return control of the document to you, try pressing the Esc key.

4. **Go back to the document you were collaborating on, and save the document.**

   You have to do this step to save the changes that were made during the collaborating session.

Be aware that when you collaborate on a document, the other collaborators can open your files from the shared application by using the File⇨Open command or save files by using the File⇨Save or File⇨Save As command. Because you're collaborating, you can see the actions your collaborator is taking, although it's probably a good policy to collaborate only with people you trust.

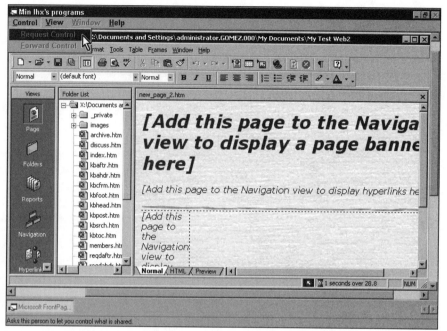

Figure 15-7:
Collabor-
ating on a
document.

Meeting Adjourned

It has been a good meeting, but now it's time to leave.

To end a call when you see the Current Call list, click the Hang Up button. (You can also choose Call⇨Hang Up at any time.)

To exit NetMeeting, close the NetMeeting window or choose Call⇨Exit.

Part V

The Part of Tens

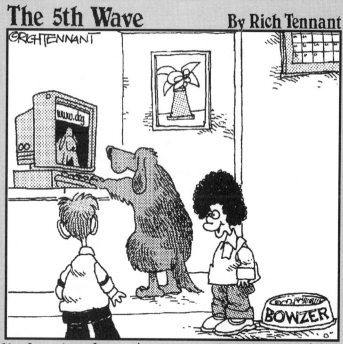

The 5th Wave By Rich Tennant

"He found a dog site over an hour ago and has been in a staring contest ever since."

In this part . . .

There's lots to know about lots of stuff before you begin to master the Internet. Stuff we couldn't fit anywhere else we put here, in The Part of Tens. We're fond of quoting Tom Lehrer, who said, "Base eight is just like base ten, really — if you're missing two fingers." So you may find that some of our lists have ten items on them in a more symbolic than literal way. We'll help you, though, with common pitfalls, frequently asked questions, places to find things, and things you absolutely, positively, shouldn't even think about doing.

Chapter 16

Ten Problems and Solutions

In This Chapter

▶ Problems most Internauts encounter

▶ What to do about them

"Loading Web Pages Takes Forever on My Computer"

The Internet promises many exciting possibilities, but it provides nothing except tedium when each page takes half a minute or more to appear. Not all Internet slowdowns are under your control, although you can take steps to speed things up:

✔ **Set your browser to load images only when you ask for them, as explained in Chapter 9.**

✔ **Get a faster modem.** If your modem is 28.8 kilobits per second or slower, it's high time to upgrade. If you're using a 28.8 Kbps unit, however getting a 33.6 Kbps modem will show only a modest improvement. Bite the bullet and get a 56 Kbps modem; they're available for as little as $30.

✔ **Switch to a higher-speed service, such as cable, xDSL, or ISDN.** All these are much faster than ordinary phone lines, although price and availability vary from region to region. Getting one of these services makes your surfing a pleasure rather than an exercise in patience (the so-called "died and went to heaven" effect). Of course, now you'll complain about the lack of broadband content (witness the freshly coined "Can't they just show all the *Star Trek* movies online and back-to-back?" effect).

"My E-Mail Inbox Is Filled with Junk Mail"

The best thing to do about junk e-mail, or *spam,* is to get good at deleting it immediately. Don't even read it if it is obviously junk. Look for telltale subject lines like "MAKE MONEY FAST!!!" or bizarre return addresses like "???@???." If you aren't sure, you should open the message — you don't want to throw out something important. You don't have to read the entire message after you realize that it's junk.

Whatever you do, don't encourage the junk e-mail industry by buying what they are selling. You may even consider getting a different account name to use on mailing lists, chat rooms, and Usenet newsgroups — all places where spammers collect addresses for their lists.

See Chapter 6 for more tips and visit http://spam.abuse.net and http://www.cauce.org for suggestions for fighting the spam problem.

"I Don't Want My Kids Exposed to Online Porn and Weirdos"

Your kid is probably safer on the Internet than he or she would be at the mall, although enough raunchy stuff is online that parents should actively supervise their kids' Internet use. Here are some tips:

✔ Although software is available that is supposed to keep kids from visiting unsuitable sites, you are relying on someone else's judgment about what is suitable. Because most sites tend to err on the side of caution, your kids see a Web that is very watered down. You can find pointers to these filtering services and many other resources for parents at http://www.smartparent.com.

✔ Be sure that you talk to your kids regularly about what they are doing online and what behavior you consider acceptable. Make sure that they know not to meet any Net friends in person without your permission and never to give out over the Internet any information that could identify them in the real world. This kind of information includes full name, street address, phone number, schools they attend, and hours they travel to and from school or other activities.

✔ The best solution, particularly for younger children, is to have a parent or other adult be with them at all times while they are online. If children are not old enough to go out on their own in the real world, they are not old enough to go out on their own online.

"I'm Afraid to Use My Credit Card Online"

If you are doing business with a reputable firm that offers a secure Web page for entering credit card information, you are probably safer than when you use your credit card at a restaurant or gas station. You can tell whether a page is secure by looking for an unbroken lock or key logo in the lower-left corner of your browser window.

For the highest level of security, we recommend that you get a version of your browser with the U.S., or 128-bit, security feature. The international, or 40-bit, versions can in principle be broken by hackers, though we have yet to hear of credit card info being stolen in transit over the Net.

"My Computer Crashes Frequently While I'm Online"

Computers have no good reason to crash as much as they do, and — hopefully — someday they won't. In the meantime, here are a few steps you can take to make crashes happen less often:

- ✔ Make sure that your computer has enough memory (RAM). We recommend at least 32 megabytes.

- ✔ Make sure that you have the latest version of your browser and helper software, although you should stay away from beta versions. The word *beta* means that the software has been sent out without being completed so that it can be tested. You can probably wait for the officially released version, which will have enough problems.

Remember the Greek alphabet? Good, because alpha comes *before* beta. Don't think of alpha as being *above* beta because software in the alpha stage is even less tested then beta-grade software.

"I Can't Find a Friend's E-Mail Address"

The best solution to this problem is to call your friend on the phone and ask for his address. Right now, no perfect way exists to find out someone's e-mail address. Here are some other suggestions:

- Keep an e-mail address book. Both Netscape and Outlook Express have this feature. When someone you care about sends you a message, copy the address, which is in the message's From field, and paste the address in your electronic address book.

- If you have the person's business card or stationery, see whether it lists an e-mail address.

- Try searching for the person's name by using AltaVista (at `http://www.altavista.com`) and DejaNews (at `http://www.deja.com`).

- All the value-added service providers — such as America Online, CompuServe, and Prodigy Internet — have ways for you to look up the addresses of other subscribers to that service. You have to be a subscriber on that provider's service, however. The address directory is one of the added values of a commercial service.

Several groups have set up Internet white pages directory services. None is close to complete. Still, you can try any of these services, such as `http://people.yahoo.com` or `http://www.whowhere.lycos.com`, to find long-lost friends or enemies.

"I Keep Getting '404 File Not Found' Messages"

If you typed the URL from a printed source, for example, make sure that you typed it exactly as it was printed, including capitalization.

If you're sure that you typed the URL correctly or if you clicked a hypertext link, the data on the site may have been reorganized. Try "walking up" the URL by deleting the portion to the right of the last slash character, and then the next-to-last slash character, and so on. If you get a "File Not Found" message when you try this address, for example:

```
http://world.std.com/~reinhold/pubs/mathmovies/
```

try this one instead:

```
http://world.std.com/~reinhold/pubs/
```

Then try this one:

```
http://world.std.com/~reinhold/
```

or even this one:

```
http://world.std.com/
```

At one of these levels, you may find a hint about where the file you seek can be found.

You can also use a search engine by including in the URL both the filename or topic you seek and the domain name. In the preceding example, you would search for `world.std.com` and `mathmovies`.

"My Eyes Hurt, My Back Aches, and My Arm Is Sore"

Spending a great deal of time at the computer can be hard on your body and can even lead to debilitating injury.

✔ Make sure that your computer is set up in a way that minimizes stresses while you work. The top of your monitor should be at or slightly below eye level and positioned to minimize reflections and glare. Your chair should give good back support and keep your thighs horizontal and your feet flat on the floor. Your forearms should be horizontal and in a straight line with your wrists and hands while typing.

✔ A good computer desk and chair are excellent investments if you plan to use your computer frequently.

✔ Take frequent short breaks. Look out the window several times an hour.

✔ If you do notice pain or discomfort, see your doctor sooner rather than later. Treatments for injuries related to computer use are usually more successful if the problems are caught early.

Yahoo has a collection of sites dealing with computer health problems, at `http://dir.yahoo.com/Health/Diseases_and_Conditions/Repetitive_Strain_Disorders/`.

"I Don't Have Enough Time to Try All Those Interesting Web Sites"

Give up television. The average American watches 2.6 hours of television and videos a day. Although many sites on the Web are a waste of time, compared to sitting on the couch in front of the idiot box, surfing the Internet is positively purposeful. Some Web sites even tell you what you missed on TV last night. Besides, if you learn something that you didn't want to learn, you've still learned something, right?

Unlike TV, the Web can save you time. Internet shopping can be very convenient. More and more government agencies have forms available online. For example, you can get passport forms at http://www.state.gov. You can look up zip codes at http://www.usps.gov. For almost any kind of information, in fact, the Internet is becoming the first place to look.

"I Spend Too Much Time Online"

The Internet can be addictive. The standard advice is "Get a life!" If you are truly enjoying what you're doing and it's bringing you in contact with others, don't be too hard on yourself.

The best test for whether you have gone overboard in your Internet usage is to ask whether the Internet is interfering with your most important relationships and activities, such as family and work. Here are some suggestions if you think that you are hooked and want to cut back:

- ✔ Talk to family and friends and get their honest appraisal of your online activities.

- ✔ Sign up for real-world activities that get you out of the house and away from the Net, such as evening classes, a health club membership, theater subscriptions, or political groups. Of course, you can spend hours on the Internet finding these activities.

- ✔ Put yourself on an Internet diet — budgeting the hours you are online each week — and stick to it.

- ✔ Pick one day a week when you do not log on, not even to check your mail.

- ✔ Let a family member change your password so that you have to ask her to log you in.

- ✔ If the Internet is ruining your life, give away your computer. People got along fine before the Net existed, and you may be better off without it.

- ✔ Get professional help, but don't look for it online!

Chapter 17

Ten Frequently Asked Questions

In This Chapter

▶ Straight (but not narrow) answers to vexing questions about the Internet

▶ Our opinions about what's useful and what's not

▶ A few myths debunked

*T*he Internet is a big subject; it seems like it's a subject that's on every-body's mind nowadays. As a result, we get asked lots of questions about the Internet. Many of the answers to those questions are sprinkled through-out this book, although some of them don't fit neatly under any specific sub-ject. You can find those questions, and our answers, here.

Now, whenever someone asks us one of these questions, we can — rather than answer it — tell them to get a copy of this book and read the chapter. Heh, heh.

If you have more than ten remaining questions after you read this book, surf to our Web site, at `http://net.gurus.com`, where we tell you where to find hundreds of answers.

It used to be that the most frequently asked questions about the Internet were things like "What kind of computer should I buy?" or "What software should I use?" If you're reading this book, you've probably decided on Windows Me and a computer that can run it, so we don't have to deal with those questions here. That leaves room for more interesting questions.

"How Important Is This Internet Stuff?"

Darned important. In a minute, we talk about all the wonderful things you can do on the Internet and all the wonderful reasons you *should* bother with the Internet. For now, however, let's talk about why you have to understand the Internet, whether you really want to or not.

Back when computers were just beginning to emerge from their big, glass houses, a visionary friend of ours, Ted Nelson, wrote a book subtitled "You can and must understand computers now!" He was absolutely right. If you don't have a clue about how computers work, you'll have a frustrating day dealing with everything from the microwave oven to the automatic-teller machine to the voice information system when you call the auto-parts store.

The future is about information, and the Internet is about getting information to people. It's not that you *can't* get by without information; of course you can. You can get by without electricity too. If you're in a community where information counts, however, whether it's school, business, or the job market, you have much more access to information if you're comfortable with the Internet. Besides, there's plenty of fun stuff to do on the Internet.

"Why Bother with the Internet, and What Can I Do with It, Anyway?"

Our favorite real-life version of this question came from one of our cousins who's not particularly technically savvy. The way he put it was, "The Internet — isn't that the new advertising thing companies are trying to get people to use so that they can sell us more stuff?" All he ever saw of the Internet were the Web addresses that started showing up on everybody's advertisements for everything.

We like to think that what motivates advertisers to put their Web addresses in their ads is a symptom of why the Net is so useful, and not a cynical attempt to force more of their product down your throat. (Actually, we suspect that companies put their Web addresses on their ads because it's the with-it thing to do, and it makes them look like they're on the cutting edge.)

The Internet is about information and communication. In Chapter 1, we talk all about the different things you can do on the Internet, and all of them revolve around getting information in different ways or communicating with people in different ways. If you're not interested in either of those things, chances are that the Internet is not for you. On the other hand, chances are that whatever you *are* interested in has an information aspect or a communication aspect to it, whether it's finding out about the latest product from some company, finding out about the latest design ideas in your favorite craft, chatting with people who share the same challenges you do, or finding people who want to buy your products or services. And *that's* why advertisers put their Web addresses in their advertisements: The Net is about information.

If you're curious about some product, chances are slim that you would pick up the telephone and call in for some information and even slimmer that you would still be interested when printed material arrived in your mailbox. With the Internet, however, in a few seconds you can be looking at a page full of information about a product, and in a second or two more you can decide that you don't care about it or that you are really interested. No matter that you live in deepest, darkest suburbia, if you want to chat about keeping chickens, you can connect with other chicken fanciers from all over the world and share stories and advice.

All the things we list in Chapter 1 that you can do with the Internet are not ends in themselves — they're means to other ends. To put it succinctly, it's not what you do with the Internet — it's what the Internet lets you do with the rest of your life. Now that so many other people are on the Internet, relevant information and people are on the Internet no matter *what* you do with the rest of your life.

"Are the Internet and the World Wide Web the Same Thing?"

No. Next question, please.

If you've read Chapters 1 and 8 in this book and the distinction between the Internet and the World Wide Web still isn't clear, we forgive you. People use the terms almost interchangeably, and, in casual conversation, sometimes we do too. We shouldn't, of course, although as it becomes increasingly true that anything you can do on the Internet you can also do through the World Wide Web, it's hard to keep the distinction uppermost in one's mind without sounding like a nitpicky academic.

Analogies abound for the Internet, and most of them make some kind of useful point and leave out some kind of important distinction: The Internet is the highway, and the World Wide Web is one kind of traffic that travels on the highway, just as cars, trucks, and buses share the physical highways; the Internet is the engine that powers the information revolution, and the World Wide Web is the dashboard we all use to control the engine; the Internet is like a cable TV system, and the World Wide Web is like the programs that go over the cable system.

Specifically, the Internet started out in 1969 as a way to connect computers. The World Wide Web, born in 1989, is a system of interconnected information (in the form of Web pages) that you can access via the Internet. In the past couple of years, the Web has become the most common way of using the Internet. By now, you can use a World Wide Web browser program to send and receive e-mail (at `http://www.hotmail.com` and `http://mail.yahoo.com`), find Usenet newsgroups (at `http://www.deja.com`), and chat with other computer users (at `http://chat.yahoo.com`), all traditionally functions that happened *through* the Internet, by using technologies other than the World Wide Web. So, though they are *not* the same thing, they're beginning to look like the same thing.

"How Much Does It Cost to Be on the Internet?"

At the moment we're writing this chapter, the short answer is "Twenty dollars a month." Obviously, there's more to it than that. Do you need another telephone line just for your computer, or can you share a telephone line between your computer, yourself, and the other people in your house? You have to figure out what telephone lines cost in your area.

Will your telephone calls to your Internet Service Provider be free (included in your basic service), or will you have to pay by the minute? Or will you pay by the minute and hit some kind of a billing cap? Margy's rural telephone service charges two cents a minute to call the next-door neighbor, so her telephone bill for Internet access works out to about $300 per month, except for the fact that those nice folks at the Vermont Department of Public Utilities put a $30 cap on local telephone fees. Good for her, but not so good for the telephone company. John's equally rural phone service in New York charges nothing for local calls. Go figure. If you're going to be on the Internet frequently, it may pay to understand your telephone bill.

After you have your telephone straightened out, you'll find that most Internet Service Providers have an all-you-can-eat plan for about $20, and a pay-as-you-go plan for between $5 and $10 for three to five hours, and about $2 for each additional hour. Early in 1998, some large providers started limiting your trips to the all-you-can-eat salad bar at about 100 hours, charging $2 for each additional hour, so what you pay depends on what you use (a radical capitalist notion). A few providers offer access for less than $10 per month, but they're depending on subsidies from "reciprocal compensation," a telephone regulation quirk that is likely to go away sometime in 2001.

If you're willing to hunt around, you may even find access to the Internet for free (at least, free after you make the telephone call). If you're affiliated with an educational institution (university, college, community college, high school, and even some elementary schools) you may be able to get dial-up access to the Internet. If you're not, check out Netzero (www.netzero.net, Freei (www.freei.net, and the free Net-access CDs handed out at places like your local department store. They all offer free access using special software that shows ads while you're online, but for many it's no worse than watching TV.

Finally, check out your local public library. Most of them have computers connected to the Internet, where you can get a taste of what's going on out there. You are, however, stuck using whatever software the library decided to install on its computers.

"Who Should I Sign Up with to Be on the Internet?"

Much of Chapter 2 is dedicated to answering this question, although it would be downright dishonest to claim to have a list of frequently asked questions that doesn't include this question, which we get asked most frequently of all.

The answer, obviously, is that it depends. You trade off four things: price, technical support, local telephone access, and speed. How much of which you get from each Internet Service Provider may be difficult to determine. The details are in Chapter 2.

"What's an Internet Address?"

Although nobody ever asks this question in just this way, from the amount of confusion we see over slashes, at-signs, and .htmls, we think that it's a question people ought to ask. If they could just figure out that they *are* confused, it's a question people would ask. Two kinds of addresses are on the Internet: Web addresses and e-mail addresses. They're pretty easy to tell apart after you know what they are but can be really confusing if you don't even know that they're different:

  - ✔ **E-mail addresses** have at-signs (@) in them. Always. (Okay, some really old-fashioned addresses have exclamation points instead, but you won't run into them.) E-mail addresses almost never have slashes in them, and they don't include www in them or .htm or .html either. They always have the form someone@somewhere.com. Sometimes it's more complicated, like someone@somecomputer.somewhere.com or even Your_Name_at_PO. Jade@smtplink.somecompany.com. The form is always the same, however: something that identifies a person, an at-sign, and something that identifies a computer.

  - ✔ **Web addresses** have slashes (/) in them. They never have at-signs (@) in them, and they usually start with http:// and end with .html. We talk a great deal about Web addresses (also called *URLs*) in Chapter 8, including the fine points about ones that start with things like ftp://.

What creates confusion is that almost all Web addresses start with http://www, and most of them end with index.html. Because we're lazy, most of us forget about those parts. Rather than say "Look for our Web page at http://www.gurus.com/index.html," people say "Find us on the Net at gurus.com" and assume that you'll figure out the rest. Then, when you hear something like "E-mail me, I'm Joe Smith at gurus.com," you're tempted to start putting https on the beginning and slashes on the end of poor Joe Smith's e-mail address, when all the mail system is looking for is JoeSmith@gurus.com.

Remember: E-mail is someone@somewhere.com, and Web addresses are http://www.somewhere.com.

"Are There Any Good Places to Shop on the World Wide Web?"

We've been saying over and over again that the Internet is about information and communication. Information is what the market economy is all about: The more information buyers have about products and prices, the better decisions they can make about what they want and whether it's worth the price. That's why Web commerce (buying and selling stuff on the World Wide Web) is such an interesting subject for so many people.

By all accounts, the runaway success in selling things on the Internet has been the bookseller Amazon.com (at http://www.amazon.com). It claims to have access to pretty much every book that's in print in English, and its Web site lets you browse the first chapter of many books. It also provides services that may be hard to get from a regular bookstore, like watching out for new books from a particular author you may be interested in. Best of all, Amazon discounts the list price. As you may imagine, its success has drawn the attention of traditional booksellers, and BarnesAndNoble.com and Borders.com are hot on its heels. Everyone we know who has ordered from Amazon has positive things to say about it.

Intent on duplicating the success of Amazon.com, CDNow (at http://www.cdnow.com) lists a host of CDs on the World Wide Web. For many of its CDs, you can hear a 30-second audio clip. You'll find, after all the hype is cleared away, that the sound quality is almost good enough to give you an idea of what the music is like. You certainly wouldn't listen to sound that bad for pleasure. Still, it's better than just reading the promo material on the CD case.

If you can buy CDs and books, why not groceries? PeaPod (at http://www.peapod.com) was one of the first to try this concept and it has worked hard on its user interface. You have to be in one of the seven markets it serves, however.

The idea of putting small shops together in a mall on the Internet is clearly an appealing one. Yahoo (the Web directory) lists no fewer than 811 malls on the Internet. It's hard for us to figure out what value you get from a mall, however, because on the Internet, everyone is next-door to everyone else already. It doesn't cost a small shop much to put up its own store on the World Wide Web, and none of the malls we've seen promotes itself well enough to become a Web destination. Estimates were made in 1997 that many mall proprietors made more money selling Internet commerce seminars than actually selling goods on the Internet.

For a sampling of what small shops can do on their own, check out our entry, at `http://www.greattapes.com`. We specialize in harder-to-find audio- and videotapes for children; we characterize them as the kind you see at a neighbor's house and ask "Where did you find that, anyway?" It has been an interesting experiment in Web commerce, and we must say that we're enthused about the concept. We started it because we were looking for some videos and just assumed that they would be available on the Internet. They weren't! Well, they are now! This site shows how easy it is to run a small retail business on the Web (because it's hard to know less about retail than we do).

Commerce on the Web isn't just about small-ticket items. Edmund's (`http://www.edmunds.com`) is an excellent online version of the venerable car-buying guides; AutoByTel (`http://www.autobytel.com`) can get you a good deal on a new or used car you select. Especially for new cars, with their dizzying array of options, the amount of information you can gather on the Internet from both the manufacturer's Web sites and sites such as Edmund's means that when you walk into the showroom, you and the sales rep are on a much more equal footing.

This discussion is just the tip of the iceberg. Online commerce is changing every day, and, in the main, it's getting better. So, yes, there are many good places to shop on the Internet. You just have to find them.

"Is It Safe to Use My Credit Card on the Net?"

Yes. Could we make that any clearer? Yes, period.

All right, there are subtleties here. In one sense, it's *never* safe to use a credit card anywhere. Anyone at the establishment where you're using your card can copy down the number and the expiration date and even your signature. What's to stop that person from using your card and your number? And then there's your cordless telephone. Any joker with a scanner from Radio Shack can drive down your street and listen to you order from Lands End or L.L. Bean; then that person has the same credit card information you just gave a reputable merchant. We like that example because it's much like what could happen on the Internet: Just as millions and millions of cordless telephone calls are made every day, only a tiny fraction of which mention credit card numbers, billions and billions of bytes of messages are sent on the Internet every day, only a tiny fraction of which mention credit card numbers. Get the picture? It *could* happen, although if you're really worried about credit card safety, stop using your cordless telephone before you stop using the Internet. Your cordless (or cellular) telephone is much riskier.

Now suppose — just suppose — that someone gets your credit card number as you're making a purchase on the Internet. We ignore the fact that at the time this chapter was written, the number of cases of credit card fraud resulting from credit card numbers being stolen from shoppers on the Internet was exactly zero — none — zip — never happened. Suppose that you make history and you're the unlucky first victim. Your liability is limited by U.S. federal law to $50. Although that amount may hurt, it won't wipe out all your assets (or, if it does, you need to think about why you're using a credit card anyway). If you report the theft as soon as you notice it, your liability may be $0.

So why all the hype about fraud on the Internet? It's new, and people are uneasy about new things, especially when it comes to money. That's not unreasonable. Back when buying things over the telephone was new, people worried about the same thing; and back when credit cards were new, people worried about that too. The flames have been fanned, however, by a bunch of consultants out to make a name for themselves by scaring people and a bunch of companies that wanted to make a bunch of money by selling the Internet's next great payment system. Although fearmongering makes for a great reputation, the dismal business results of the companies trying to sell "digital cash" and other such schemes would seem to indicate that people don't really feel that they need them.

If, after this harangue, you still don't want to send your plastic over the Net or you're one of the fiscally responsible holdouts who doesn't do plastic, most online stores are happy to have you call in your number over the phone or send them a check.

"How Can I Make Money on the Net?"

We can't remember exactly how many trillions of dollars of business opportunity the Internet represents according to the people who claim to know about these things. We do see that businesses rely on communication. As a new medium of communication, the doors of the Internet are being flung open for new ways of doing business.

Rather than try to figure out how to make money in the Internet business, spend time getting to know the Net extensively — by checking out newsgroups and mailing lists in addition to exploring the World Wide Web. The more you see, the more you can think about organic ways in which your business can use the Net. Follow your loves: Find newsgroups and mailing lists that excite you. You will meet all kinds of interesting people and get new ideas. We think that what you can find out from the Net can help you find for yourself where your unique opportunities lie.

We have found that the best way to make money on the Net is to write books about it! Then again, we were writing books when dirt was two days old and playing with the Internet for longer than that. If we weren't in the book business, we probably would look at business-to-business commerce, either online services or Net-related "real world" business services, as the most likely candidates.

"Can People Steal Information from My Computer If I'm on the Internet?"

No. This question hasn't generated as much heat and light as credit cards on the Internet, which is surprising. Because, although the answer in general is "No," you can make a number of different slip-ups that do make it easier for people to "tap in" to your computer after you're on the Internet.

The biggest security hole we know of relates to cable and DSL access. We talked about them in Chapter 2. If they're available in your area, we think that they're a terrific idea for fast Internet access. If your cable modem is set up incorrectly, you may find that you can look at the computer of everyone else on your street who has a cable modem. People tend to spot this situation pretty quickly, however, and the cable companies are usually eager to fix it, so it's not a situation that's likely to last long. Although DSL connections don't suffer from that particular nuisance, other dangers exist that are just as unpleasant.

Windows Me occasionally displays a message about disabling file and printer sharing on your Internet connection, usually if your computers are connected in a Local Area Network. Although it's theoretically possible for someone to gain access to your computer if you ignore this message, they would have to be looking specifically for you and employ a certain amount of technical sophistication. How smart are your enemies? Tell Windows to disable file and printer sharing anyway.

For the rest of us, however, unless you go out of your way to allow people to look at your computer, it's safe. Again, analogies to items we're more familiar with are useful. Your telephone answering machine is connected to the telephone network (just like your computer). Unless your answering machine has a remote message-retrieval feature, however, no one can listen to your telephone messages. The same thing goes for your computer: Unless you've installed a feature to access your computer remotely, you're safe.

Chapter 18

Ten Cool Places on the Internet

● ●

In This Chapter

▶ Some of our favorite Web sites

● ●

A Fact-Filled Feature for Flick Fans

*E*ver get into an argument about how many Oscars *Gone With The Wind* was awarded? (It won eight, plus five more nominations, including Clark Gable's. Robert Donat won best actor that year for his performance in *Goodbye, Mr. Chips.*)

If you're interested in movies, the Internet Movie Database, at `http://www.imdb.com`, is *the* place to look. It has comprehensive information about nearly every major movie ever made and links to other movie pages, including the official page every movie must have these days. Best of all, you can add your own trivia tidbits.

The Spook's Almanac

If that movie you just found sparks your curiosity about some far-off place, don't mess around. Get the information you need from the U.S. Central Intelligence Agency. The *CIA World Fact Book,* at `http://www.odci.gov/cia/publications/factbook/index.html`, is filled with facts, statistics and even maps you can download. Don't expect hotel and restaurant recommendations, though; those are still classified.

Getting There Needn't Be a Pain

Now that you know where to go, you have to make plane reservations. Travelocity, at `http://www.travelocity.com`, lets you tap in to the same computer system — Sabre — that many travel agents use. Although you have to set up an account for yourself, Travelocity is free and a great place to look for airfare bargains. For more info about making travel arrangements over the Internet, visit `http://www.iecc.com/airline` to see John's lengthy pontifications on the topic.

Old-Fashioned Books

The Web is fine and dandy, although most of us prefer to relax curled up with a page-turner made of genuine forest-grown paper. You probably will need several books for that long plane ride to Nepal. Amazon.com, at `http://www.amazon.com` (of course), is the Internet's biggest virtual bookstore, has an enormous selection to choose from, offers steep discounts, and provides excellent service.

All the News That Links

You will want to check for late-breaking developments before taking that trip. *The New York Times*, at `http://www.nytimes.com`, considered by many to be the best newspaper in the world, has an extensive Web presence. Many other newspapers are on the Web too. You can find an up-to-date list at `http://www.yahoo.com/Business_and_Economy/Companies/News_and_Media/`.

Read the Future

If you tire of traditional media, you may want to try material written especially for the Web. Hundreds of newsletters and journals are on the Web. Perhaps the best is *Slate,* at `http://www.slate.com`, the well-funded Microsoft attempt to break into culture. The writing is good, and you aren't killing any trees.

Get a New Computer Custom-Built for You

If you bought this book in anticipation of buying a computer or if you know someone who is planning to buy, a few major computer companies let you order a computer the way you want it online and then build it pronto for delivery in a couple of days. Dell Computers, at `http://www.dell.com`, pioneered this concept. If Windows Me hasn't met all your expectations, you can see what the competition offers at the Apple custom e-store, at `http://www.apple.com`.

Share That Ware

You need some software to make that new computer do its stuff. Perhaps the coolest place to get it is at TUCOWS, at `http://www.tucows.com`. TUCOWS stands for The Ultimate Collection of Winsock Software, although this site does much more than collect software these days. Don't forget to encourage those dedicated shareware authors by paying your shareware fees.

Lost Romance

Old-flame surfing is the latest rage. Can't forget that cute kid in senior English you used to flirt with — before you understood what flirting was really all about — and then lost track of after high school? The Internet is the place to reconnect. Try the telephone white pages listings at WhoWhere, at `http://www.whowhere.lycos.com`, or Four11, at `http://people.yahoo.com`. Sometimes the regular search engines, such as AltaVista (`http://altavista.com`, can produce surprising results when you search for someone's name.

If that special someone of whom you have been thinking about all those years turns out to be married with three kids and doesn't even remember who you are, closure is worth something, isn't it?

Ring Around the Web

Oodles of interesting personal Web sites are out there in addition to a great deal of junk. One cool place to find sites you may enjoy visiting is the Webring page, `http://www.webring.com`. The Web ring idea is simple: People with common interests link to one another. You keep clicking along until you get back to where you started — that is, if you don't get lost following other links you find along the way. The Webring page serves a master jumping-off point, with topical lists and a search engine.

Immerse Yourself in Cyberspace

Many sites on the Web can help you find what you're looking for. Yahoo, at `http://www.yahoo.com`, stands out as the best place to find what you aren't looking for. Just poking around in the many Yahoo categories is bound to stimulate your curiosity.

Yahoo also encourages you to make its site your home page with a customizable version called My Yahoo. Visit `http://my.yahoo.com` and follow the instructions to build your own personal news report that is customized every time you sign on to the Web.

If You Liked This Book . . .

You'll love our Web site, `http//net.gurus.com`. In addition to more of our inimitable prose, you will find

- ✔ **Updates and corrections:** The Internet changes so fast that any printed information runs a risk of being out of date.
- ✔ **Information that wouldn't fit:** The best of what we don't have room for gets posted here.
- ✔ **Links we find interesting:** When we find something cool, we try to let our readers know about it.

Be sure to register your book while you're there!

Chapter 19

Ten Stupid Internet Moves to Avoid

*T*he Internet is an exciting place. If you haven't figured that out by now, perhaps you're reading the wrong book. Like most exciting places, however, it's full of excitable people, and those excitable people sometimes go careening off in all directions. One of the surest ways to set them off is to act like a clueless newbie or, even worse, to act obnoxiously even though it looks like you've been around for a while. Finally, it's true that the Internet is well integrated into Windows Me, although you can still do some things that really mess things up on your computer.

In this chapter, we try to keep you out of trouble with some do's and don'ts, for both Net behavior and good housekeeping on your computer. When we're done, you'll look like the coolest Web surfer on your block.

Fitting In

The moment you get your new Internet account, you may have an overwhelming urge to begin sending out lots of messages to mailing lists, chat groups, and anybody else whose online address you can get. *Don't do it!*

Read mailing lists, Web pages, and other Net resources for a while before you send anything out. You then can figure out where best to send your messages, which makes it both more likely that you will contact people who are interested in what you say and less likely that you will annoy people by bothering them with irrelevancies because you sent something to an inappropriate place.

One of the nicest innovations that is creeping from the Internet back to the rest of communications is the list of *Frequently Asked Questions,* or *FAQs.* We talk a little about them on our Web site, at http://net.gurus.com, where we point out that most Usenet newsgroups have one. As we mention there, you can find Usenet FAQs at the FTP site ftp://rtfm.mit.edu. You can also find Usenet FAQs at DejaNews (http://www.deja.com) and Yahoo (http://www.yahoo.com), although you have to search for the word *FAQ* and the name of the newsgroup you're interested in.

Many Web sites also have FAQs. Practically all mailing lists have FAQs. When you subscribe to a mailing list, you usually get the FAQ automatically. It's a long message you'll be tempted to skip over. *Don't!* It contains a great deal of information that will help you be a valued member of the list rather than a nuisance. After you've read the message, save it (some of us have a mail folder named Reference or Registrations that's full of these things — see Chapter 6 for tips on how to do it).

Before you go telling other people on the list how to behave, read the rules again. Some officious newbie, newly subscribed to JAZZ-L, began flaming the list and complaining about the off-topic threads. JAZZ-L encourages this kind of discussion — it says so right in the introduction to the list. As you may imagine, that was not a way to become a valued member of the list.

To reiterate: Before you go asking questions in a newsgroup or discussion group or mailing list, *read the FAQ.* They're not called *frequently asked questions* for nothing — more often than not, our questions have been answered there.

Netiquette 101

The primary tool you use to make a fool of yourself on the Internet is your e-mail program. Face it — it's hard to do much damage when you're just reading someone else's Web page. After you join a mailing list or begin to correspond with friends and acquaintances or begin to post to a Usenet newsgroup, however, the possibilities for embarrassment are endless. Keep in mind the advice in this section while your fingers do the talking.

Speling counts

Many Net users feel that because Net messages are short and informal, spelling and grammar don't count. Some even think that strange spelling makes them K00L D00DZ. If you feel that wey, theirs' not much wee can do abowt it. We think that sending out a sloppy, misspelled message is similar to showing up at a party with big grease stains on your shirt — although your friends will know that it's you, people who don't know you will tend to conclude that you don't know how to dress yourself.

Many mail programs have spell checkers. If you have installed the Microsoft Spelling Checker (it comes with Microsoft Office, Word, and Excel), Outlook Express uses it to check the spelling of your e-mail messages. While you're composing your message, choose Tools⇨Spelling. If you didn't purchase one of the other Microsoft products, you're out of luck, though.

Netscape 4.0 always comes with a spell checker. After you've composed your message, choose Tools⇨Check Spelling from the menu, or click the Spelling button on the toolbar.

Eudora Pro (the commercial version of Eudora) checks your spelling when you click the dictionary icon (the *ABC* one) on the toolbar or choose Edit⇨Check Spelling from the menu. Eudora can also automatically check outgoing messages for spelling errors; choose Tools⇨Options and find the Spell Checking screen; make sure that the box labeled Check when messages queued or sent has a check mark in it.

STOP SHOUTING — I CAN HEAR YOU

You can shout in your e-mail, just like in real life: JUST TYPE YOUR ENTIRE MESSAGE IN CAPITAL LETTERS. People don't like it, any more than they like being shouted at in real life. It's likely to get you some snappy comments suggesting that you do something about the stuck Shift key on your keyboard. Except for Apple computers, keyboards have handled lowercase letters since about 1970, so avail yourself of this modern technical marvel and aid to literate writing.

Now and then, we get mail from someone who says, "i dont like to use capital letters or punctuation its too much work" You can get away with this technique if you're e. e. cummings; from anybody else, we find it tedious.

If you don't have anything to say, don't say it

Avoid trying to sound smart. When you do, the result is usually its opposite. One of the stupidest things we have seen was on the mailing list TRAVEL-L. Someone posted a legitimate request for information about some travel destination. Then came the edifying comment "Sorry, Bud, Can't Help You." We would have thought that people who don't know anything could keep their mouths shut, but apparently we were wrong.

Each message you post to a list goes to the entire list. Each list member is there on a voluntary basis. If other members are like us, they often wonder whether a subscription to any particular mailing list is worthwhile: Does the good content of the list outweigh the noise and inanity? The more inanity flourishes, the more sensible subscribers unsubscribe and the list deteriorates. What you do *and don't* post has a direct effect on how worthwhile the list is. If you're going to participate, find a constructive way to do so.

"Can someone tell me how to unsubscribe from this list?"

Signing up for a mailing list is a cool thing. We tell you all about how to do it in Chapter 7. We also tell you how to unsubscribe from a mailing list. Still, one of the most common ways of looking like a klutz is to send a message to the whole list asking to be taken off the list. This mistake is doubly absurd: Everyone on the list has to read the message, although it doesn't even get the sender taken off the list.

In case you missed Chapter 7, subscribe and unsubscribe requests go to the *list server program* (not to the list itself) in a particular format; in the case of lists that are not automated, address them to the list owner. Read Chapter 7 carefully please, lest you be the next person impressing every list member with your newbieness.

The netiquette police: Police yourself

Sooner or later, you see something that cries out for a cheap shot. Sooner or later, someone sends you something you shouldn't have seen and you want to pass it on. Don't do it. Resist cheap shots and proliferating malice. The Net has plenty of jerks — don't be another one. (See the suggestion later in this chapter about what to do when you're tempted to flame.) Be tolerant of newbies — you were once one yourself.

Still, you may be motivated by the best of intentions. Okay, someone makes a mistake, such as sending to the entire mailing list a message that says "subscribe" or posting a message that says, "Gee, I don't know!" in response to a request for help with a newsgroup. Yes, it's true, someone made a dumb move. Don't compound it, however, by posting additional messages complaining about it. Either delete the message and forget about it or respond privately, by e-mail addressed only to the person, not to the mailing list. The entire mailing list probably doesn't want to hear your advice to the person who blew it.

Your message doesn't have to be long and preachy either. For example, you can send a private e-mail message saying, "In the future, send subscription and unsubscription messages to `eggplants-request`, not to `eggplants`, okay?" or "This is a list about domestic laying hens, so could you post your message about cats somewhere else?"

Signing off

All mail programs let you have a *signature,* a file that gets added to the end of each mail or news message you send. The signature is supposed to contain something to identify you. Snappy quotes quickly became common, to add that personal touch. Here's John's signature, for example:

```
Regards,
John Levine, johnl@iecc.com, Primary Perpetrator of "The
          Internet for Dummies,"
Information Superhighwayman wanna-be, http://iecc.com/johnl,
          Sewer Commissioner
```

(Yes, he really is the sewer commissioner.) Some people's signatures get way out of hand, going on for 100 lines of "ASCII art," long quotations, extensive disclaimers, and other allegedly interesting stuff. Although this type of signature may seem cute the first time or two, it quickly gets tedious and marks you as a total newbie.

Keep your signature to four lines or fewer. All the experienced Net users do.

Don't get attached

Attachments are a useful way to send files by e-mail. That also makes it tempting to e-mail them to whatever mailing list you happen to be on. "Look, I found this really cool picture of a Barred Rock Rooster. I knew that you would all want to see it, so I've attached it to this message." This idea is a very, very bad one. Your picture (or sound clip or word-processing file or whatever) is probably half a megabyte of information (or more). Multiply that by the number of people who are on the mailing list, and you soon have a very large number of bytes, enough to clog up the mail server and portions of the Internet for some time.

A friend of ours administers a number of academic lists and has just gone through the exercise of smoothing all the ruffled feathers that resulted from an attachment to a mailing list post. One entire university's medium-size

Internet connection was tied up for several hours by this multimegabyte message. What's worse (and what's also common) is that the file that was attached was already on the World Wide Web. In a case like that, you have absolutely no excuse — none — ever — to attach the file to a mail message. Just tell people where to get it. "I found this cool picture of a Barred Rock Rooster on the Web, at `http://www.cyborganic.com/people/ feathersite/`." On the off chance that people who want it don't have Web access, they can e-mail you *privately* for a copy of the file, and you can e-mail it to them *privately.*

Even if you're just e-mailing a friend, you should remember some things about attachments. First, we reiterate this: Do you really need to send it as an attachment, or is it already on the Web? You would be surprised at how often we get attachments of things we could just as well get off the Web ourselves if *we* decide that it's worth it. Second, remember that your attached file is useful to the recipient only if she uses an e-mail program that can handle attachments done the way your e-mail program does them *and* she has a program that can read the file or files you are sending. For example, if you send a WordPerfect document to someone who doesn't have a word-processing program, the file is unreadable. Ditto for graphics files, sound files, and other files you may want to send around.

Third, it can take a long time to download an attachment. Nothing is more frustrating than waiting for an important e-mail and watching two megabytes of who-knows-what downloading because someone sent you an attachment you didn't ask for. The moral of the story: Ask *first* before sending an attachment.

Warning: Do not use e-mail in the presence of open flame

For some reason, it's easy to get VERY, VERY UPSET ABOUT SOMETHING SOMEONE SAYS ON THE NET. (See, it happens even to us.) Sometimes it's something you find on the Web, and sometimes it's personal e-mail. You may be tempted to shoot a message right back telling that person what a doofus he is. Guess what? He will almost certainly shoot back. This type of overstated outrage is so common that it has its own name: *flaming.* Now and then, it's fun (if you're certain that the recipient will take it in good humor), but it's always unnecessary.

You have several things to think about here. One, e-mail messages always come across as crabbier than the author intended. Two, crabbing back hardly ever makes the person more reasonable. Three, flaming someone seldom makes him go away and certainly doesn't end the discussion. Instead, he'll get back to you with 150 reasons why he's right and you're wrong. And, if you're talking on a mailing list or discussion group, someone else will pick one point of what you said and dispute it. Before you know it, you're spending all your time talking about something you probably didn't even want to talk about in the first place.

A technique we often find helpful when we're tempted to flame (or respond to a flame) is to write the strongest, crabbiest response possible, full of biting wit and skewering each point in turn. Then we throw it away rather than send it. It makes us feel better and saves everybody a great deal of time.

Junk Mail — Retail and Wholesale

Junk mail seems to be one of those facts of modern life — it's hard to arrange your life so that more or less often you end up with something in your physical mailbox that you know should go directly to recycling. The same has become true of the electronic world. Although bits of computerized information are easier to recycle than pieces of paper, you still have to figure out what it is that you're ignoring, and that can take time. You're likely to run into two kinds of junk mail in your electronic in-box: chain letters from "friends" and acquaintances, and industrial-strength junk mail. *You* may even be tempted to indulge in the odd chain letter or unsolicited advertisement from time to time. Don't do it.

The chain gang

Sending a chain letter on the Net is easy: Just click the Forward button, type a few names, and send your letter off. It's a lousy idea. We have never, ever gotten a chain letter that was worth passing along. A bunch of classic chain letters have been circulating around the Net for a decade (see Chapter 6 for details about the boy who doesn't want cards, the phantom good-times virus, the nonexistent modem tax, the overpriced recipe that isn't, and a way that you won't make money fast). Regardless of where they come from, please just throw them away.

It seems that new chain letters crop up every day. Friends (yes, even relatives) of ours have been victims of what has come to be called the "gullibility virus": Just because they read it in an e-mail and because it's easy, they believe that if they just forward this one e-mail to us and all our coauthors and friends, they will help save the whales or save National Public Radio or acquire some Microsoft software or make money fast — you name it. Needless to say, our esteem for these people falls a little with every chain letter we receive. Don't embarrass your friends and do the same thing to them.

Wholesale junk mail, also known as spam

One of the least pleasant online innovations in recent years is *spamming,* or sending the same message — usually selling something that was rather dubious in the first place — to as many e-mail addresses or Usenet groups as possible. This practice is annoying, and we talk all about it in Chapter 6. You should remember, however, that the spammer is liable in many cases for her provider's expenses in cleaning it up. Spamming newsgroups is also ineffective because automatic systems identify and cancel most Usenet spams within minutes after they occur. Even spamming individual mailboxes isn't what it used to be because an increasing number of providers offer e-mail filtering, and most recipients, including us, presume that anything advertised by spam must be fraudulent.

If you do any kind of business on the Net (for profit, nonprofit, or even volunteer), you may find that you accumulate a list of addresses of people who have contacted you for one reason or another. You may be tempted to write to them about some new venture you have, more or less related to the reason they got in touch with you in the first place. Our experience is that this situation is a classic slippery slope, and it's hard to decide where the legitimate "If you were interested in that, you may be interested to know about this" ends and the "If I just send this message to everyone I can find and 1 percent of them respond" reasoning begins. Our advice is to avoid the whole thing. (We're thinking about sending notifications of new editions of this book, for example, to people who write to us at `internetme@gurus.com`. Let us know if you would like to get news from us or if you would consider it spam.)

Don't Cause a Run on the Bank

The Internet, the telephone system, and the banking system all share at least one characteristic: If everyone tries to use them at one time, there's not enough to go around. Most of us are familiar with this concept when we think of a run on a bank: The bank doesn't have enough money in the vault for every depositor to get all his money on the same day. The telephone system is similar: If everyone picks up her telephone at the same time, there aren't enough dial tones to go around. The Internet is the same: If everyone tries to download information as fast as her modem can go, the whole Net slows down like molasses on a cold day.

Unlike the bank and telephone examples, you don't have to be there to bog down the Internet. Unbelievable amounts of material are on the Net: programs, documents, pictures, megabyte after megabyte of swell stuff — all free for the taking. All you have to do is set your computer, like the sorcerer's apprentice, to download it all for you. Don't. Go ahead and take whatever you're likely to use, but don't download entire directories full of stuff "just in case."

Your Internet provider sets its charges based on the resources a typical user uses. A single user can use a substantial fraction of the provider's Net connection by sucking down files continuously for hours at a time. Just like a bank, which typically a keeps a small percentage of its depositors' money on hand, Internet providers typically "overcommit" their Net connection by a factor of three or so. In this case, if every user tried to transfer data at full speed at the same time, it would require three times as fast a connection as the provider has. Because real users transfer for a while and then read what's on-screen for a while, sharing the connection among all the users works out okay. (The provider is not cheating you by using this method any more than the bank is; it's a sensible way to provide access at a reasonable cost. If you want guaranteed connection performance, you can get it, but at a stiff price.) If users begin using several more connections than the provider budgeted for, prices go up.

Hang up, already!

This advice applies particularly to providers who offer unlimited connect time per month. Don't leave your computer connected if you're not using it. Most Net software packages have a time-out feature that hangs up if no data is transferred to or from the Net for a specified period. We leave ours set to 15 minutes on our dial-up connections. Most Internet providers do the same thing from their end: If your connection has no activity for a set period, it hangs up on you.

You can get little programs that fool Windows Me and your Internet Service Provider into thinking that you're doing something and thus keep your telephone connection open. Call us old-fashioned, but we think that this technique is an irresponsible, dog-in-the-manger approach to the Internet. If you're using your Net connection, great. If you're not using it, however, let someone else use it. That's much nicer than "I'm not using that telephone connection to my Internet provider, but you can't use it either, and I don't care whether you get a busy signal when you try to connect."

Stunts like that have caused many large Internet Service Providers to put a cap on their "unlimited" connect-time plans, usually at around 100 hours. Of course, none of this applies to cable or DSL connections because they were meant to remain connected all the time.

Audio and video pigs

Internet Phone and the like present a particular problem on the Net because they put a much, much heavier load on both the local provider and the Net in general than do other Internet services. When you're transferring voice information over the Net, you're pumping data through as fast as your connection will let you. Video connections are even worse: When sites with fast Net connections begin sending video programs around to each other, the entire Net slows down.

For the moment, few enough people are using Internet Phone that it hasn't become a big problem. If the product becomes popular enough, providers will have to provide "no phone" and "phone" accounts, with the latter costing much more, to keep reasonable access for all their users.

Some Web Wisdom

Windows Me is convenient because it gives you everything you need to create your own pages on the Web and even to put your PC on the Internet as a Web server. (Check out our Web site, at `http://net.gurus.com/`, if you want to find out all about how to do it.) Because what you put on your Web page is all that most people will know about you, this section provides a few suggestions.

Small is beautiful, Part I

When you're creating your Web pages, you see them right on your own computer. Quickly. After all, they don't have to come in over the telephone line — they're right on your hard drive. Remember that most people who look at your Web page are connected by using a dial-up line and a modem. Those pictures that appeared so quickly when you were creating your Web pages take a long time to load over the phone. If your home page contains a full-page picture that takes 12½ minutes to load, you may as well have hung out a Keep Out sign. Keep the pictures small enough that the page loads in a reasonable amount of time. If you have a huge picture that you think is wonderful, put a small "thumbnail" version of it on your home page and make it a link to the full picture for people with the time and interest to look at the big version.

Small is beautiful, Part II

Small pages that fit on a screen or two work better than large pages. Small pages are easier to read, and they load faster. If you have 12 screens full of stuff to put on your Web page, break up your page into five or six separate pages, 2 screens full each, with links among them. A well-designed set of small pages makes finding stuff easier than does one big page because the links can direct readers to what they want to find.

If we want the White House, we know where to find it

No Web page (or set of Web pages, as we just suggested) is complete without some links to the author's other favorite pages. For some reason, every new user's Web page used to have a link to http://www.whitehouse.gov and maybe to Yahoo, Netscape, and a few other sites that every Net user already knows about. Cool Web sites give you links to interesting pages you *don't* already know about.

Let a hundred viewers blossom

Whenever you create a new Web page, look at it with as many Web browsers as possible. Yes, most people use some version of Netscape or Internet Explorer, but Prodigy and AOL users (close to 10 million possible visitors to your site) use the browsers that come with those services, and users with dial-up shell connections use the text-only browser Lynx. Take a look at your pages to make sure that they're at least legible regardless of which browser people are using.

Don't be dumb

Don't put information on your Web page that you don't want everyone in the world to know. In particular, you may not want to include your home address and phone number. We know at least one person who received an unexpected phone call from someone she met on the Net and wasn't too pleased about it. Why would Net users need this information, anyway? They can send you e-mail!

Glossary

Active Desktop: A Windows 95 and Windows 98 feature that lets you display Web pages on your Windows desktop. Although most of the components remain, Active Desktop as a Microsoft technology is pretty much dead.

ActiveX: A Microsoft standard for computer program building blocks, known as *objects.* Not very secure.

address: Internet users encounter two important types of addresses: e-mail addresses (for sending e-mail to someone; e-mail addresses almost always contain a @) and Web page addresses (more properly called URLs).

ADSL (Asymmetric Digital Subscriber Line): A technology that lets you transmit data over phone lines faster — as much as 9 million bps — in one direction than in the other.

AltaVista: A search engine used for finding things on the World Wide Web. Its true name is `http:// www.altavista.com`.

America Online (AOL): A value-added online service that provides many services in addition to Internet access, including access to popular chat groups.

anonymous FTP: A way of using the FTP program to log on to another computer to copy files, even though you don't have an account on the other computer. When you log on, you type `anonymous` as the username and your e-mail address as the password.

applet: A small computer program written in the Java programming language. You can download applets by using a Web browser. Applets must obey special rules that make it difficult for the programs to do damage to your computer.

archive: A single file containing a group of files that have been compressed and glommed together for efficient storage. You have to use a program such as WinZip, PKZIP, tar, or StuffIt to get the original files back out.

ASCII: American Standard Code for Information Interchange, the way most computers store *text files.*

attachment: A computer file electronically stapled to an e-mail message and sent along with it.

backbone: The high-speed communications links that connect Internet providers and other large Internet sites.

baud: The number of electrical symbols per second a modem sends down a phone line. Often used as a synonym for bps (bits per second); although this usage is incorrect, only 43 people on the entire planet know why or care. Named after J. M. E. Baudot, the inventor of the teletypewriter.

BCC: *B*lind *c*arbon *c*opy. BCC addressees get a copy of your e-mail without other recipients knowing about it. *See also* CC.

binary file: A file which contains information that does not consist only of text. For example, a binary file may contain an archive, a picture, sounds, a spreadsheet, or a word-processing document that includes formatting codes in addition to text characters.

bit: The smallest unit of measure for computer data. Bits can be *on* or *off* (symbolized by 1 or 0) and are used in various combinations to represent different types of information.

bitmap: Little dots put together to make a black-and-white or color picture.

bookmark: The address of a Web page to which you may want to return. Netscape lets you maintain a list of bookmarks to make it easy to go back to your favorite Web pages.

bounce: To return as undeliverable or redeliver to the appropriate address. If you mail a message to a bad address, it bounces back to your mailbox. If you get e-mail intended for someone else, you can bounce it to her.

bps (bits per second): A measure of how fast data is transmitted. Often used to describe modem speed.

browser: A superduper, all-singing, all-dancing program that lets you read information on the World Wide Web.

byte: A group of eight bits, enough to represent a character. Computer memory is usually measured in bytes.

cable modem: A box that connects your computer to the Internet via your cable TV supplier. Cable modems are much faster than ordinary dial-up phone connections.

CC: *C*arbon *c*opy. CC addressees get a copy of your e-mail, and other recipients are informed of it if they bother to read the message header.
See also BCC.

CGI: A system used on Web servers to process user forms and other user requests. The programs that run via CGI are known as CGI *scripts*.

channel: In IRC, a group of people chatting together. Called "rooms" by value-added providers who use "channel" to mean a major interest area you can get to easily, like a TV channel. In Windows 98, a Web site to which you have subscribed.

chanop: In IRC, the *chan*nel *op*erator is in charge of keeping order in a channel. The chanop can throw out unruly visitors.

chat: To talk (or type) live to other network users from any and all parts of the world. To chat on the Internet, you use an Internet Relay Chat (IRC) program like or mIRC or Microsoft Chat. America Online and CompuServe have similar services.

Classic style: A Windows 98 option that makes your computer behave like older versions of Windows, with double clicks opening files and programs. See *Web style*.

client: A computer that uses the services of another computer, or server (such as Usenet, Gopher, FTP, or the Web). If you dial in to another system, your computer becomes a client of the system you dial in to (unless you're using X Windows — don't ask.) *See also* server.

client/server model: A division of labor between computers. Computers that provide a service other computers can use are known as *servers*. The users are *clients*. *See also* client, servers.

com: When these letters appear the last part of an address (in `net.gurus.com`, for example), it indicates that the host computer is run by a commercial organization, probably in the United States.

CompuServe (CIS): A value-added online service that provides many services in addition to Internet access, including forums for many popular business topics.

cookie: A small text file stored on your computer by a Web site you have visited, used to remind that site about you the next time you visit it.

country code: The last part of a geographic address, which indicates in which country the host computer is located, such as `us` for the United States. Country codes are always two letters.

cyber-: A prefix meaning the use of the computers and networks that comprise the Internet, typically in the form of a metaphorical comparison to things with which we are familiar in real life, such as cyberspace or cybercop. Also short for cybersex. (Don't ask.)

digest: A compilation of the messages that have been posted to a mailing list during the past few days.

Dial-Up Networking: The built-in Internet communication program in Windows 95 and Windows 98.

domain: Part of the official name of a computer on the Net — for example, `gurus.com`. To register a domain name, go to `http.//www.internic.net/`.

domain name server (DNS): A computer on the Internet that translates between Internet domain names, such as `xuxa.iecc.com`, and Internet numerical addresses, such as `140.186.81.2`. Sometimes just called a name server.

download: To copy a file from a remote computer "down" to your computer.

DSL: Digital Subscriber Line, a fast, permanent Internet connection via a phone line.

dummies: People who don't know everything but are smart enough to seek help. Used ironically.

edu: When these letters appear as the last part of an address (in `www.middlebury.edu`, for example), it indicates that the host computer is run by an educational institution, usually a college or university in the United States.

e-mail: Electronic messages sent via the Internet.

Eudora: A popular mail-handling program.

extranet: An Internet technology used to connect a company with its customers and business partners.

FAQ (Frequently Asked Questions): An article that answers questions that come up often. Many mailing lists and Usenet newsgroups have FAQs that are posted regularly. To read the FAQs for all newsgroups, FTP to `rtfm.mit.edu`.

Favorites: A list of files or Web pages you plan to use frequently. Internet Explorer lets you maintain a list of your favorite items to make it easy to see them again. Click the Start button and choose Favorites.

flame: To post angry, inflammatory, or insulting messages. Don't do it!

flame war: A great deal of flaming between two or more individuals. To stop one, let the other guy have the last word.

firewall: A specially programmed computer that connects a local network to the Internet and, for security reasons, lets only certain kinds of messages in and out.

FTP (File Transfer Protocol): A method of transferring files from one computer to the other over the Net.

gateway: A computer that connects one network with another, where the two networks use different protocols.

GIF (Graphics Interchange Format): A patented type of graphics file originally defined by CompuServe and now found all over the Net. Files in this format end in .gif and are called GIF files or just GIFs. Pronounced "jif" unless you prefer to say "gif."

giga-: Prefix meaning one billion (a thousand million).

Gopher: An Internet system that lets you find information by using menus, mostly made obsolete by the Web.

gov: When these letters appear as the last part of an address (in cu.nih.gov, for example), it indicates that the host computer is run by some government body, probably the U.S. federal government.

header: The beginning of an e-mail message containing To and From addresses, subject, date, and other gobbledygook important to the programs that handle your mail.

home page: The entry page, or main page, of a Web site. If you have a home page, it's the main page about you. A home page may contain links to other Web pages.

host: A computer on the Internet (chico.iecc.com, for example).

HTML (Hypertext Markup Language): The language used to write pages for the World Wide Web. This language lets the text include codes that define fonts, layout, embedded graphics, and hypertext links. Don't worry — you don't have to know anything about it to use the World Wide Web. Web pages are stored in files that usually have the extension .htm or .html.

HTTP (HyperText Transfer Protocol): The way in which World Wide Web pages are transferred over the Net. URLs for Web pages start with http://.

HTTPS: A variant of HTTP that encrypts messages for security.

hypertext: A system of writing and displaying text that enables the text to be linked in multiple ways, be available at several levels of detail, and contain links to related documents. The World Wide Web uses both hypertext and hypermedia.

ICQ: A technology that lets you exchange personal messages with other ICQ members who are online at the same time you are. See http://www.icq.com.

Internet: All the computers that are connected together into an amazingly huge global network so that they can talk to each other. When you connect your puny little computer to your Internet Service Provider, your computer becomes part of that network.

Internet Explorer: A Web browser vigorously promoted by Microsoft that comes in Windows, Mac, and UNIX flavors.

Internet Relay Chat (IRC): A system that enables Internet folks to talk to each other in real-time (rather than after a delay, as with e-mail messages).

InterNIC: The Internet Network Information Center, a central repository of information about domain names.

intranet: A private version of the Internet that lets people within an organization exchange data by using popular Internet tools, such as browsers.

ISDN (Integrated Services Digital Network): A faster, digital phone service that operates at speeds as high as 128 kilobits per second.

Java: A computer language invented by Sun Microsystems. Because Java programs can run on any modern computer, Java is ideal for delivering application programs over the Internet.

JPEG: A type of file for storing scanned photographs, found all over the Net. Files in this format end in .jpg or .jpeg and are called JPEG (pronounced "JAY-peg") files. Stands for Joint Photographic Experts Group.

K56flex: The Rockwell International modem technology for downloading data at 56,000 bps. Competed with *x2*. The ITU has negotiated a compromise standard, called *V.*90.

Kbyte: 1,024 bytes. Also written *KB* or just plain *K.* Usually used as a measure of a computer's memory or hard disk storage, or as a measure of file size.

kilo-: Prefix meaning one thousand (1,000) or often, with computers, 1,024.

LDAP: Lightweight Directory Access Protocol, a new Internet standard that lets applications access "address book" directory services.

link: A hypertext connection that can take you to another document or another part of the same document. On the World Wide Web, links appear as text or pictures that are highlighted. To follow a link, you click the highlighted material. *See also* hypertext, WWW.

ListProc: Like LISTSERV, a program that handles mailing lists.

LISTSERV: A family of programs that automatically manages mailing lists, distributing messages posted to the list and adding and deleting members, for example, which spares the list owner the tedium of having to do it manually. The names of mailing lists maintained by LISTSERV often end with -L.

Linux: A free version of the UNIX operating system that runs on personal computers and is supported by a dedicated band of enthusiasts on the Internet.

lurk: To read a mailing list or chat group without posting any messages. Someone who lurks is a lurker. Lurking is okay and is much better than flaming.

Lynx: A character-based World Wide Web browser. No pictures, but it's fast.

mailbot: A program that automatically sends or answers e-mail.

mail server: A computer on the Internet that provides mail services for mail clients.

mailing list: A special type of e-mail address that remails all incoming mail to a list of subscribers to the mailing list. Each mailing list has a specific topic, so you subscribe to the ones that interest you.

Majordomo: Like LISTSERV, a program that handles mailing lists.

MBone: The multicast backbone. A special Internet subnetwork that transmits live video and other multimedia to many different places on the Net simultaneously.

mega-: Prefix meaning one million.

Microsoft Network (MSN): A commercial online service that provides many Internet services, including e-mail and access to the World Wide Web.

mil: When these letters appear as the last part of an Internet address or domain name (the zone), it indicates that the host computer is run by some part of the U.S. military.

MIME: Multipurpose Internet Mail Extension. Used to send pictures, word-processing files, and other nontext information through e-mail.

mirror: An FTP or Web server that provides copies of the same files as another server. Mirrors spread out the load for more popular FTP and Web sites.

modem: A gizmo that lets your computer talk on the phone or cable TV. Derived from *mo*dulator/*dem*odulator.

moderator: The person who looks at the messages posted to a mailing list or newsgroup before releasing them to the public. The moderator can nix messages that are stupid, redundant, wildly off the topic, or offensive.

MPEG: A type of video file found on the Net. Files in this format end in .mpg. Stands for Moving Picture Experts Group.

MUD (Multi-User Dungeon): Started as a Dungeons and Dragons type of game that many people can play at one time; now, it's an Internet subculture. For information about joining a MUD, consult the Usenet newsgroup `rec.games.mud.announce`.

Netscape Navigator: A popular Web browser that comes in Windows, Mac, and UNIX flavors. The latest version of Navigator comes as part of Netscape Communicator.

net: A network, or (when capitalized) the Internet itself. When these letters appear as the last part of an address (in `www.abuse.net`, for example), it's supposed to indicate that the host computer is run by a networking organization, but often is used as an alternative to `.com`.

NetNanny: A program that tries to keep kiddies from accessing Web sites the company deems inappropriate.

network: Computers that are connected. Those in the same or nearby buildings are called Local Area Networks, those that are farther away are called Wide Area Networks, and when you interconnect networks all over the world, you get the Internet!

network computer (NC): A computer that lacks a hard disk and gets all its data instead over a computer network, like the Internet.

newbie: A newcomer to the Internet (variant: clueless newbie). If you have read this book, of course, you're not a clueless newbie anymore!

newsgroup: A topic area in the Usenet news system. (See Chapter 8.)

newsreader: A program that lets you read and respond to the messages in Usenet newsgroups.

NIC (Network Information Center): Responsible for coordinating a set of networks so that the names, network numbers, and other technical details are consistent from one network to another. The address of the one for the United States part of the Internet is `rs.internic.net`.

nickname: In IRC, the name by which you identify yourself when you're chatting, synonymous with *screen name.*

node: A computer on the Internet, also called a host.

org: When these letters appear as the last part of an e-mail address or URL (in `www.uua.org`, for example), it indicates that the host computer is run by a nonprofit institution, usually in the United States.

Outlook Express: The latest Microsoft e-mail and Usenet newsreading program.

packet: A chunk of information sent over a network. Each packet contains the address it's going to and the address from which it came.

page: A document, or hunk of information, available by way of the World Wide Web. Each page can contain text, graphics files, sound files, video clips — you name it.

password: A secret code used to keep things private. Be sure to pick one that's not crackable, preferably two randomly chosen words separated by a number or special character. Something like `G12nk997ssR4` or `spleen2325hotdog` is good. Something like `mypassword` or `11111` are no good and will get guessed lickety-split. Don't use a single word that is in a dictionary or any proper name; we hear that the world's most popular and easily guessed password is `Susan`.

PDF file: A method for distributing formatted documents over the Net. You need a special reader program named Acrobat. Get it at `http://www.adobe.com/acrobat`.

PGP (Phil's Pretty Good Privacy): A program that lets you encrypt and sign your e-mail, written by Phil Zimmerman. See `http://www.pgp.com` or check in on `comp.security.pgp.discuss` for more information.

PICS (Platform for Internet Content Selection): A way of marking pages with ratings about what is inside. Designed to keep kids from getting at the racy stuff, although it has other applications as well.

ping: Sending a short message to which another computer automatically responds. If you can't ping the other computer, you probably can't talk to it any other way, either.

PKZIP: A file-compression program that runs in DOS (and Windows in a DOS window). PKZIP creates a ZIP file that contains compressed versions of one or more files. To restore these files to their former size and shape, you use PKUNZIP or WinZip. *See also* ZIP file.

plug-in: A computer program you add to your browser to help it handle a special type of file.

POP (Post Office Protocol): A system by which a mail server on the Net lets you pick up your mail and download it to your PC or Mac. A POP server is the computer from which you pick up your mail. Also called *POP3*.

port number: An identifying number assigned to each program that is chatting on the Net. You hardly ever have to know these numbers — the Internet programs work this stuff out among themselves.

posting: An article published on or submitted to a mailing list or Usenet newsgroup.

PPP (Point-to-Point Protocol): A scheme for connecting your computer to the Internet over a phone line. Like SLIP, only better.

protocol: The agreed-on rules that computers rely on to talk among themselves. A set of signals that mean "go ahead," "got it," "didn't get it, please resend," and "all done," for example.

public key cryptography: A method for sending secret messages whereby you get two keys: a public key you give out freely so that people can send you coded messages and a second, private key that decodes them.

QuickTime: A video file format invented by Apple Computer and widely used on the Net.

RealAudio: A popular streaming audio file format that lets you listen to programs over the Net. You can get a player plug-in at http://www.real.com.

router: A computer that connects two or more networks.

RTFM (Read The Manual): A suggestion made by people who feel that you have wasted their time by asking a question you could have found the answer to by looking it up in an obvious place. A well-known and much used FTP site named rtfm.mit.edu contains FAQs for all Usenet newsgroups.

search engine: A program used to search for things on the Web, or a Web site where you can use such a program.

secure server: A Web server than uses encryption to prevent others from reading messages to or from your browser. Web-based shopping sites usually use secure servers so that others can intercept your ordering information.

serial port: The place on the back of your computer where you plug in your modem. Also called a communications port or comm port.

server: A computer that provides a service — such as e-mail, Web data, Usenet, or FTP — to other computers (known as clients) on a network. *See also* client.

shareware: Computer programs that are easily available for you to try with the understanding that, if you decide to keep the program, you will send the requested payment to the shareware provider specified in the program. It's an honor system. A great deal of good stuff is available, and people's voluntary compliance makes it viable.

Shockwave: A program for viewing interactive multimedia on the Web. For more information about Shockwave and for a copy of the program's plug-in for your browser, go to `http://www.macromedia.com/shockwave/`.

SLIP (Serial Line Internet Protocol): An obsolete software scheme for connecting your computer to the Internet over a serial line. *See also* PPP.

smiley: A combination of special characters that portray emotions, such as :-) or :-(. Although hundreds have been invented, only a few are in active use, and all are silly.

S/MIME: Secure Multipurpose Internet Mail Extension. An extension to MIME that includes encryption.

SMTP (Simple Mail Transfer Protocol): The misnamed method by which Internet mail is delivered from one computer to another. An SMTP server is the computer to which you send your outgoing e-mail.

socket: A logical "port" a program uses to connect to another program running on another computer on the Internet. You may have an FTP program using sockets for its FTP session, for example, and have Eudora connect by way of another socket to get your mail. Winsock is the standard way that Windows Internet programs use sockets.

spam: The act of sending e-mail to thousands of uninterested recipients or of posting inappropriate messages to many uninterested newsgroups or mailing lists. It's antisocial and ineffective.

SSL (Secure Socket Layer): A Web-based technology that lets one computer verify another's identity and allow secure connections.

Start button: A gizmo that appears in the lower-left corner of your computer's screen when you move the mouse cursor there. Clicking the Start button brings up a menu of programs and other options.

streaming audio: A system for sending sound files over the Net that begins playing the sound before the sound file finishes downloading, letting you listen with minimal delay.

surf: To wander around the World Wide Web and look for interesting stuff.

T1: A telecommunications standard that carries 24 voice calls or data at 1.44 million bps over a pair of telephone lines.

TCP/IP: Short for Transfer Control Protocol/Internet Protocol, the way networks communicate with each other on the Net.

telnet: A program that lets you log in to some other computers on the Net.

terminal: In the olden days, a computer terminal consisted of just a screen and a keyboard. If you have a personal computer and want to connect to a big computer somewhere, you can run a program that makes it *pretend* to be a brainless terminal — the program is called a terminal emulator, terminal program, or communications program.

text file: A file that contains only textual characters, with no special formatting, graphical information, sound clips, video, or what-have-you. Because most computers, other than some IBM mainframes, store their text by using a system of codes named ASCII, these files are also known as ASCII text files. *See also* Unicode.

thread: An article posted to a mailing list or Usenet newsgroup, together with all the follow-up articles, the follow-ups to follow-ups, and so on.

Unicode: An up-and-coming extension of ASCII that attempts to include the characters of all active written languages.

UNIX: A geeky operating system originally developed at Bell Labs. Used on many servers on the Net.

upload: To copy your stuff to somebody else's computer.

URL (Uniform Resource Locator): A standardized way of naming network resources, used for linking pages on the World Wide Web.

Usenet: A system of thousands of newsgroups. You read the messages by using a newsreader. *See also* newsreader. (See the Web page http://net.gurus.com/ usenet for a description of Usenet newsgroups.)

uuencode/uudecode: A method of sending binary files as e-mail. Older and cruddier than MIME.

viewer: A program to show you files that contain stuff other than text.

virtual reality: A 3-D visual computer simulation that responds to your input so realistically that you feel you are inside another world.

VRML: A language used for building virtual reality pages on the Web.

WAV file: A popular Windows format for sound files (.wav files) found on the Net.

Web page: A document available on the World Wide Web.

Web style: A Windows option that makes your computer behave like a Web page, with single clicks opening files and programs. See also *Classic style*.

WebTV: An online Internet service from Microsoft (who else?) that includes hardware (an Internet terminal and remote control) you connect to your TV.

Winsock: A standard way for Windows programs to work with TCP/IP. You use it if you directly connect your Windows PC to the Internet, with either a permanent connection or a modem by using PPP or SLIP.

WWW (World Wide Web): A hypermedia system that lets you browse through lots of interesting information. The Web will be the central repository of humanity's information in the 21st century.

WinZip: A file-compression program that runs under Windows. It reads and creates a zip file that contains compressed versions of one or more files.

x2: USRobotics modem technology for downloading data at 56,000 bps. Competes with *K56flex*. Now superseded by V.90.

X.400: A cumbersome, ITU-blessed mail standard that competes with the Internet SMTP mail standard, but isn't winning.

X.500: A standard for white-pages e-mail directory services. It isn't quite as broken as X.400, and Internet people are trying to use it.

XML: Extensible Markup Language, a more powerful replacement for HTML.

Yahoo!: A set of Web pages that provide a subject-oriented guide to the World Wide Web. Go to the URL http://www.yahoo.com.

ZIP file: A file with the extension .zip that has been compressed using PKZIP, WinZip, or a compatible program. To get at the files in a ZIP file, you usually need WinZip, PKUNZIP, or a compatible program.

zone: The last part of an Internet host name. Also known as a *top-level domain*. If the zone is two letters long, it's the country code in which the organization that owns the computer is located. If the zone is three letters long, it's a code indicating the type of organization that owns the computer.

Index

• *Numbers* •

800 numbers for ISPs, 44

• *A* •

Active Desktop, 244–245
  Subscription Wizard, 250
  Web pages displayed on, 246–247
Active Desktop items
  channels, 249
  displaying, 249
  exposing, 250
  hiding, 248, 250
  moving, 248
  overview, 248
  passwords for Web pages,
    providing, 250
  scheduling when to get Web pages, 251
  several pages from same Web site,
    retrieving, 250
  sizing, 248
address book
  Eudora, 137–138
  Netscape, 136
  Outlook Express, 135–136
  overview, 135
advertising on search systems, 224
Aladdin Expander
  downloading, 294–295
  installing, 295
  using, 296
AltaVista, 220–221, 223
  options, 224
  Yahoo! used with, 223
Amazon, 269, 366

America Online, 26, 28
  advantages of, 29
  chat room categories, 307
  chatting, 306–307
  creating chat rooms, 309
  disadvantages of, 30–31
  e-mail, 112, 126
  ignoring people in chat rooms, 308
  Instant Message, 308
  Internet connection through, 77
  local access numbers, 29
  master screen name, 309
  private chat rooms, 310
  profile of people in chat room, 308–309
  reporting people in chat rooms, 311
  sample conversation in chat room,
    309–310
  technical chat rooms, help from people
    in, 309
American Century, 267
Ameritrade, 268
anonymity online, 20
anonymous FTP, 279
Apple Computer, 270
ARPANET, 13
ASCII files, 280
AskJeeves, 225
AT&T WorldNet, Internet connection
    through, 77
attachments, e-mail, 143, 146–147
audioconferencing, 328
autodialing, 85, 87–88
automatic disconnection, 89
AutoUpdater, 253–254

• *B* •

bandwidth, 31
banking online
  overview, 19, 265
  PayPal, 266
  USAccess, 265
  Wachovia, 265
  Wingspan, 265
Berners-Lee, Tim, 176
Bigfoot, 232
binary files, 280
blind carbon copy, 121
bookmarks, 199, 201
Borders, 269
bouncing e-mail, 140
broadband, 79–80
browsers, 47–48
  address line, 182
  Back button, 183
  cookies, 208–209
  Forward button, 183
  FTP and, 280, 282
  Fullscreen mode, 183
  History button, 184
  logo, 184
  multitasking with, 207–208
  overview, 12, 179
  printing from, 208
  Refresh/Reload button, 183
  remembering sites, 197
  Status area, 183
  Stop button, 183
  window, 181
built-in FTP program, 297
businesses, searching for, 227, 229–230

• *C* •

cable access, 27, 32, 79–80
Cabot Creamery, 272
cache, 203–204

Canada 411, 232
canceling your Internet account, 93
carbon copy, 121
case-sensitivity, 83
CDNow, 269
chain letters (e-mail), 144–145, 375
  "dying boy wants greeting cards" chain
    letter, 144
  "make money fast" chain letters, 144
  "modem-tax rumor" chain letter, 144
channels for online chat, 300
Charles Schwab, 267
chat rooms, 12
chatting. *See* online chat
CIA World Fact Book, 365
collaborative working, 48
Companies Online, 230
CompuServe, 26, 28
  advantages of, 29
  disadvantages of, 30–31
  e-mail, 112
  Internet connection through, 77
  local access numbers, 29
computer crashes, 351
Computer Discount Warehouse, 270
computer networks, 10–11
connection software, 47
connections, Internet. *See* Internet
  connections
Consummate Winsock Applications
  page, 189
Control Panel, 66
  Dial-Up Networking, 69–70
  modems, 66
  TCP/IP, setting up, 71, 73–74
cookies, 208–209
  online shopping and, 261
  overview, 21
CoolList, 168
copyright of Web pages, 207
credit cards used for shopping online,
  258–259, 351

• D •

DALNet, 312
Dell Computers, 270, 367
desktop computers, setting local
    telephone numbers, 96–98
desktop, Dial-Up Networking connection
    shortcut on, 91
Dial-Up Networking connection, 73–74
  connection statistics, 90
  Control Panel, 69–70
  creating, 75–76
  desktop, creating shortcut on, 91
  disconnecting, 85
  local telephone numbers, 94
  monitoring, 89–90
  password, saving, 94–95
  shortcut, creating, 90–92
  Start menu, creating shortcut on, 92
  starting, 82–84
dialing locations, 96, 98
  creating new, 99
digests, 158
directory
  index compared, 214
  overview, 214
disconnecting from Internet, 89
DNS addresses, 73
domain names, 73
domains, 108–109
  new domains, 110
  registering, 109
  sending messages to someone in
    same, 110
double-clicks, when to use, 63–64
downloading, 275–276
  files, 278
  pictures, 277
  programs, 277
  Web pages, 276–278
DSL, 32–34, 79–80

• E •

E-Mail For Dummies, 23
e-mail
  abbreviations, list of common, 125
  address book. _See_ address book
  America Online, 112
  attachments, 143, 146–147, 373–374
  blind carbon copy, 121
  bouncing, 140
  capitalization, 371
  carbon copy, 121
  chain letters, 144–145, 375
  CompuServe, 112
  content of message you are replying to,
    including, 135
  deleting, 142
  editing forwarded mail, 139
  effective use of, 151
  encryption, 115
  etiquette, 131, 370–371, 373–375
  filters, 148
  flaming, 131
  forwarding mail, 138–140
  forwarding service, 39
  free e-mail accounts, 112
  information your e-mail program needs
    to know, 113–114
  junk e-mail, 149
  LAN e-mail accounts, 113
  links, adding, 143
  mail servers, 110–111
  mailbots, 147
  managing, 148
  overview, 11
  party you are replying to, checking
    address of, 134
  postmaster, 130
  privacy issues, 115
  redirecting, 140
  remailing, 140
  replying to, 134–135

e-mail (*continued*)
  robots, 147
  saving, 140–142
  signatures, 373
  smileys, 132
  spam, 149–150, 350, 375–376
  spelling, 370–371
  unsolicited commercial e-mail, 149
  Web-based mail, 113
e-mail address, 107–108
  described, 359
  domains, 108–109
  finding someone's, 351–352
  finding your own, 110
  mailbox, 108
  searching for, 231
  username, 108
eBay, 271
EDGAR, 229
EFnet, 312
Egg Farm Dairy, 272
eGroups, 168–170
electronic commerce, 12
  overview, 18
  security, 18–19
emoticons, 304–305
encryption, 19, 22, 115
ergonomics, 353
error messages, 352–353
etiquette
  e-mail, 131, 373–375
  Internet, 369–374
  mailing lists, 371–372
  online chat, 302–303
Eudora, 111
  address book, 137–138
  e-mail attachments, 147
  getting, 126
  overview, 125
  reading mail, 129
  replying to mail, 134
  saving mail, 142
  sending mail, 127, 129
  setting up, 126–127
Excite, 226
external modems, 37, 89

FAQs, 370
Fatbrain, 269
Favorites, 198–199
Fidelity Investments, 267
file transfer, 275
filters, 148
financial resources online
  American Century, 267
  Ameritrade, 268
  Charles Schwab, 267
  Fidelity Investments, 267
  MoneyCentral Investor, 268
  Morgan Stanley Dean Witter Online, 267
  mutual funds, 267
  My Snap, 268
  My Yahoo, 268
  overview, 266
  portfolio tracking, 268
  Reuters Moneynet, 268
  Salomon Smith Barney, 268
  stockbrokers, 267
  Vanguard Group, 267
firewalls, 33
flaming, 131, 374–375
Flash, 241–242
forms, 205
forwarding e-mail, 138–140
Four11, 367
free e-mail accounts, 112
freenets, 41–42
FreeWWWeb, 41–42
FTP, 275
  anonymous FTP, 279
  ASCII files, 280

binary files, 280
built-in FTP program, 280, 297
client, 279–280
mirrors, 279
NetLoad, 284
Netscape Navigator, 291
overview, 279
server, 279
time for transfering files, length of, 290
URL for, 281–282
Web browser used for downloading
    files, 280, 282
Winsock program, 280
wrong mode, transferring files in, 289
WS_FTP, 283–289, 291

• *G* •

games, 12–13
Gap, 270
Go Network, 226
Good Times virus hoax, 144
Google, 225
Gurus search page, 215

• *H* •

hackers, 34–35
handle, 301
help
  ListProc, 163
  LISTSERV, 160
  Majordomo, 161
  online, 252
helper applications, 47
home pages, viewing, 186
Hoover, 229
hostnames, 73
HotBot, 226
HTTP, 180, 276
hypertext, 176–178

• *I* •

IBM, 270
iChat, 211–212
image maps, 185
images, viewing, 202
Inc. magazine, 230
incoming mail server, 110
index
  directory compared, 214
  overview, 214
InfoBeat, 167
information retrieval, 12
installing downloaded programs, 298
instant messaging, 48, 308
internal modems, 37
Internet
  anonymity and, 20
  businesses, finding, 16
  cost of connection to, 358
  education, 17
  etiquette, 369–374
  geographical scope of, 16
  history of, 13
  importance of, 355–357
  investing, 17
  marketing and sales, 17
  medical information and support, 17
  money made on, 362–363
  nonprofit organizations, 17
  organizing events, 17
  overuse of, 377
  overview, 9–11, 13–14
  people, finding, 16
  privacy, 21–22
  products, finding, 16
  research, 16
  safety, 20–21
  services, finding, 16
  travel, 17

Internet *(continued)*
  unlimited connection time, 377
  uses of, 16–17
  World Wide Web compared, 357
Internet access
  elements needed for, 65
  overview, 15
Internet Autodial, 88
Internet Connection Wizard
  ISPs, already signed up with, 54–58
  ISPs, signing up with, 53–54
  modems, picking yourself, 61, 64
  modems, recognizing, 60–61
  options, 51
  overview, 45, 49–50
  running, 50–53
  signup information, saving, 54
Internet connections
  America Online, 77
  AT&T WorldNet, 77
  autodialing, 85, 87–88
  cable access, 27
  choices for, 26–27
  CompuServe, 77
  ISPs, 26
  MSN, 78
  online services, 26
  pre-existing connections, checking
      for, 27
  Prodigy, 78
  XDSL, 27
Internet Explorer, 47
  cache, 203
  downloading, 189–193
  Favorites, 198–199
  getting, 188–193
  images, 202
  installing, 194–195
  organizing favorite Web sites, 198–199
  shutting down Internet connection, 85
  start page, changing, 201
  starting, 86–88
  toolbar, 204
  versions, 190

Internet Movie Database, 365
Internet Secrets, 23
Internet Service Providers. *See* ISPs
Internet software, 47
  chatting, 48
  collaborative working, 48
  connection software, 47
  helper applications, 47
  instant messaging, 48
  Usenet, 48
  Web browser plug-ins, 47
  Web browsers, 47–48
Internet technology, 16
IP address, 35
IRC, 12
  channels, 312–313
  commands, 320–322
  lags, 313
  netsplits, 313
  nicknames, 314
  overview, 311
  rules for, 322
IRCnet, 312
ISDN, 36
ISPs
  800 numbers, 44
  canceling your account, 93
  choosing, 39, 42–44, 359
  comparing, 39
  finding local, 40
  information on, 75–76
  Internet accounts, 26
  Internet Connection Wizard, 53–54,
      56–58
  local telephone numbers, 41
  modem speed, 43
  overview, 31
  payment plans, 44
  price, 42–43
  signing up with, 45–46
  support, 43, 101
  traffic, 43

• J •

Jazz Lover's List, 168
JC Penney, 272
junk e-mail, 149

• K •

Kitchen Link, 272
Knowledge Base, 252

• L •

lags, 313
LAN
  connecting to Internet via, 75
  e-mail accounts, 113
Lands End, 269
laptops, local telephone numbers and,
    96, 98–100
Liberal Judaism, 168
list box, 205
list charter, 171
ListProc
  help, 163
  messages, 163
  signing off, 162
  subscribing, 162
LISTSERV
  digests, 159
  files, 159
  help, 160
  overview, 156–157
  people on list, finding out who are, 159
  signing off, 157
  subscribing, 157
  temporary stop mail, 158
  your messages, 159
local telephone numbers, 29
  desktop computers, 96–98
  Dial-Up Networking connection, 94
  laptops, 96, 98–100
  remote users, 96, 98–100

lurking, 302
Lycos, 226

• M •

mail servers, 11, 110–111
mailbots, 11, 147
mailbox, 108
mailing lists, 11
  automatic management, 154
  bouncing messages, 164
  CoolList, 168
  creating, 170–171
  differences between major, 162
  digests, 158
  eGroups, 168–170
  errors in posting, 155
  etiquette, 371–372
  FAQ document, 172
  first message, sending, 163
  InfoBeat, 167
  Jazz Lover's List, 168
  Liberal Judaism, 168
  list charter, 171
  ListProc. *See* ListProc
  LISTSERV. *See* LISTSERV
  Majordomo. *See* Majordomo
  management of, 154
  moderator, 163
  Net-Happenings Digest, 167
  newcomer errors, 155
  overview, 153–154
  Privacy Forum Digest, 167
  registering, 169–170
  replying to messages, 164
  Risks Digest, 167
  running, 168, 171–172
  searches, 233
  signing on, 154
  TipWorld, 167
  Topica, 168
  Travel-L, 167
  types of, 166
  Usenet newsgroups and, 165

Majordomo
  commands, list of, 161
  help, 161
  overview, 160
  subscribing, 160
  unsubscribing, 160
master screen name, 309
Microsoft Chat
  channels, 317
  comic displays in chat rooms, 319
  installing, 315
  joining chat rooms, 318
  nicknames, 318
  owning channels, 319–320
  private channels, 320
  private conversations, 319
  public channels, 320
  secret channels, 320
  types of channels, 320
  using, 316
Microsoft technical support, 102
MIME, 145
MIRC, 315
modems
  Control Panel, 66
  defined, 39
  described, 36
  external, 37
  internal, 37
  Internet Connection Wizard and,
    60–61, 64
  ISDN, 36
  PC Card, 37–38
  speed, 37
Modems Properties dialog box, 66
  properties of modems, 68
  testing modems, 67
moderator, 163
MoneyCentral Investor, 268
Morgan Stanley Dean Witter Online, 267
MP3 files, 237

MSN, 30
  Internet connection through, 78
MUD, 12
Multi-User Dimension. _See_ MUD
multimedia
  Flash, 241–242
  MP3 files, 237
  overview, 236–237
  protocol errors, 243–244
  QuickTime, 240
  RealPlayer, 237–239
  Shockwave, 241–242
  Windows Media Player, 242
multithreaded programs, 207
mutual funds, 267
My Snap, 268
My Yahoo, 268

• N •

Nelson, Ted, 178
Net-Happenings Digest, 167
NetLoad, 284
NetMeeting
  Adjust Audio Volume/View Participant
    List button, 332
  answering calls, 338
  applications, sharing, 343
  audioconferencing, 328
  calling people, 334–335
  Chat button, 332
  Chat window used to conduct a
    meeting, 339
  connections, 331
  Directory button, 332
  documents, sharing, 344
  drawings, changing, 342
  End Call button, 332
  exiting, 345
  files, sending, 340
  locking the whiteboard, 342

logging on, 328
people on different servers, finding, 334
Picture-in-Picture button, 332
Place Call button, 332
private conversations, 340
server, trying alternate, 333–334
setting up, 328–329, 331
setting up a meeting, 338–339
Share Program button, 332
Start Video button, 332
start-up screens, 329–331
starting, 328
talking to people, 335
Transfer Files button, 332
video connection, 336
video options, 337
videoconferencing, 328
Whiteboard button, 332
whiteboard, use of, 341–342
window, 332–333
Netscape, 47. *See also* Netscape Mail;
    Netscape Messenger; Netscape
    Navigator
bookmarks, 199, 201
cache, 203
images, 203
organizing Web sites, 199, 201
start page, changing, 202
toolbar, 205
Netscape Mail
address book, 136
e-mail attachments, 146
reading mail, 124
receiving mail, 124
running, 123
sending mail, 125
Netscape Messenger, 111
e-mail attachments, 146
reading mail, 123
receiving mail, 123
replying to mail, 134
running, 122

saving mail, 141
sending mail, 123
Netscape Navigator
downloading, 189–193
FTP, 291
getting, 188–193
installing, 194–195
versions, 190
netsplits, 313
New York Times, 366
nicknames, 301, 314
Nordstrom, 272
Northern Light, 227

• *O* •

online chat
AOL, 306–311
bad behavior, 305
channels, 300
DALNet, 312
EFnet, 312
emoticons, 304–305
etiquette, 302–303
first time, tips for, 301
handle, 301
IRC, 311–322
IRCnet, 312
lurking, 302
mIRC, 315
MSN Chat, 323–324
nickname, 301
overview, 299–300
rooms, 300
safety guidelines, 303
sample conversation, 300, 309–310
screen name, 301
shorthand, list of, 304–305
Undernet, 312
Web-based chat sites, 322–323
online help, 252
online services, 26, 28

outgoing mail servers, 111
Outlook Express, 23, 48, 111
  address book, 135–136
  e-mail attachments, 146
  reading mail, 120–121
  replying to mail, 134
  running for the first time, 114, 116, 118
  saving mail, 141
  sending mail, 119–120

• P •

paging, 12
passwords
  Dial-Up Networking password, saving,
    94–95
  disclosing your, 20
  saving, 83
PayPal, 266
PC Card modems, 37–38
PC Connection, 270
Peapod, 272
Pegasus, 111
PEM, 115
people, searching for, 230, 232–233
permanent IP address, 73
PGP, 23, 115
phone numbers, searching for, 231
PKUNZIP, 292
PKZIP, 292
plug-ins
  iChat, 211–212
  overview, 210
  QuickTime, 211
  RealPlayer, 211–212
  Shockwave, 211
  using, 211
POP servers, 110
POP3, 110
pornography, 350
port numbers, 180
portfolio tracking, 268

postmaster, 130
PPP account, 31
privacy, 21–22
  e-mail and, 115
Privacy Forum Digest, 167
Prodigy, 30
  Internet connection through, 78
push technology, 245

• Q •

QuickTime, 211, 240
QVC, 272

• R •

radio buttons, 205
RealPlayer, 211–212, 237–239
redirecting e-mail, 140
REI, 270
remailing, 140
remote users, local telephone numbers
  and, 96, 98–100
Reuters Moneynet, 268
Risks Digest, 167
robots, 147

• S •

safety, 20–21
Salomon Smith Barney, 268
Save password check box, 83
saving
  e-mail, 140–142
  Web pages, 206
screen name, 301
search engines, 12, 215
searches
  advertising supporting, 224
  AltaVista, 220–221, 223
  AskJeeves, 225
  businesses, 227, 229–230

dead links, 223
e-mail addresses, 231
Excite, 226
Go Network, 226
Google, 225
Gurus search page, 215
HotBot, 226
Lycos, 226
Northern Light, 227
overview, 213–215
people, 230, 232–233
phone numbers, 231
shopping information, 233
spelling and, 222
WebCrawler, 225
Yahoo!, 216, 218, 220
second telephone lines, 38
security, 363
electronic commerce, 18–19
encryption, 19
firewalls, 33
online chats, 303
Shockwave, 211, 241–242
shopping online, 360–361
advantages of, 257
airline tickets, 258, 263–264
auctions, 270–271
books, 258, 268–269
cable shopping outlets, 272
CDs, 258
checklist for, 273
clothes, 269–270
computers, 258, 270
cookies, 261
credit cards, 258–259, 351, 361–362
department stores, 272
disadvantages of, 258
example, complex, 262–263
example, simple, 260
food, 272
mail-order catalog items, 258

mutual funds, 258
stocks, 258
travel arrangements, 258
signatures, 373
single-clicks, when to use, 63–64
Slate, 366
smileys used in e-mail, 132
SMTP server, 111
SN Chat, 323–324, 328
spam, 149–150, 350, 375–376
Start menu, Dial-Up Networking
     connection shortcut on, 92
static IP address, 35
stockbrokers, 267
subscription, 236
Subscription Wizard, 250

• _T_ •

TCP/IP, 71, 73–74
technical support
   from computer company, 102
   from friends, 103
   from Microsoft, 102
   ISPs, 101
telephone calling cards, use of, 100
telephone line, getting a second, 38
TipWorld, 167
top-level domain, 109
Topica, 168
Travel-L, 167
Travelocity, 366
troubleshooters, 102
troubleshooting Internet
     connections, 101
TUCOWS, 189, 277, 298, 367

• _U_ •

Undernet, 312
unencoding, 145

Uniform Resource Locator. *See* URLs
United Computer Exchange, 271
unsolicited commercial e-mail, 149
Update Wizard, 253
updates, 253–254, 257
uploading, 275–276
URLs, 178
  described, 359
  error messages, 352–353
  file, 180
  FTP, 180, 281–282
  mailto, 180
  structure of, 180
USAccess, 265
Usenet FAQs, 370
Usenet newsgroups, 48, 148
  mailing lists, 165
usernames, 108
  case-sensitivity, 83

• *V* •

Vanguard Group, 267
videoconferencing, 328
virus scans, 296

• *W* •

Wachovia, 265
Web address
  See URLs, 359
Web browser plug-ins, 47
Web browsers. *See* browsers
Web pages
  Active Desktop, displayed on, 246–247
  browsers used to view, 379
  copyright, 207
  downloading, 276–278
  links on, 379
  loading, speed of, 349
  personal information on, 379
  saving, 206
  small size of, 378

Web sites, 12
  Amazon, 366
  authors of this book, 368
  CIA World Fact Book, 365
  Dell Computers, 367
  Four11, 367
  Internet Movie Database, 365
  New York Times, 366
  Slate, 366
  time to visit, 354
  Travelocity, 366
  TUCOWS, 367
  Webring, 368
  WhoWhere, 367
  Yahoo!, 368
Web-based chat sites, 322–323
Web-based mail, 113
WebCOMBO, 41–42
WebCrawler, 225
WHOIS, 228
WhoWhere, 232, 367
Windows ME help file, 101–102
Windows Media Player, 242
Wingspan, 265
Winsock, 46, 280
WinZip
  extracting files, 294
  installing, 293
  overview, 292
  running, 293
  unzipping files, 294
World Wide Web. *See* WWW
World Wide Web Consortium, 176
WS_FTP, 283
  Connect button, 289
  downloading, 284–285
  downloading files, 288
  exiting, 289
  FTP server, connecting to, 285–287
  Local system, 287
  Remote system, 287
  uploading files, 291
  using, 285

WWW
   clicking on links, 184
   exiting, 188
   garbled pages, 187
   history of, 176
   Internet compared to, 357
   overview, 11–12, 175
   recommended links, 187
   structure of, 177

• •

XDSL, 27

• •

Yahoo People Search, 232
Yahoo!, 187, 216, 218, 220, 223, 368
Yahoo! Auctions, 271
Yellow Pages, 230

• Z •

zones, 109

Notes

Notes

Notes

YOUR ONLINE RESOURCE

WWW.DUMMIES.COM

Discover Dummies Online!

The Dummies Web Site is your fun and friendly online resource for the latest information about *For Dummies®* books and your favorite topics. The Web site is the place to communicate with us, exchange ideas with other *For Dummies* readers, chat with authors, and have fun!

Ten Fun and Useful Things You Can Do at www.dummies.com

1. Win free *For Dummies* books and more!
2. Register your book and be entered in a prize drawing.
3. Meet your favorite authors through the IDG Books Worldwide Author Chat Series.
4. Exchange helpful information with other *For Dummies* readers.
5. Discover other great *For Dummies* books you must have!
6. Purchase Dummieswear® exclusively from our Web site.
7. Buy *For Dummies* books online.
8. Talk to us. Make comments, ask questions, get answers!
9. Download free software.
10. Find additional useful resources from authors.

Link directly to these ten fun and useful things at
http://www.dummies.com/10useful

WWW.DUMMIES.COM

For other technology titles from IDG Books Worldwide, go to
www.idgbooks.com

Not on the Web yet? It's easy to get started with *Dummies 101®: The Internet For Windows® 98* or *The Internet For Dummies®* at local retailers everywhere.

IDG BOOKS WORLDWIDE

Find other *For Dummies* books on these topics:

Business • Career • Databases • Food & Beverage • Games • Gardening • Graphics • Hardware
Health & Fitness • Internet and the World Wide Web • Networking • Office Suites
Operating Systems • Personal Finance • Pets • Programming • Recreation • Sports
Spreadsheets • Teacher Resources • Test Prep • Word Processing

IDG BOOKS WORLDWIDE
BOOK REGISTRATION

Register This Book and Win!

We want to hear from you!

Visit **http://my2cents.dummies.com** to register this book and tell us how you liked it!

- ✔ Get entered in our monthly prize giveaway.

- ✔ Give us feedback about this book — tell us what you like best, what you like least, or maybe what you'd like to ask the author and us to change!

- ✔ Let us know any other *For Dummies®* topics that interest you.

Your feedback helps us determine what books to publish, tells us what coverage to add as we revise our books, and lets us know whether we're meeting your needs as a *For Dummies* reader. You're our most valuable resource, and what you have to say is important to us!

Not on the Web yet? It's easy to get started with *Dummies 101®: The Internet For Windows® 98* or *The Internet For Dummies®* at local retailers everywhere.

Or let us know what you think by sending us a letter at the following address:

For Dummies Book Registration
Dummies Press
10475 Crosspoint Blvd.
Indianapolis, IN 46256

FOR DUMMIES ™

BESTSELLING BOOK SERIES